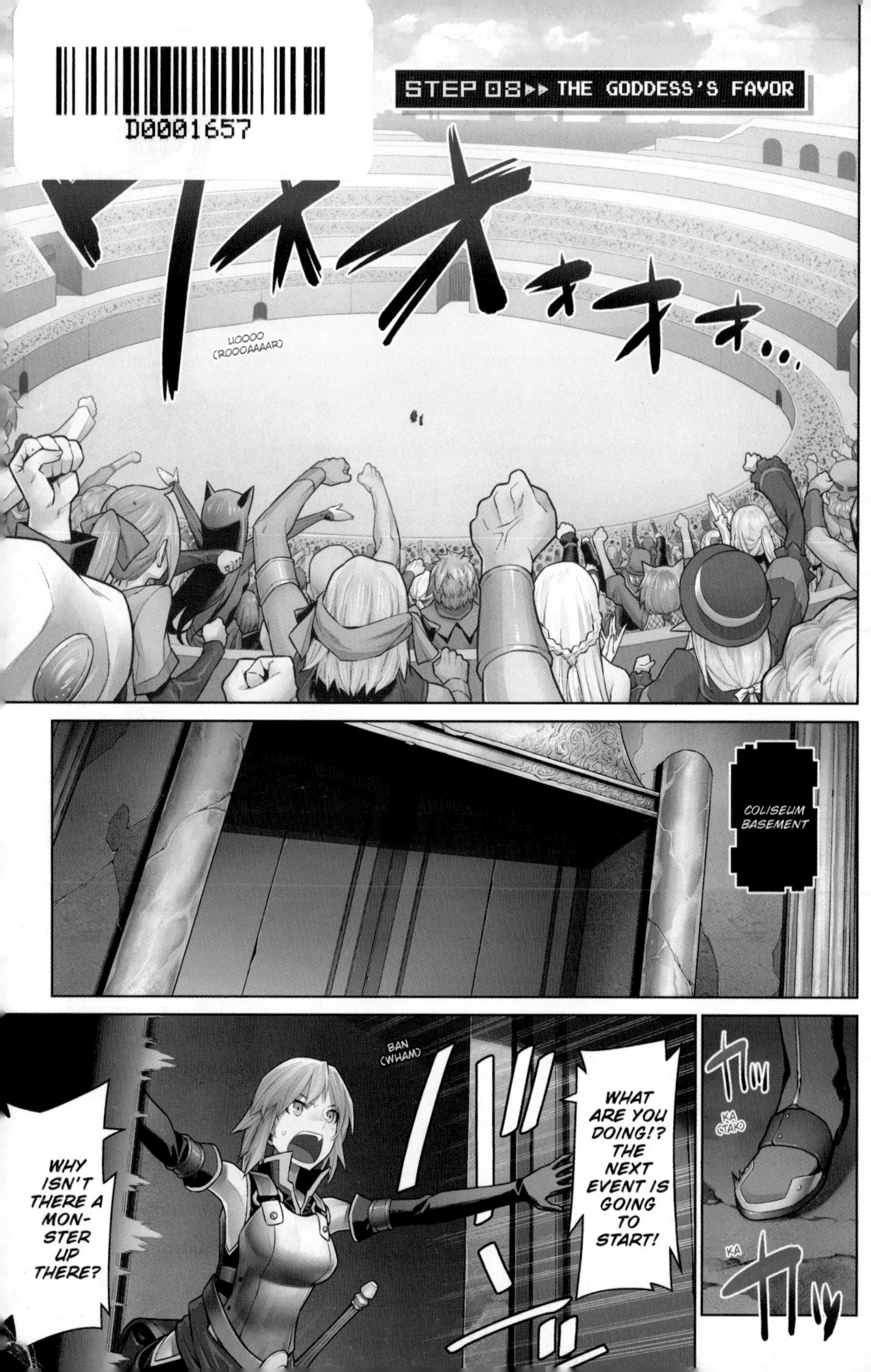
STEP 08 ▸▸ THE GODDESS'S FAVOR
UOOOO
(ROOOAAAAR)
COLISEUM BASEMENT
KA
(TAK)
KA
WHAT ARE YOU DOING!? THE NEXT EVENT IS GOING TO START!
BAN
(WHAM)
WHY ISN'T THERE A MON-STER UP THERE?

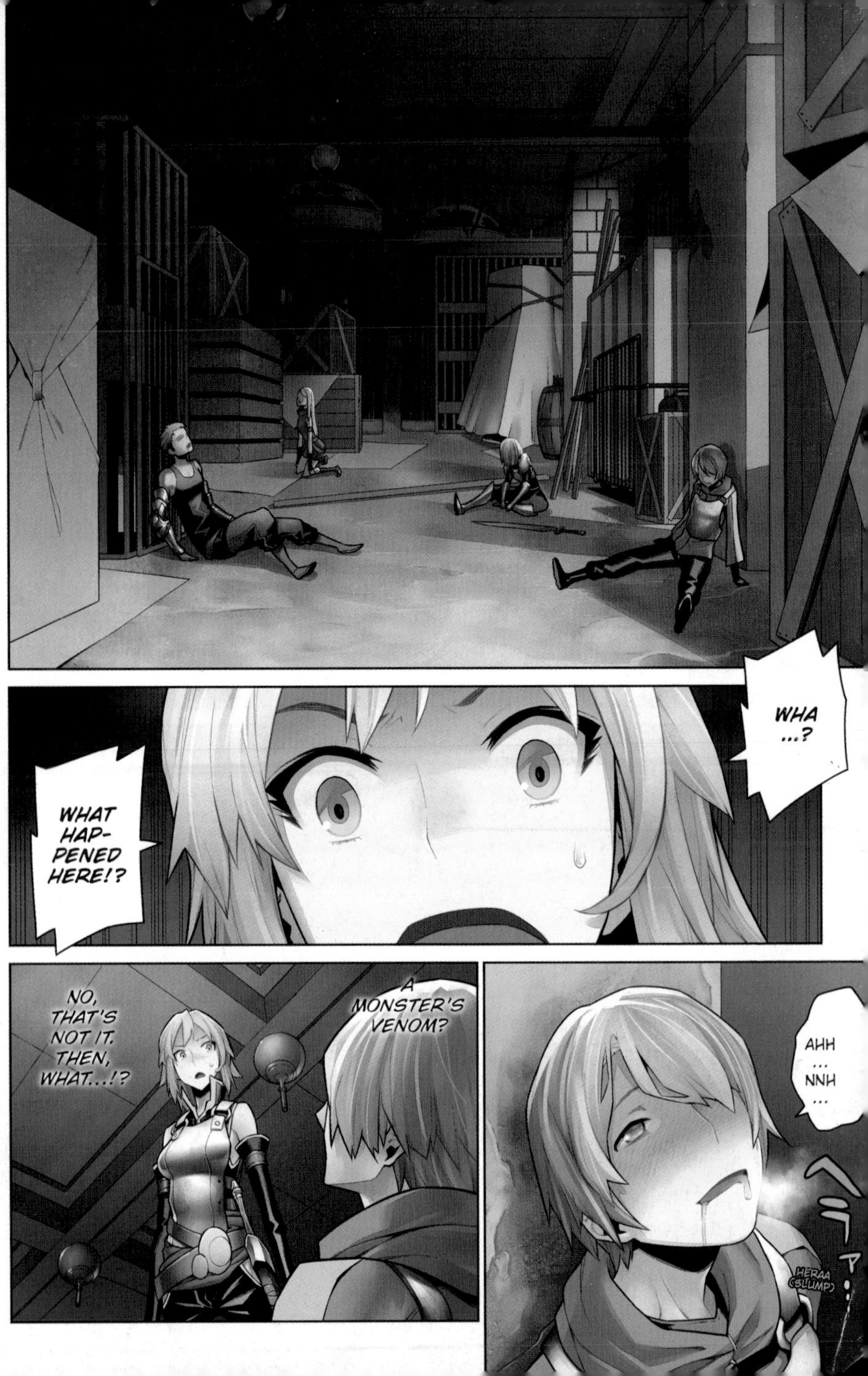
WHA ...?
WHAT HAP-PENED HERE!?
AHH ... NNH ...
HERAA (SLUMP)
A MONSTER'S VENOM?
NO, THAT'S NOT IT. THEN, WHAT...!?

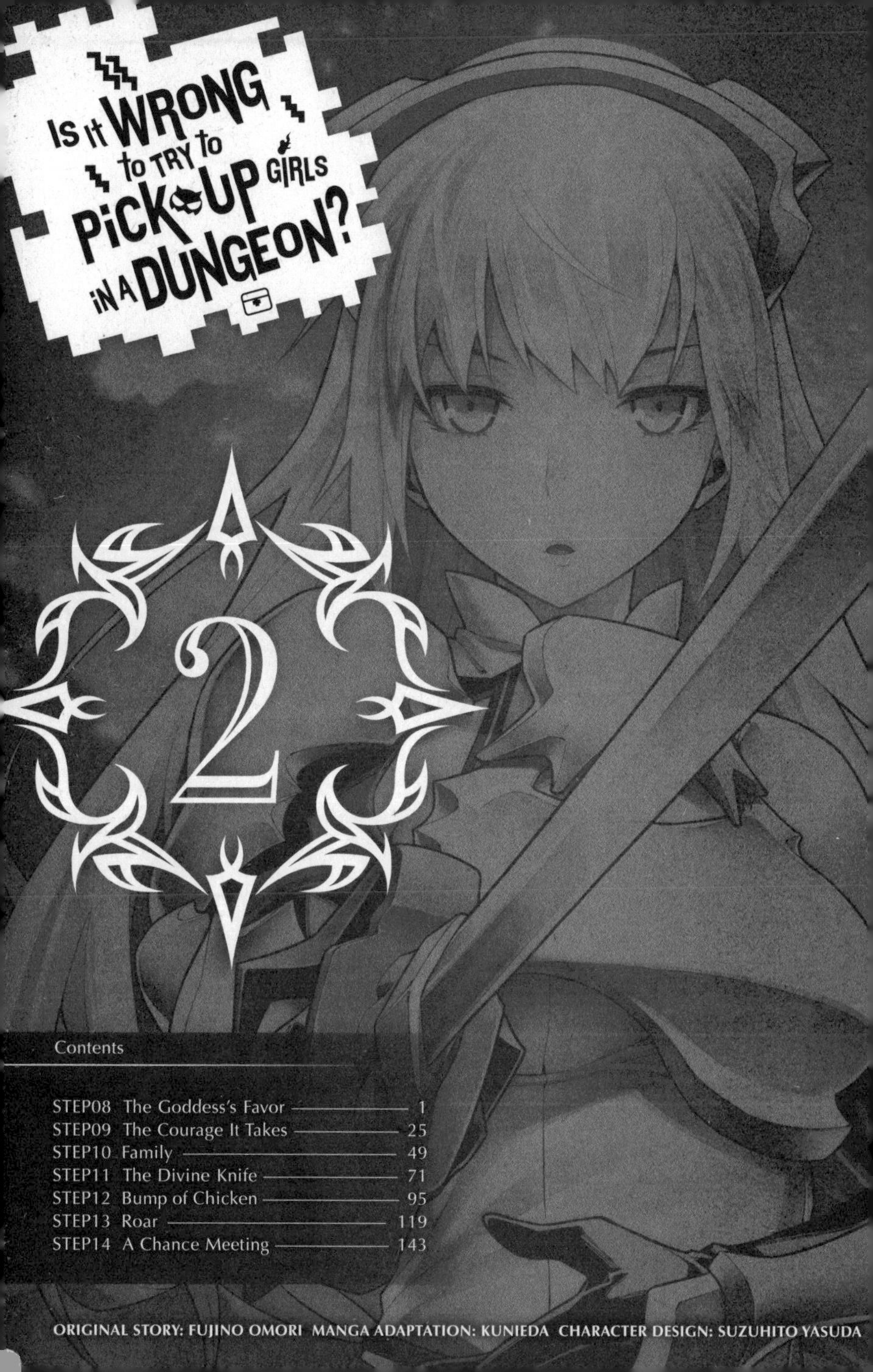
Is it WRONG to TRY to PiCK UP GIRLS iN A DUNGEON?
2

Contents

ORIGINAL STORY: FUJINO OMORI MANGA ADAPTATION: KUNIEDA CHARACTER DESIGN: SUZUHITO YASUDA

Is it WRONG to TRY to PiCK UP GIRLS iN A DUNGEON?

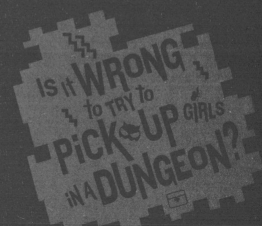

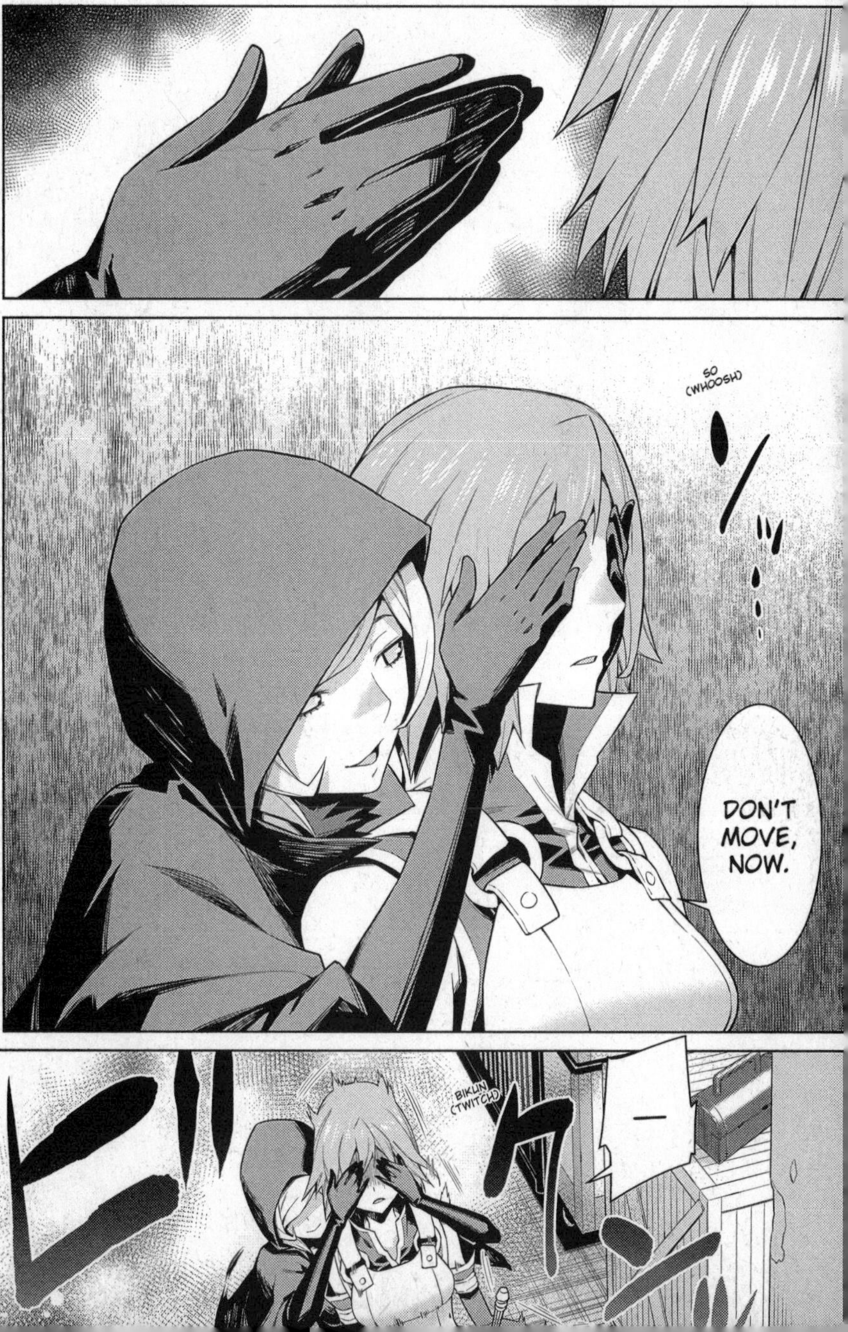
SO (WHOOSH)
DON'T MOVE, NOW.
BIKUN (TWITCH)
—

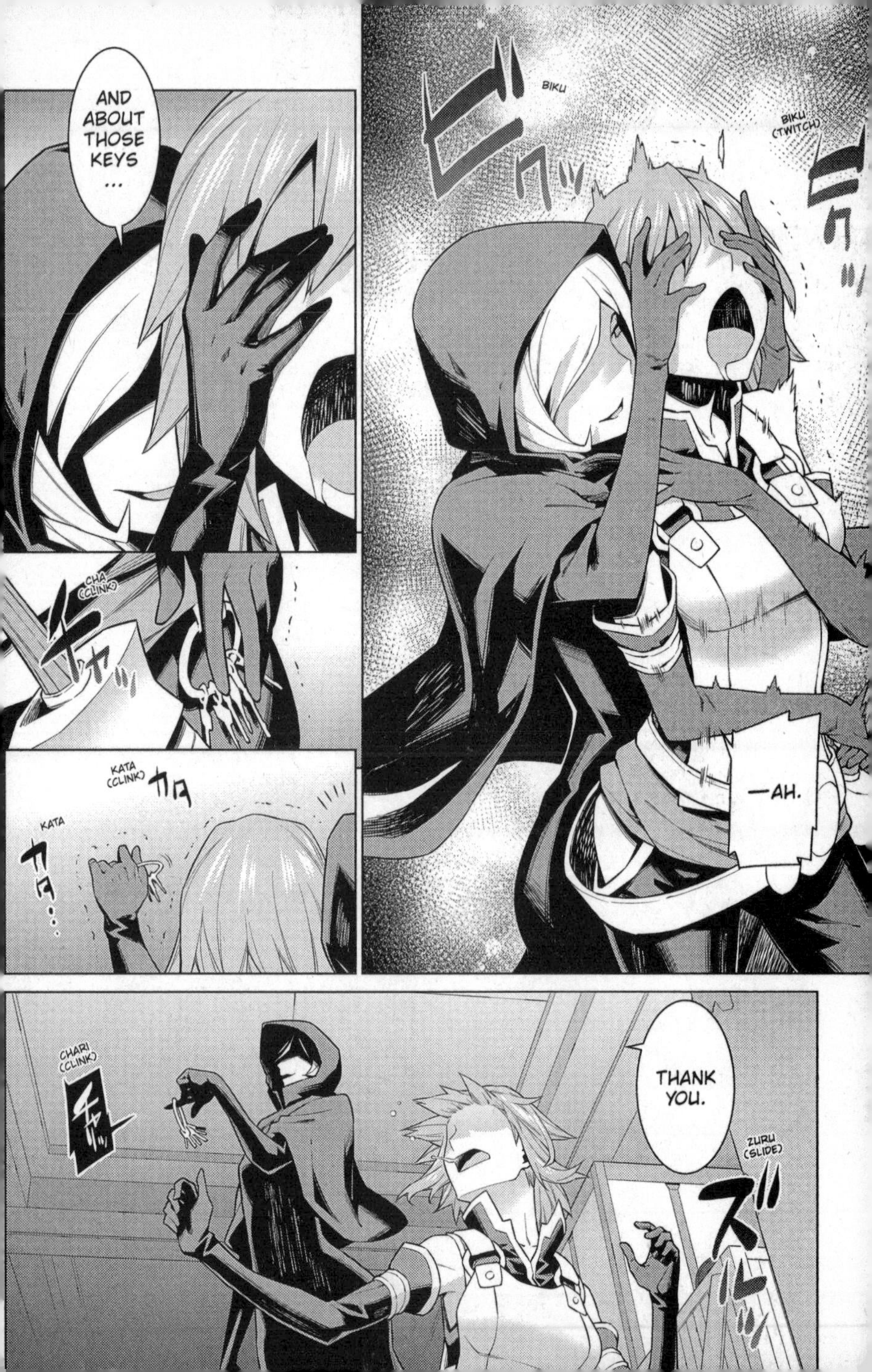
BIKU
BIKU (TWITCH)
—AH.
AND ABOUT THOSE KEYS ...
CHA (CLINK)
KATA (CLINK)
KATA
THANK YOU.
ZURU (SLIDE)
CHARI (CLINK)

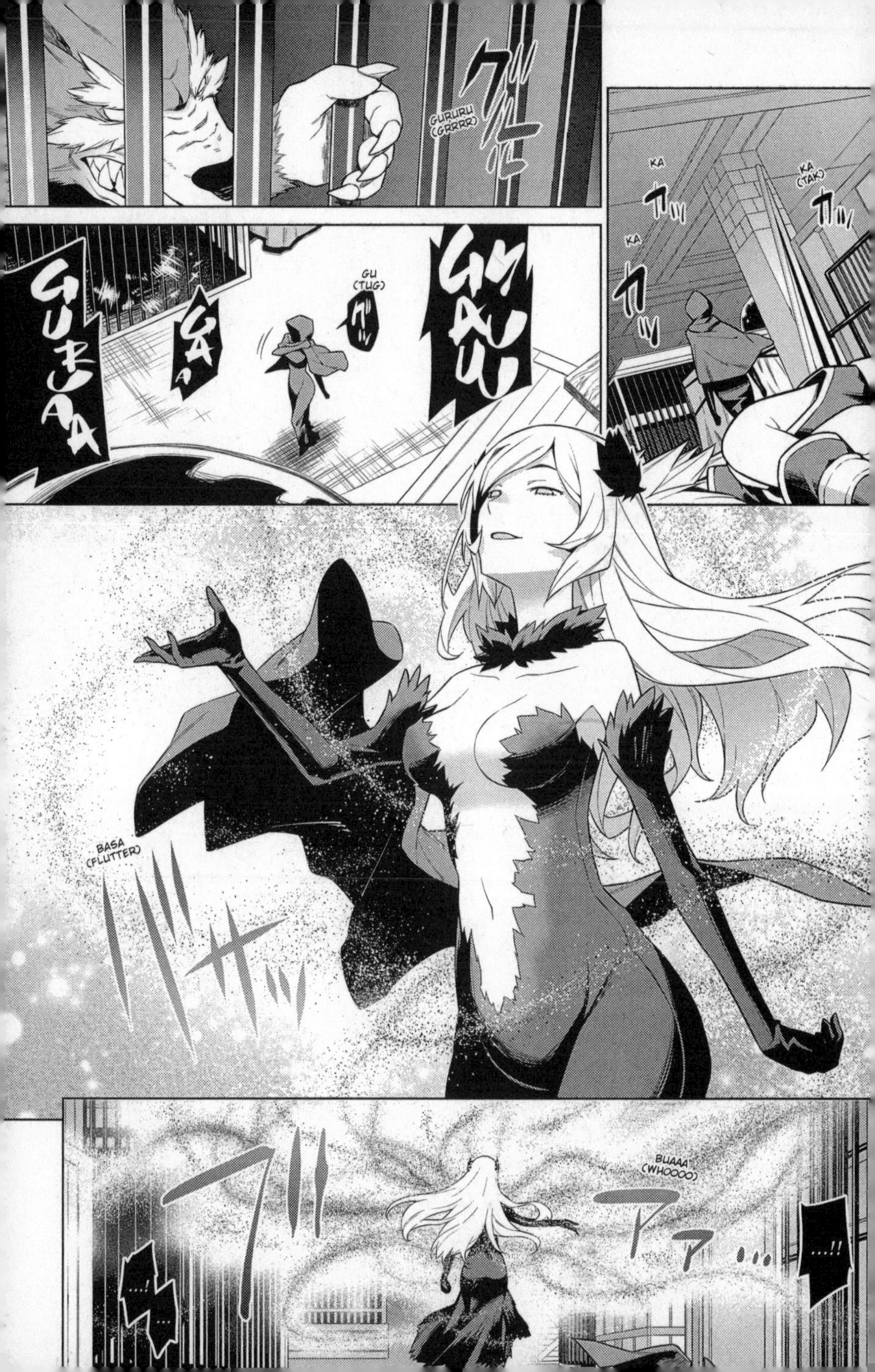
KA (TAK)
KA
KA
GURURU (GRRRR)
GAU
GU (TUG)
GA
GURUAA
BASA (FLUTTER)
BUAAA (WHOOOO)
...!!
...!

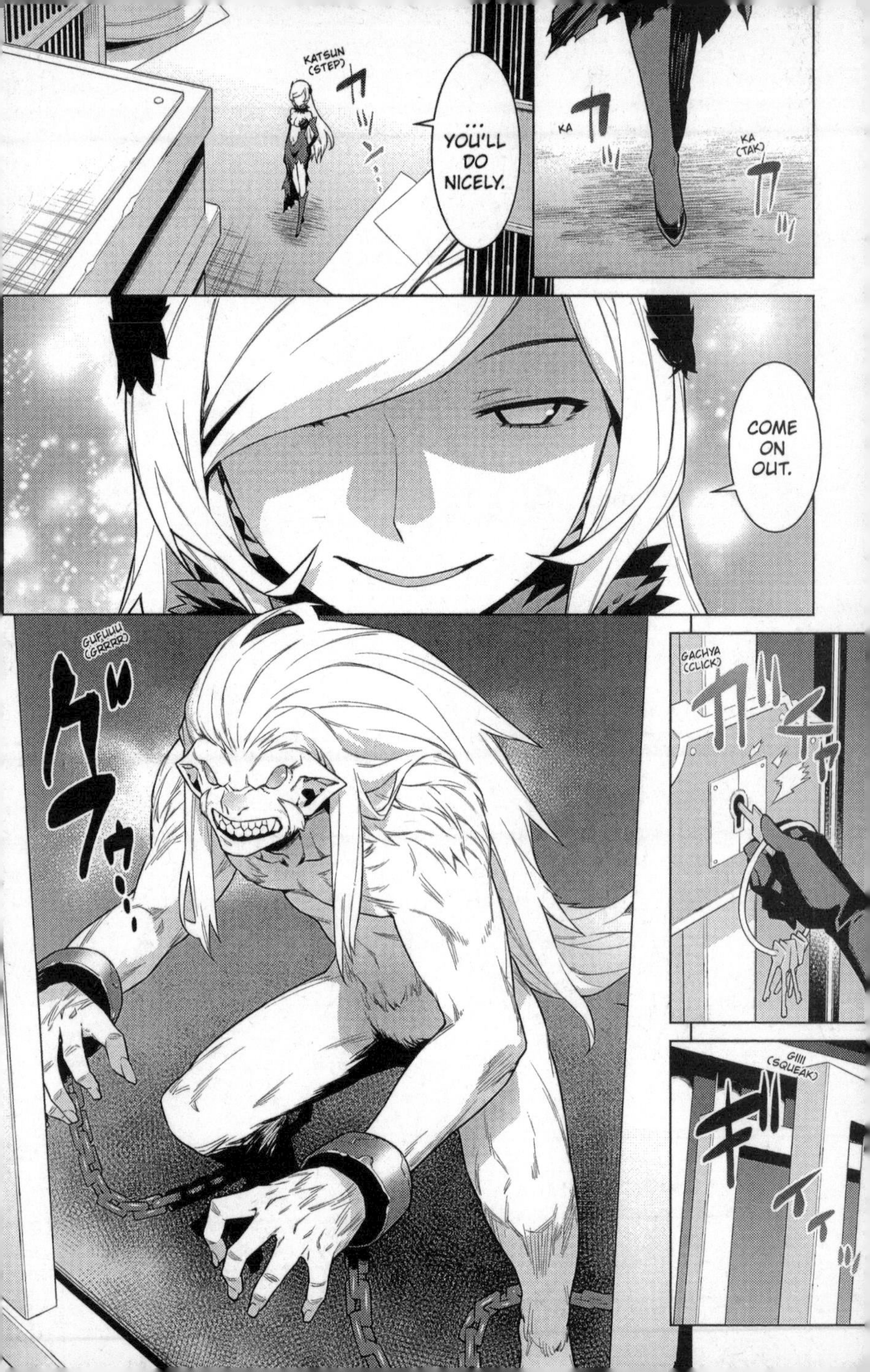
KA
KA (TAK)
KATSUN (STEP)
... YOU'LL DO NICELY.
COME ON OUT.
GACHYA (CLICK)
GIIII (SQUEAK)
GUFUUU (GRRRR)

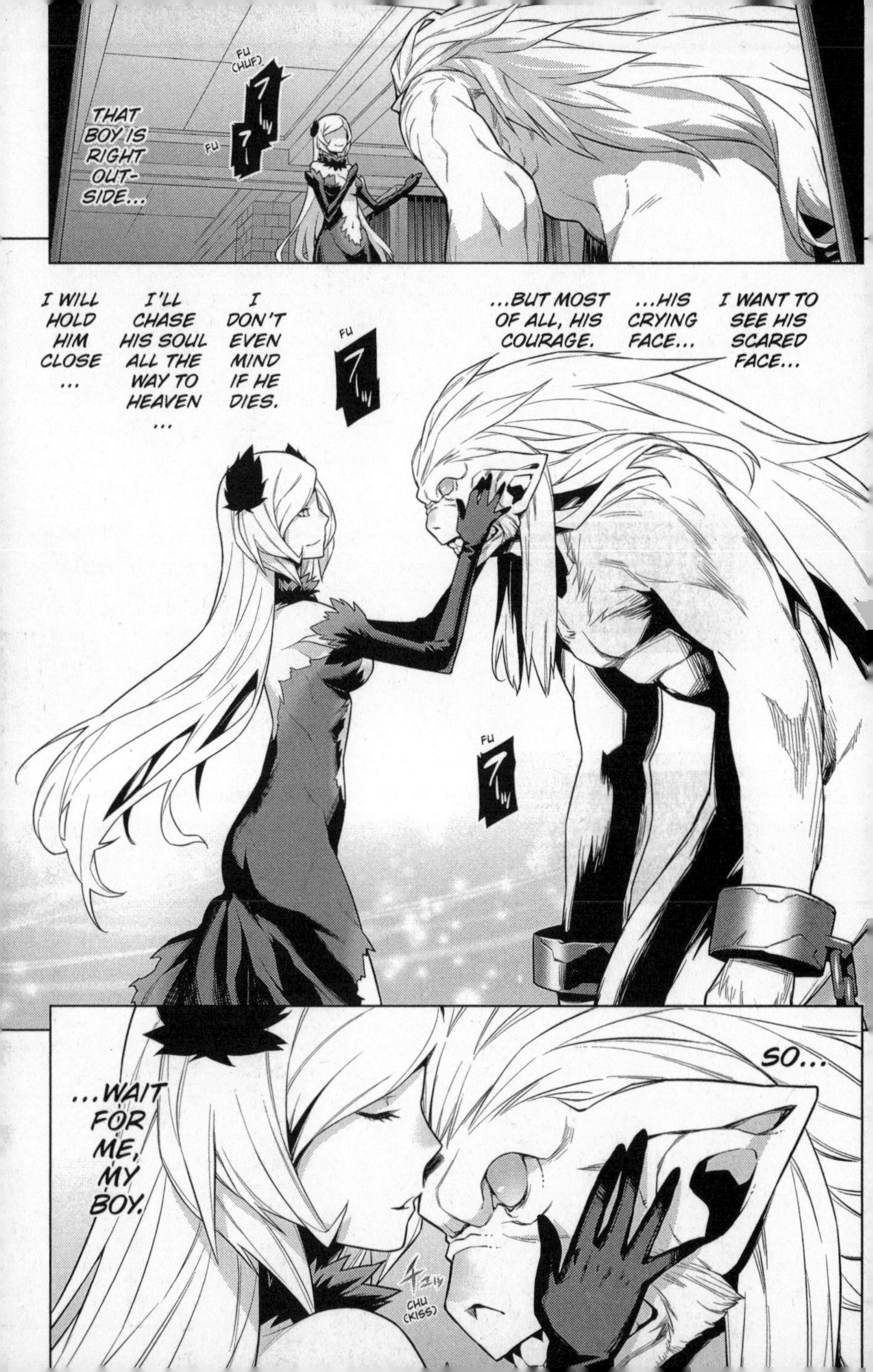
FU (HUF)
FU
THAT BOY IS RIGHT OUTSIDE...
I WANT TO SEE HIS SCARED FACE...
...HIS CRYING FACE...
...BUT MOST OF ALL, HIS COURAGE.
FU
I DON'T EVEN MIND IF HE DIES.
I'LL CHASE HIS SOUL ALL THE WAY TO HEAVEN...
I WILL HOLD HIM CLOSE...
FU
SO...
...WAIT FOR ME, MY BOY.
CHU (KISS)

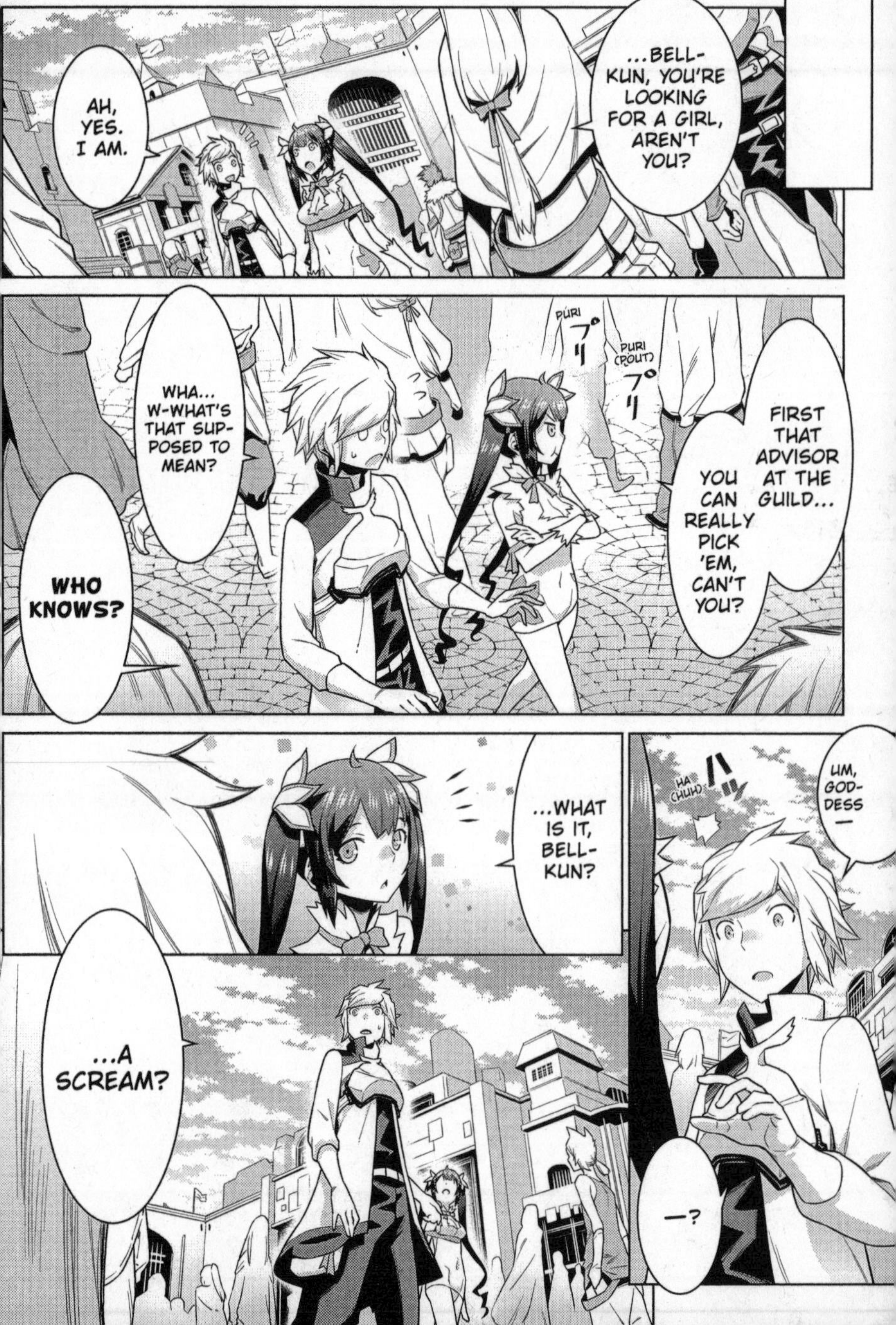
...BELL-KUN, YOU'RE LOOKING FOR A GIRL, AREN'T YOU?
AH, YES. I AM.
プリ PURI
プリ PURI (POUT)
FIRST THAT ADVISOR AT THE GUILD...
YOU CAN REALLY PICK 'EM, CAN'T YOU?
WHA... W-WHAT'S THAT SUPPOSED TO MEAN?
WHO KNOWS?
UM, GOD-DESS—
ハッ HA (HUH)
—?
...WHAT IS IT, BELL-KUN?
...A SCREAM?

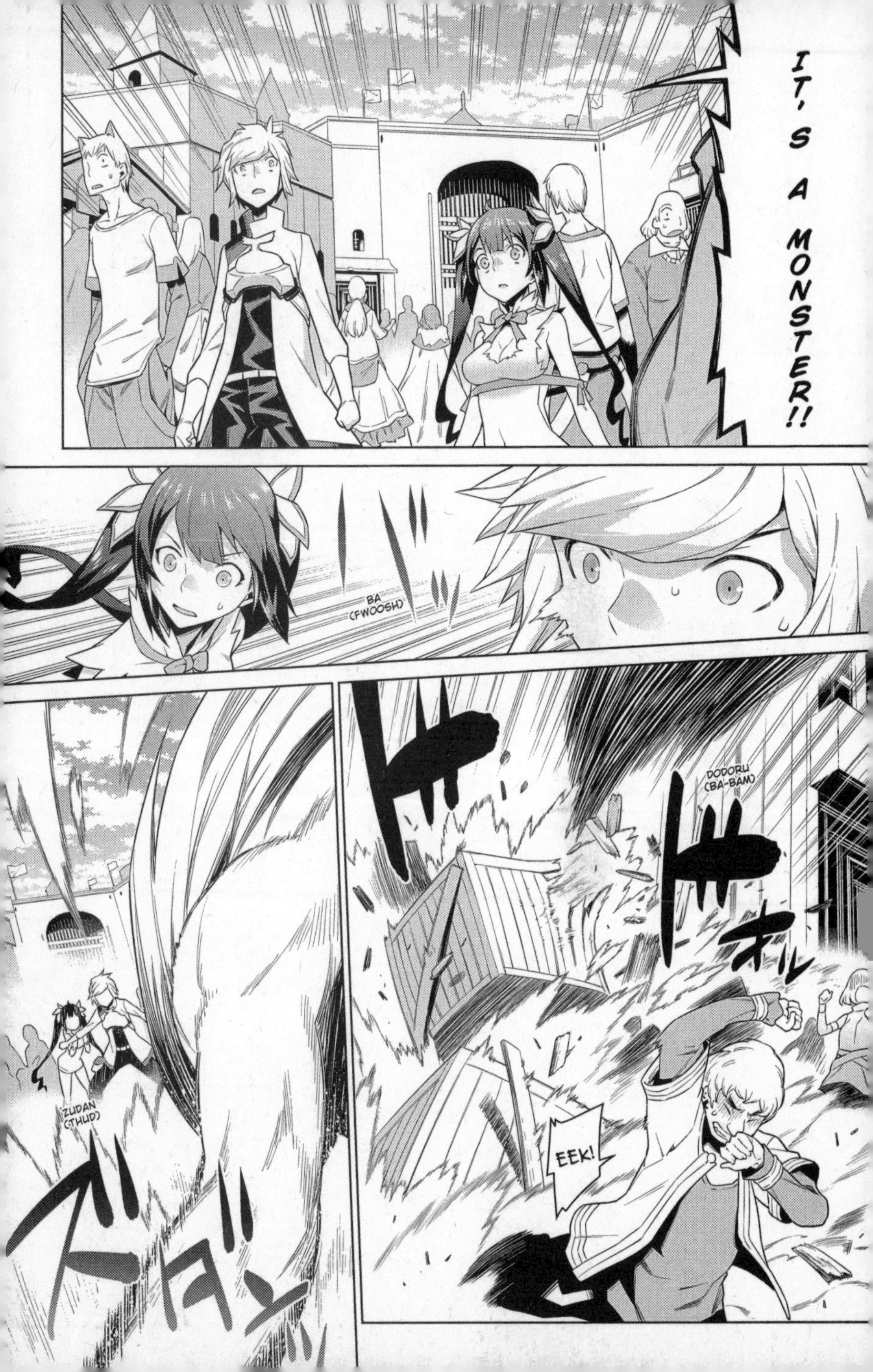
IT'S A MONSTER!!
BA
(FWOOSH)
DODORU
(BA-BAM)
EEK!
ZUDAN
(THUD)

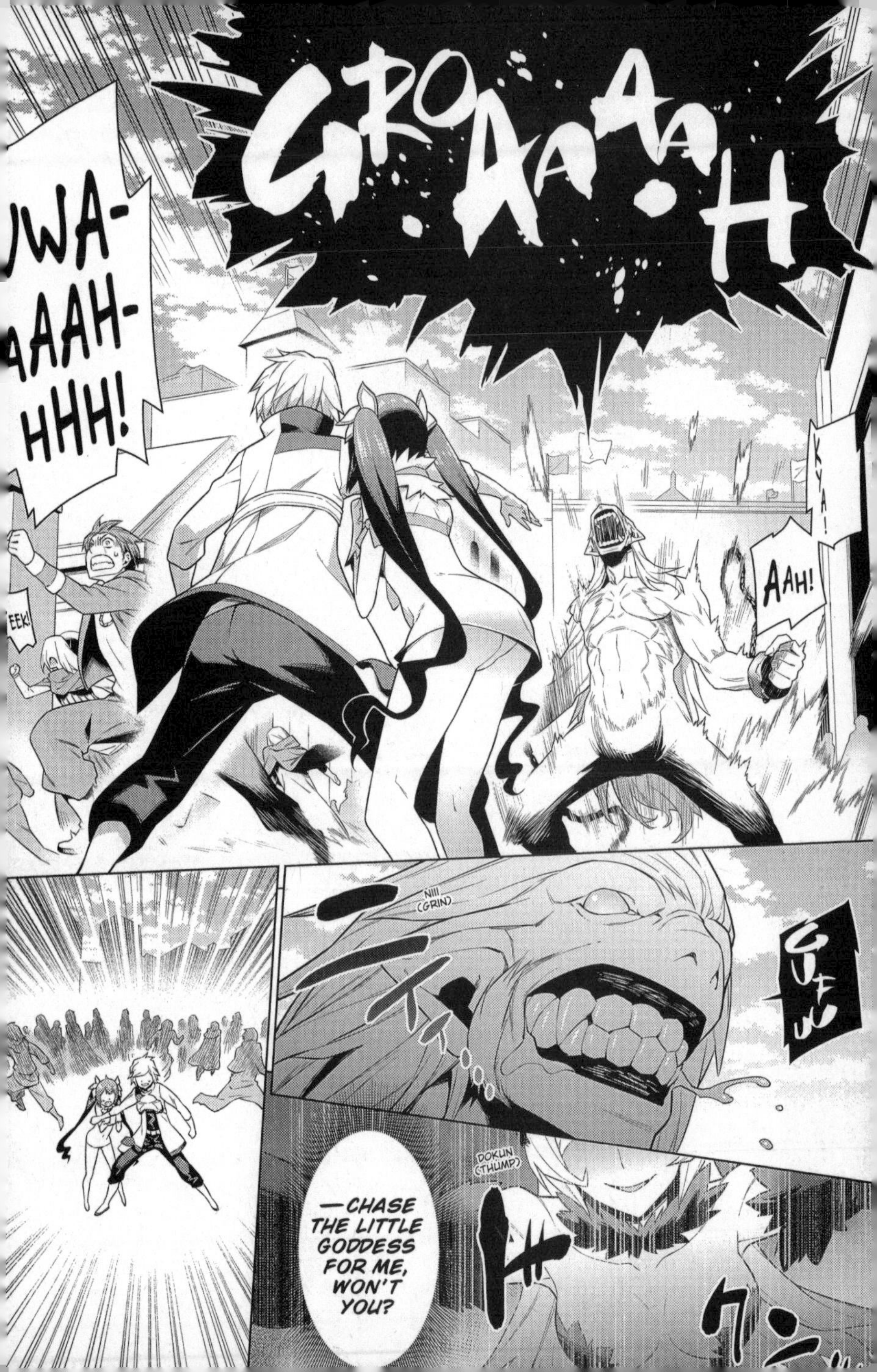
GROAAAAH
KYAA!
AAH!
UWA-AAAH-HHH!
EEK!
GUFUU
NIII (GRIN)
DOKUN (THUMP)
—CHASE THE LITTLE GODDESS FOR ME, WON'T YOU?

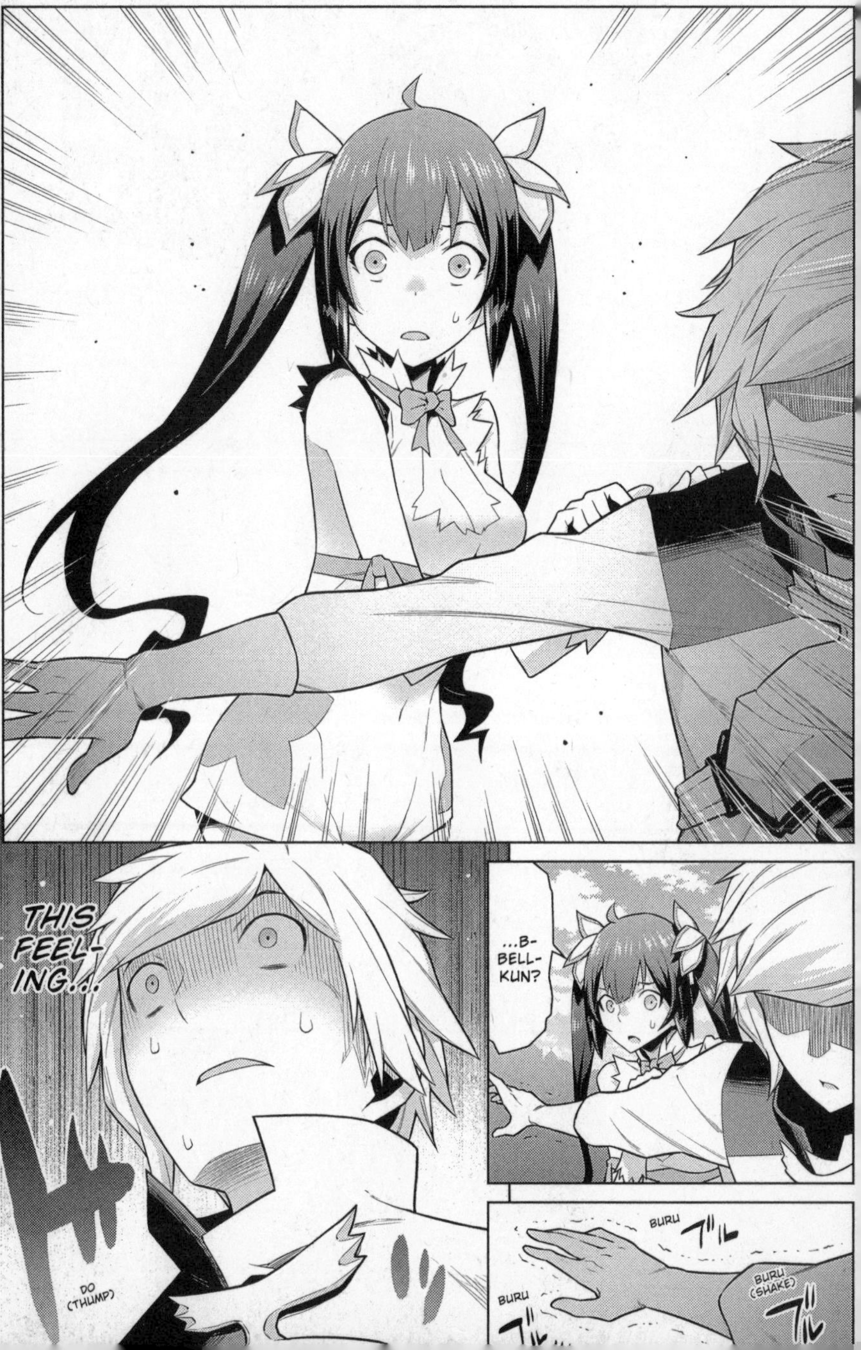
...B-BELL-KUN?
BURU
BURU (SHAKE)
BURU
THIS FEEL-ING...
DO (THUMP)

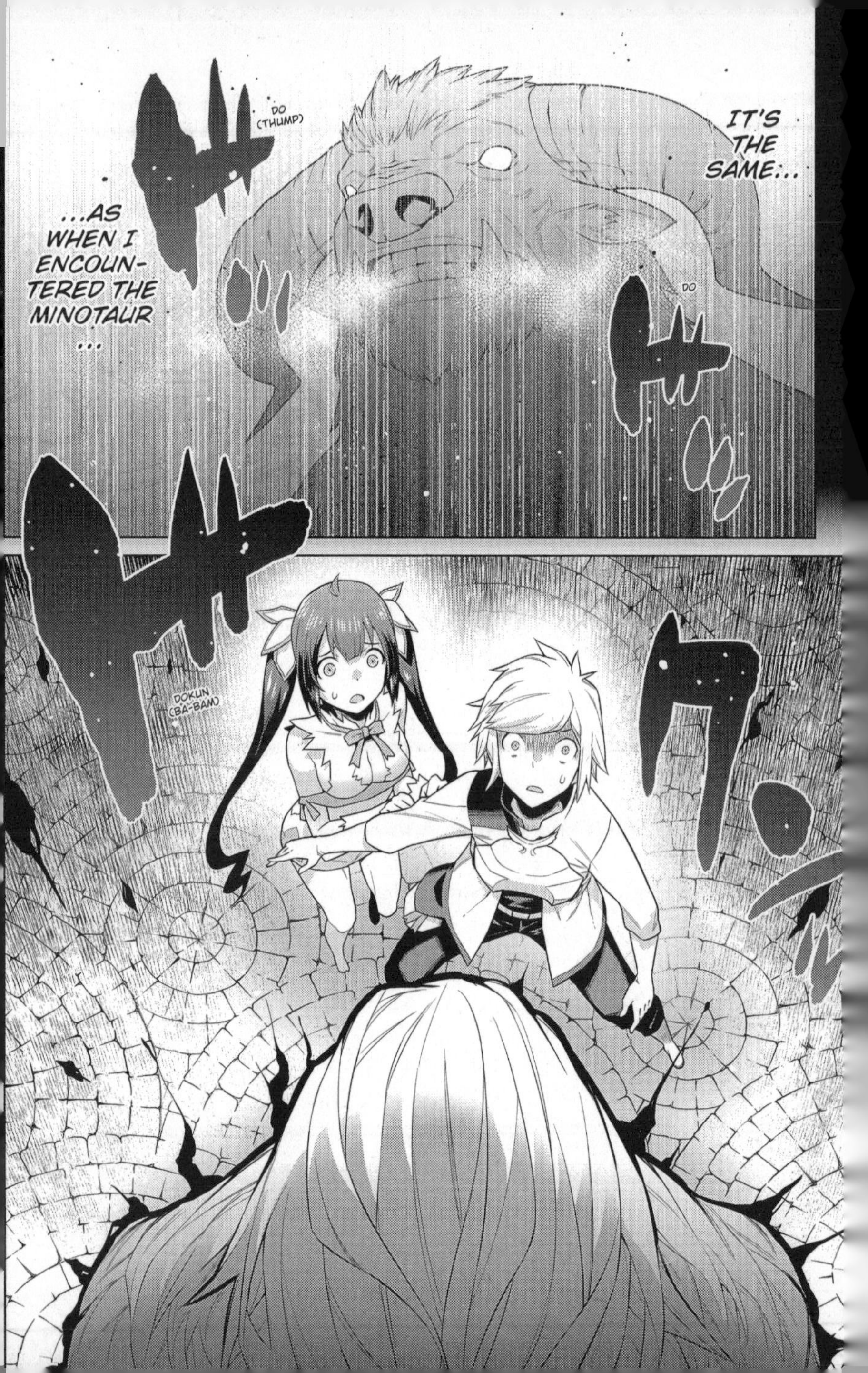
IT'S THE SAME...
DO
DO (THUMP)
...AS WHEN I ENCOUN-TERED THE MINOTAUR...
DOKUN (BA-BAM)

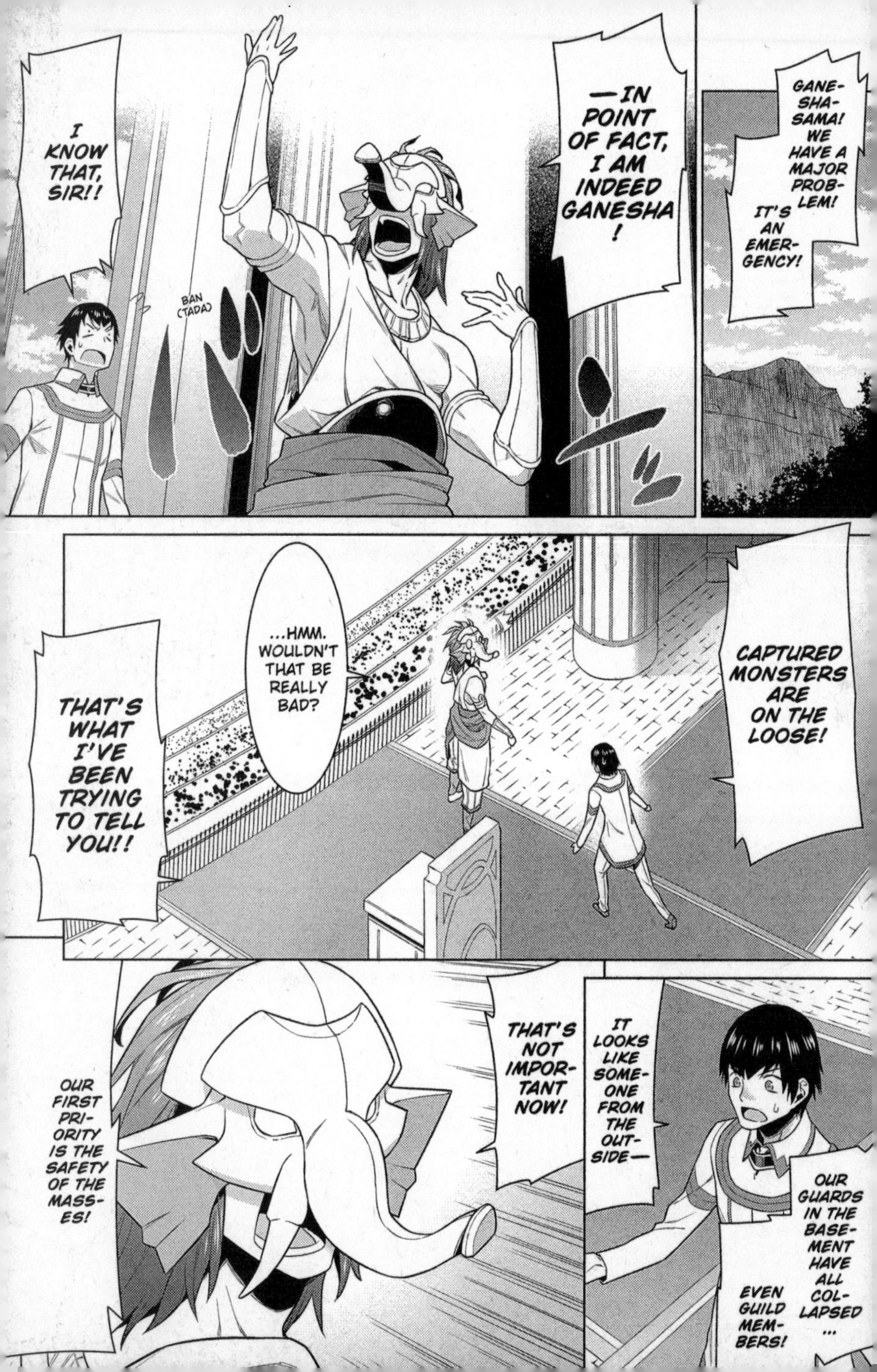
GANESHA-SAMA! WE HAVE A MAJOR PROBLEM!
IT'S AN EMERGENCY!
—IN POINT OF FACT, I AM INDEED GANESHA!
BAN (TADA)
I KNOW THAT, SIR!!
CAPTURED MONSTERS ARE ON THE LOOSE!
...HMM. WOULDN'T THAT BE REALLY BAD?
THAT'S WHAT I'VE BEEN TRYING TO TELL YOU!!
OUR GUARDS IN THE BASEMENT HAVE ALL COLLAPSED...
EVEN GUILD MEMBERS!
IT LOOKS LIKE SOMEONE FROM THE OUTSIDE—
THAT'S NOT IMPORTANT NOW!
OUR FIRST PRIORITY IS THE SAFETY OF THE MASSES!

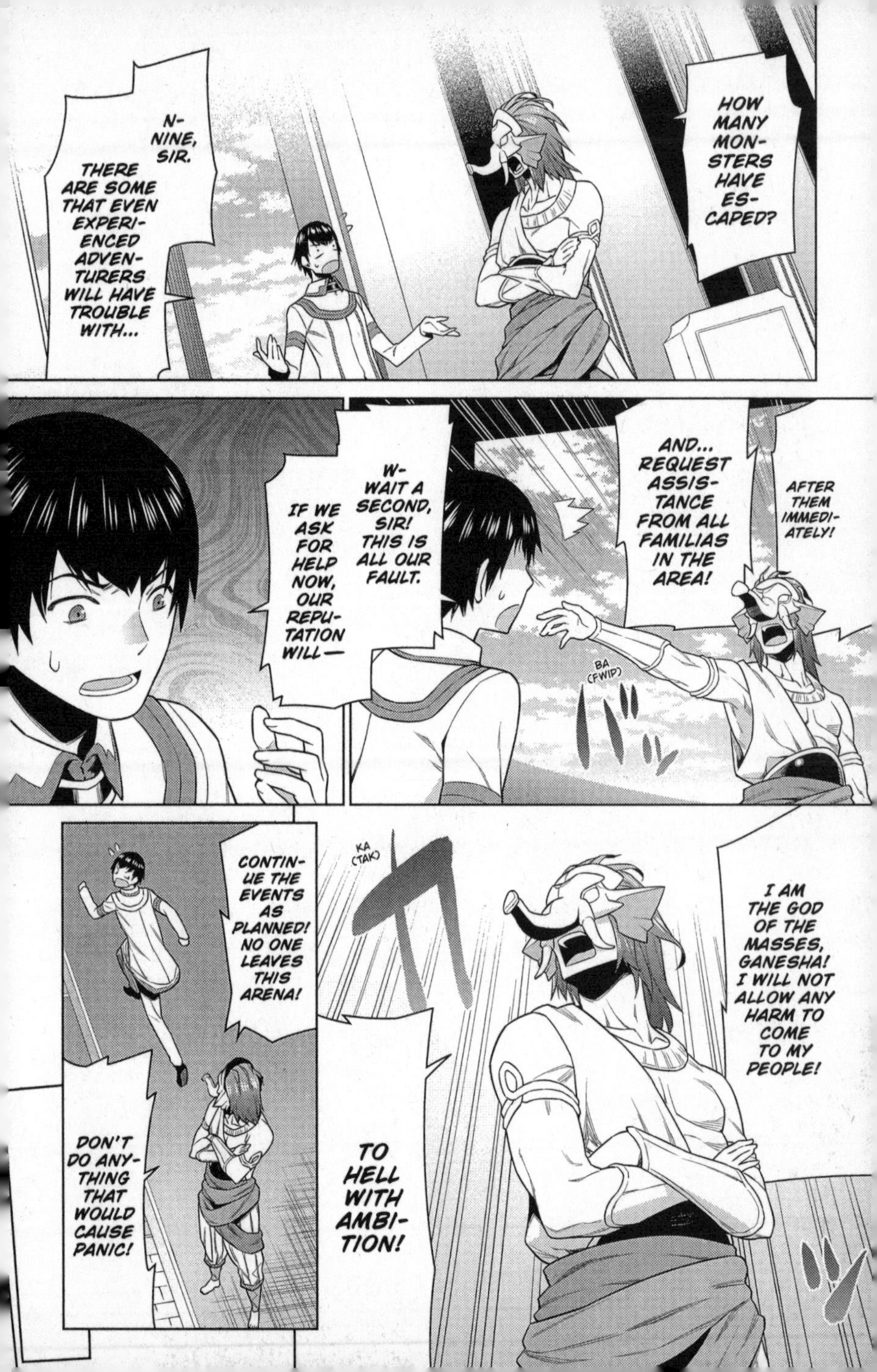
HOW MANY MONSTERS HAVE ESCAPED?
N-NINE, SIR.
THERE ARE SOME THAT EVEN EXPERIENCED ADVENTURERS WILL HAVE TROUBLE WITH...
AFTER THEM IMMEDIATELY!
AND... REQUEST ASSISTANCE FROM ALL FAMILIAS IN THE AREA!
BA (FWIP)
W-WAIT A SECOND, SIR! THIS IS ALL OUR FAULT.
IF WE ASK FOR HELP NOW, OUR REPUTATION WILL—
I AM THE GOD OF THE MASSES, GANESHA! I WILL NOT ALLOW ANY HARM TO COME TO MY PEOPLE!
KA (TAK)
TO HELL WITH AMBITION!
CONTINUE THE EVENTS AS PLANNED! NO ONE LEAVES THIS ARENA!
DON'T DO ANYTHING THAT WOULD CAUSE PANIC!

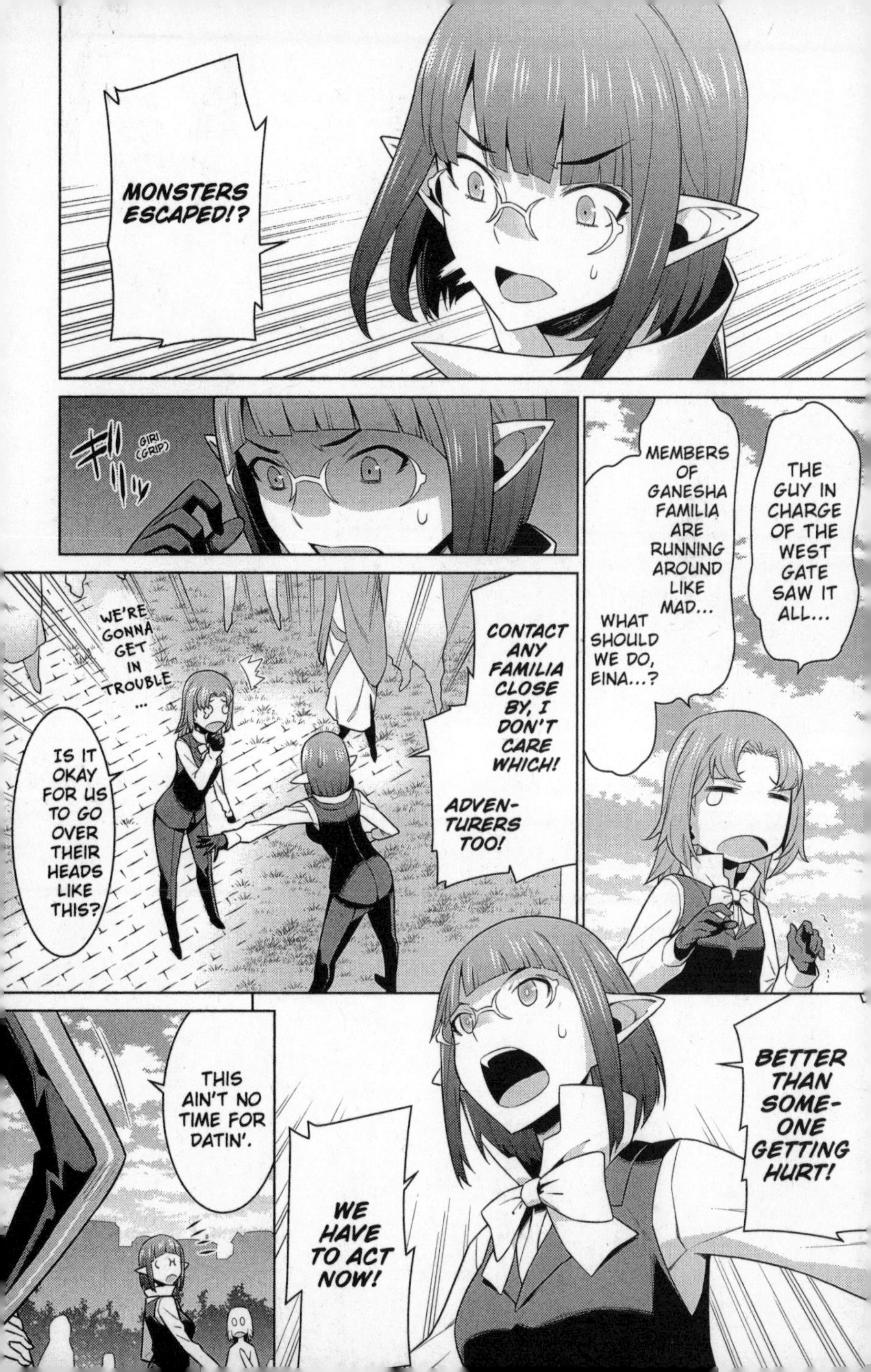

MONSTERS ESCAPED!?
THE GUY IN CHARGE OF THE WEST GATE SAW IT ALL...
MEMBERS OF GANESHA FAMILIA ARE RUNNING AROUND LIKE MAD...
WHAT SHOULD WE DO, EINA...?
GIRI (GRIP)
CONTACT ANY FAMILIA CLOSE BY, I DON'T CARE WHICH!
ADVEN-TURERS TOO!
WE'RE GONNA GET IN TROUBLE...
IS IT OKAY FOR US TO GO OVER THEIR HEADS LIKE THIS?
BETTER THAN SOME-ONE GETTING HURT!
WE HAVE TO ACT NOW!
THIS AIN'T NO TIME FOR DATIN'.

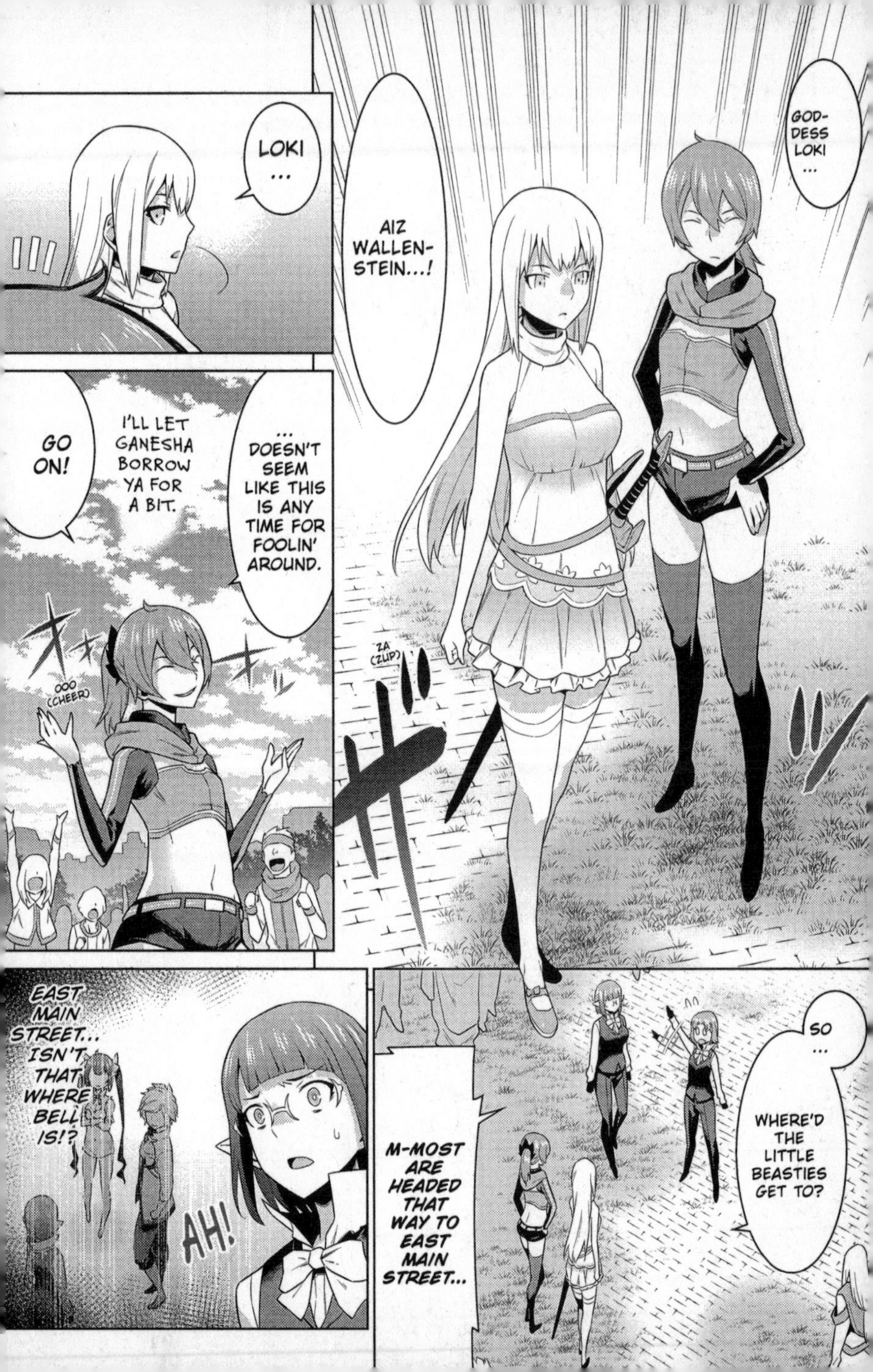
GOD-DESS LOKI ...
AIZ WALLEN-STEIN...!
ZA (ZUP)
LOKI ...
... DOESN'T SEEM LIKE THIS IS ANY TIME FOR FOOLIN' AROUND.
I'LL LET GANESHA BORROW YA FOR A BIT.
GO ON!
OOO (CHEER)
SO ...
WHERE'D THE LITTLE BEASTIES GET TO?
M-MOST ARE HEADED THAT WAY TO EAST MAIN STREET...
AH!
EAST MAIN STREET... ISN'T THAT WHERE BELL IS!?

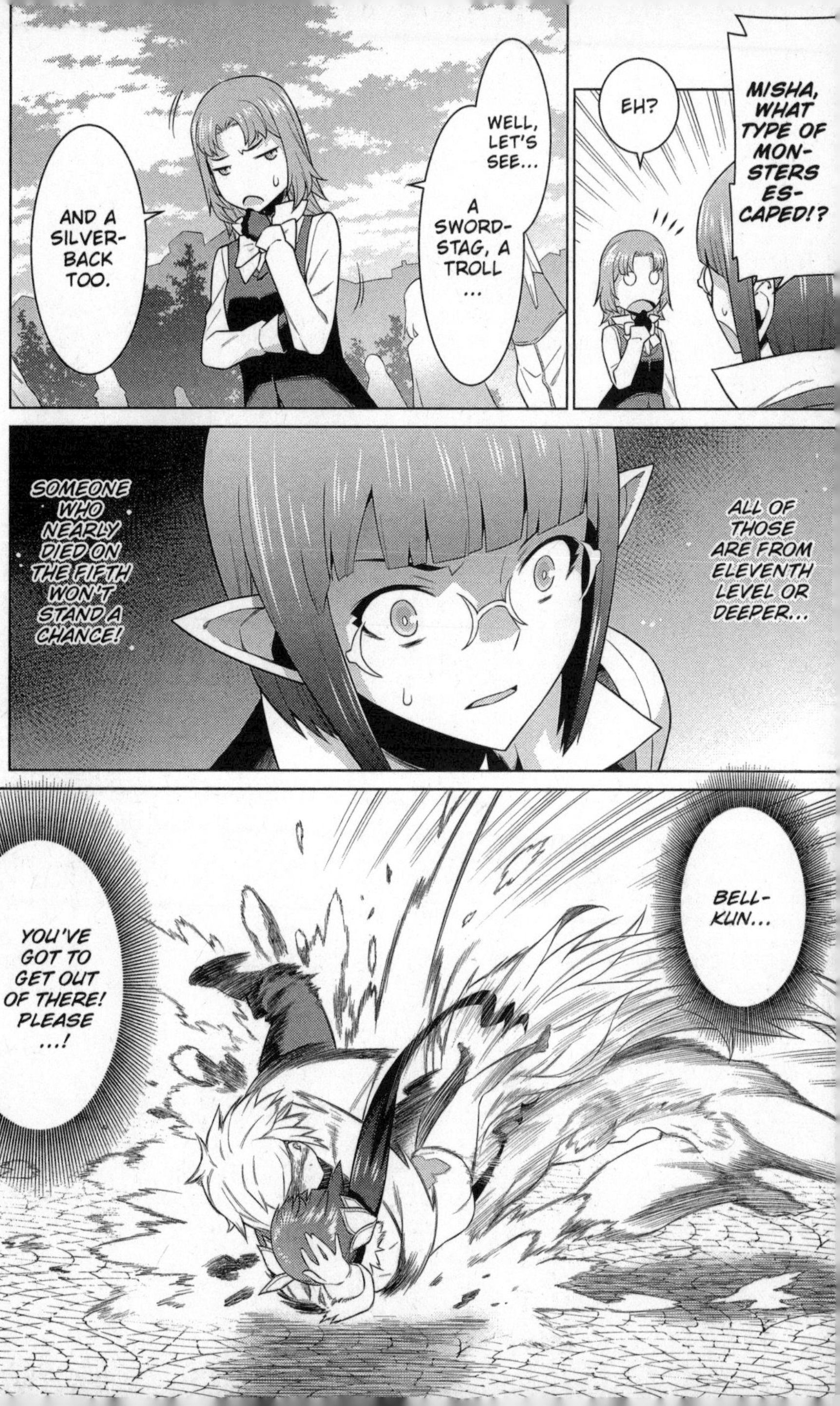
MISHA, WHAT TYPE OF MON-STERS ES-CAPED!?
EH?
WELL, LET'S SEE...
A SWORD-STAG, A TROLL ...
AND A SILVER-BACK TOO.
ALL OF THOSE ARE FROM ELEVENTH LEVEL OR DEEPER...
SOMEONE WHO NEARLY DIED ON THE FIFTH WON'T STAND A CHANCE!
BELL-KUN...
YOU'VE GOT TO GET OUT OF THERE! PLEASE ...!

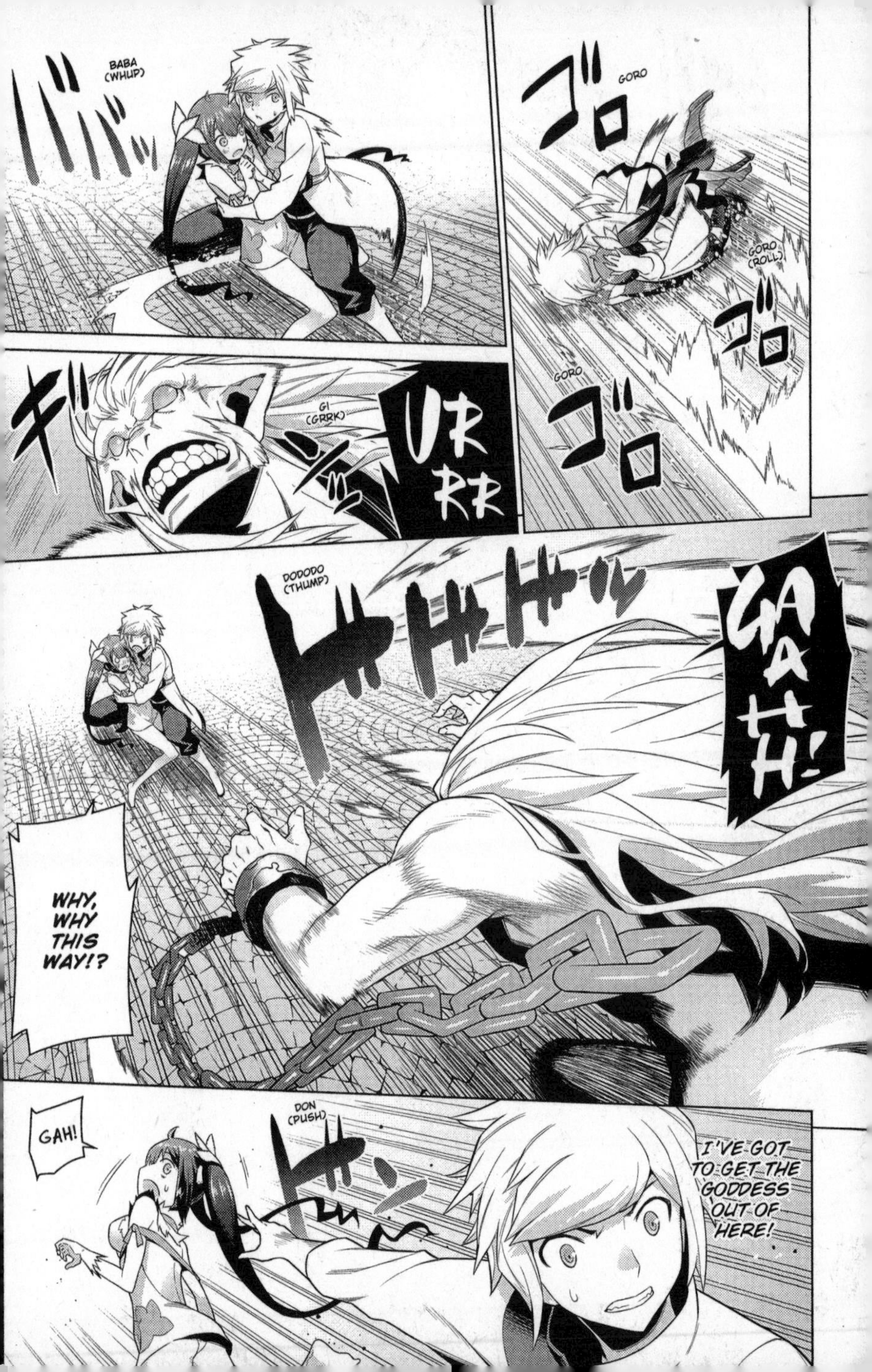
ゴロ
GORO
GORO (ROLL)
ゴロ
GORO
ゴロ
BABA (WHUP)
GI (GRRK)
URRRR
DODODO (THUMP)
GAAHH!
WHY, WHY THIS WAY!?
I'VE GOT TO GET THE GODDESS OUT OF HERE!
DON (PUSH)
GAH!

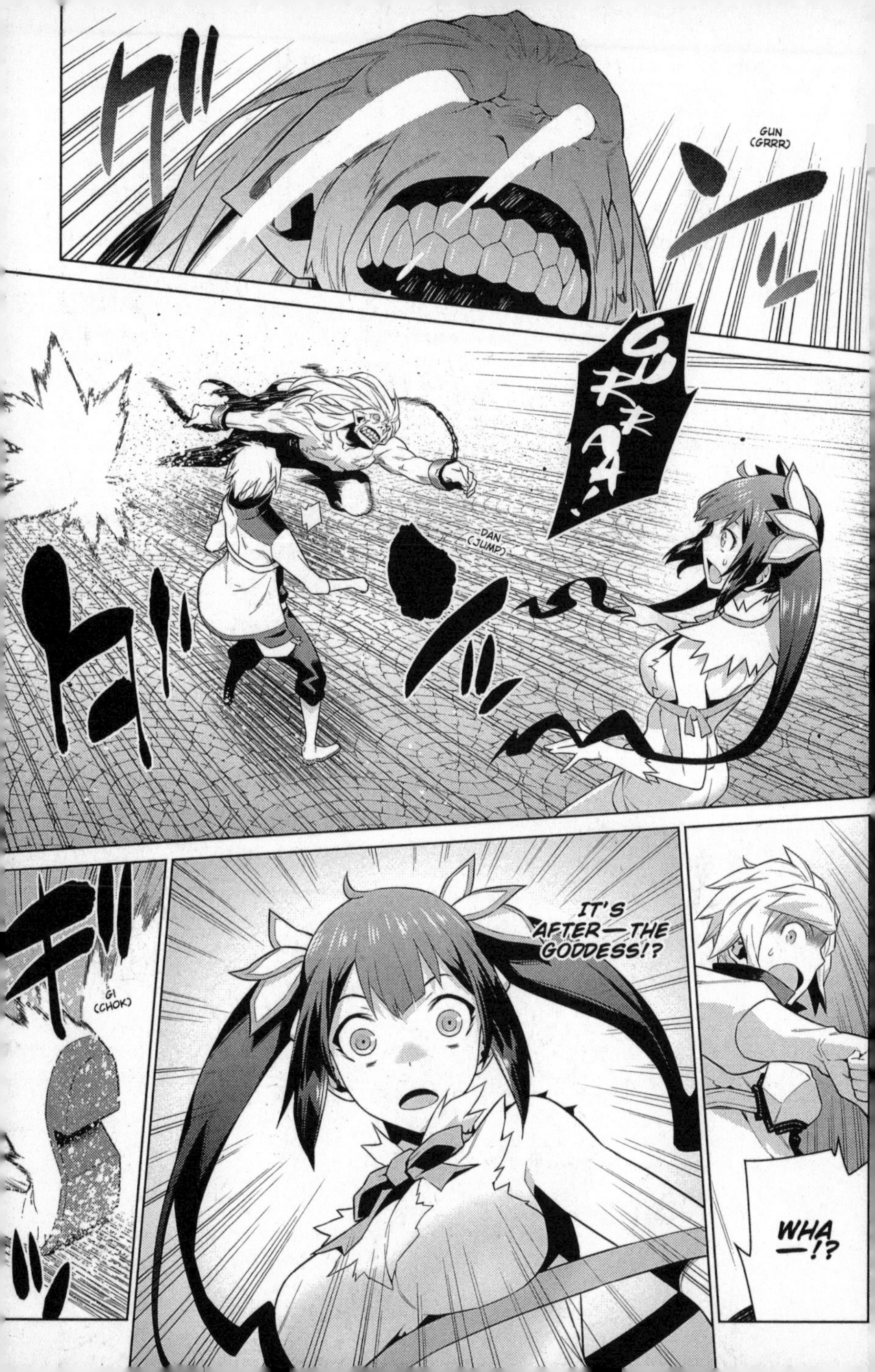
GUN
(GRRR)
GURRAA!
DAN
(JUMP)
WHA—!?
IT'S AFTER—THE GODDESS!?
GI
(CHOK)

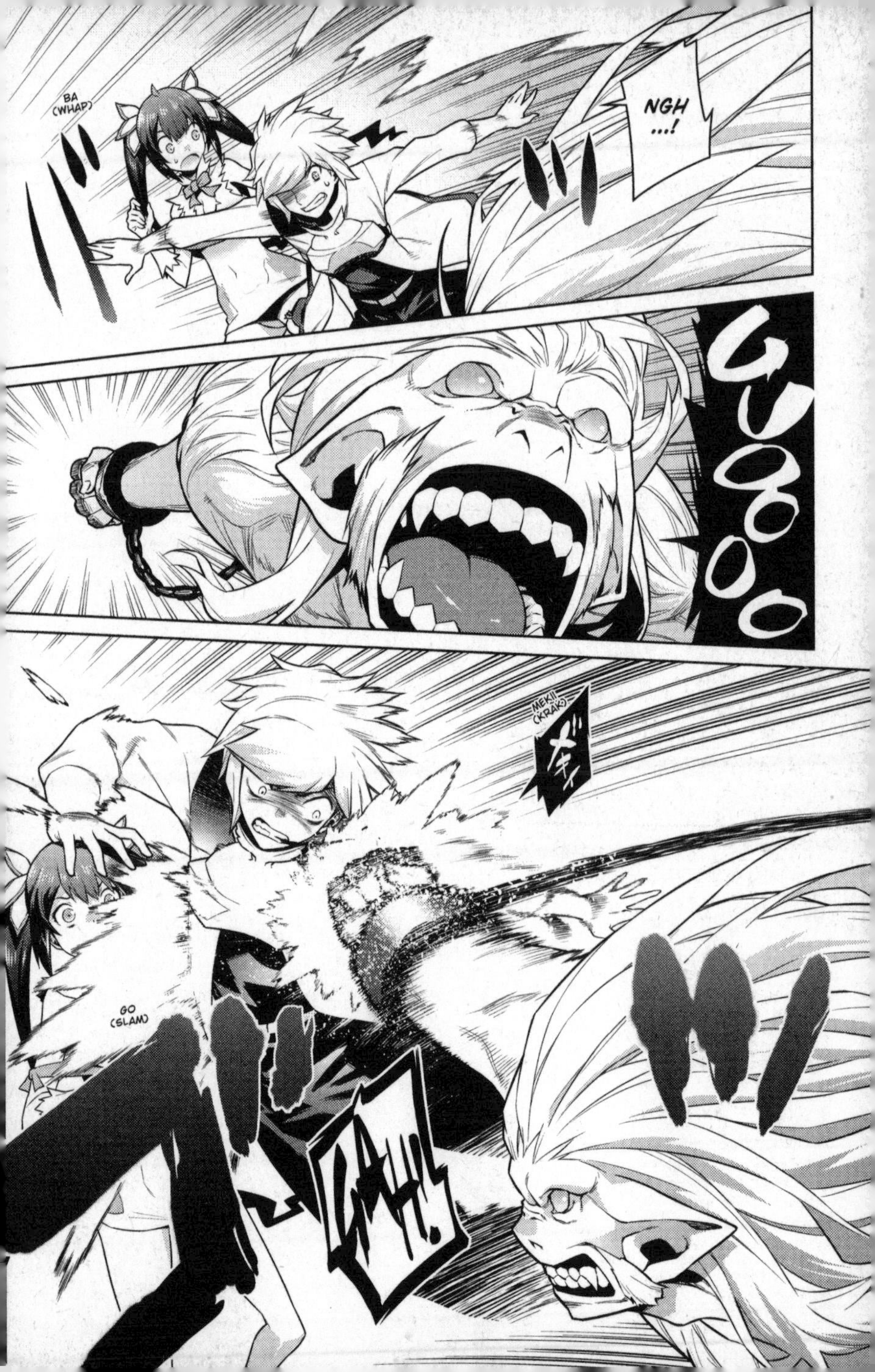
NGH ...!
BA (WHAP)
UUOOOO
MEKI! (KRAK)
GAH!!
GO (SLAM)

CITIZENS OF ORARIO

text by Fujino Omori
character rough by Kunieda

➤File 01

BELL CRANELL

The main character, he belongs to Hestia Familia. He is a human boy who ventured into the Dungeon to meet girls on the advice of his grandfather. He has a strong desire to become a hero.

CITIZENS OF ORARIO

text by Fujino Omori
character rough by Kunieda

➤File 02

HESTIA

A young goddess, she leads Hestia Familia. Very few have faith in her. A down-and-out goddess. She both understands Bell and has special feelings for him.

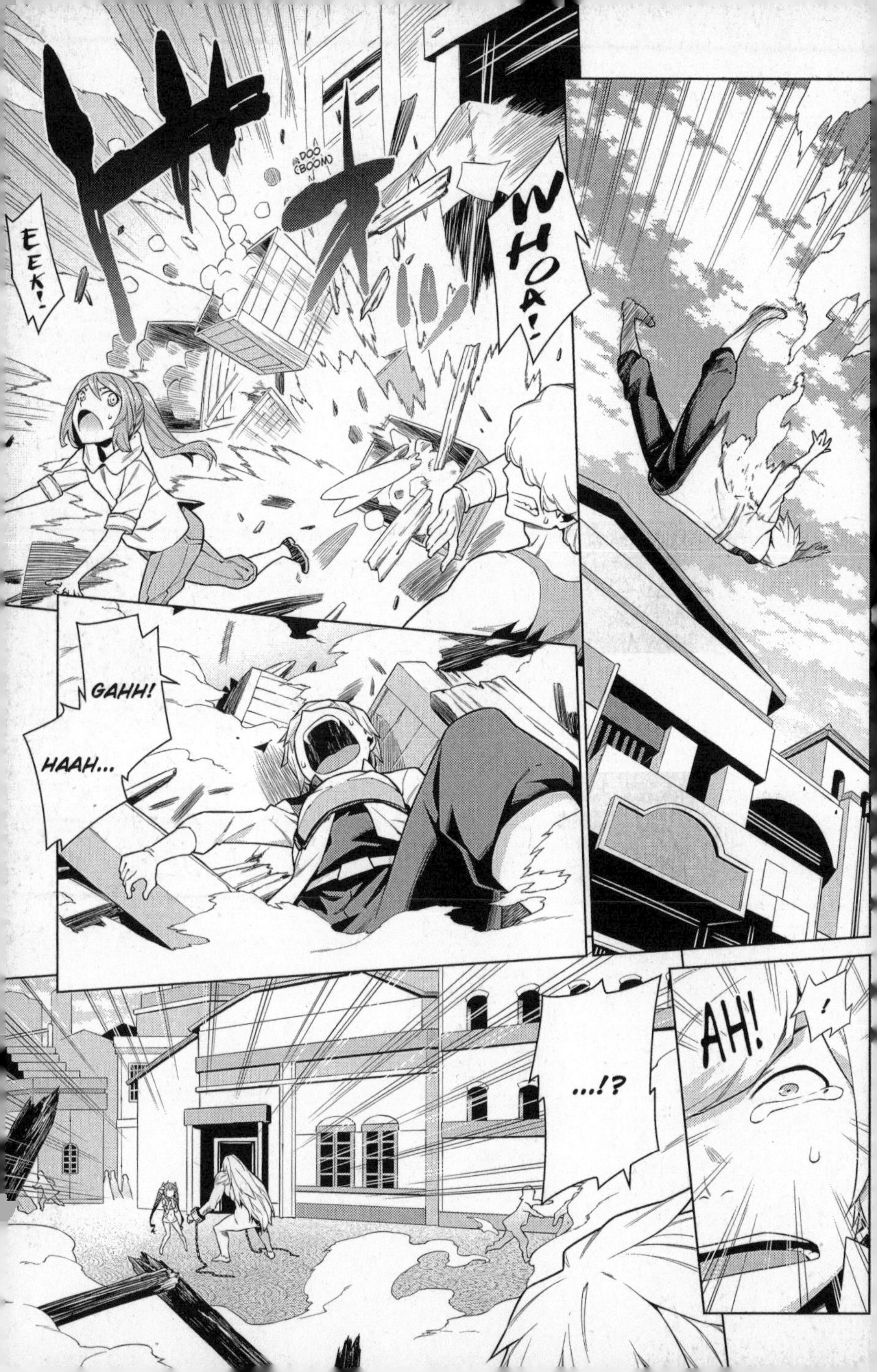
WHOA!
DOO (BOOM)
EEK!
GAHH!
HAAH...
AH!
!
...!?

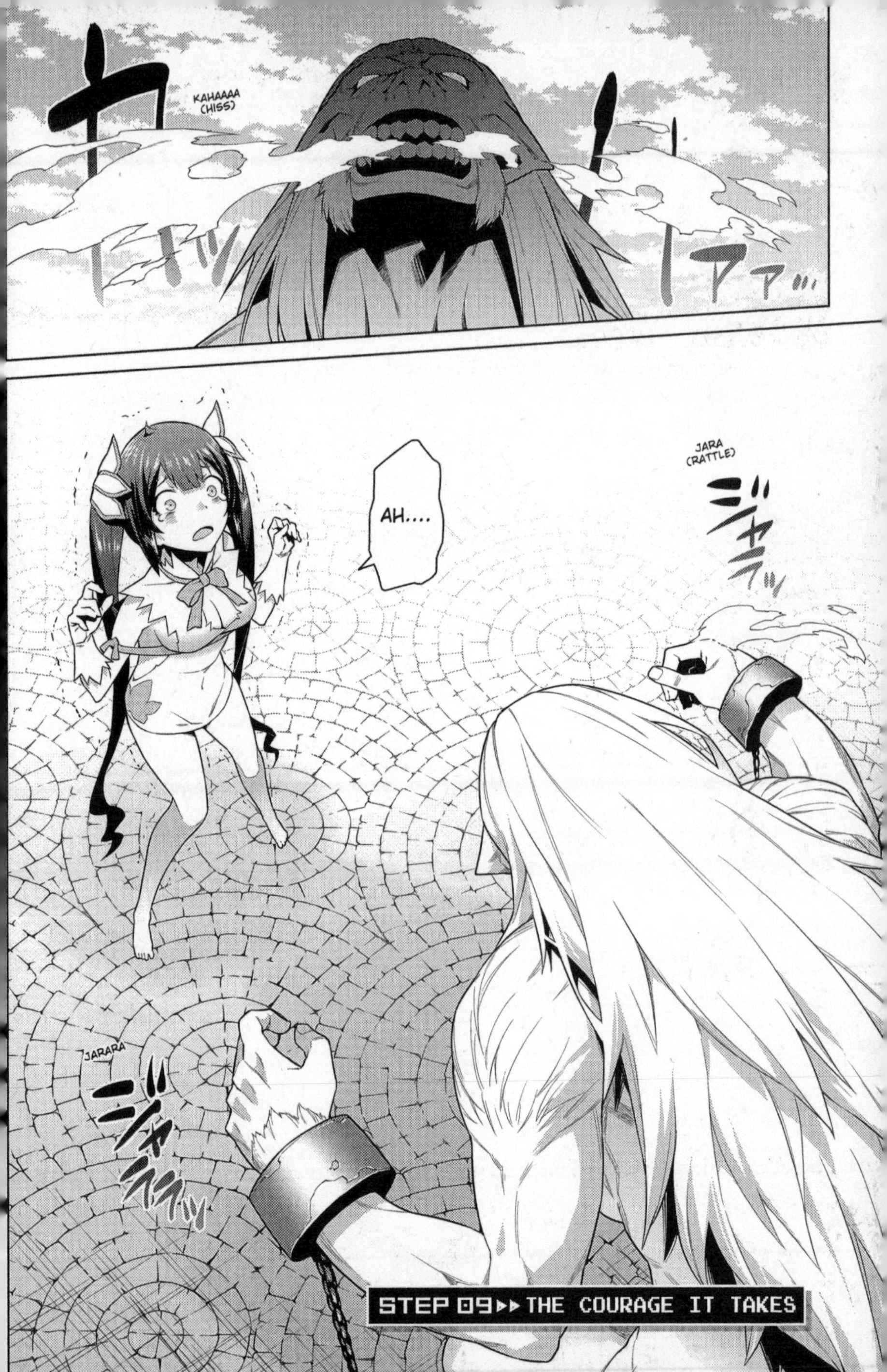
KAHAAAA (HISS)
JARA (RATTLE)
AH....
JARARA
STEP 09 ▸▸ THE COURAGE IT TAKES

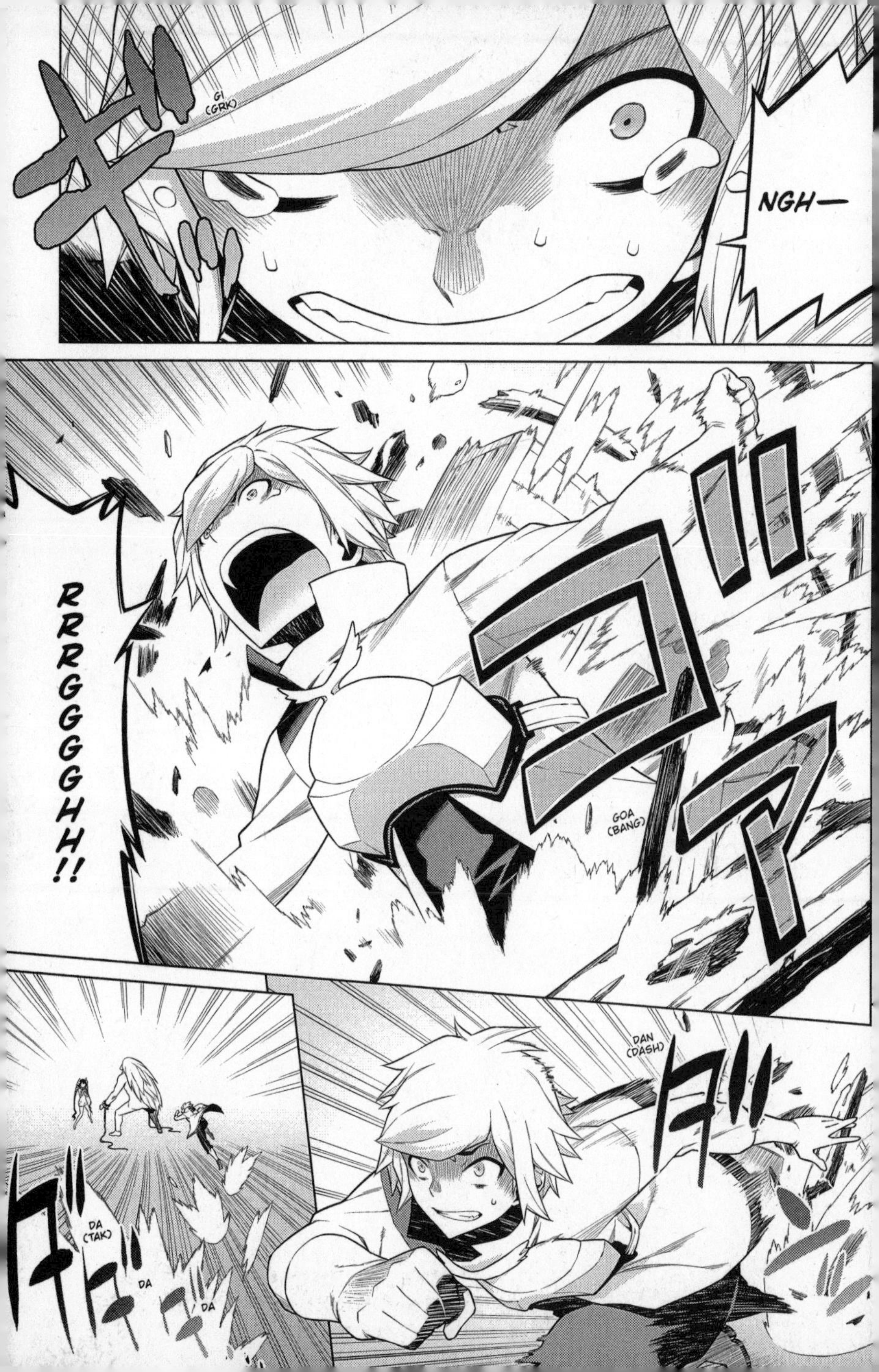
NGH—
GI
(GRK)
GOA
(BANG)
RRRGGGGGHH!!
DAN
(DASH)
DA
(TAK)
DA
DA

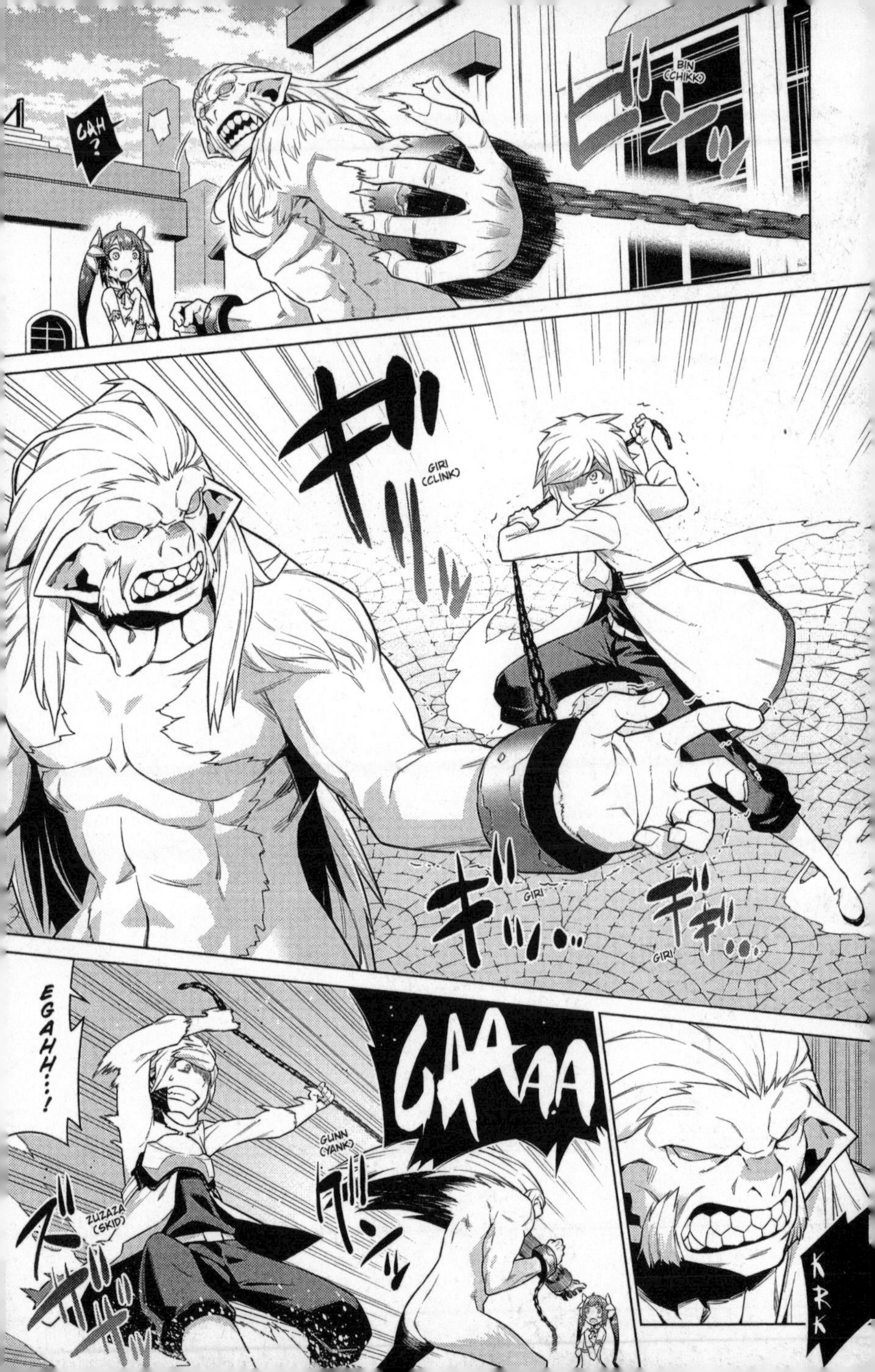

BIN (CHIKK)
GAH ?
GIRI (CLINK)
GIRI
GIRI
KRK
GAAAA
GUNN (YANK)
EGAHH...!
ZUZAZA (SKID)

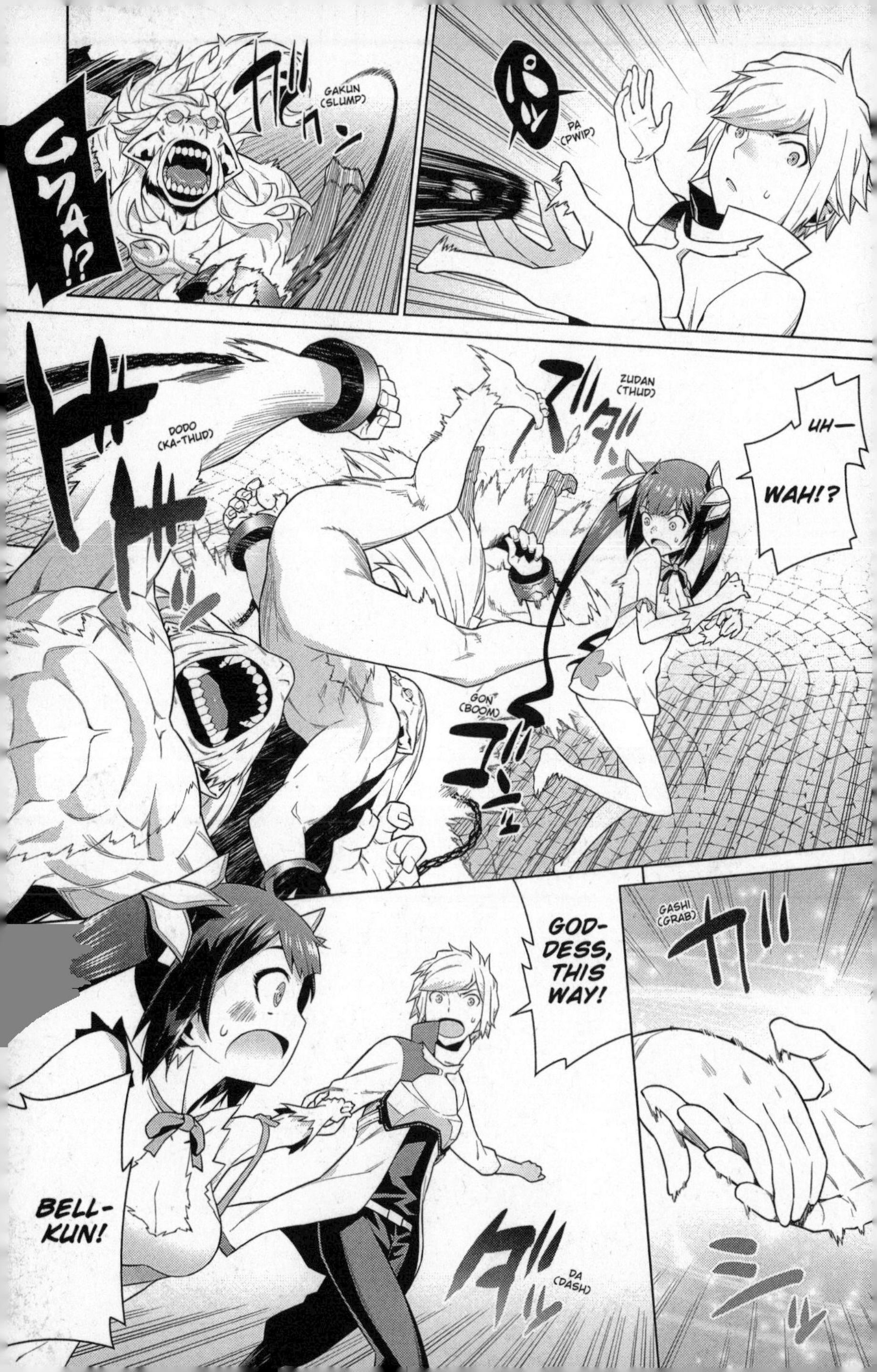
PA (PWIP)
GAKUN (SLUMP)
GYAA!?
UH— WAH!?
ZUDAN (THUD)
DODO (KA-THUD)
GON (BOOM)
GASHI (GRAB)
GOD-DESS, THIS WAY!
BELL-KUN!
DA (DASH)

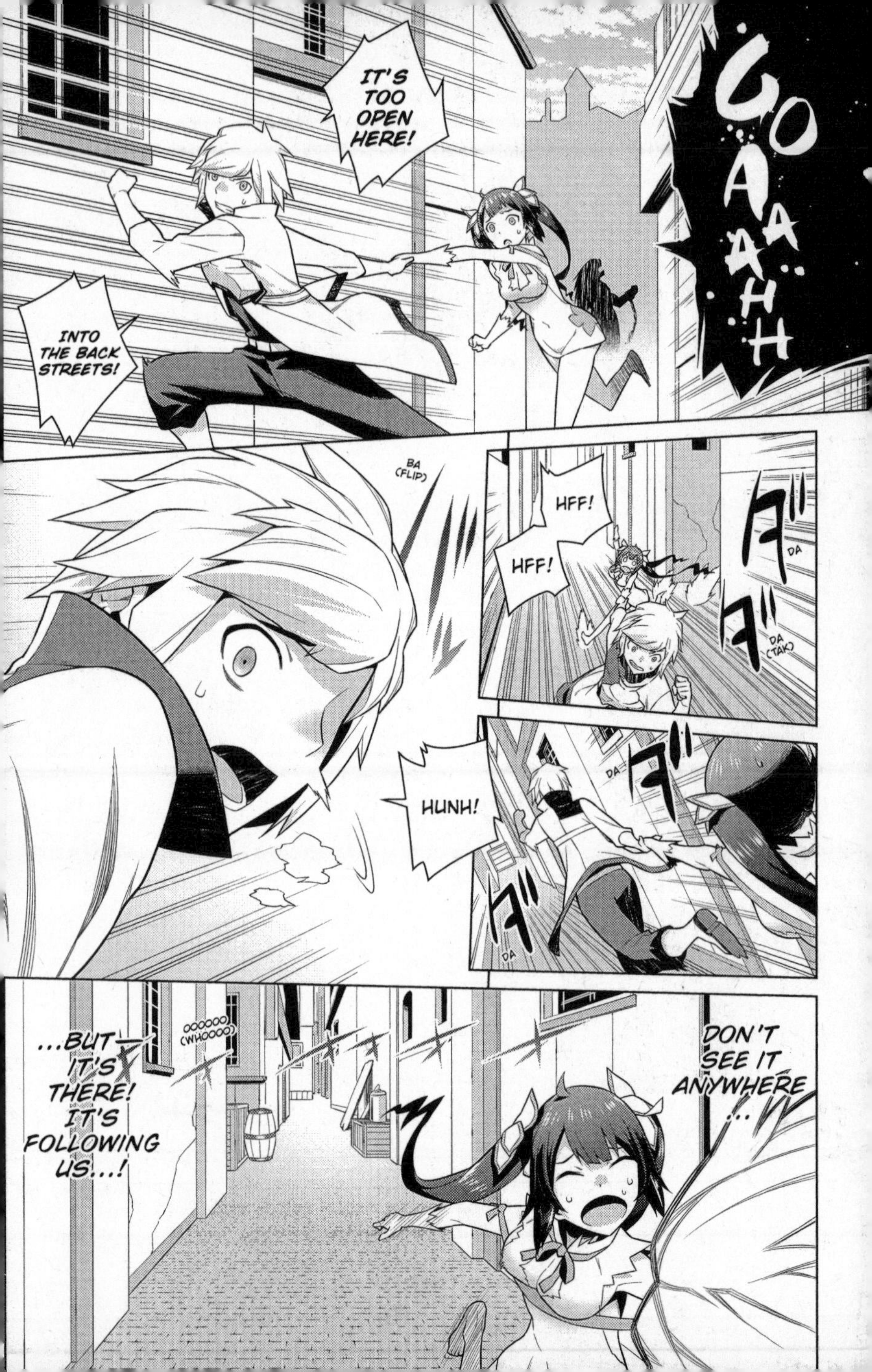
GOAAAAHH
IT'S TOO OPEN HERE!
INTO THE BACK STREETS!
HFF!
HFF!
ダ DA
ダ DA (TAK)
ダ DA
ダ DA
BA (FLIP)
HUNH!
DON'T SEE IT ANYWHERE...
OOOOOO (WHOOOO)
...BUT— IT'S THERE! IT'S FOLLOWING US...!

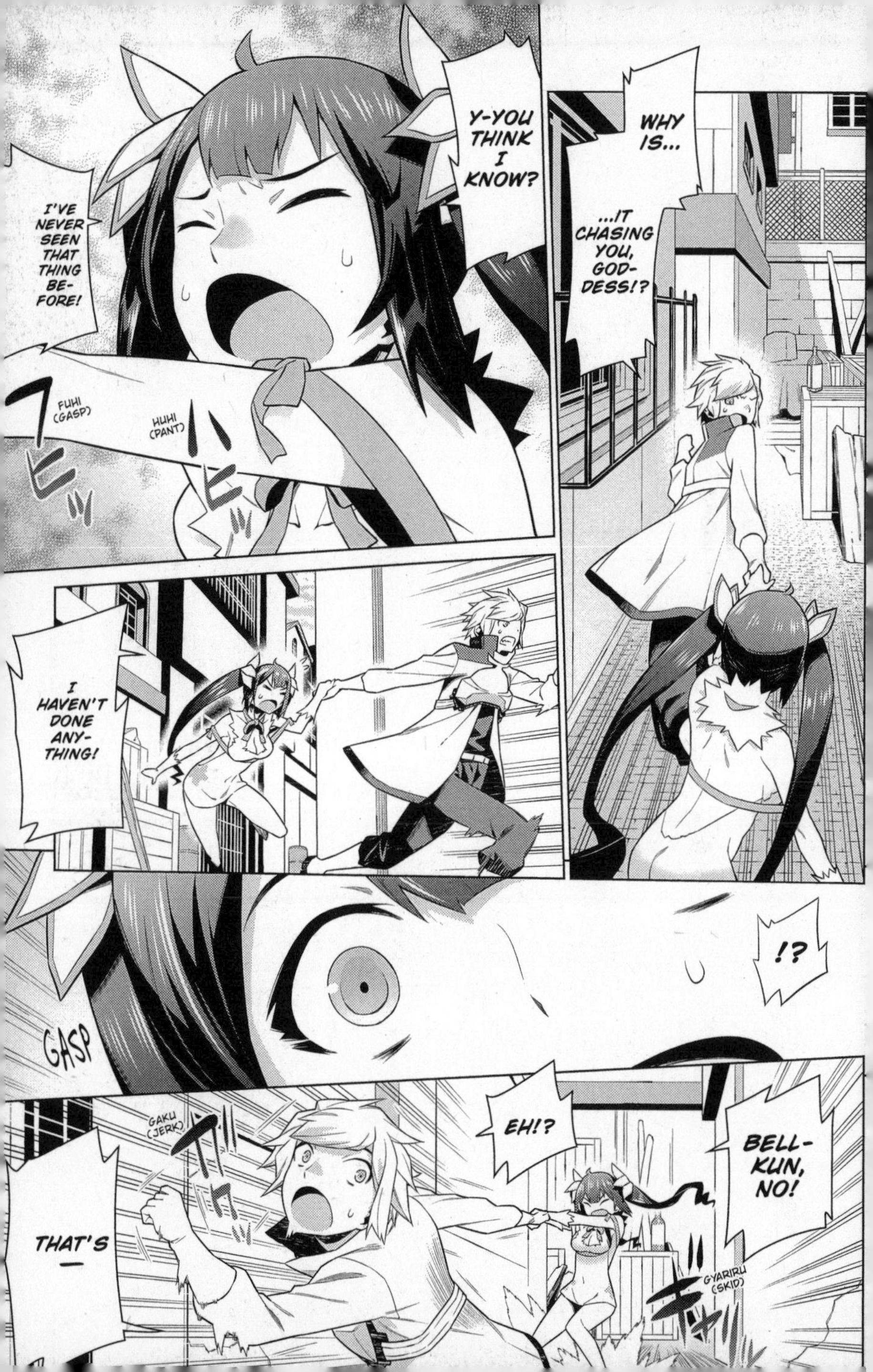
WHY IS...
...IT CHASING YOU, GOD-DESS!?
Y-YOU THINK I KNOW?
I'VE NEVER SEEN THAT THING BE-FORE!
FUHI (GASP)
HUHI (PANT)
I HAVEN'T DONE ANY-THING!
!?
GASP
BELL-KUN, NO!
GYARIRU (SKID)
EH!?
GAKU (JERK)
THAT'S —

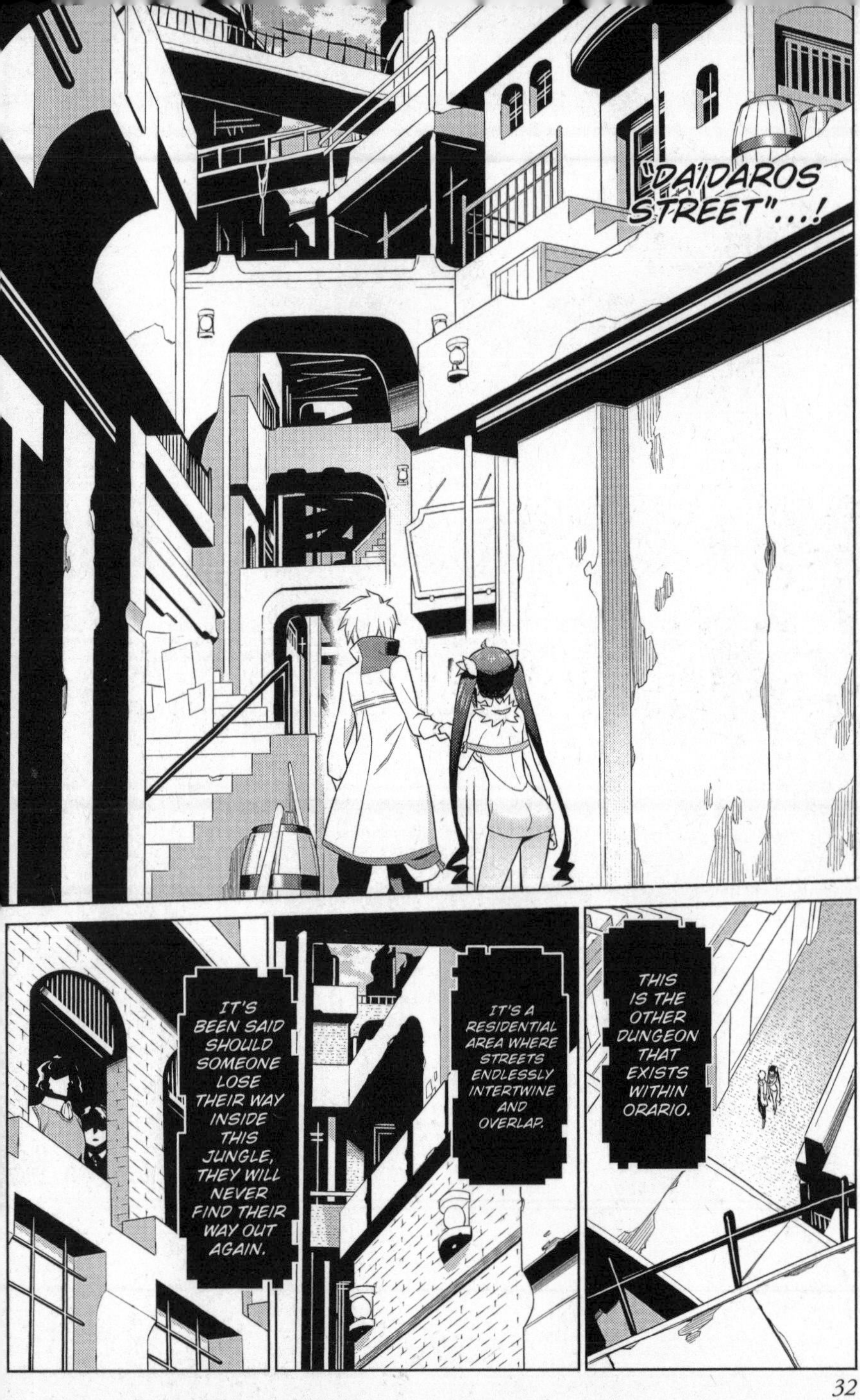
"DAIDAROS STREET"...!
THIS IS THE OTHER DUNGEON THAT EXISTS WITHIN ORARIO.
IT'S A RESIDENTIAL AREA WHERE STREETS ENDLESSLY INTERTWINE AND OVERLAP.
IT'S BEEN SAID SHOULD SOMEONE LOSE THEIR WAY INSIDE THIS JUNGLE, THEY WILL NEVER FIND THEIR WAY OUT AGAIN.

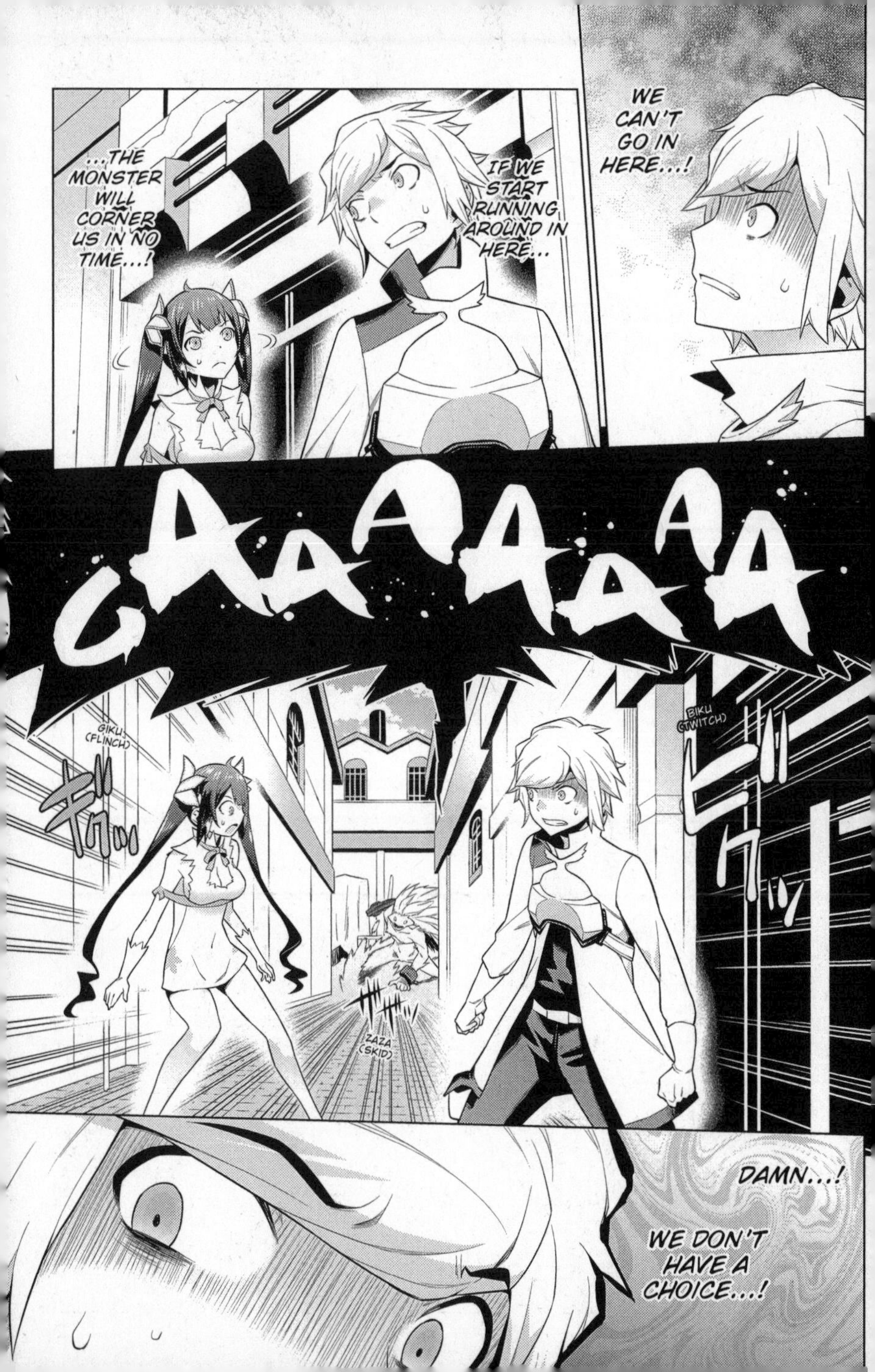
WE CAN'T GO IN HERE...!
IF WE START RUNNING AROUND IN HERE...
...THE MONSTER WILL CORNER US IN NO TIME...!
GAAAAAAA
BIKU (TWITCH)
GIKU (FLINCH)
ZAZA (SKID)
DAMN...!
WE DON'T HAVE A CHOICE...!

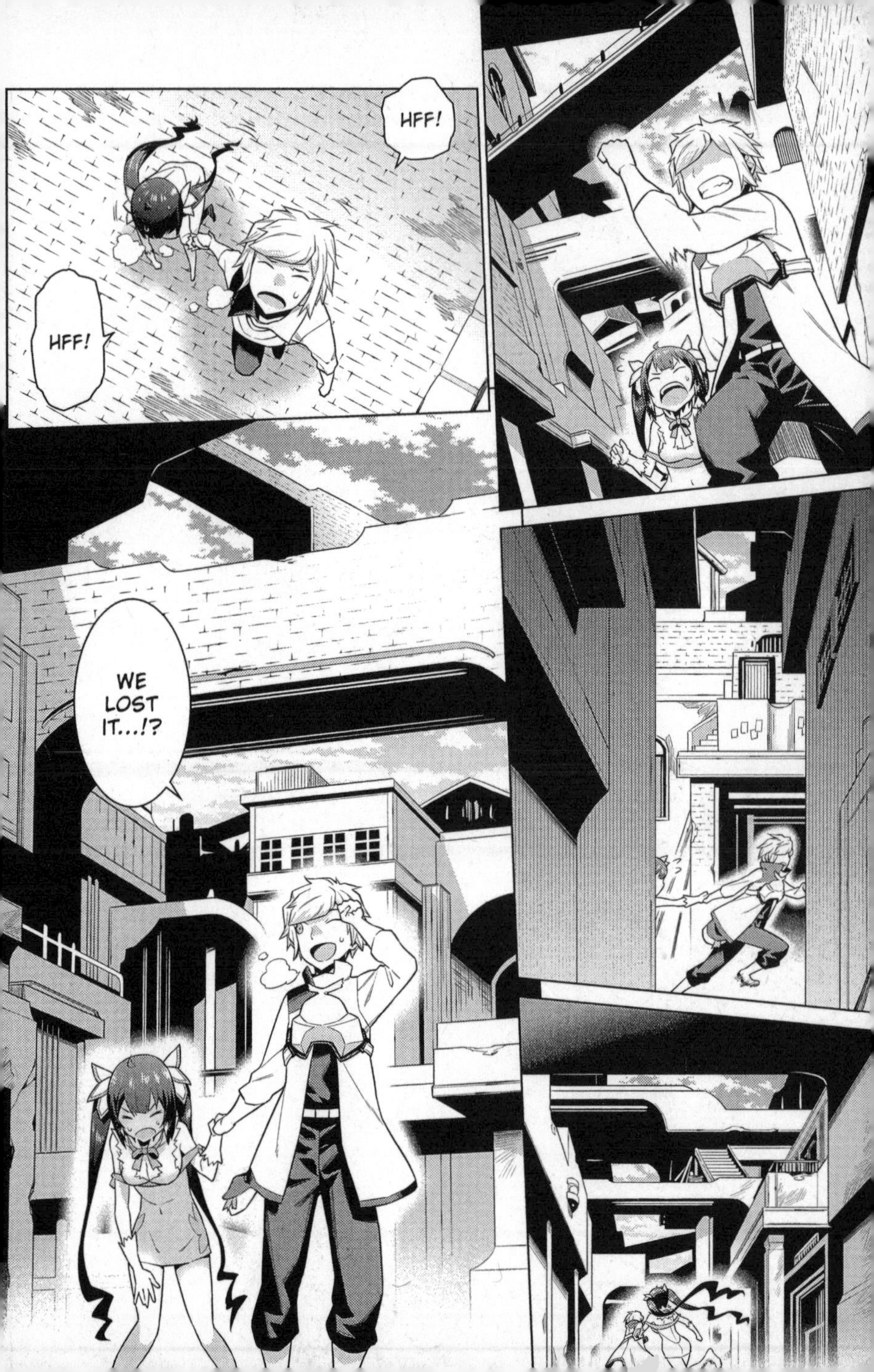
HFF!
HFF!
WE LOST IT...!?

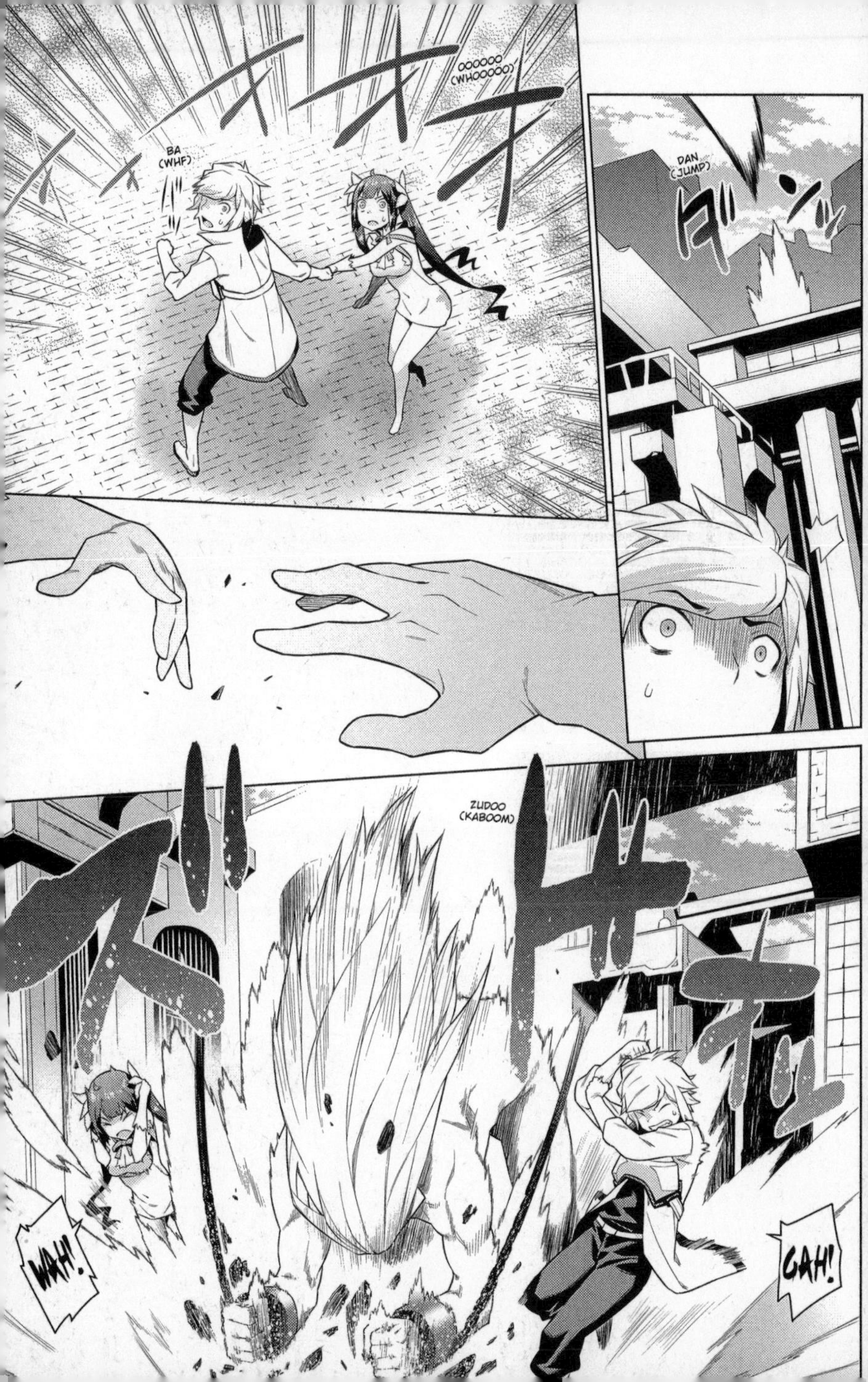
DAN
(JUMP)
OOOOOO
(WHOOOOO)
BA
(WHF)
ZUDOO
(KABOOM)
GAH!
WAH!

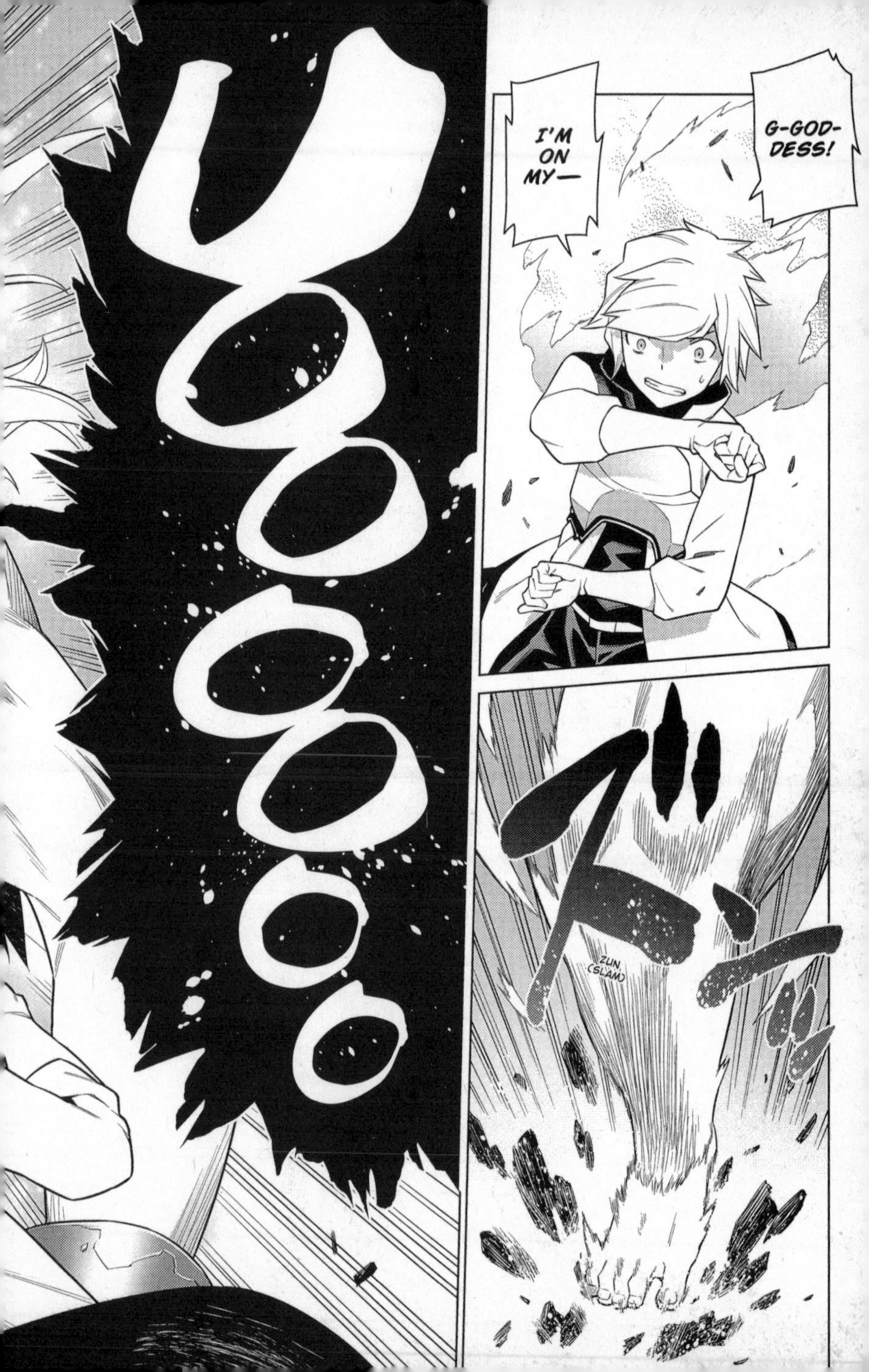
G-GOD-DESS!
I'M ON MY—
ZUN (SLAM)

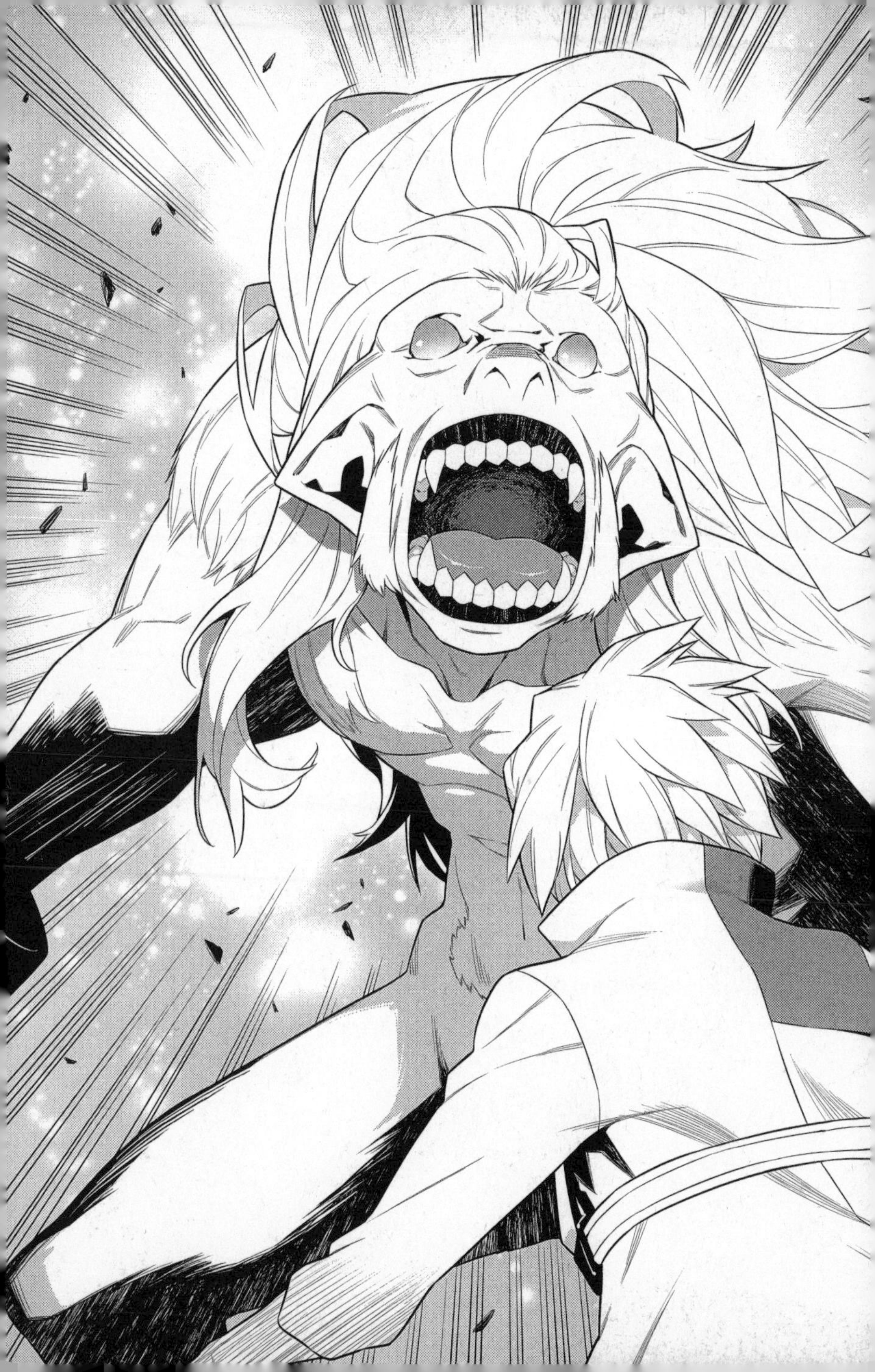

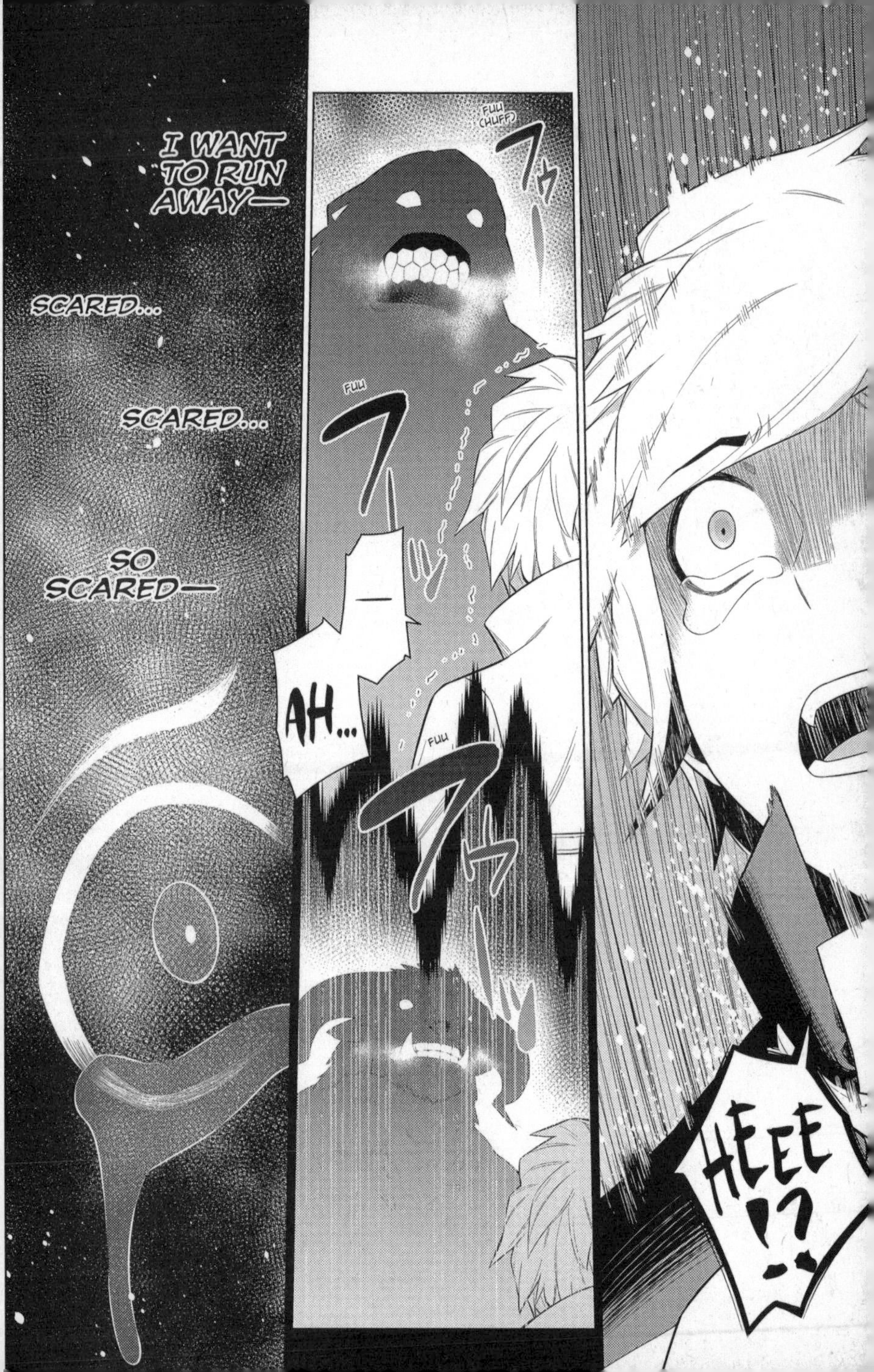
HEEE!?
FUU (CHUFF)
FUU
AH...
FUU
I WANT TO RUN AWAY—
SCARED...
SCARED...
SO SCARED—

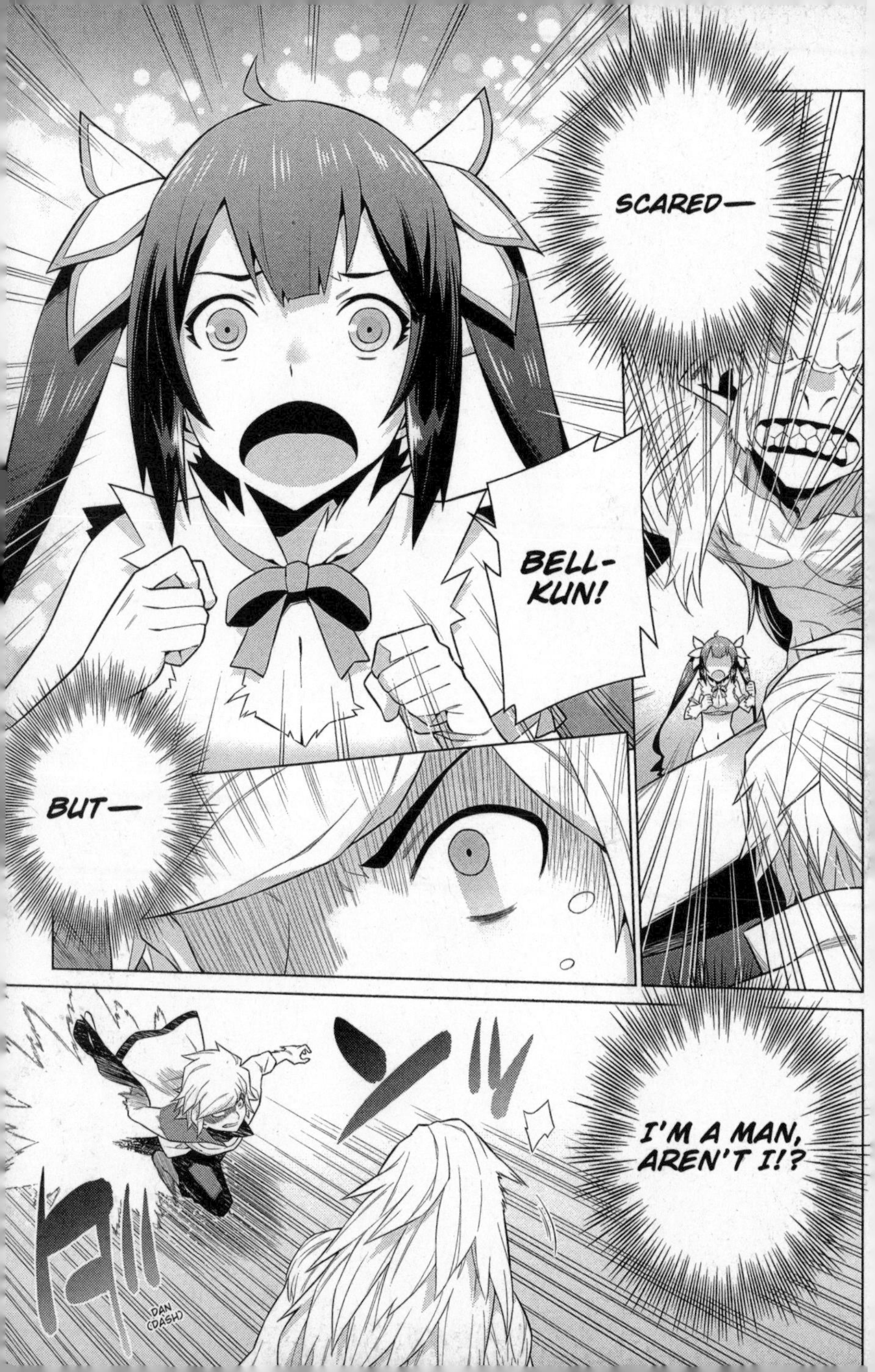
SCARED—
BELL-KUN!
BUT—
I'M A MAN, AREN'T I!?
DAN (DASH)

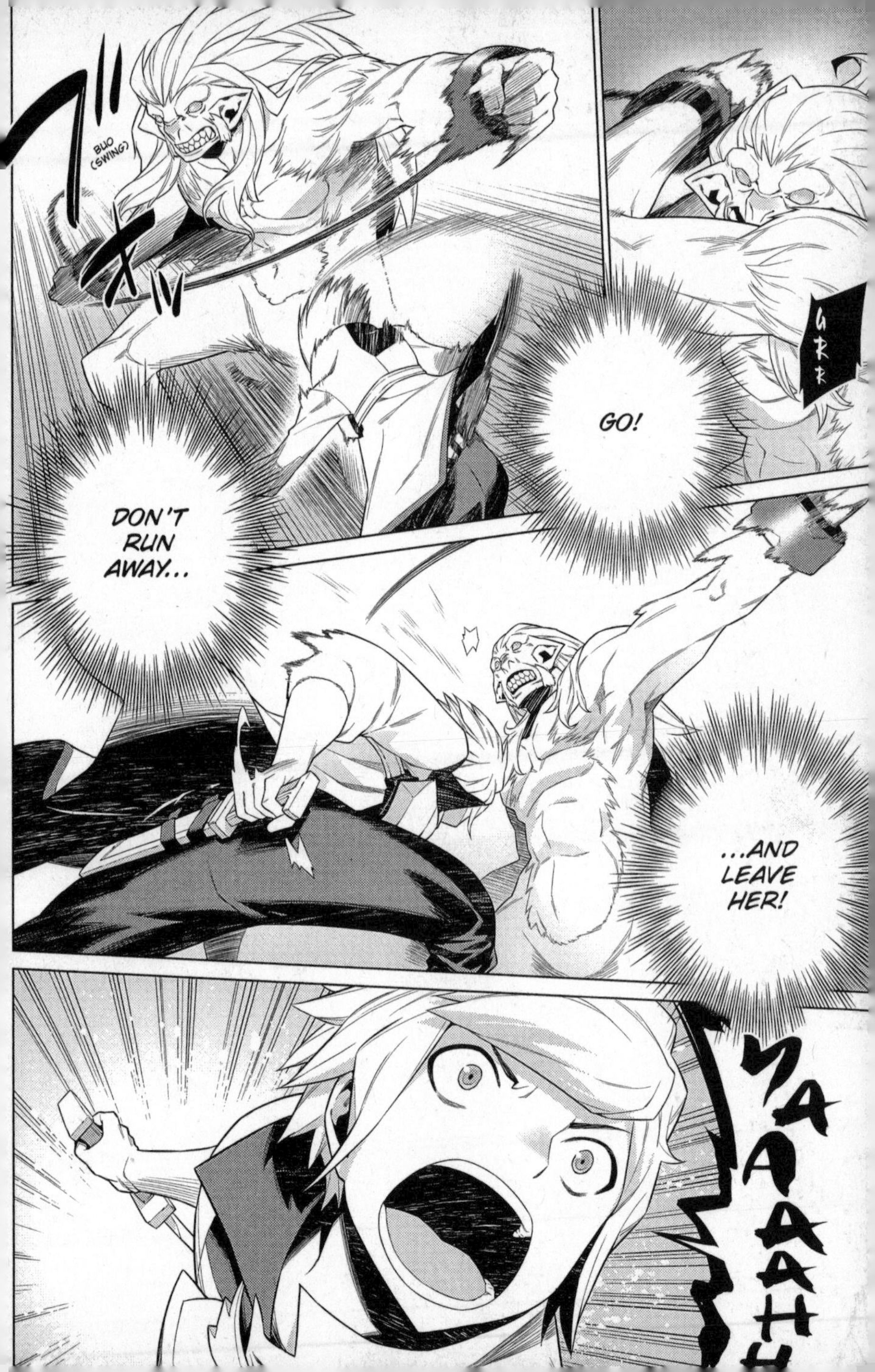
GRR
GO!
BUO (SWING)
DON'T RUN AWAY...
...AND LEAVE HER!
YAAAAAH

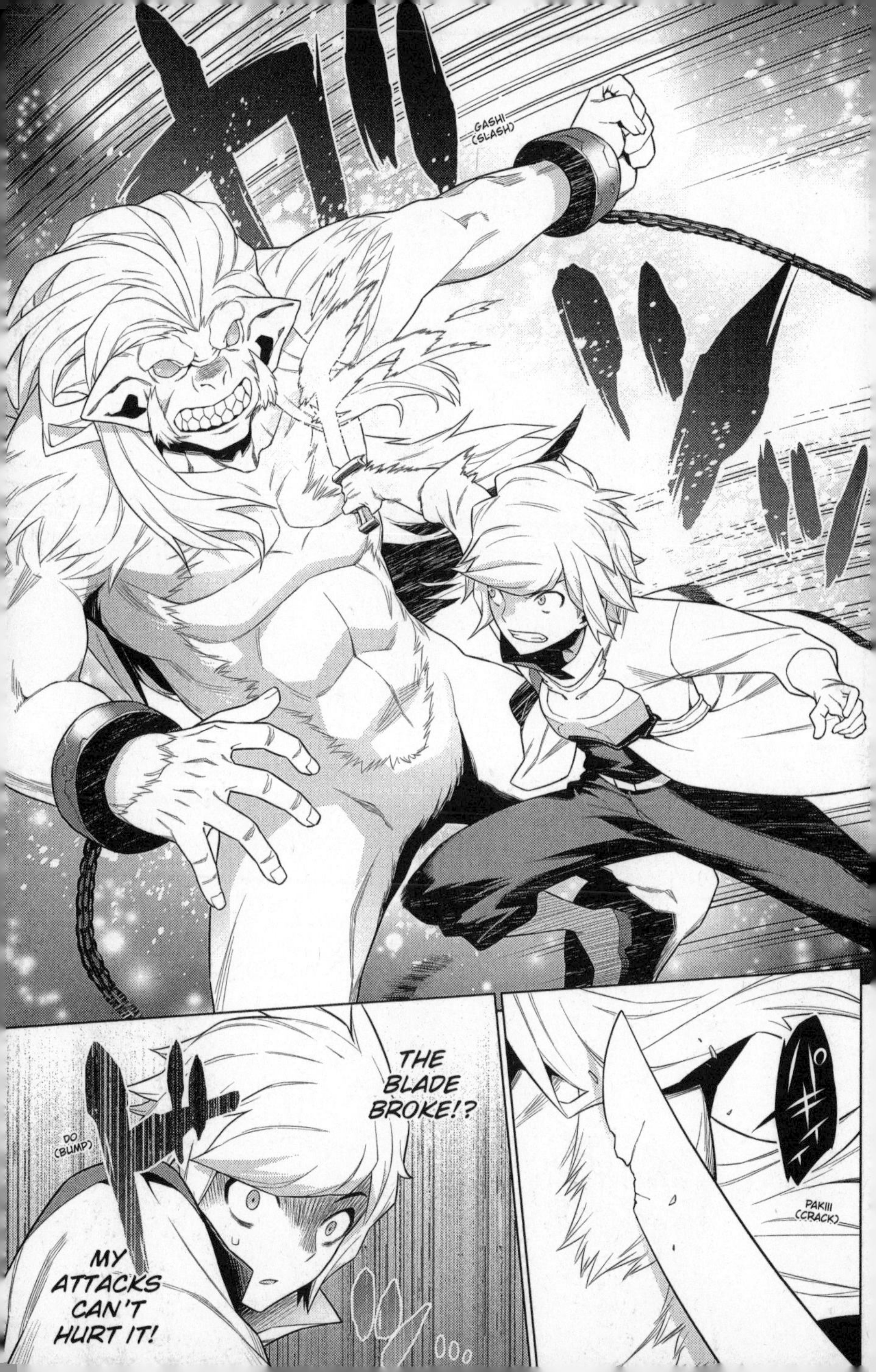
GASHI (SLASH)
PAKIII (CRACK)
THE BLADE BROKE!?
DO (BUMP)
MY ATTACKS CAN'T HURT IT!

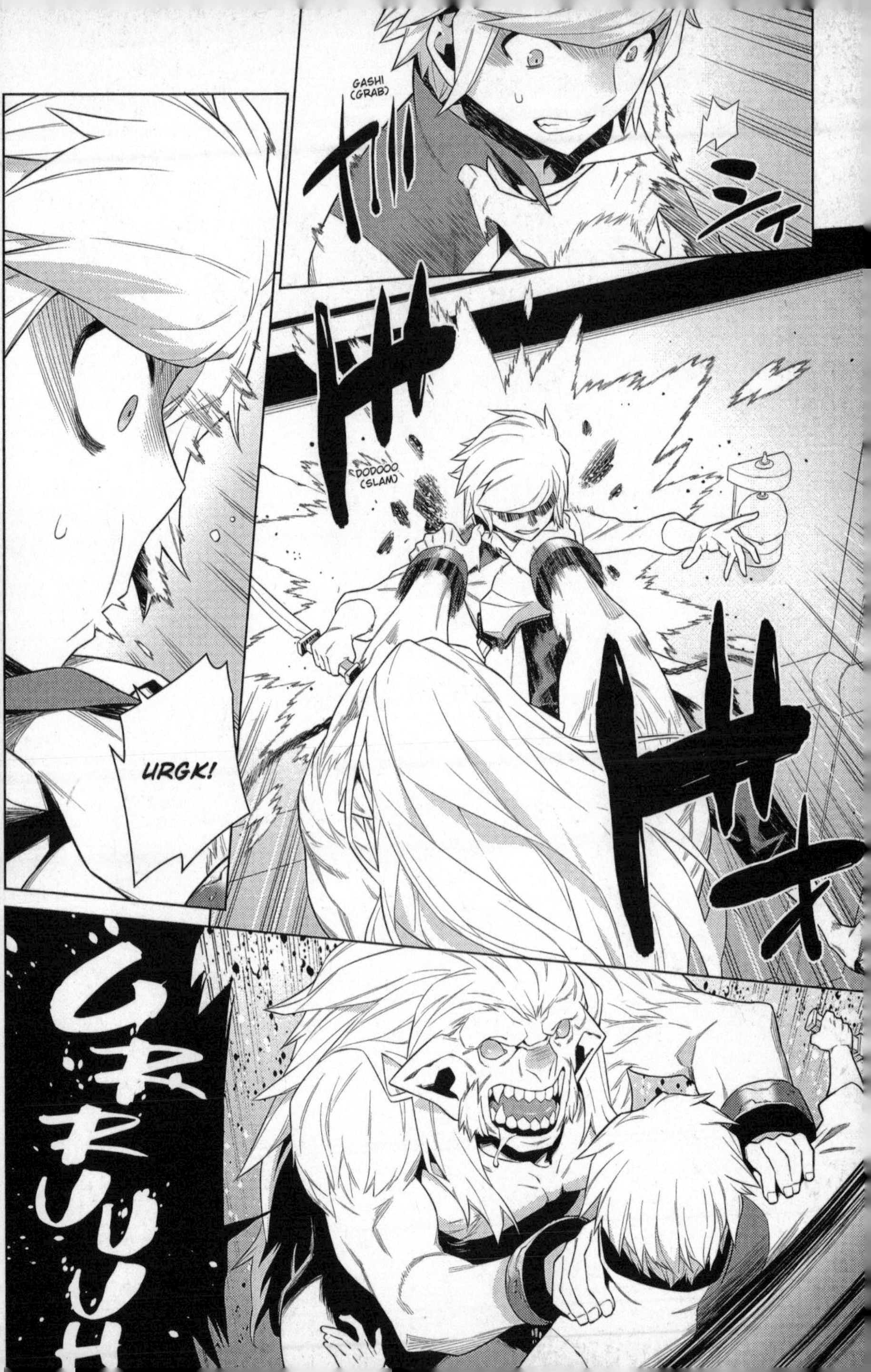
GASHI (GRAB)
DODOOO (SLAM)
URGK!

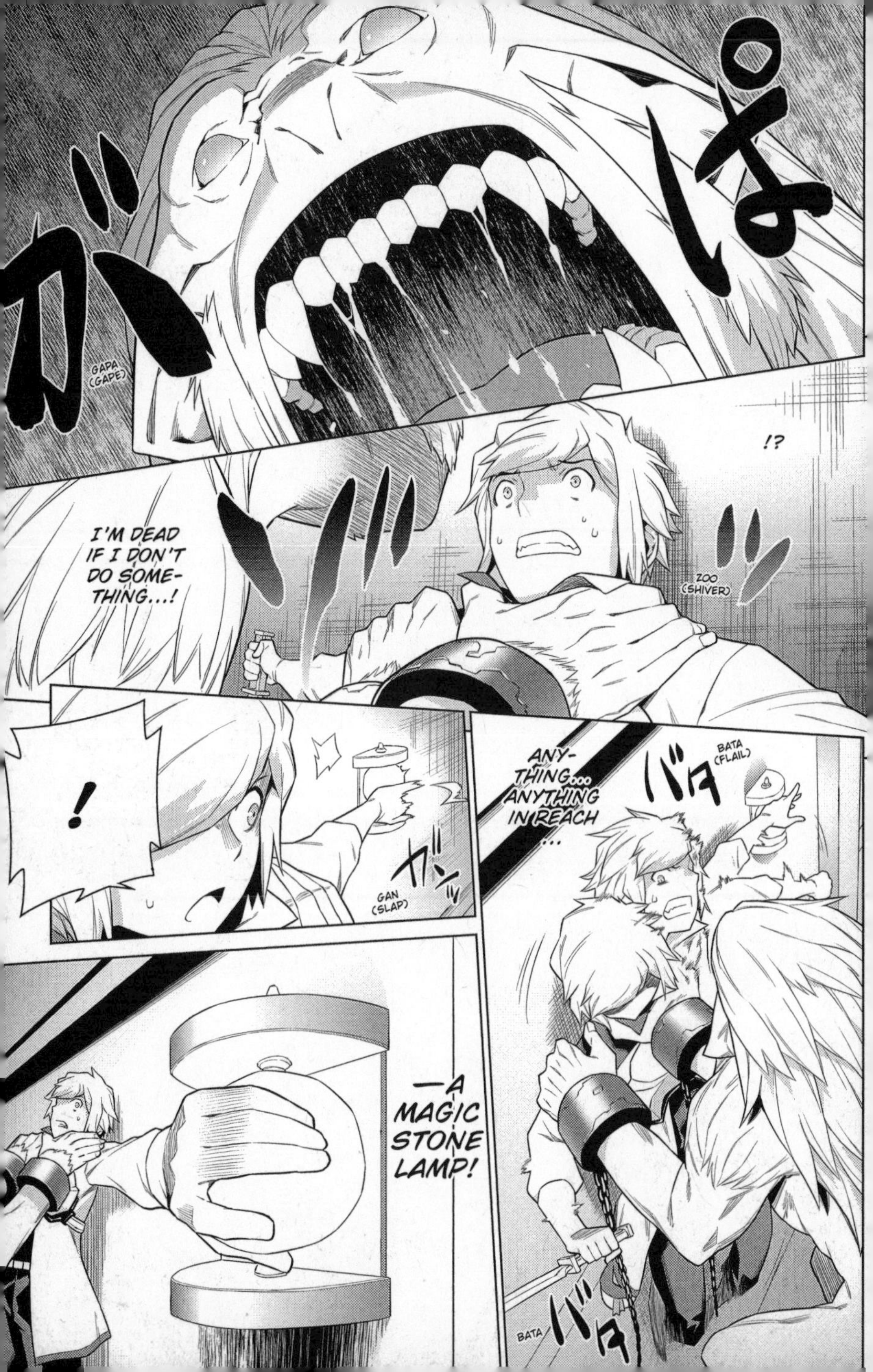
ガ
ぱ
GAPA
(GAPE)
!?
ゾッ
ZOO
(SHIVER)
I'M DEAD IF I DON'T DO SOME-THING...!
ANY-THING... ANYTHING IN REACH...
バタ
BATA
(FLAIL)
バタ
BATA
!
ガンッ
GAN
(SLAP)
—A MAGIC STONE LAMP!

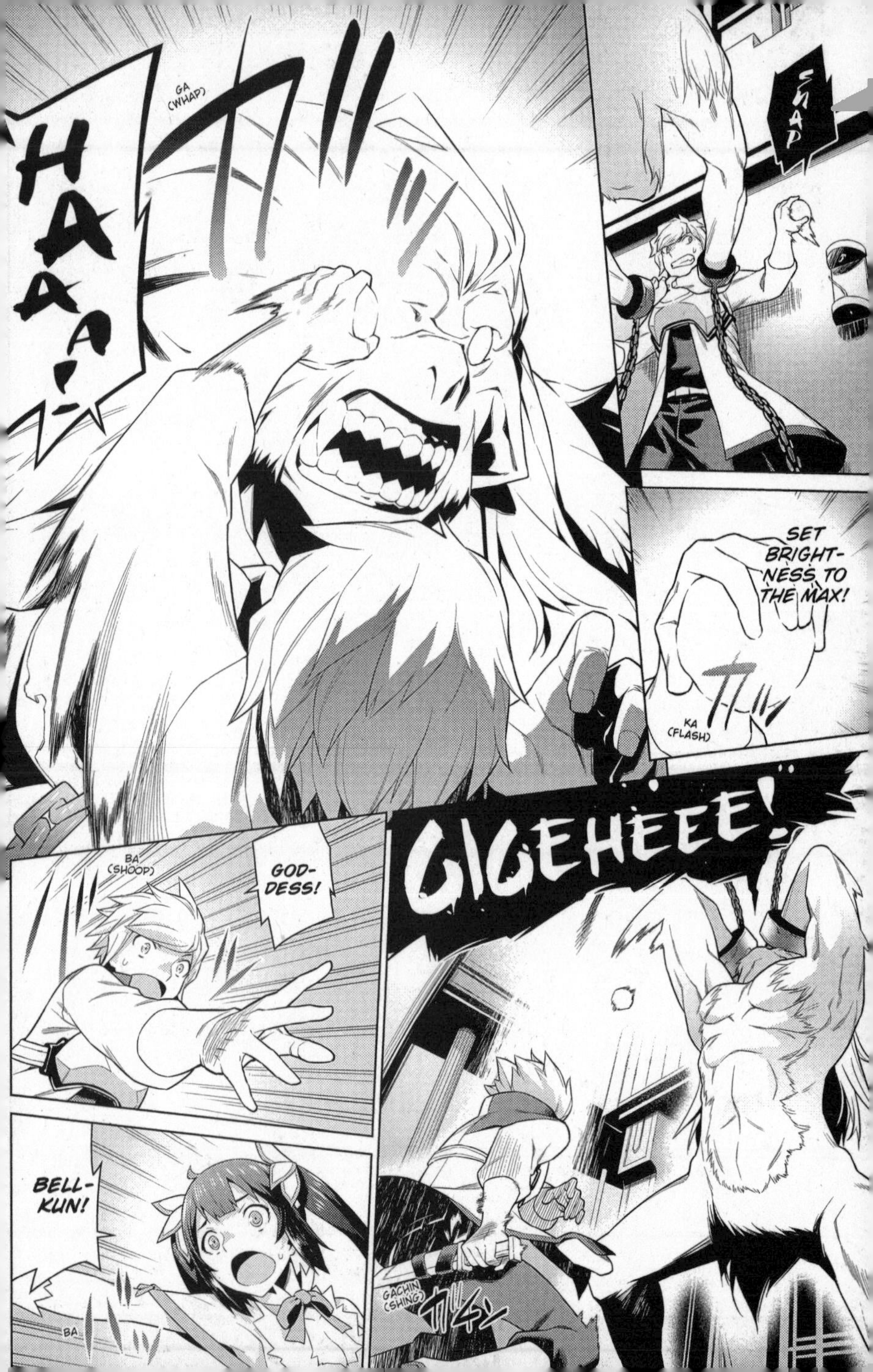
SNAP
SET BRIGHT-NESS TO THE MAX!
KA (FLASH)
HAAA!
GA (WHAP)
GIGEHEEE!
GACHIN (SHING)
GOD-DESS!
BA (SHOOP)
BELL-KUN!
BA

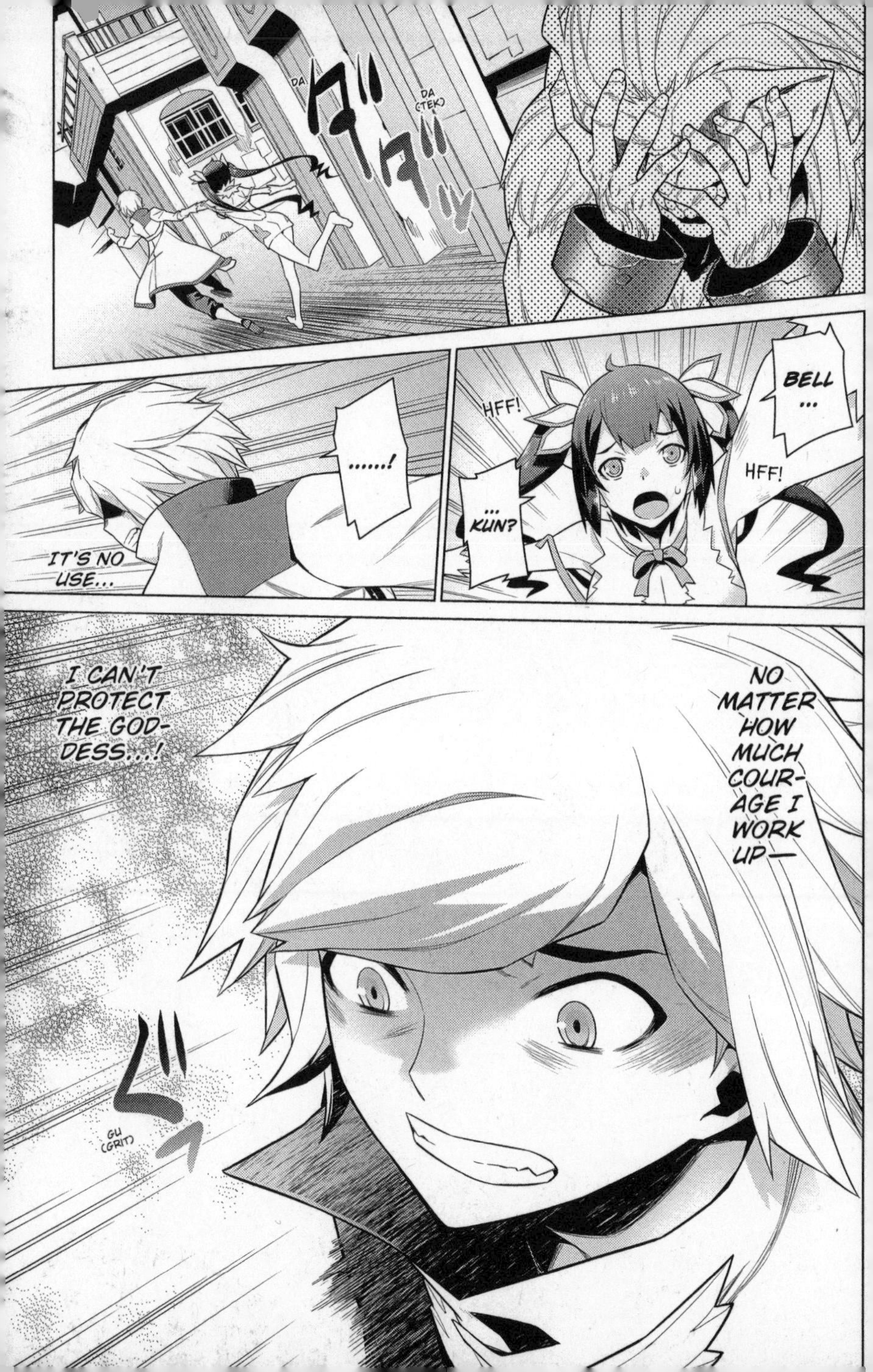
DA
DA (TEK)
BELL ...
HFF!
HFF!
... KUN?
......!
IT'S NO USE...
NO MATTER HOW MUCH COURAGE I WORK UP—
I CAN'T PROTECT THE GODDESS...!
GU (GRIT)

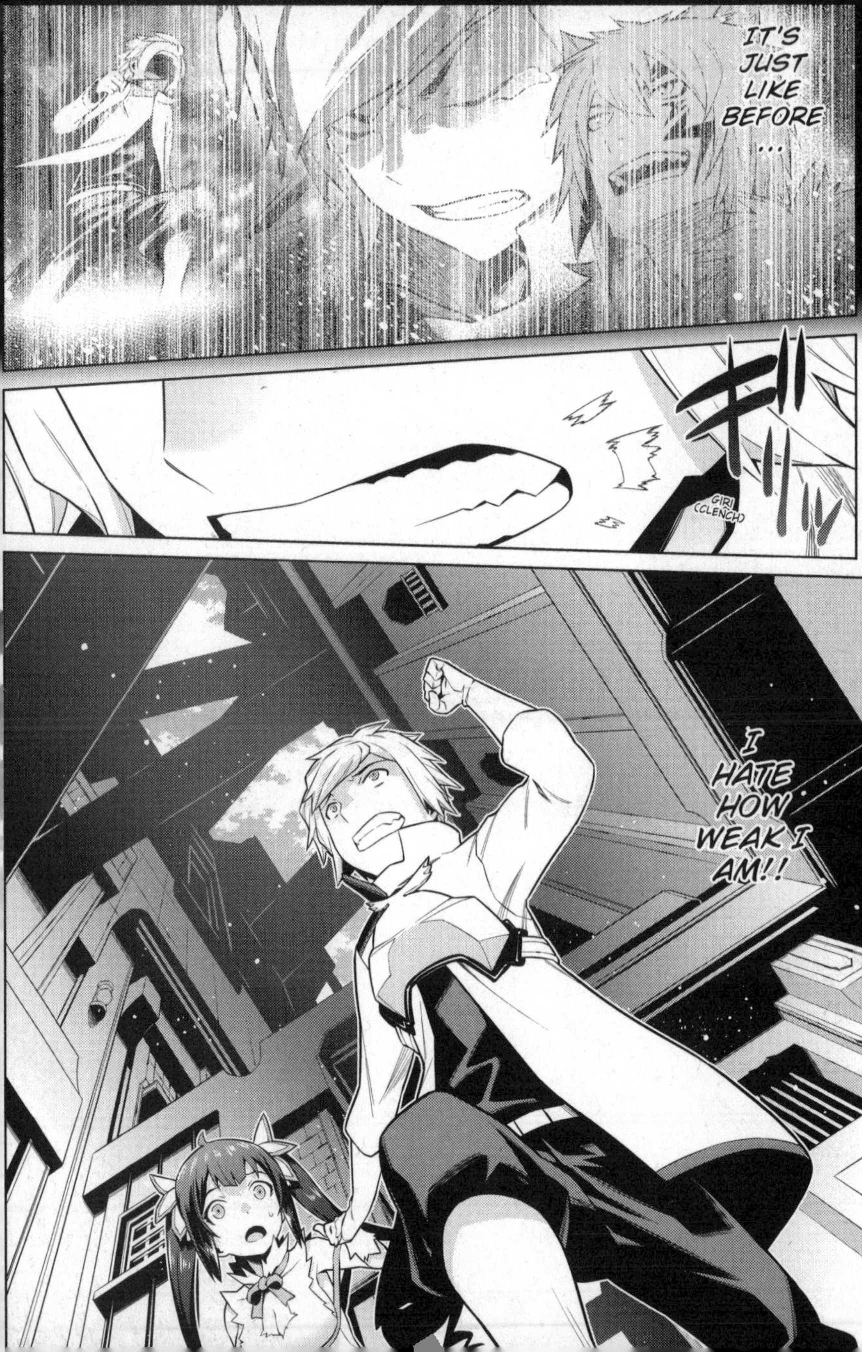
IT'S JUST LIKE BEFORE...
GIRI (CLENCH)
I HATE HOW WEAK I AM!!

**CITIZENS OF
ORARIO**

text by Fujino Omori
character rough by Kunieda

➤ File 03

AIZ WALLENSTEIN

*She's the beautiful flower, far
out of reach. Belonging to
Loki Familia and known
as "Kenki," she is one of
Orario's top adventurers.
She is also Bell's idol.*

CITIZENS OF ORARIO

text by Fujino Omori
character rough by Kunieda

➤File 04

EINA TULLE

A workaholic half-elf, she belongs to the Guild, and serves as Bell's dungeon advisor. Very popular among adventurers for being the cute receptionist.

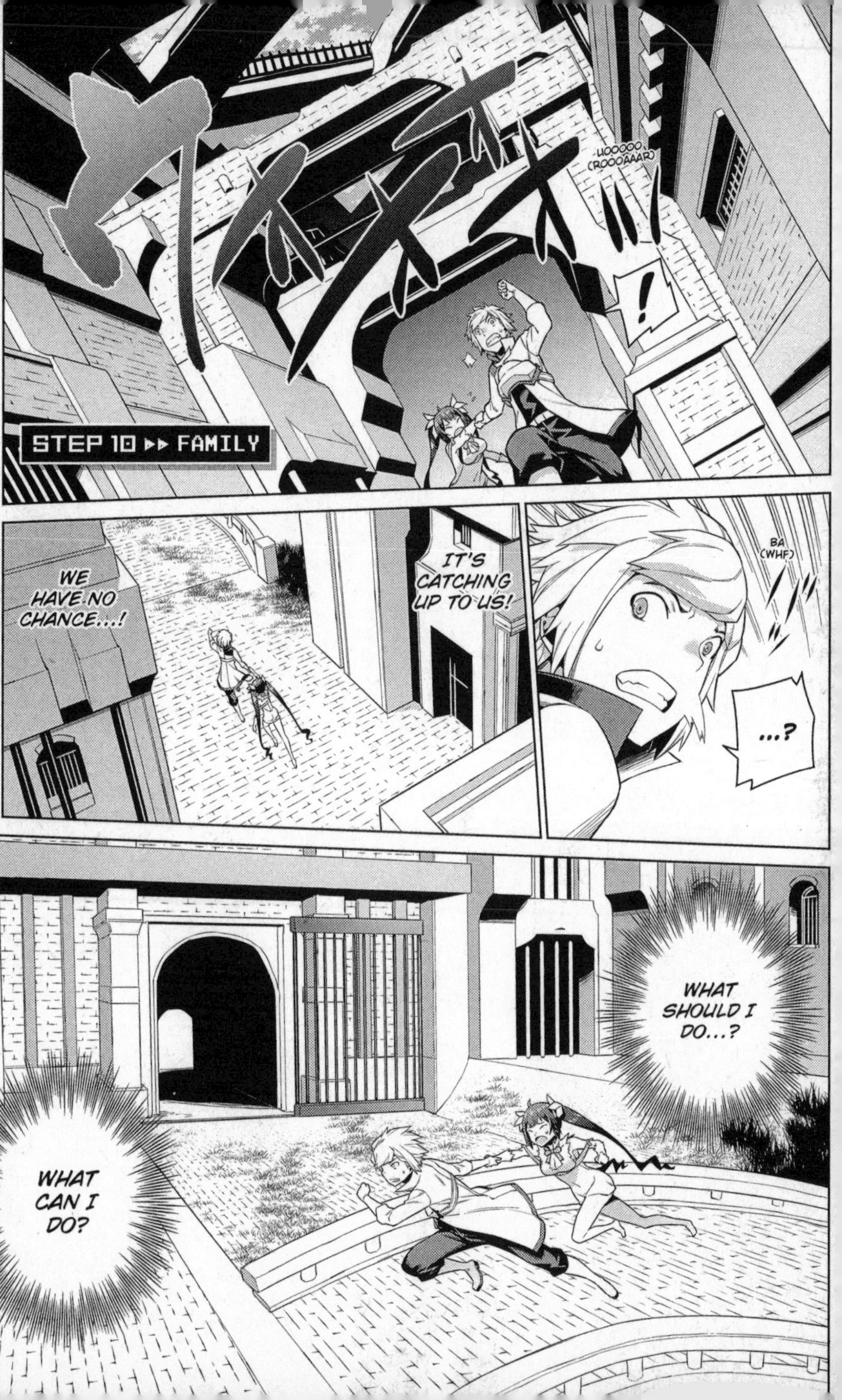
HOOOOO (ROOOAAAR)
!
STEP 10 ▸▸ FAMILY
BA (WHF)
...?
IT'S CATCHING UP TO US!
WE HAVE NO CHANCE...!
WHAT SHOULD I DO...?
WHAT CAN I DO?

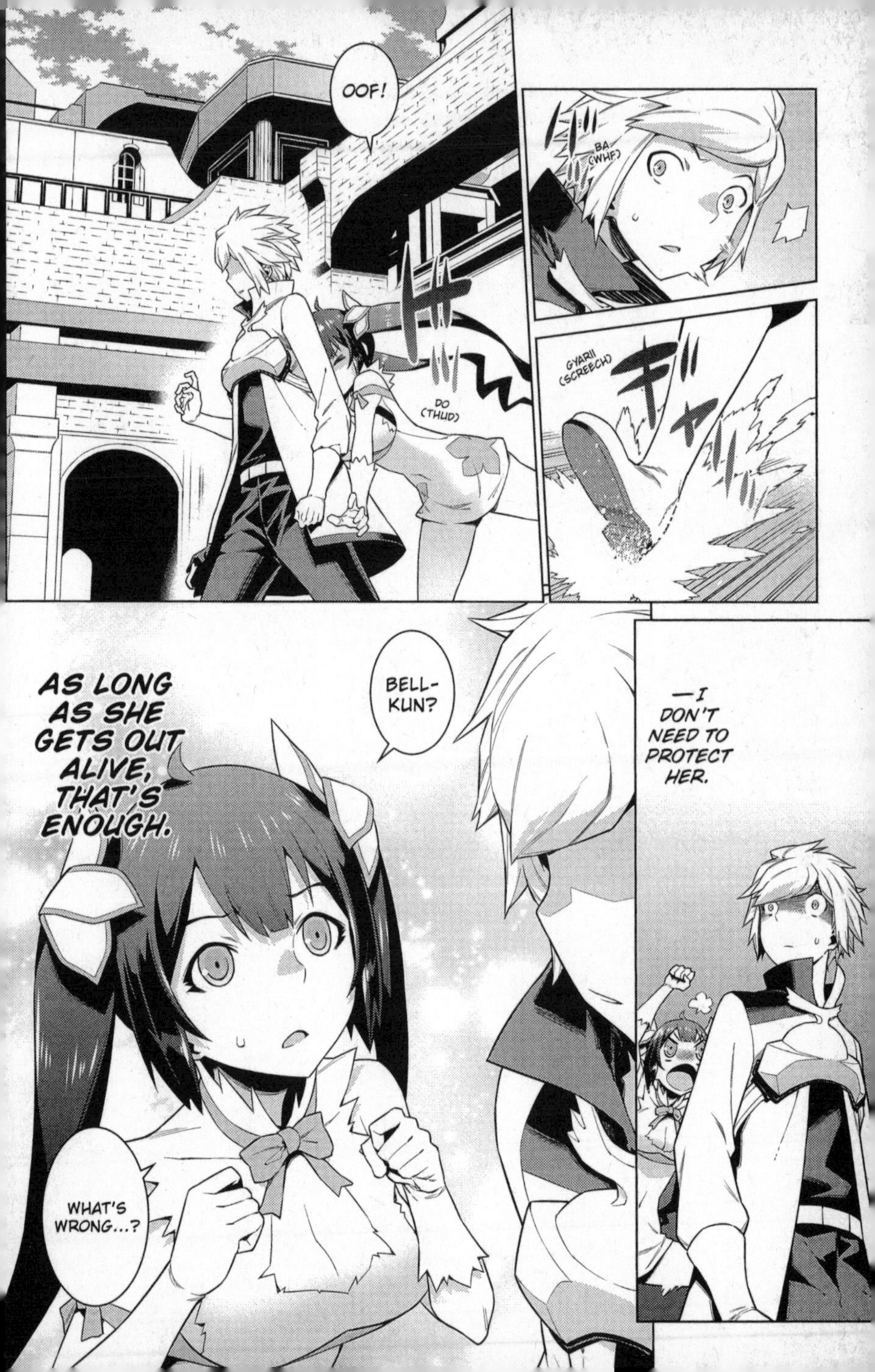
BA (WHF)
GYARII (SCREECH)
OOF!
DO (THUD)
—I DON'T NEED TO PROTECT HER.
BELL-KUN?
AS LONG AS SHE GETS OUT ALIVE, THAT'S ENOUGH.
WHAT'S WRONG...?

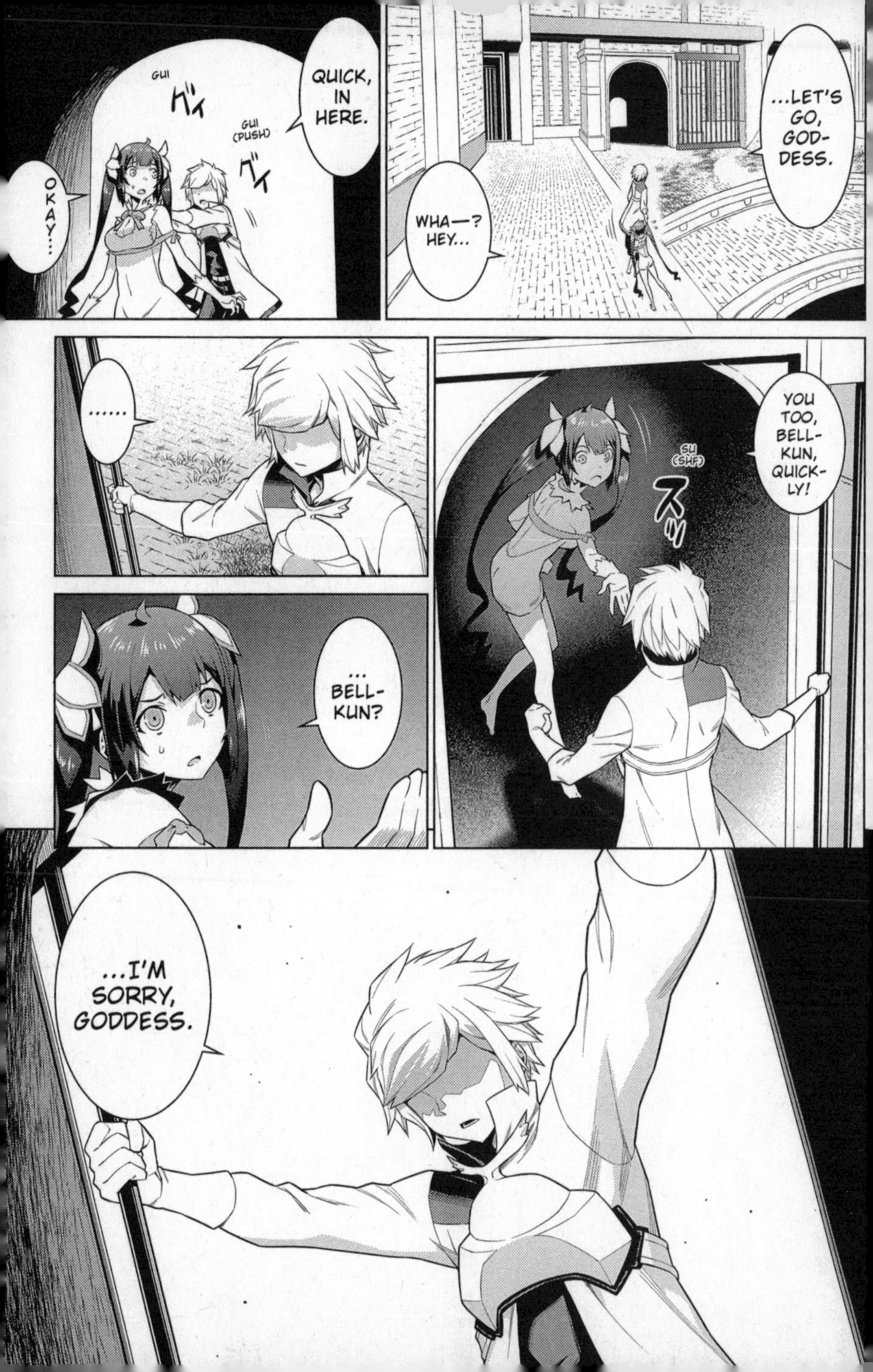
...LET'S GO, GOD-DESS.
WHA—? HEY...
QUICK, IN HERE.
GUI
グイ
GUI (PUSH)
グイ
OKAY...
YOU TOO, BELL-KUN, QUICKLY!
SU (SHF)
スッ
......
...BELL-KUN?
...I'M SORRY, GODDESS.

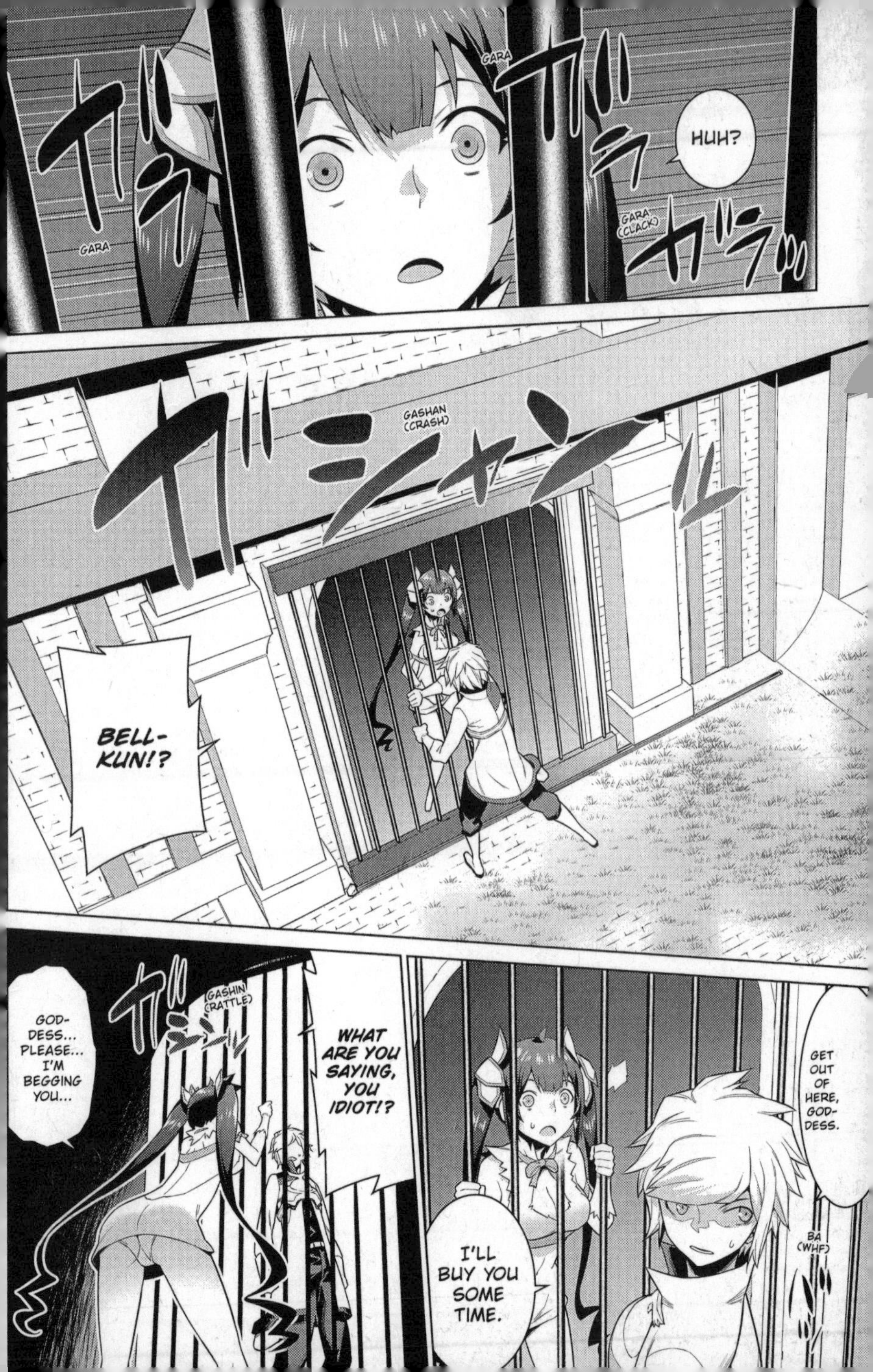
GARA
HUH?
GARA (CLACK)
GARA
GASHAN (CRASH)
BELL-KUN!?
GET OUT OF HERE, GOD-DESS.
BA (WHF)
I'LL BUY YOU SOME TIME.
WHAT ARE YOU SAYING, YOU IDIOT!?
GASHIN (RATTLE)
GOD-DESS... PLEASE... I'M BEGGING YOU...

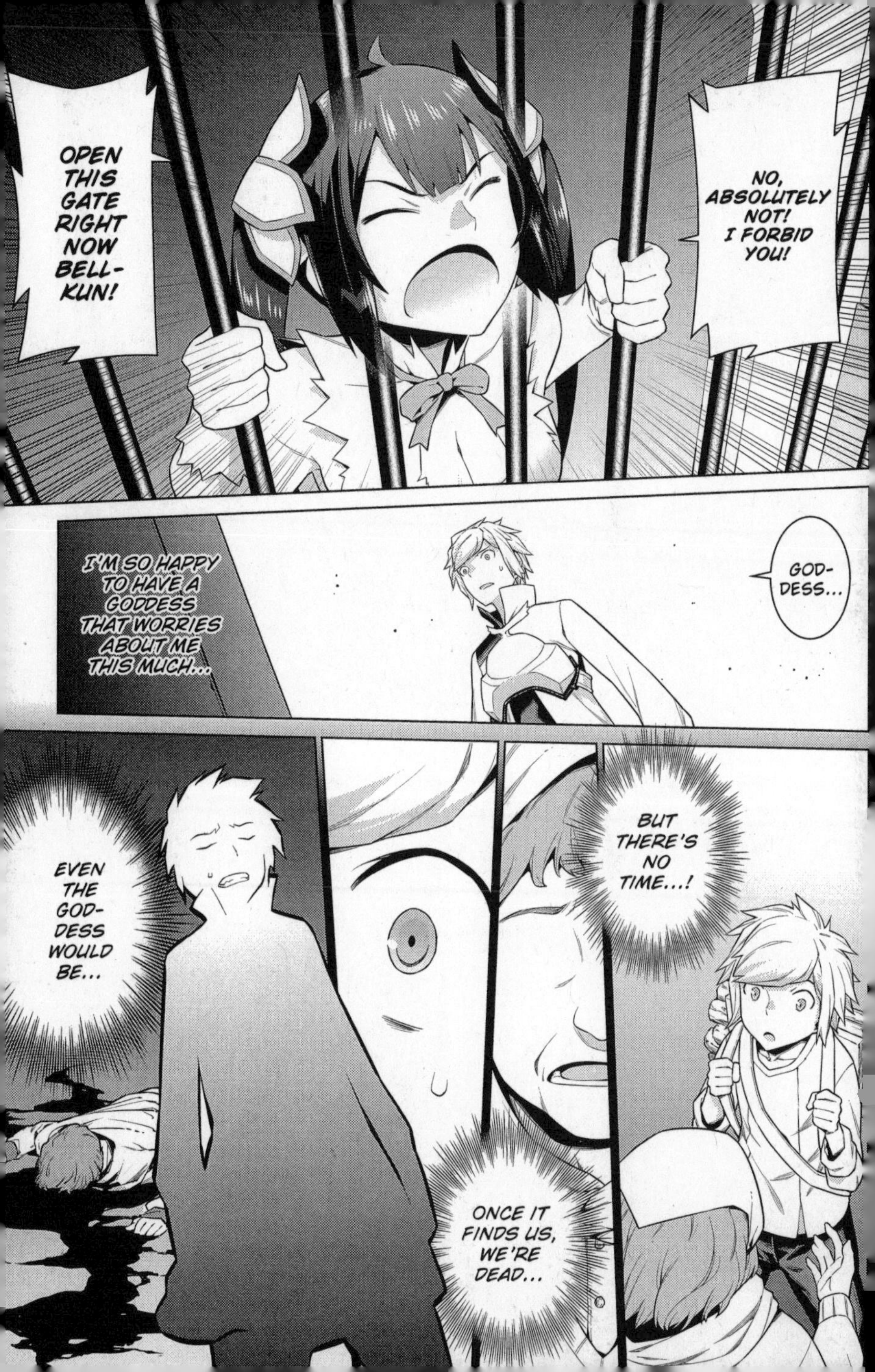

NO, ABSOLUTELY NOT! I FORBID YOU!
OPEN THIS GATE RIGHT NOW BELL-KUN!
GOD-DESS...
I'M SO HAPPY TO HAVE A GODDESS THAT WORRIES ABOUT ME THIS MUCH...
BUT THERE'S NO TIME...!
ONCE IT FINDS US, WE'RE DEAD...
EVEN THE GOD-DESS WOULD BE...

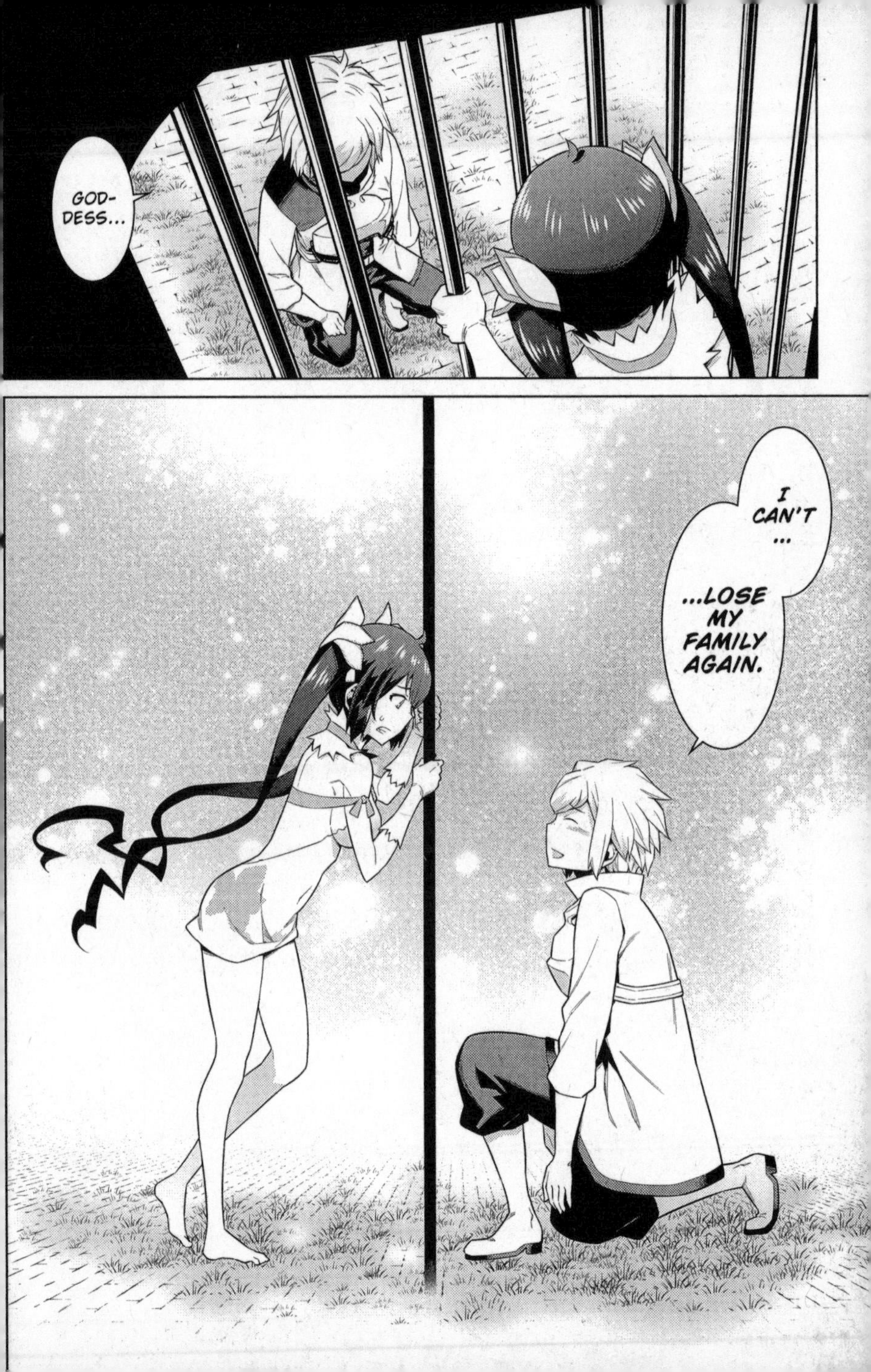
GOD-DESS...
I CAN'T ... ...LOSE MY FAMILY AGAIN.

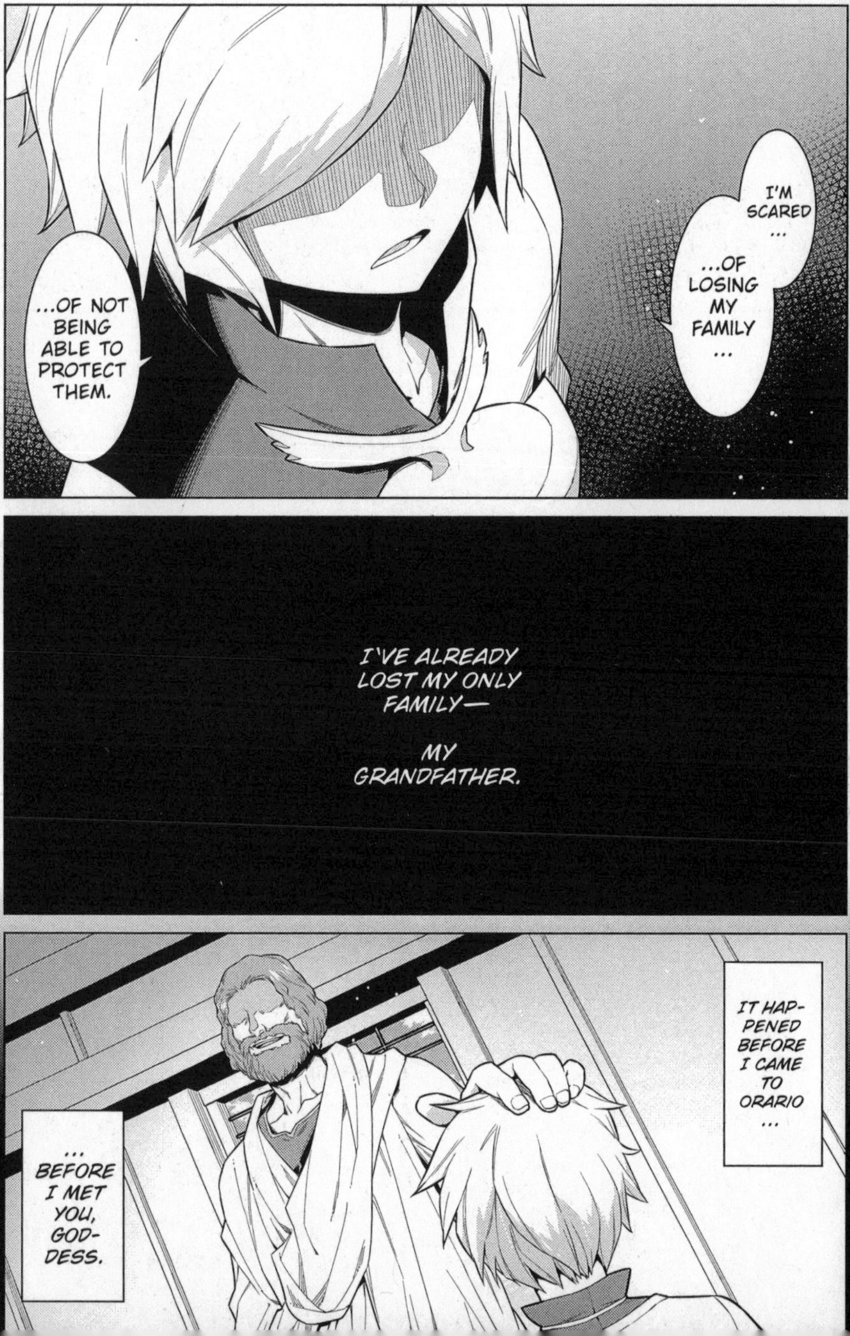
I'M SCARED... ...OF LOSING MY FAMILY...
...OF NOT BEING ABLE TO PROTECT THEM.
I'VE ALREADY LOST MY ONLY FAMILY—
MY GRANDFATHER.
IT HAP-PENED BEFORE I CAME TO ORARIO...
...BEFORE I MET YOU, GOD-DESS.

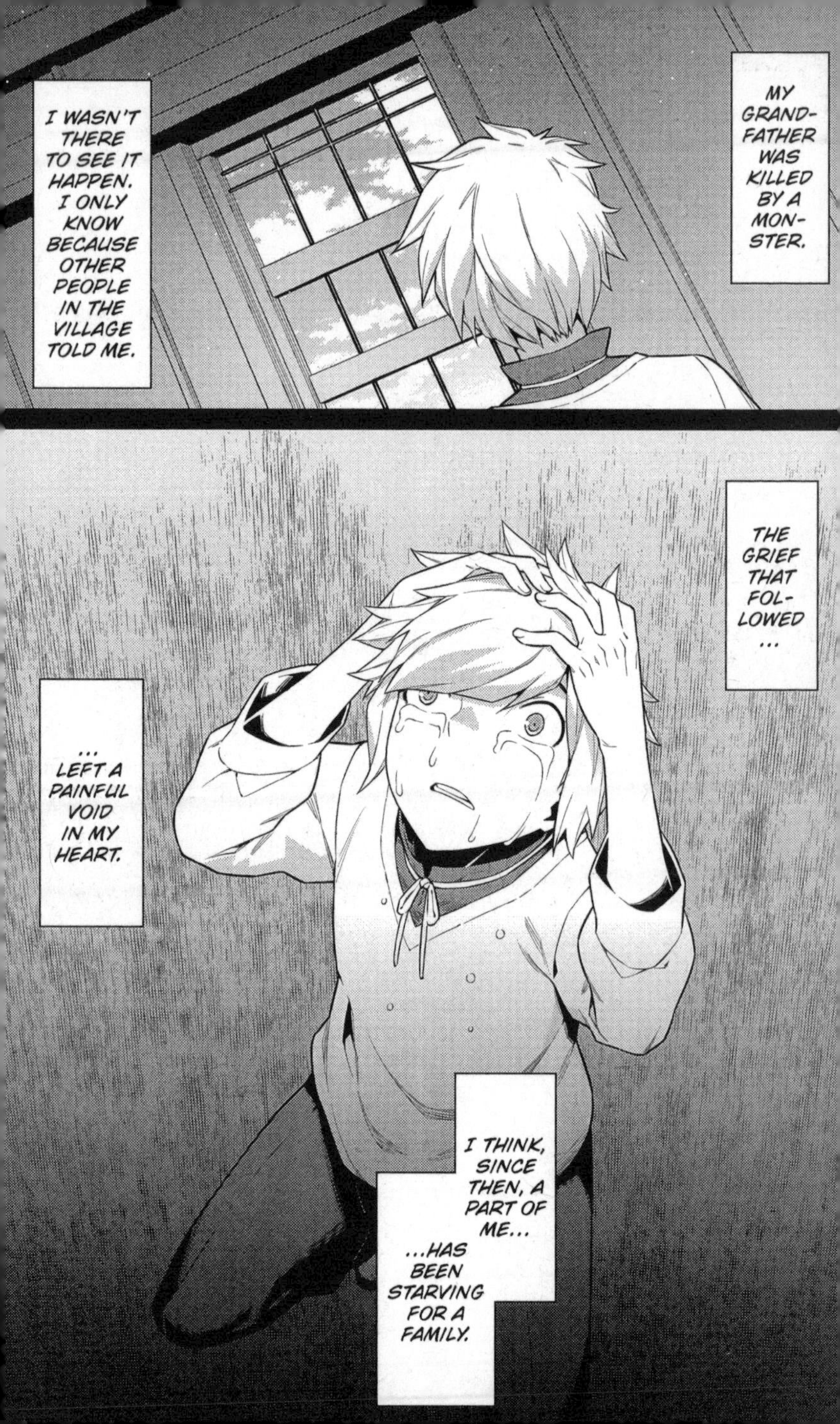
MY GRANDFATHER WAS KILLED BY A MONSTER.
I WASN'T THERE TO SEE IT HAPPEN. I ONLY KNOW BECAUSE OTHER PEOPLE IN THE VILLAGE TOLD ME.
THE GRIEF THAT FOLLOWED...
...LEFT A PAINFUL VOID IN MY HEART.
I THINK, SINCE THEN, A PART OF ME...
...HAS BEEN STARVING FOR A FAMILY.

I CAME TO ORARIO TO FIND THE GIRL OF MY DREAMS.

ZARI (STEP)

TO TEST MY BOND WITH MY GRANDFATHER, TO MAKE SURE IT WOULDN'T BREAK... ...I LOOKED FOR THE GIRL I WAS DESTINED TO BE WITH.

BUT MORE THAN THAT...

...I THINK THERE WAS SOMETHING ELSE I WAS LOOKING FOR.

THE BOND OF FAMILY, OF FAMILIA, THAT YOU GAVE ME, GODDESS.

SO PLEASE...

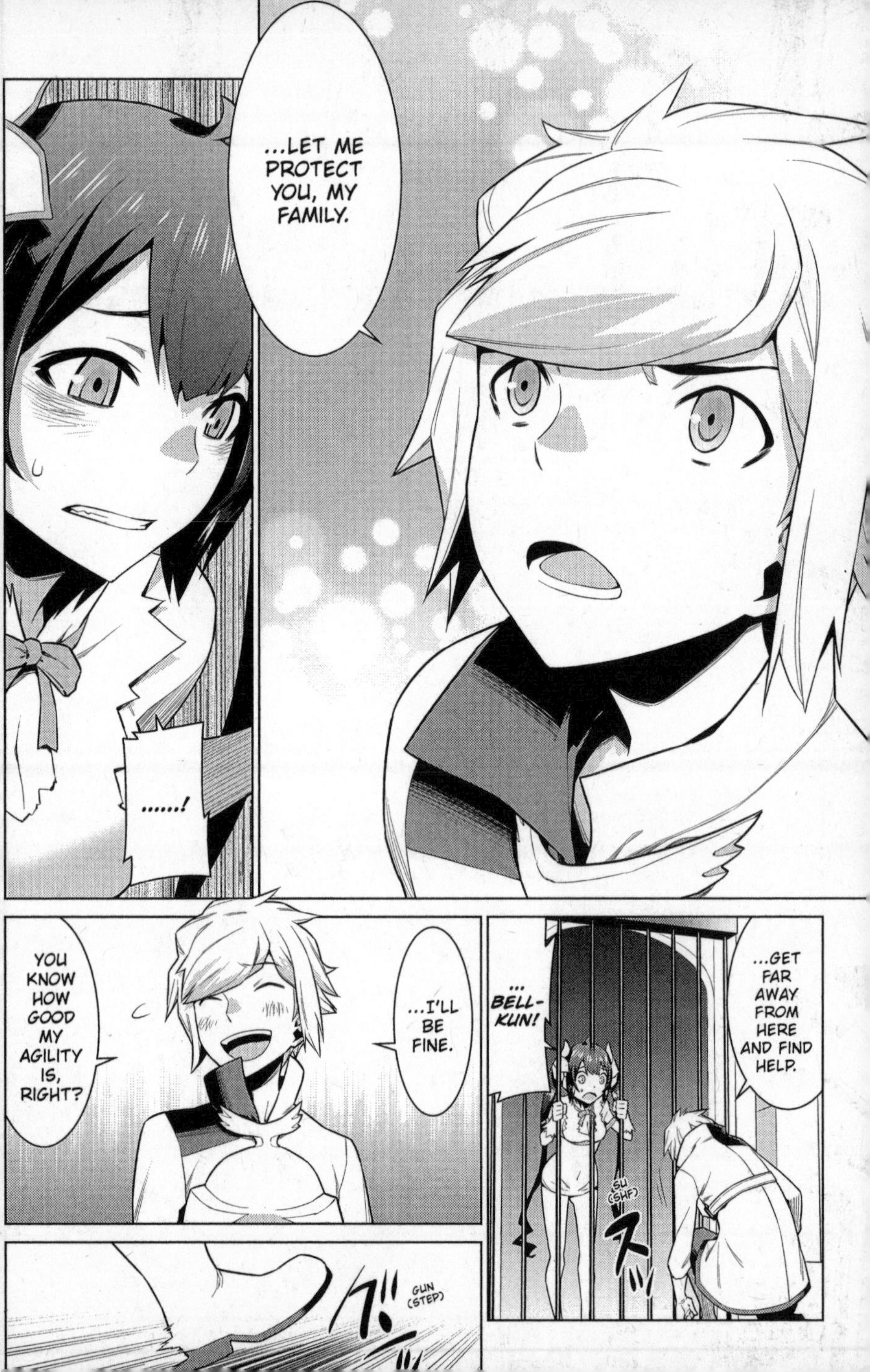
...LET ME PROTECT YOU, MY FAMILY.
......!
...GET FAR AWAY FROM HERE AND FIND HELP.
...BELL-KUN!
SU (SHF)
...I'LL BE FINE.
YOU KNOW HOW GOOD MY AGILITY IS, RIGHT?
GUN (STEP)

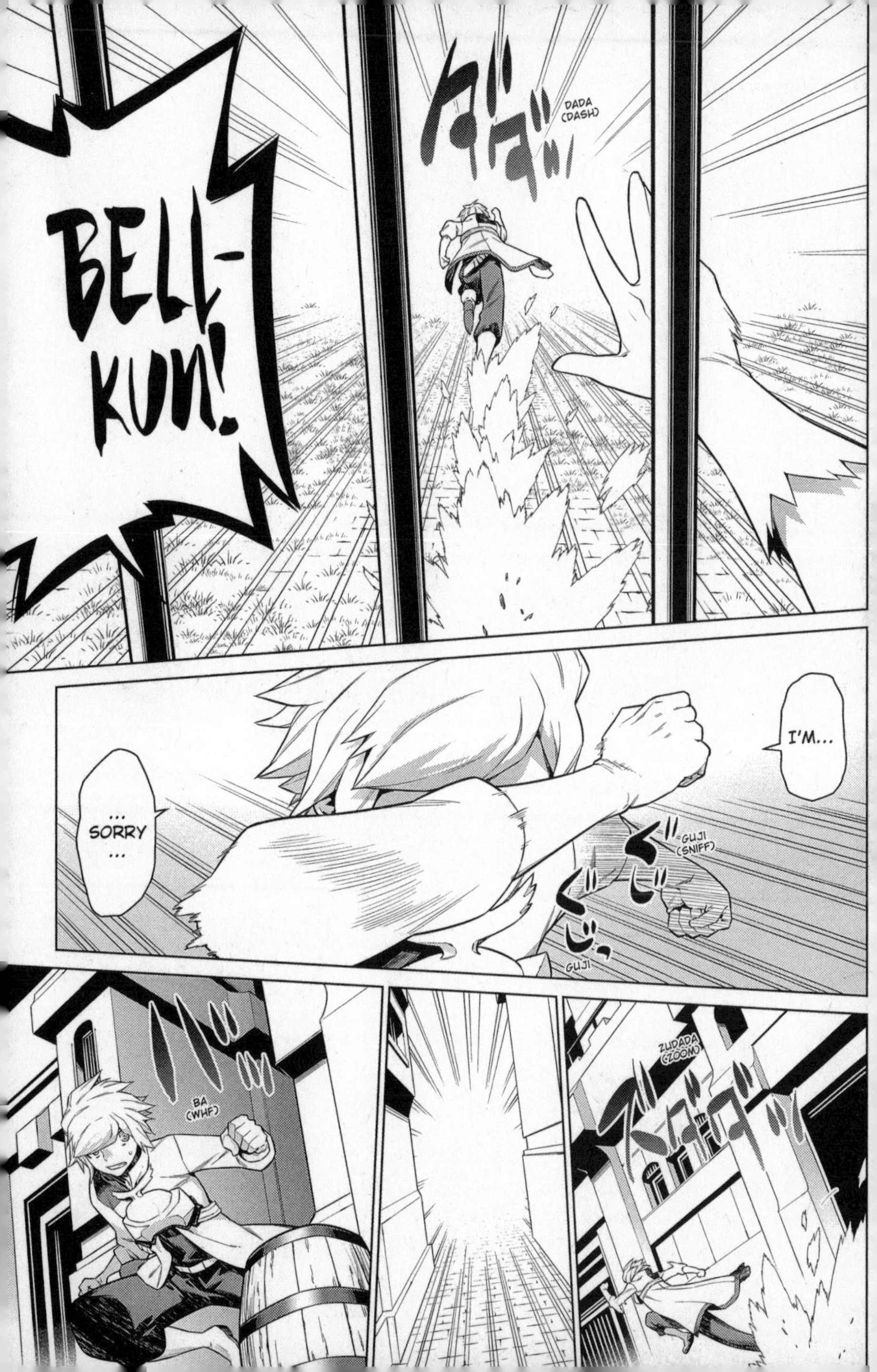
DADA (DASH)
BELL-KUN!
I'M...
GUJI (SNIFF)
GUJI
... SORRY ...
ZUDADA (ZOOM)
BA (WHF)

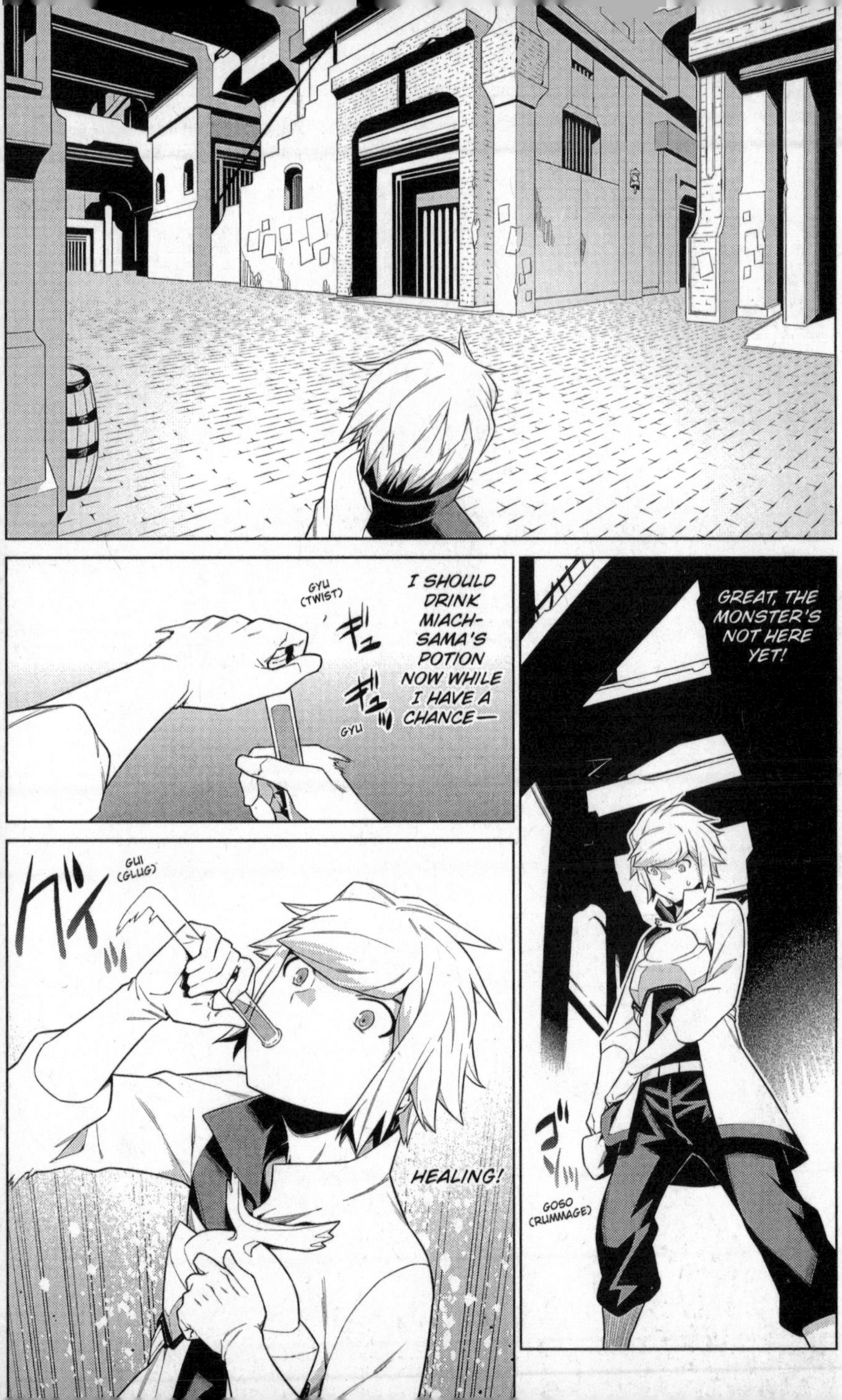
GREAT, THE MONSTER'S NOT HERE YET!
GOSO (RUMMAGE)
GYU (TWIST)
I SHOULD DRINK MIACH-SAMA'S POTION NOW WHILE I HAVE A CHANCE—
GYU
GUI (GLUG)
HEALING!

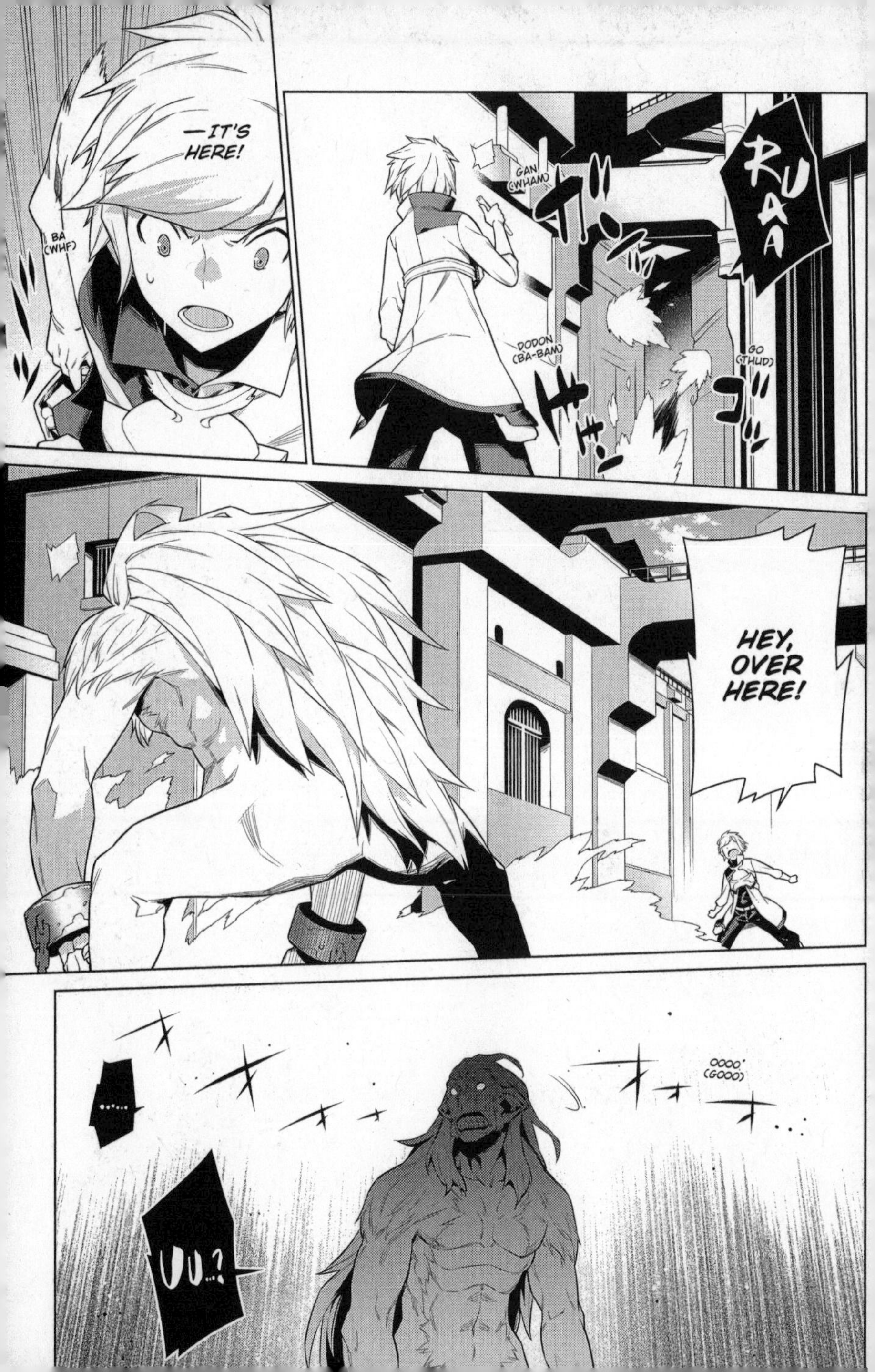
RUAA
GAN (WHAM)
GO (THUD)
DODON (BA-BAM)
—IT'S HERE!
BA (WHF)
HEY, OVER HERE!
OOOO (GOOO)
......
UU..?

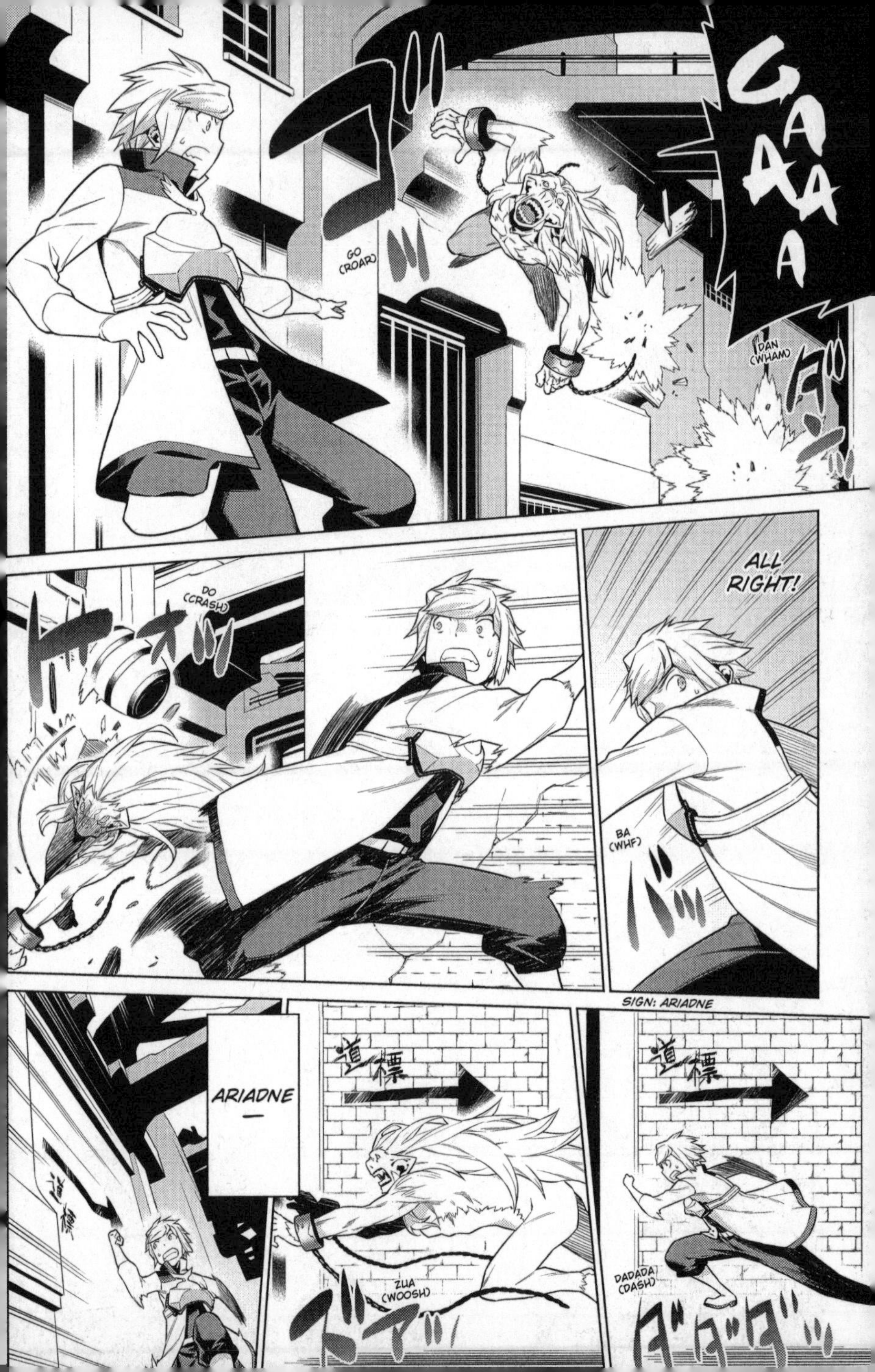
GAAAAA
GO (ROAR)
DAN (WHAM)
ALL RIGHT!
BA (WHF)
DO (CRASH)
SIGN: ARIADNE
道標
DADADA (DASH)
道標
ZUA (WOOSH)
ARIADNE —

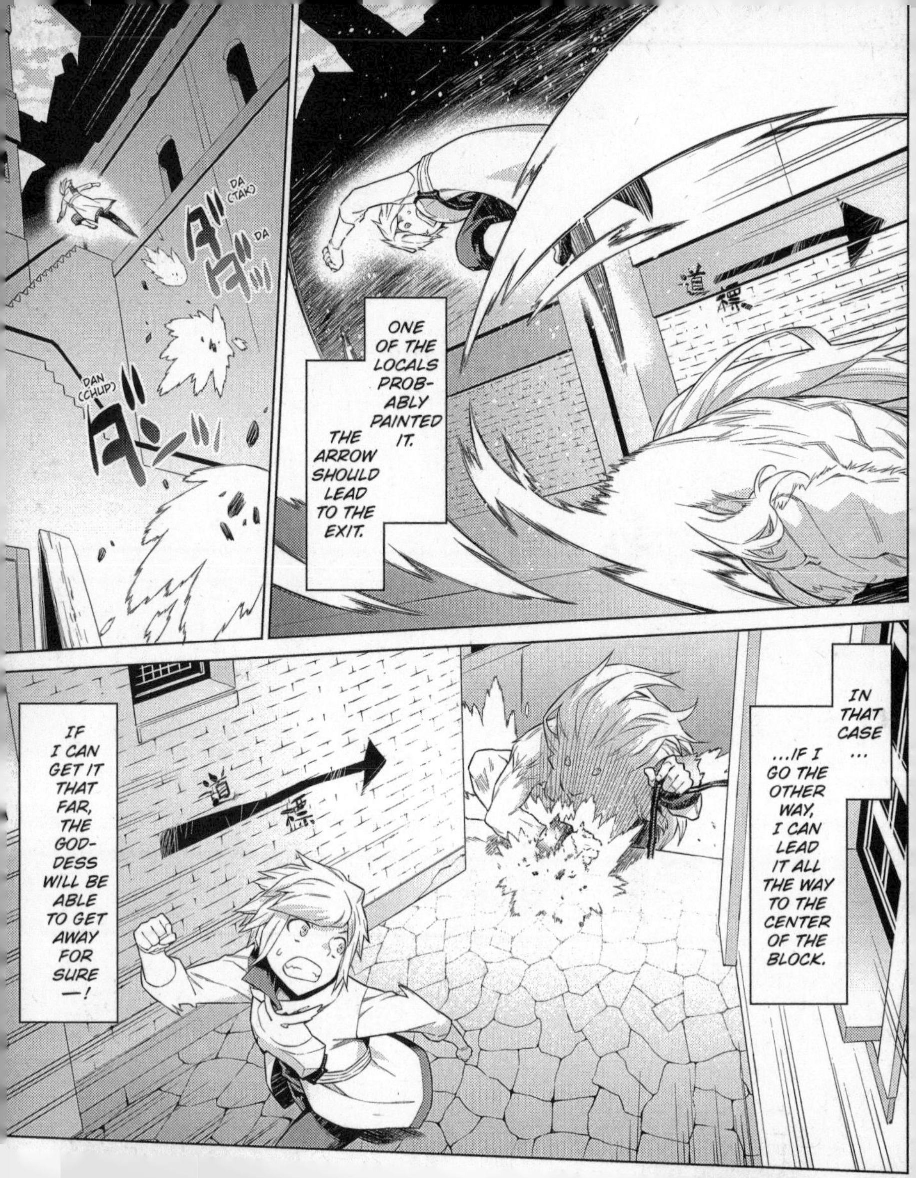
道標
ONE OF THE LOCALS PROBABLY PAINTED IT.
THE ARROW SHOULD LEAD TO THE EXIT.
DA (TAK)
DA
DAN (CHUP)
道標
IN THAT CASE...
...IF I GO THE OTHER WAY, I CAN LEAD IT ALL THE WAY TO THE CENTER OF THE BLOCK.
IF I CAN GET IT THAT FAR, THE GODDESS WILL BE ABLE TO GET AWAY FOR SURE—!

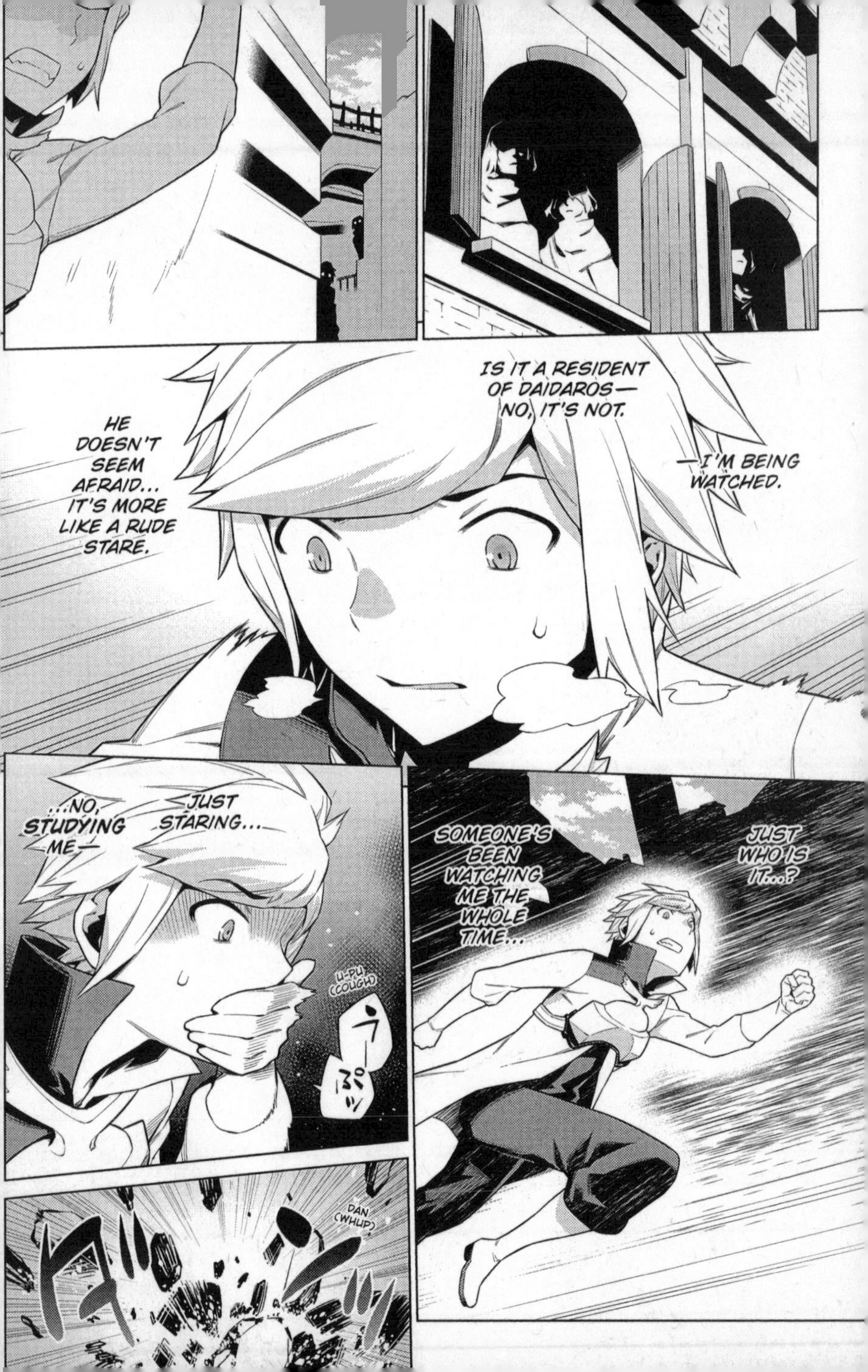
IS IT A RESIDENT OF DAIDAROS— NO, IT'S NOT.
—I'M BEING WATCHED.
HE DOESN'T SEEM AFRAID... IT'S MORE LIKE A RUDE STARE.
JUST WHO IS IT...?
SOMEONE'S BEEN WATCHING ME THE WHOLE TIME...
JUST STARING...
...NO, STUDYING ME—
U-PU (COUGH)
ウーぷッ
DAN (WHUP)
ダッ

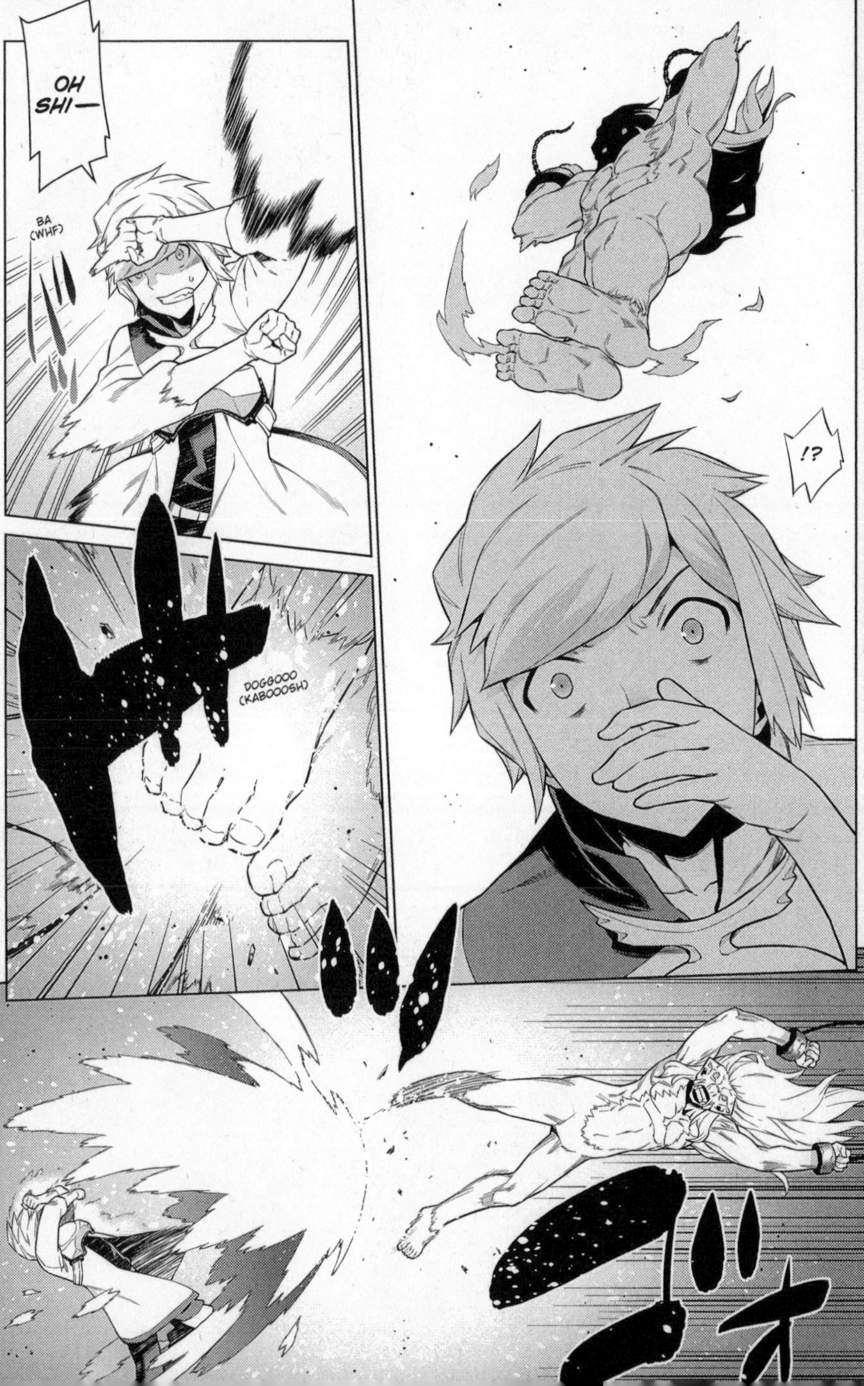
!?
OH SHI—
BA (WHF)
DOGGOOO (KABOOOSH)

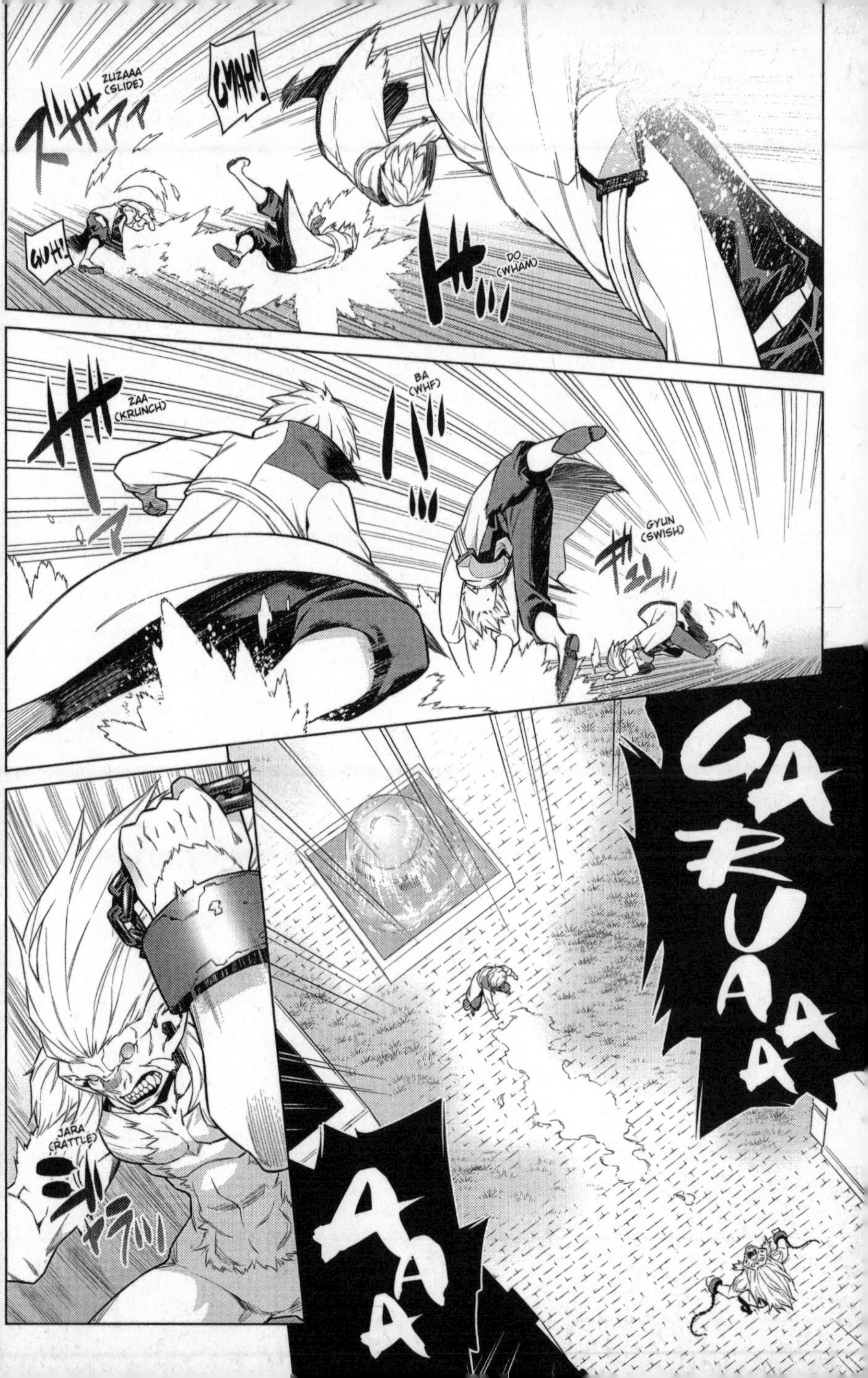
DO (WHAM)
GWAH!
ZUZAAA (SLIDE)
GUH!
BA (WHF)
GYUN (SWISH)
ZAA (KRUNCH)
GARUAAAA
AAAA
JARA (RATTLE)

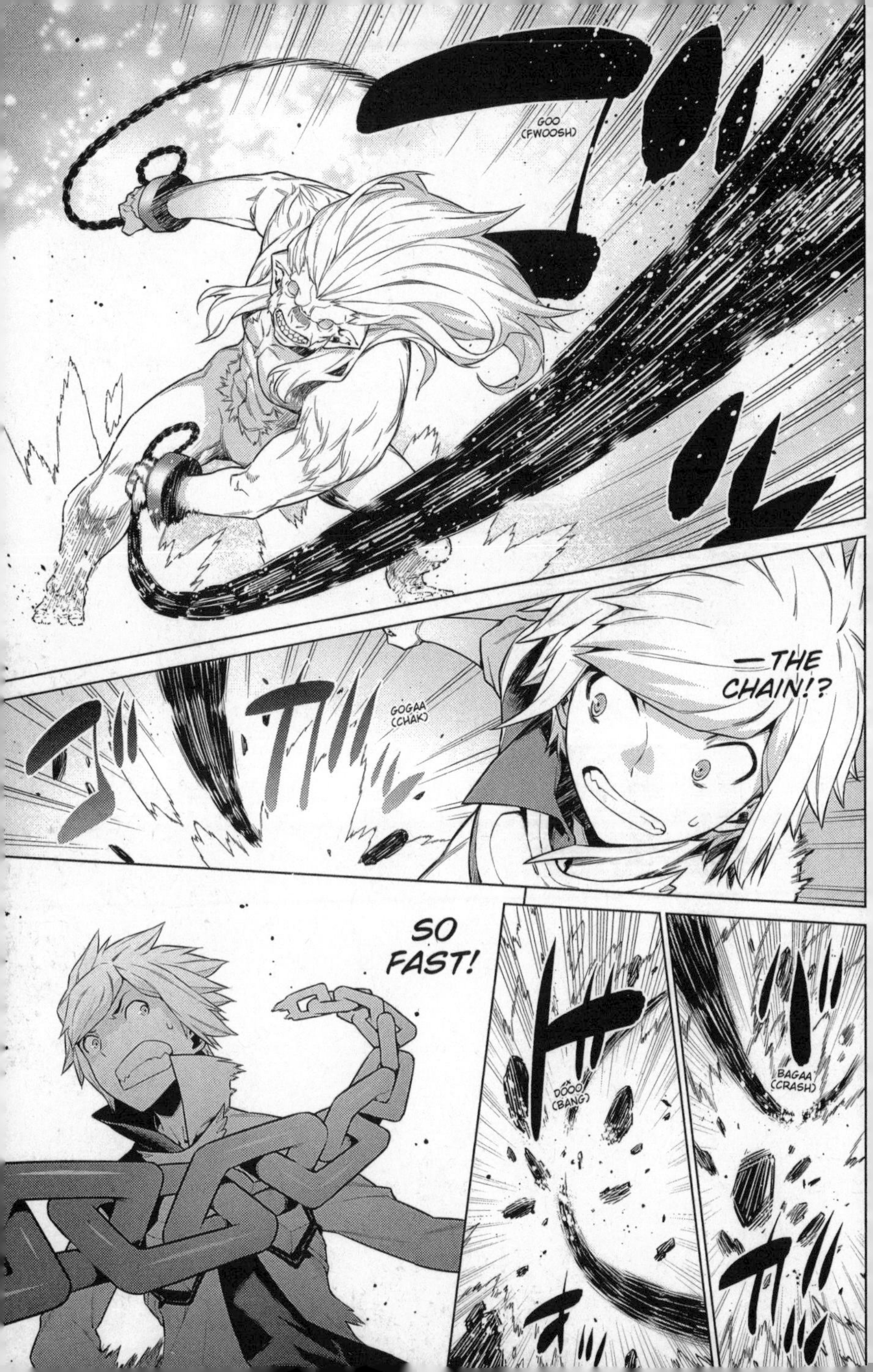
GOO
(FWOOSH)
—THE CHAIN!?
GOGAA
(CHAK)
BAGAA
(CRASH)
DOOO
(BANG)
SO
FAST!

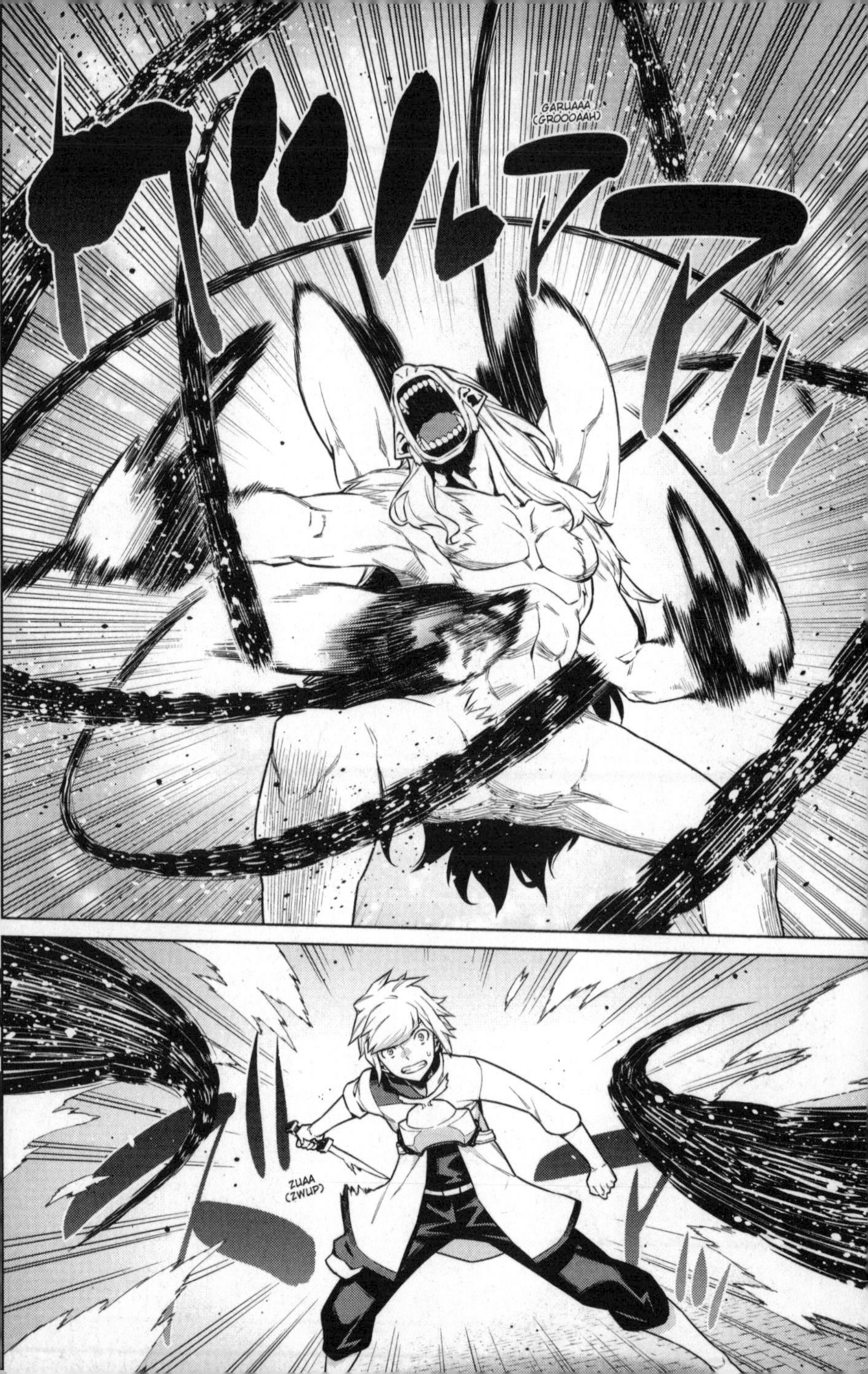
GARUAAA
(GROOOAAH)
ZUAA
(ZWUP)

CITIZENS OF ORARIO

text by Fujino Omori
character rough by Kunieda

➢File 05

FREYA

The goddess of beauty and the leader of Freya Familia. Her otherworldly good looks pair with absolutely perfect body proportions.
She is the physical embodiment of beauty and bewitches anyone who sees her.

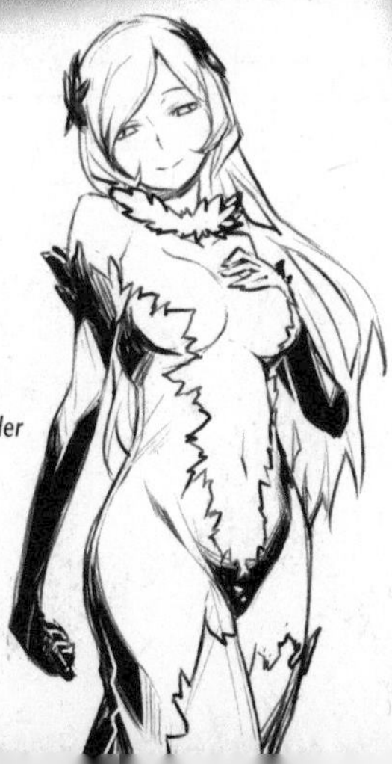

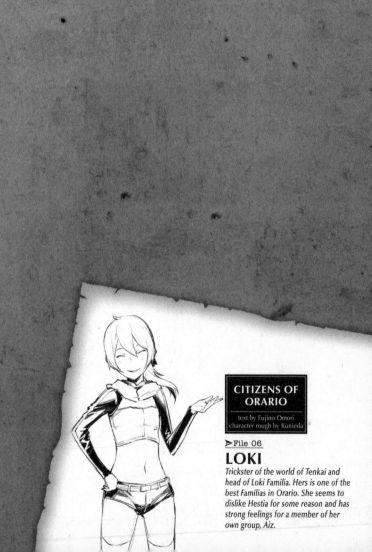

CITIZENS OF ORARIO

text by Fujino Omori
character rough by Kunieda

➤File 06

LOKI

Trickster of the world of Tenkai and head of Loki Familia. Hers is one of the best Familias in Orario. She seems to dislike Hestia for some reason and has strong feelings for a member of her own group, Aiz.

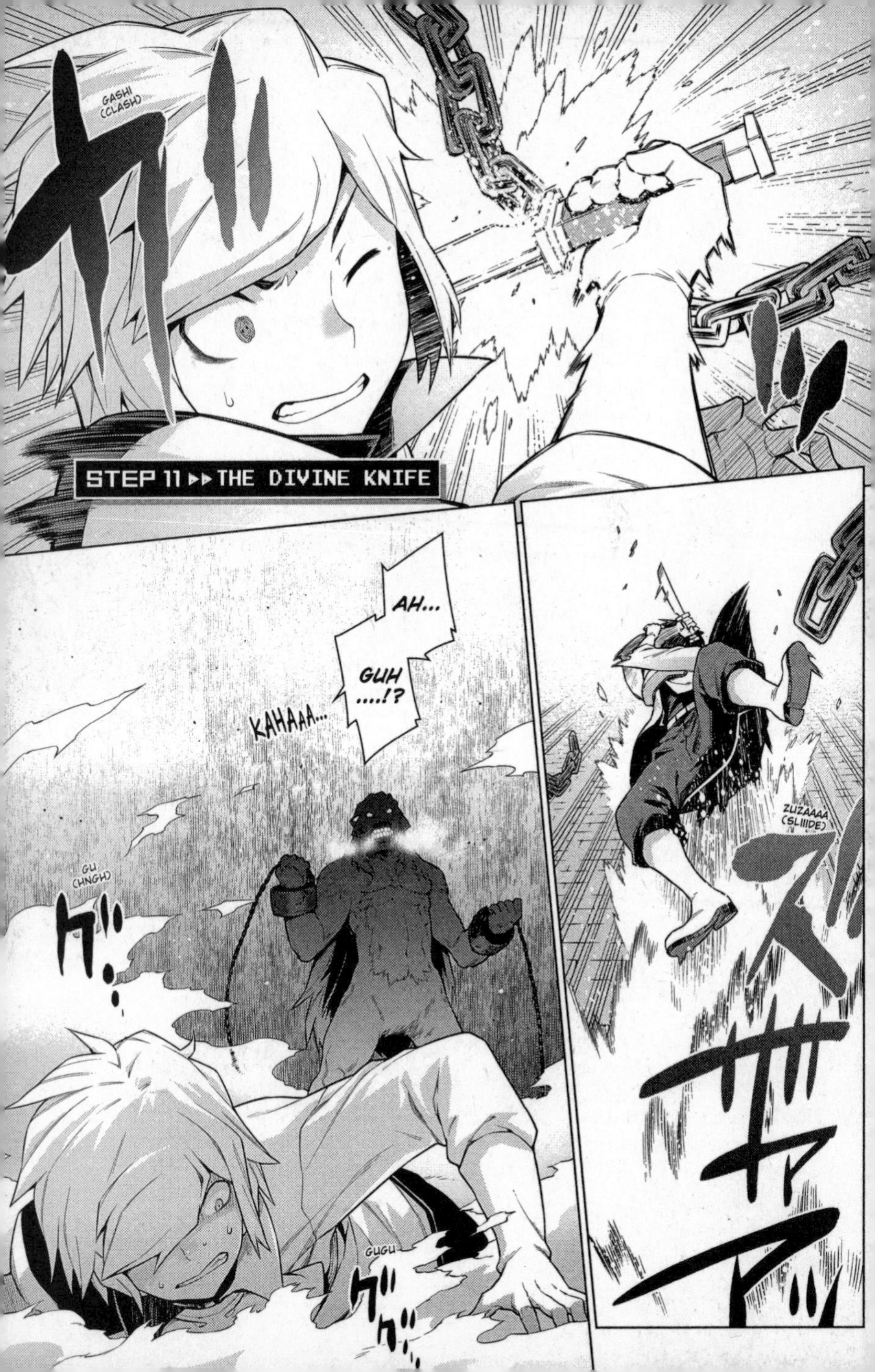
GASHI (CLASH)
STEP 11 ▸▸ THE DIVINE KNIFE
ZUZAAAA (SLIIIDE)
AH...
GUH ....!?
KAHAAA...
GU (HNGH)
GUGU

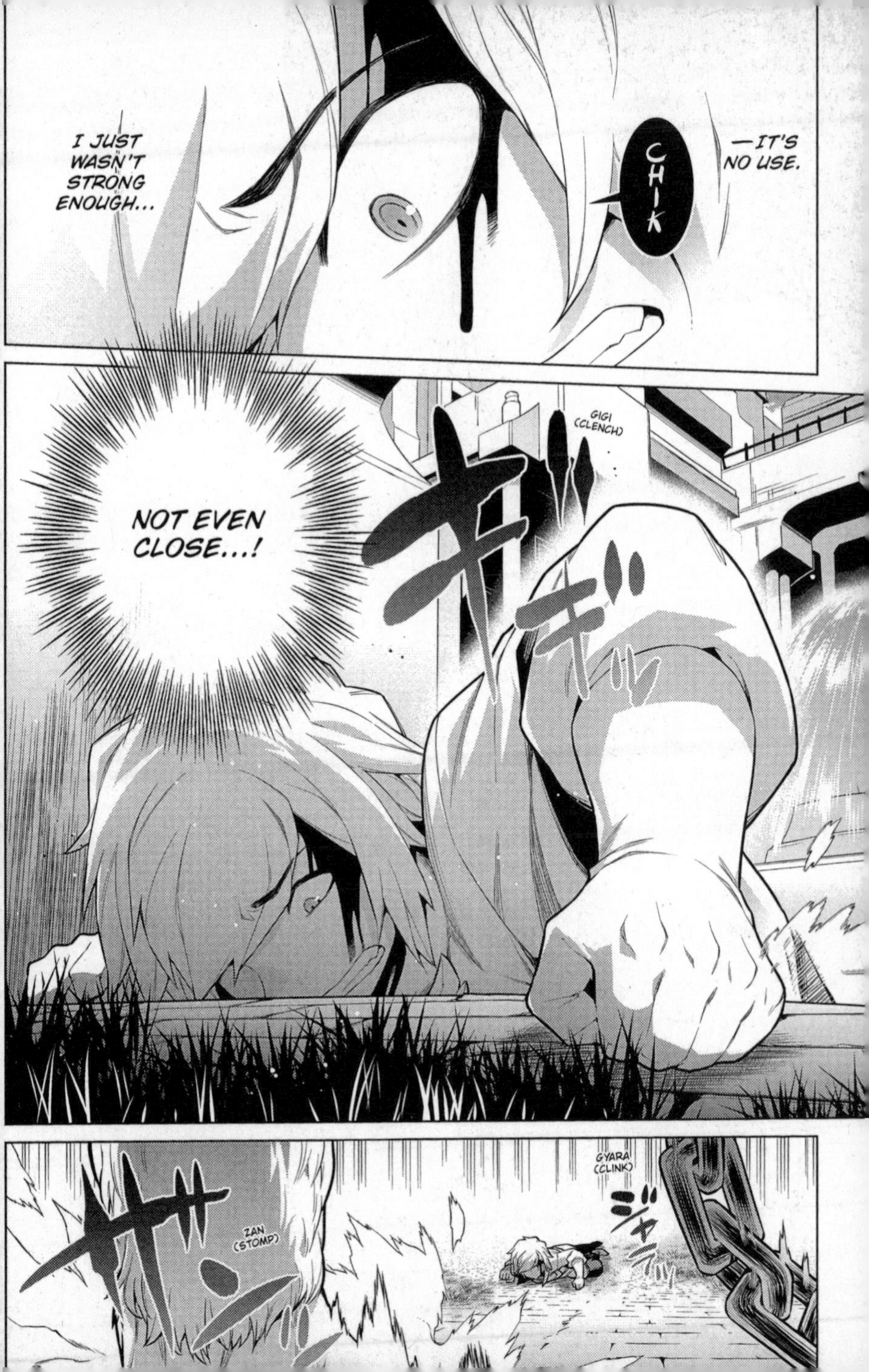
—IT'S NO USE.
CHIK
I JUST WASN'T STRONG ENOUGH...
GIGI (CLENCH)
NOT EVEN CLOSE...!
GYARA (CLINK)
ZAN (STOMP)

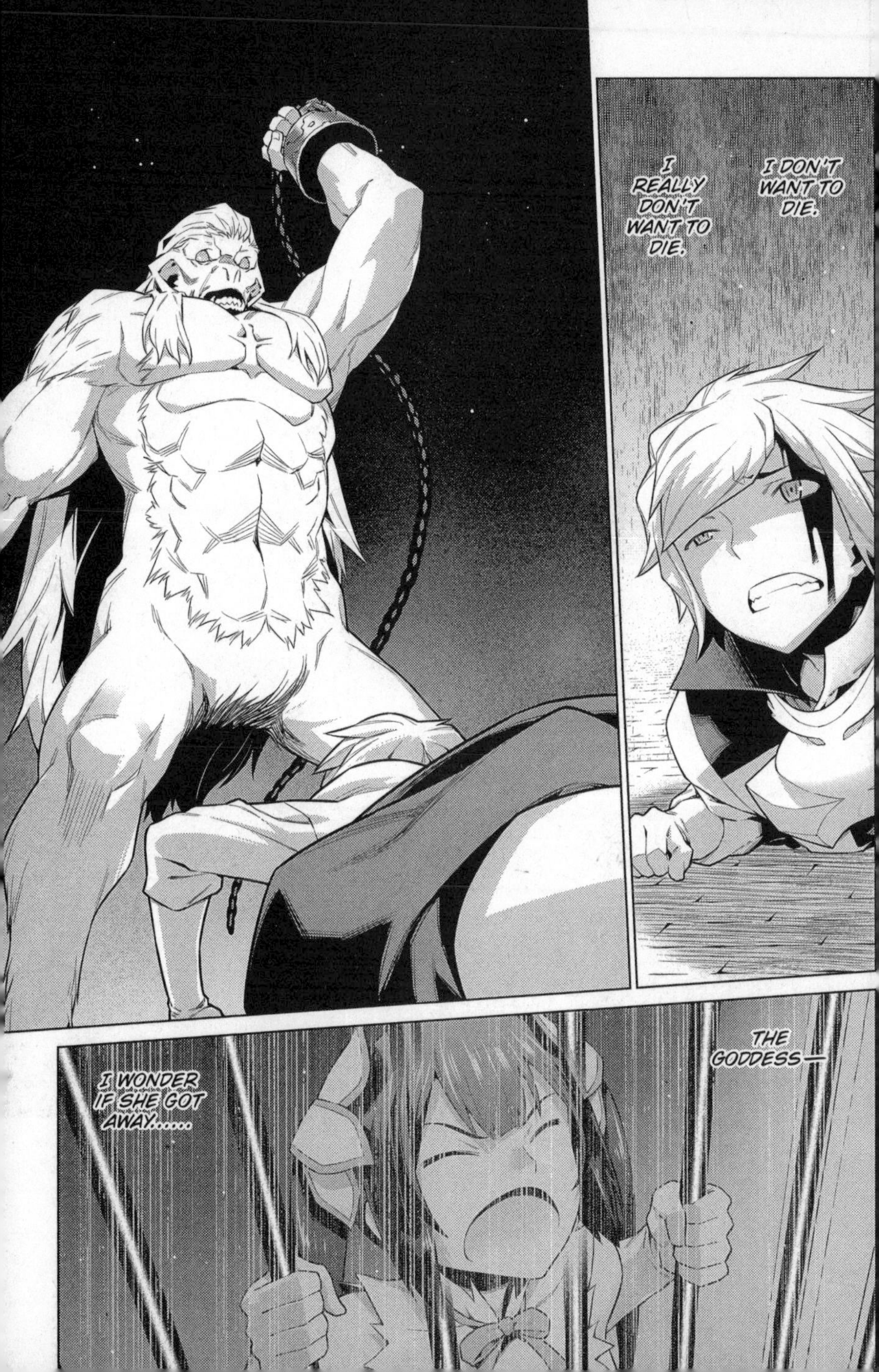
I DON'T WANT TO DIE.
I REALLY DON'T WANT TO DIE.
THE GODDESS—
I WONDER IF SHE GOT AWAY......

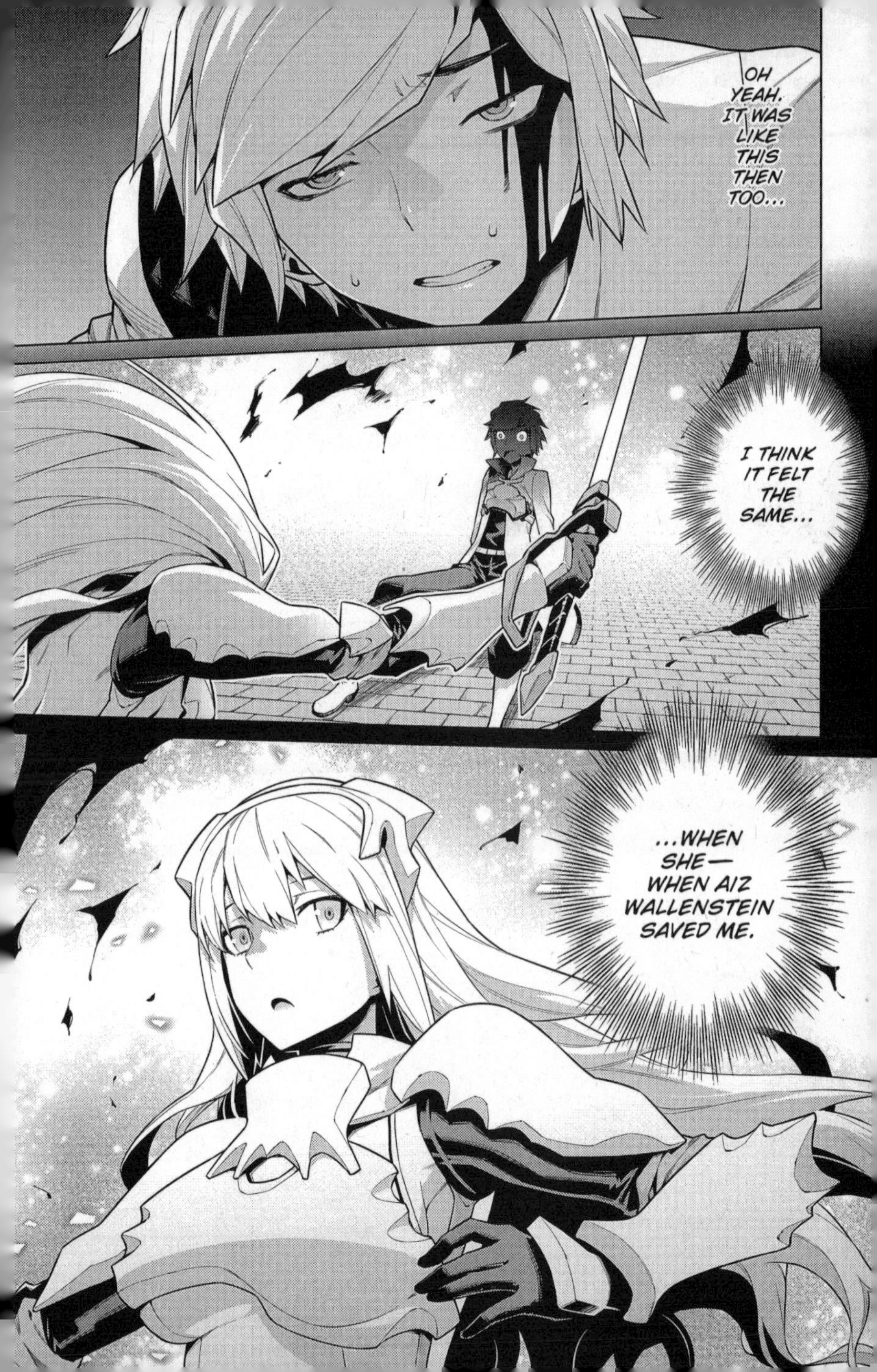
OH YEAH. IT WAS LIKE THIS THEN TOO...
I THINK IT FELT THE SAME...
...WHEN SHE— WHEN AIZ WALLENSTEIN SAVED ME.

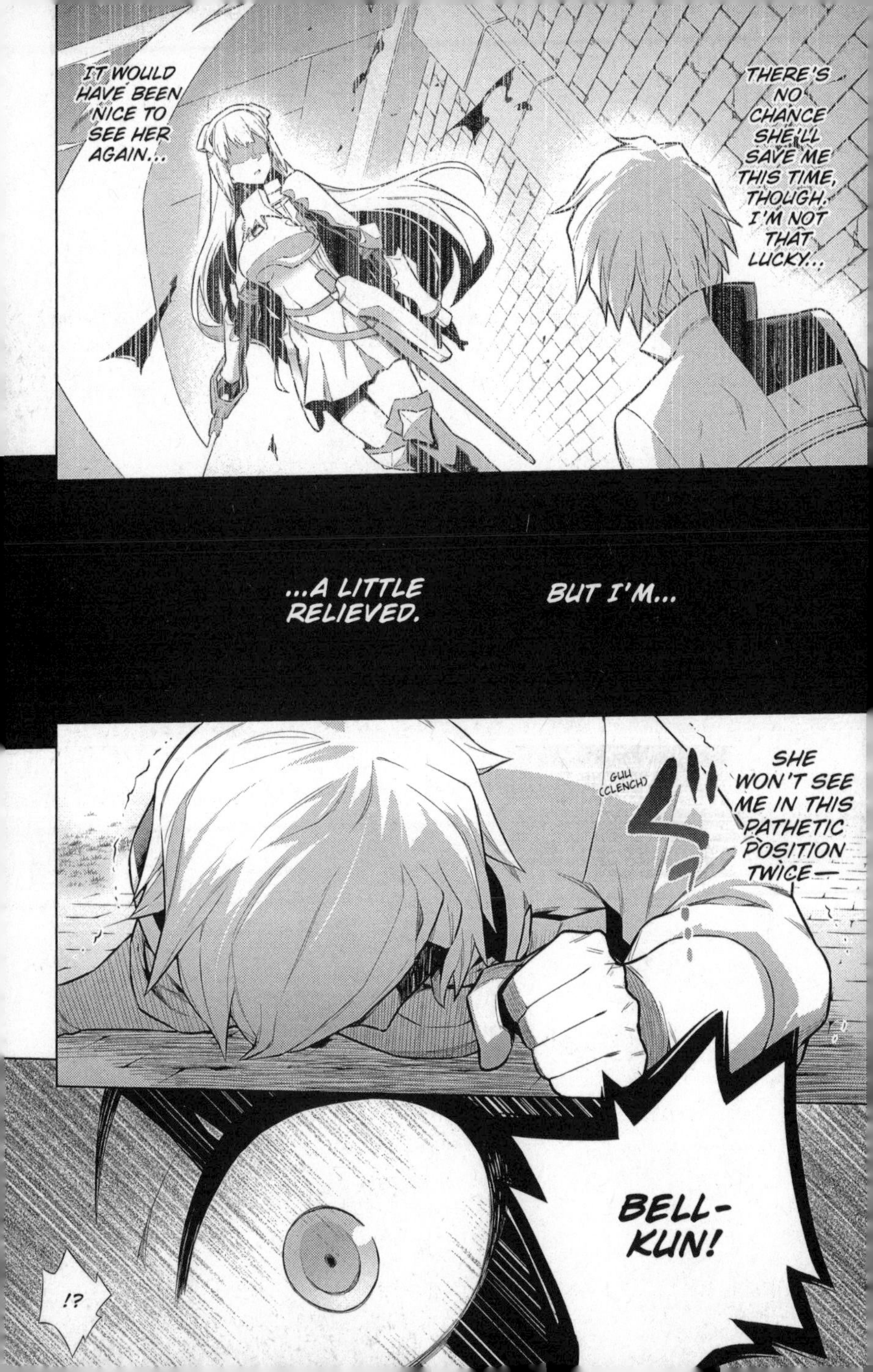
THERE'S NO CHANCE SHE'LL SAVE ME THIS TIME, THOUGH. I'M NOT THAT LUCKY...
IT WOULD HAVE BEEN NICE TO SEE HER AGAIN...
BUT I'M...
...A LITTLE RELIEVED.
SHE WON'T SEE ME IN THIS PATHETIC POSITION TWICE—
GUU (CLENCH)
BELL-KUN!
!?

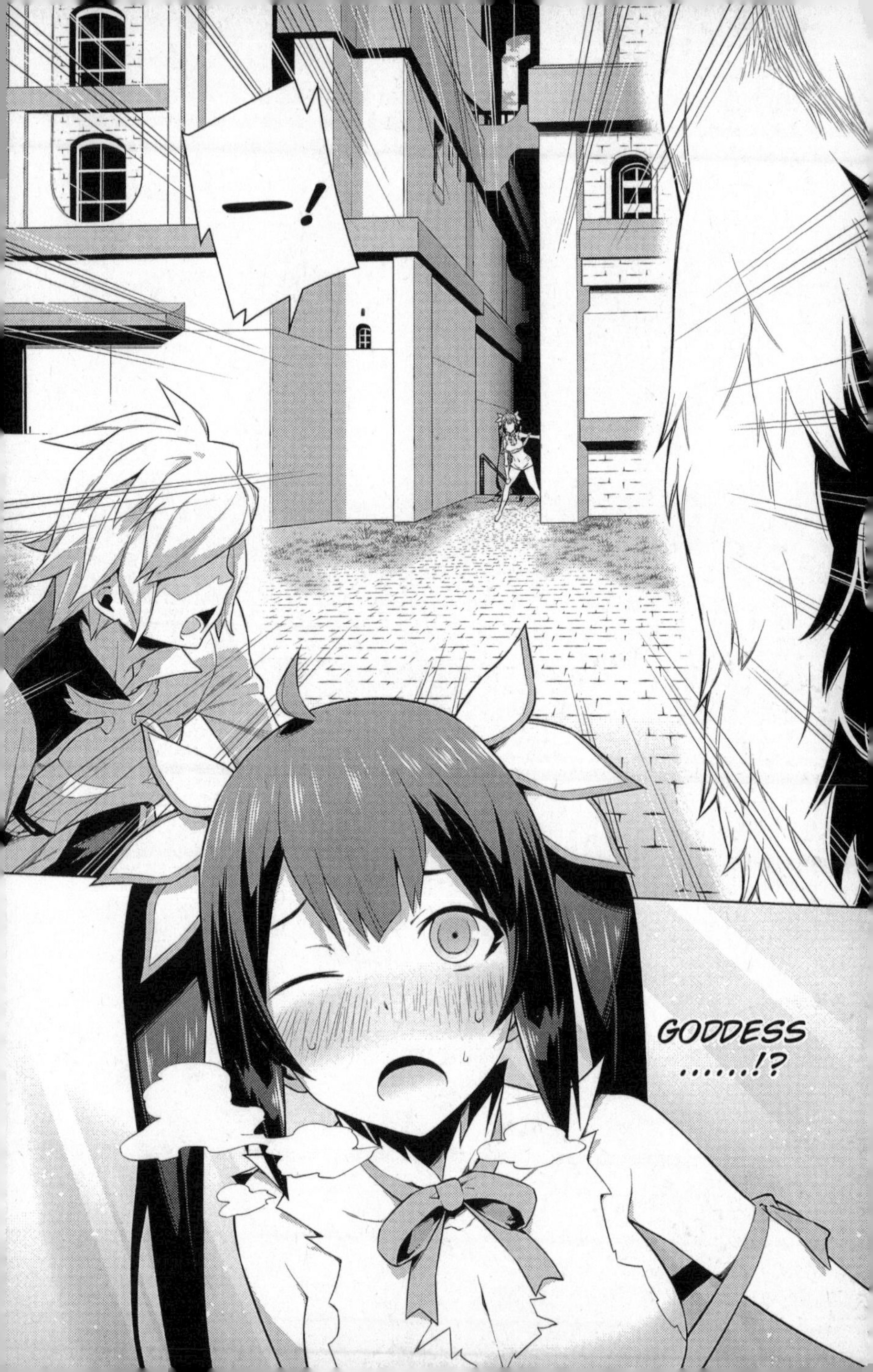
——!
GODDESS ......!?

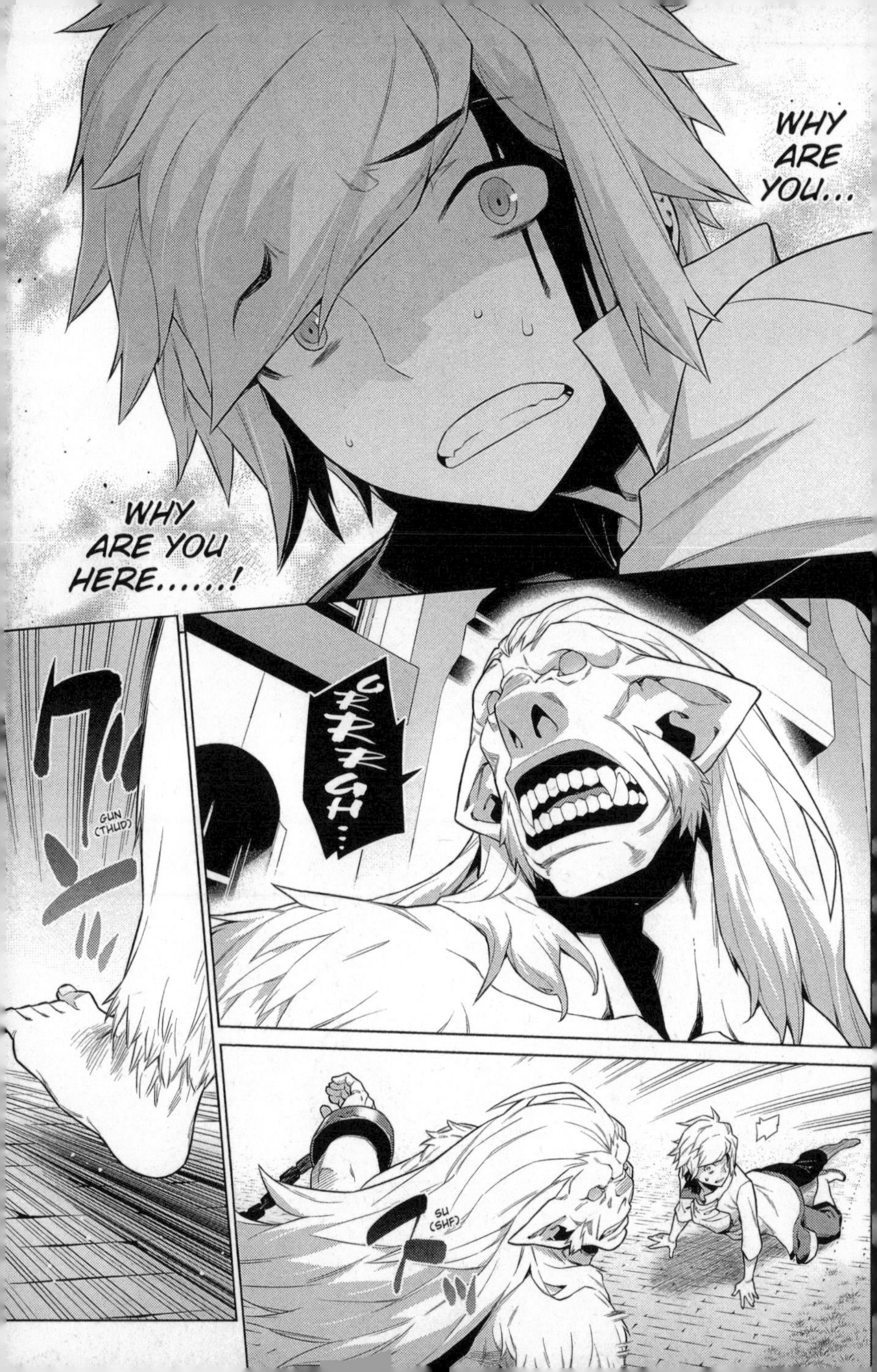
WHY ARE YOU...
WHY ARE YOU HERE......!
GRRRGH...
SU (SHF)
GUN (THUD)

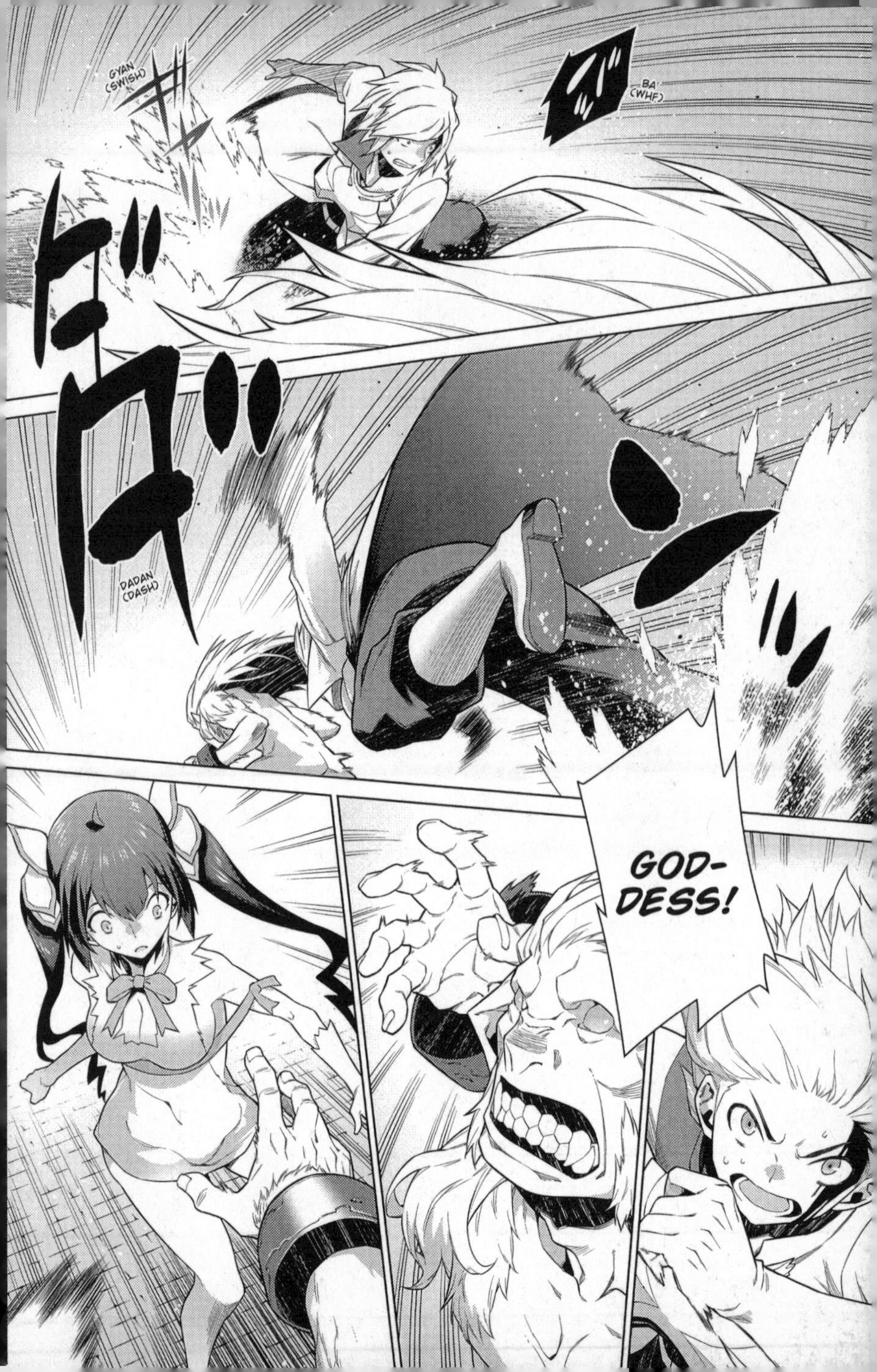
BA (WHF)
GYAN (SWISH)
DADAN (DASH)
GOD-DESS!

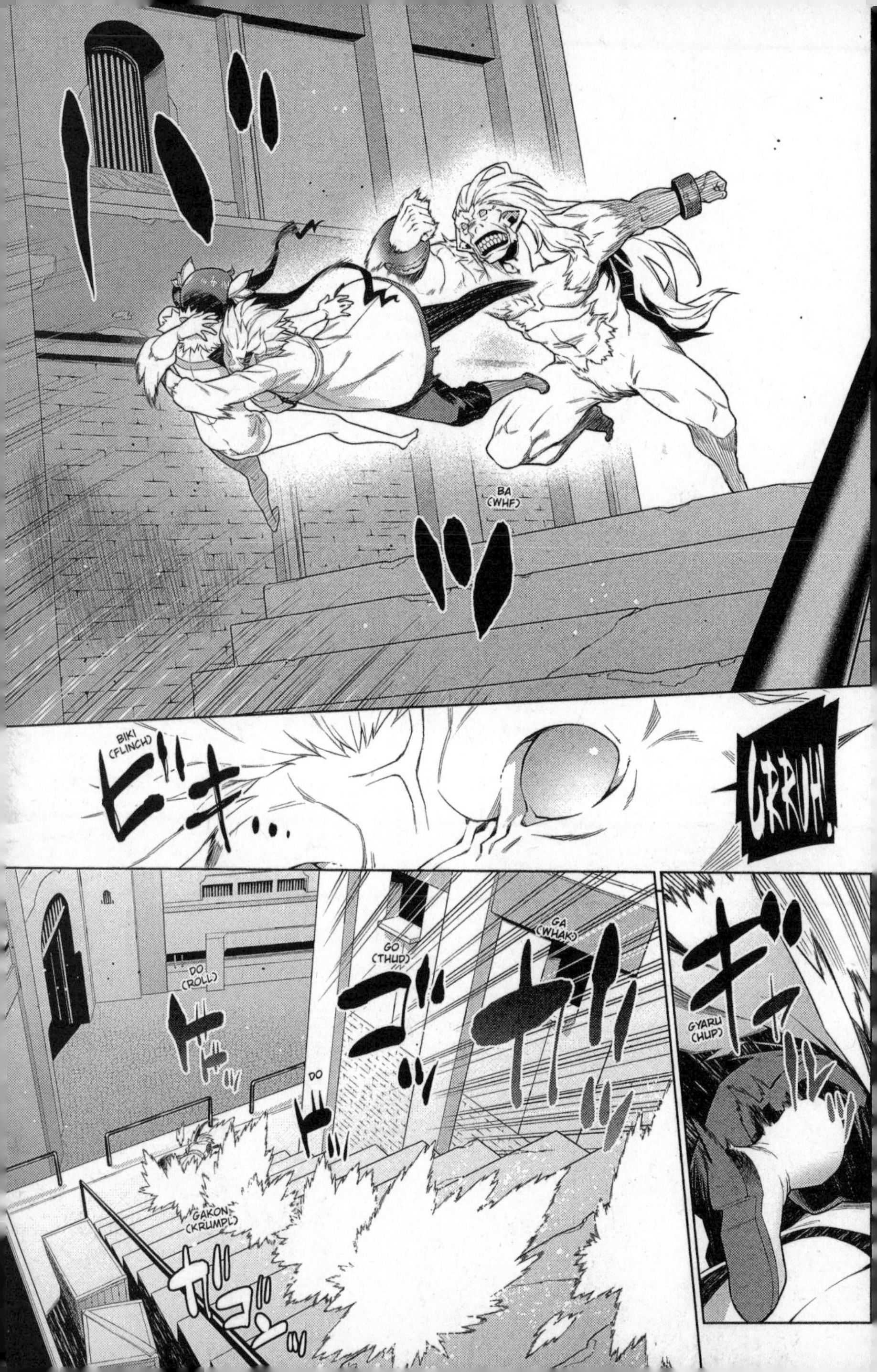

BA
(WHF)
GRRUH!
BIKI
(FLINCH)
GYARU
(HUP)
GA
(WHAK)
GO
(THUD)
DO
(ROLL)
DO
GAKON
(KRUMPL)

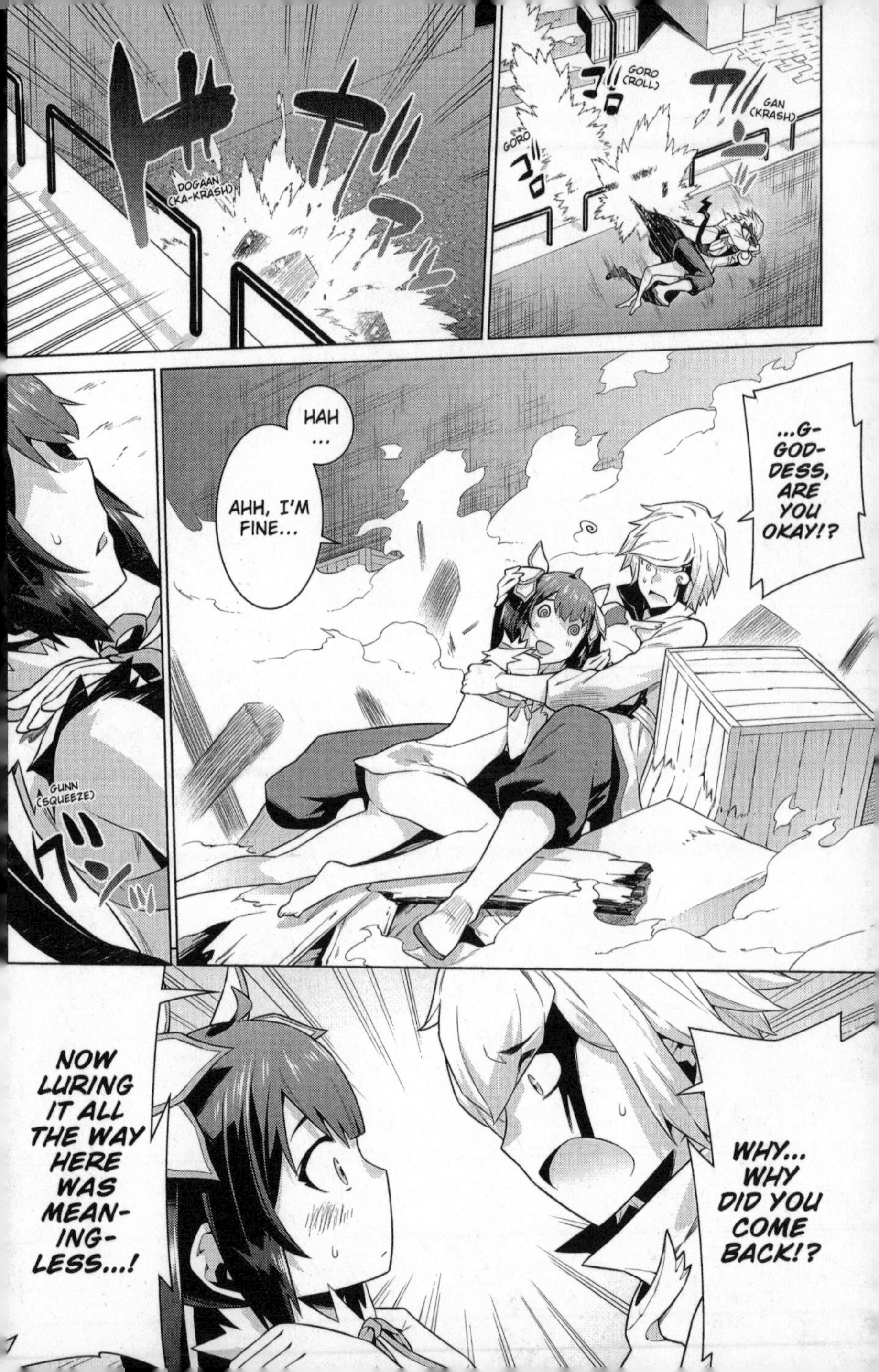
GORO (ROLL)
GORO
GAN (KRASH)
DOGAAN (KA-KRASH)
...G-GOD-DESS, ARE YOU OKAY!?
HAH ...
AHH, I'M FINE...
GUNN (SQUEEZE)
WHY... WHY DID YOU COME BACK!?
NOW LURING IT ALL THE WAY HERE WAS MEAN-ING-LESS...!

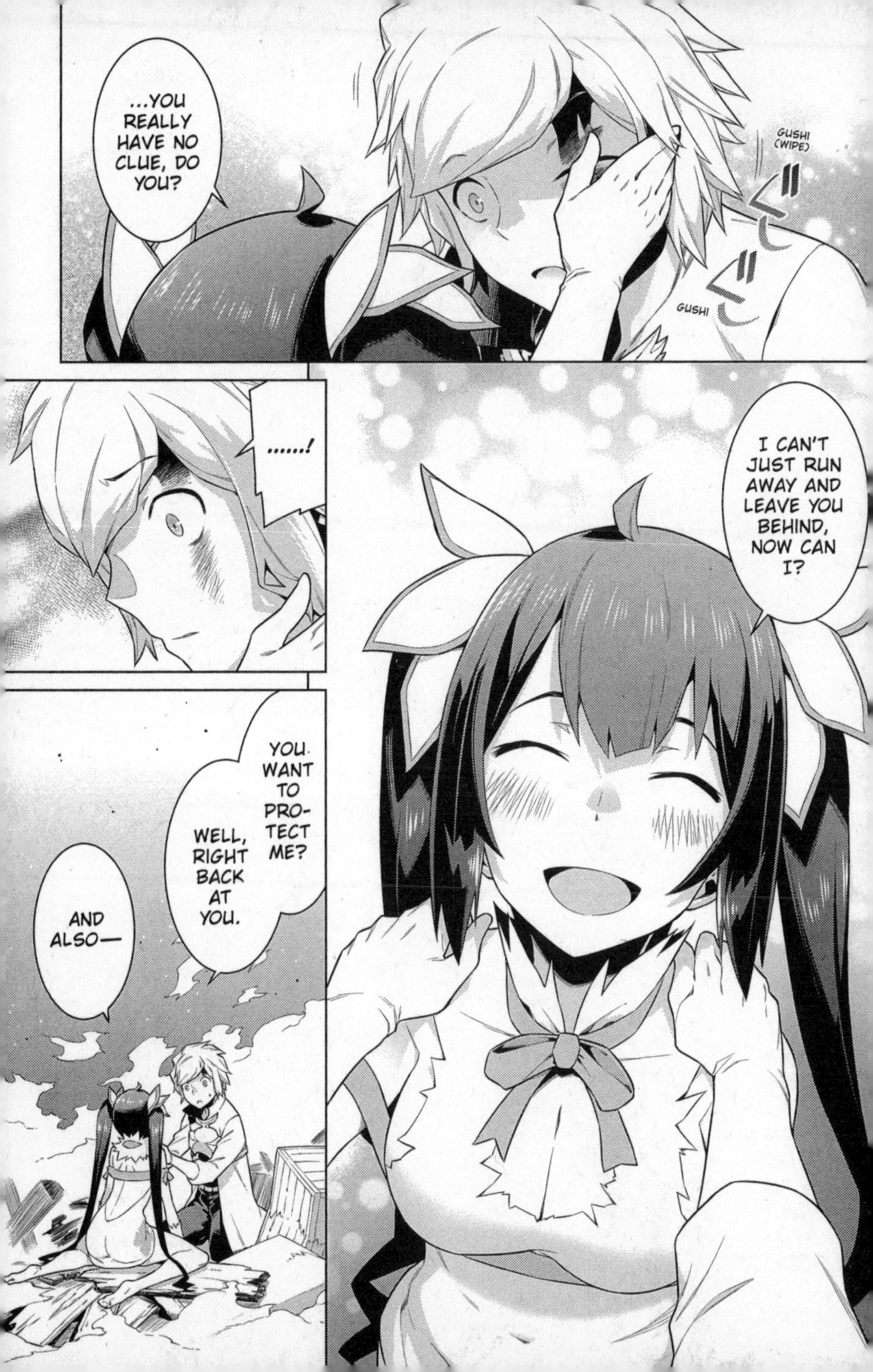
...YOU REALLY HAVE NO CLUE, DO YOU?
GUSHI (WIPE)
GUSHI
I CAN'T JUST RUN AWAY AND LEAVE YOU BEHIND, NOW CAN I?
......!
YOU WANT TO PROTECT ME?
WELL, RIGHT BACK AT YOU.
AND ALSO—

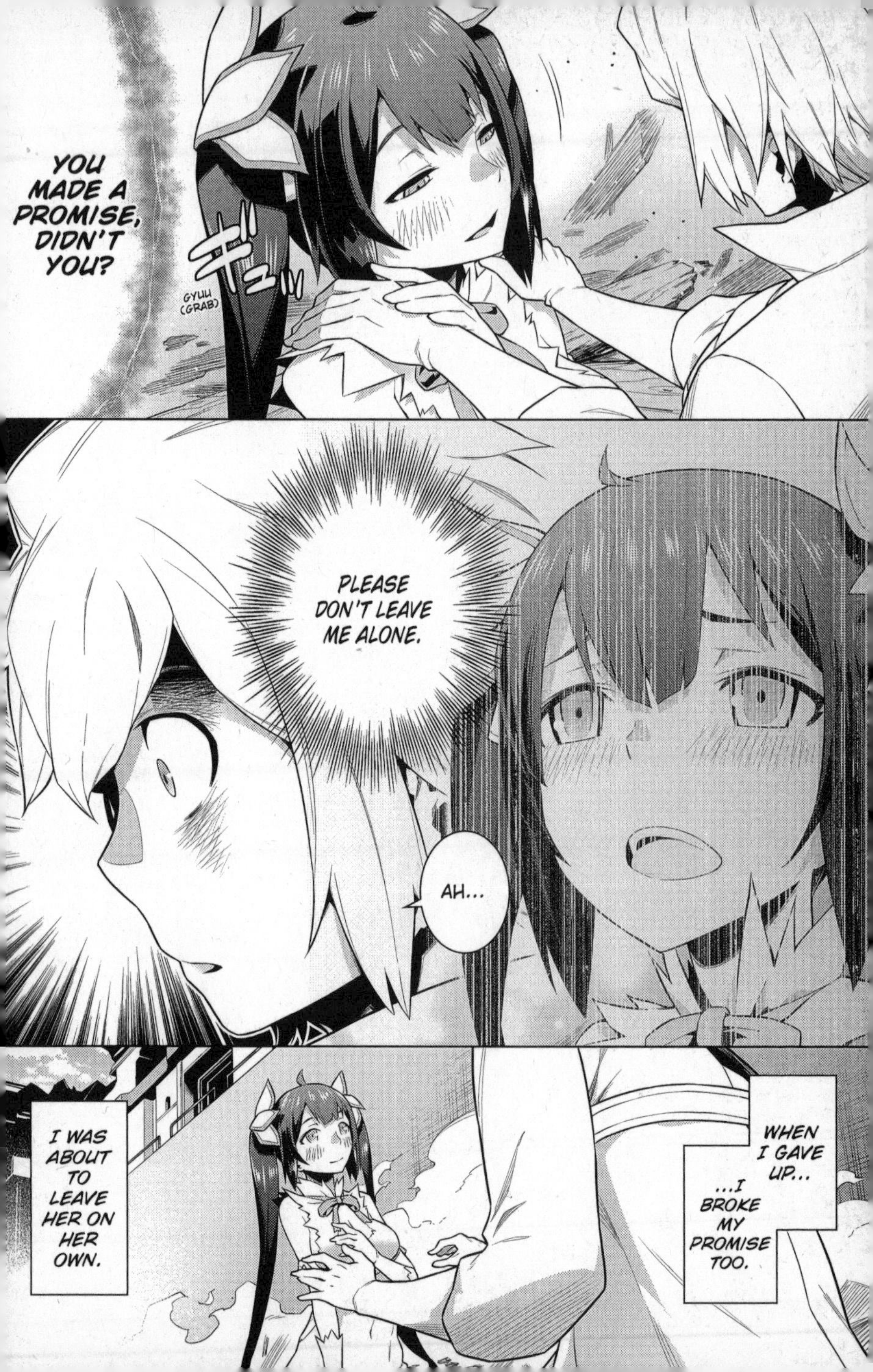

YOU MADE A PROMISE, DIDN'T YOU?
ギュッ
GYUU (GRAB)
PLEASE DON'T LEAVE ME ALONE.
AH...
WHEN I GAVE UP...
...I BROKE MY PROMISE TOO.
I WAS ABOUT TO LEAVE HER ON HER OWN.

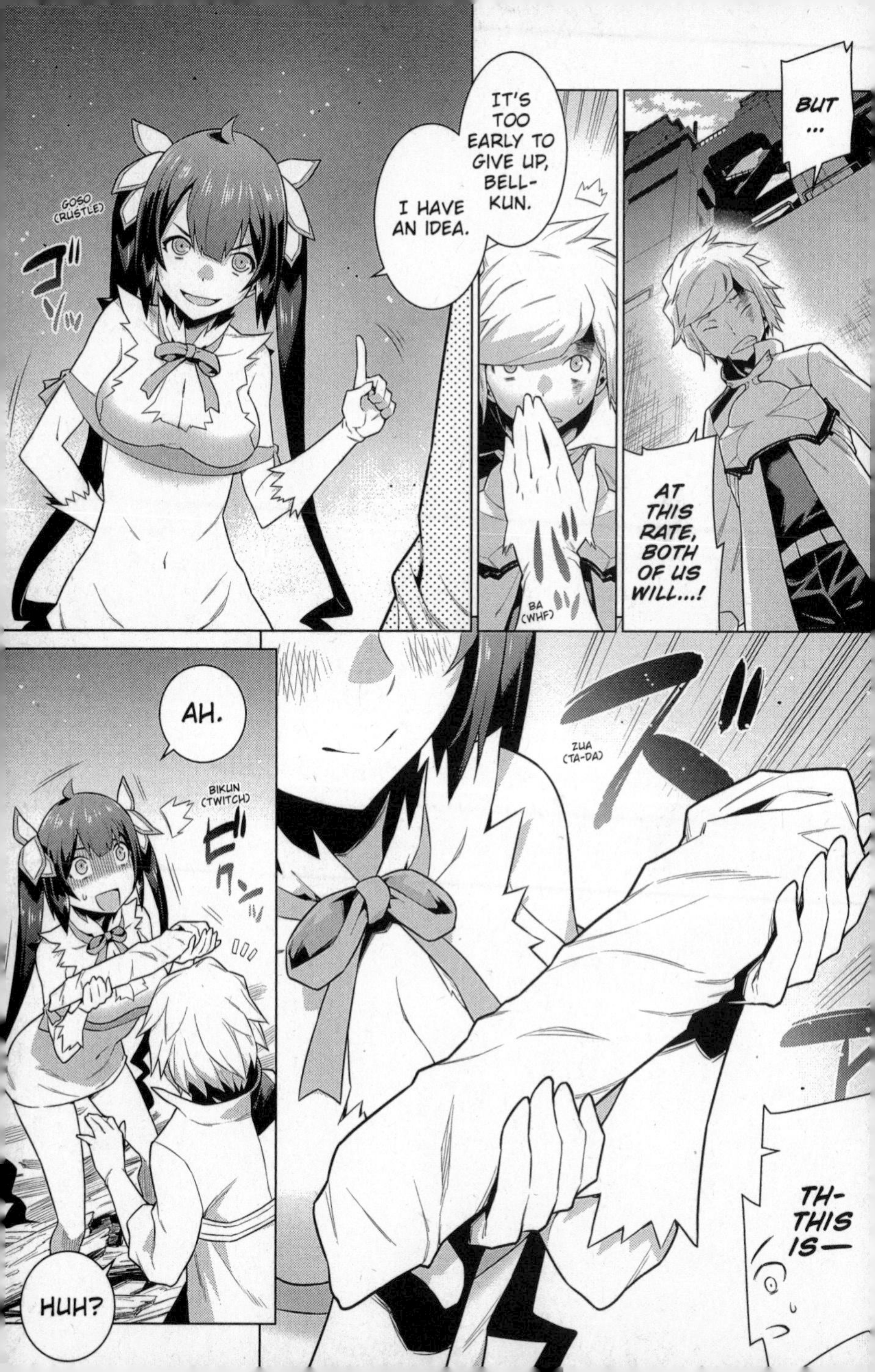
BUT ...
AT THIS RATE, BOTH OF US WILL...!
IT'S TOO EARLY TO GIVE UP, BELL-KUN.
BA (WHF)
I HAVE AN IDEA.
GOSO (RUSTLE)
ZUA (TA-DA)
TH-THIS IS—
AH.
BIKUN (TWITCH)
HUH?

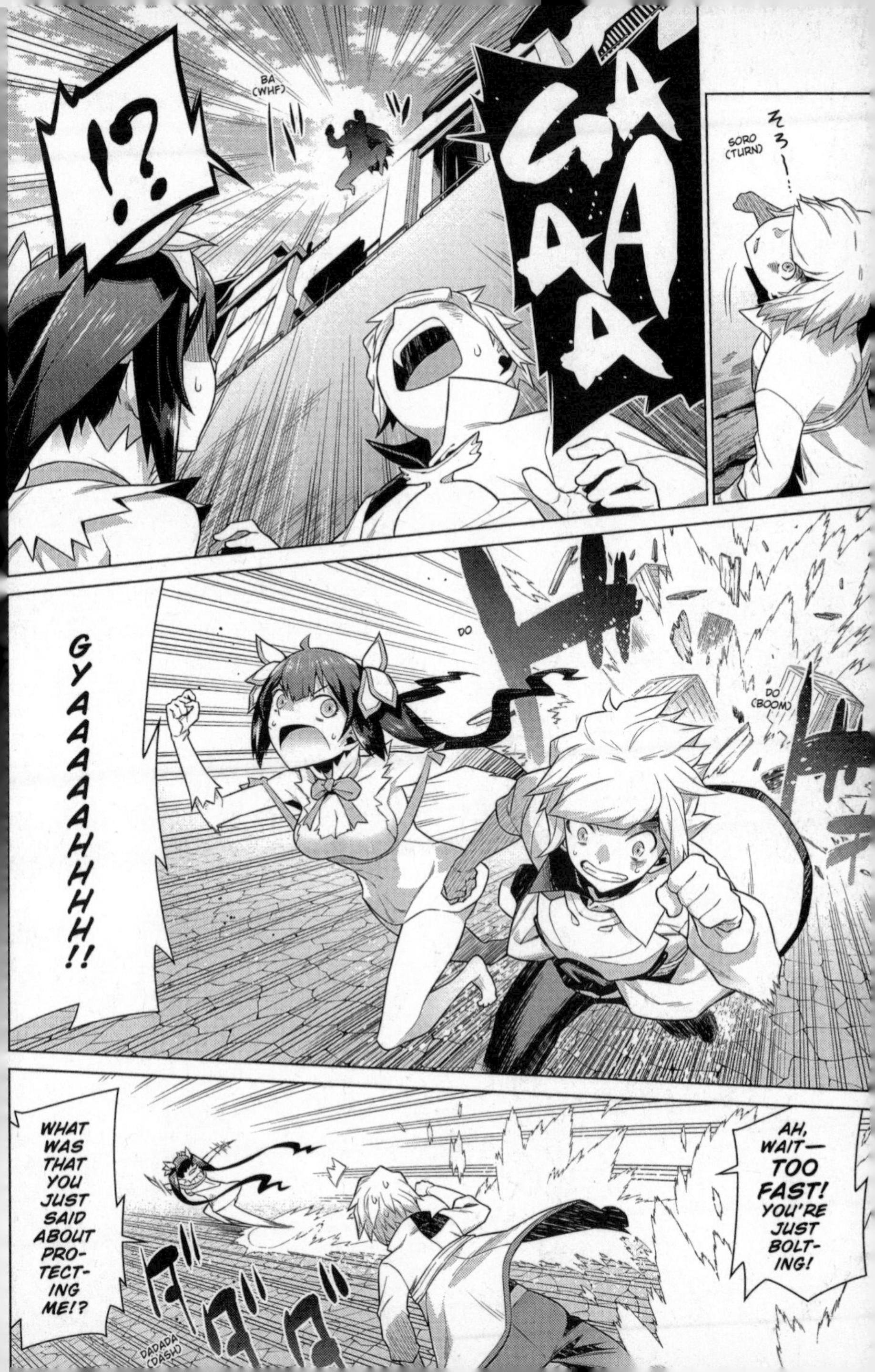
SORO (TURN)
GAAAA
BA (WHF)
!?
DO (BOOM)
DO
GYAAAAAAHHHH!!
AH, WAIT— TOO FAST! YOU'RE JUST BOLTING!
WHAT WAS THAT YOU JUST SAID ABOUT PROTECTING ME!?
DADADA (DASH)

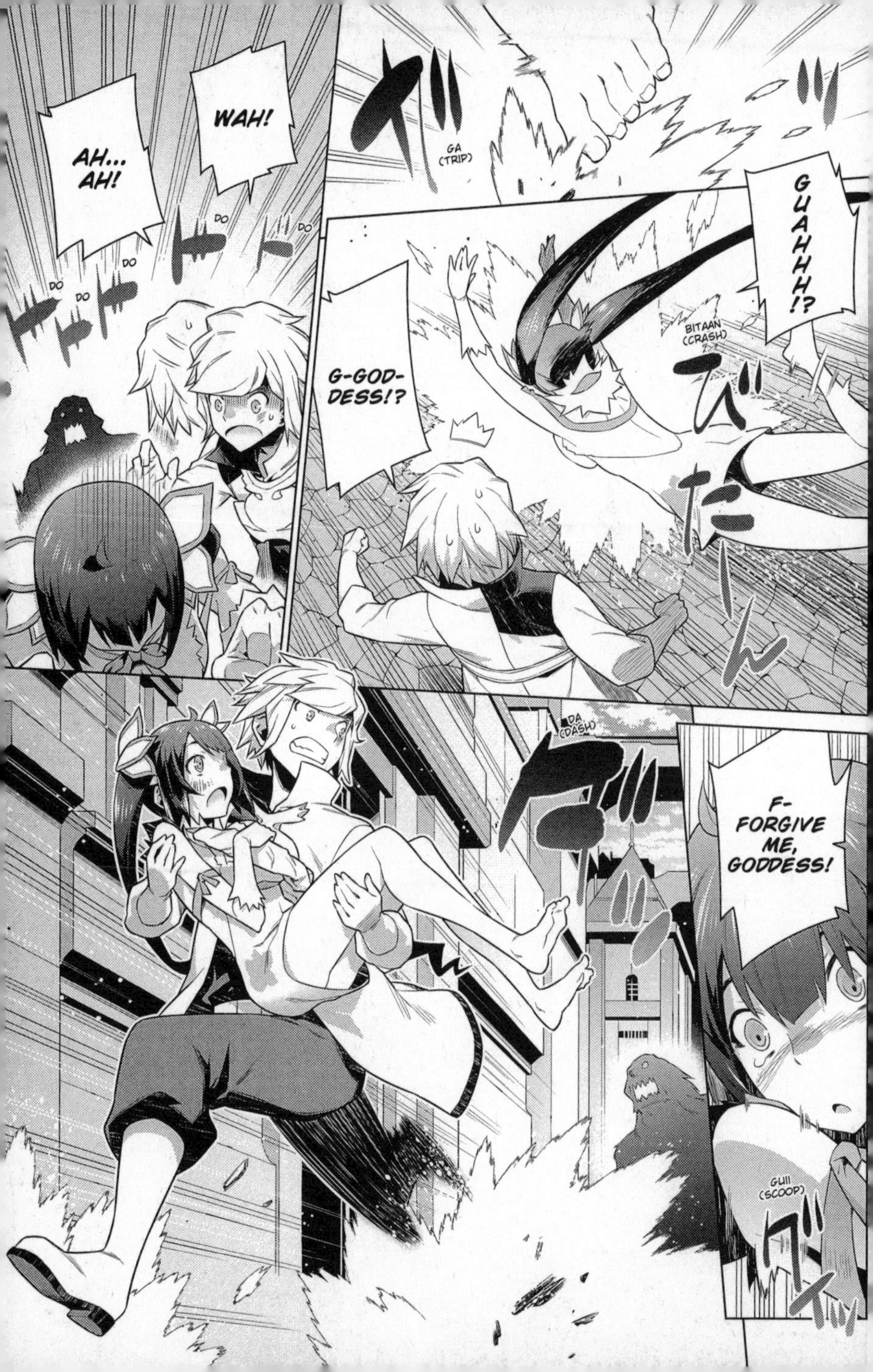

GA (TRIP)
GUAHHH!?
BITAAN (CRASH)
G-GOD-DESS!?
WAH!
AH... AH!
DO
DO
DO
DO
DO
F-FORGIVE ME, GODDESS!
GUII (SCOOP)
DA (DASH)

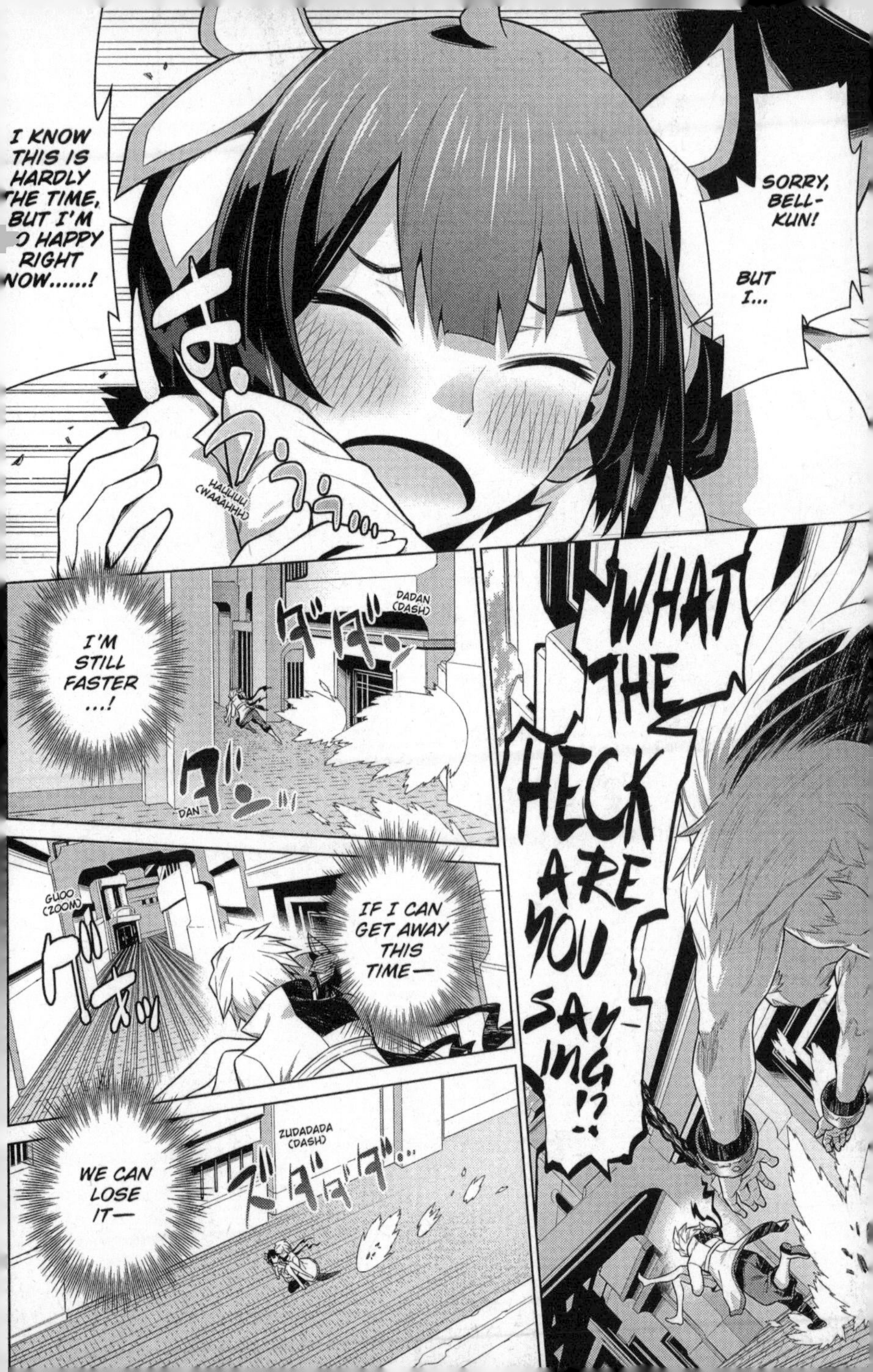
SORRY, BELL-KUN!
BUT I...
I KNOW THIS IS HARDLY THE TIME, BUT I'M SO HAPPY RIGHT NOW......!
HAUUUU (WAAAHHH)
WHAT THE HECK ARE YOU SAYING!?
DADAN (DASH)
I'M STILL FASTER...!
DAN
IF I CAN GET AWAY THIS TIME—
GUOO (ZOOM)
ZUDADADA (DASH)
WE CAN LOSE IT—

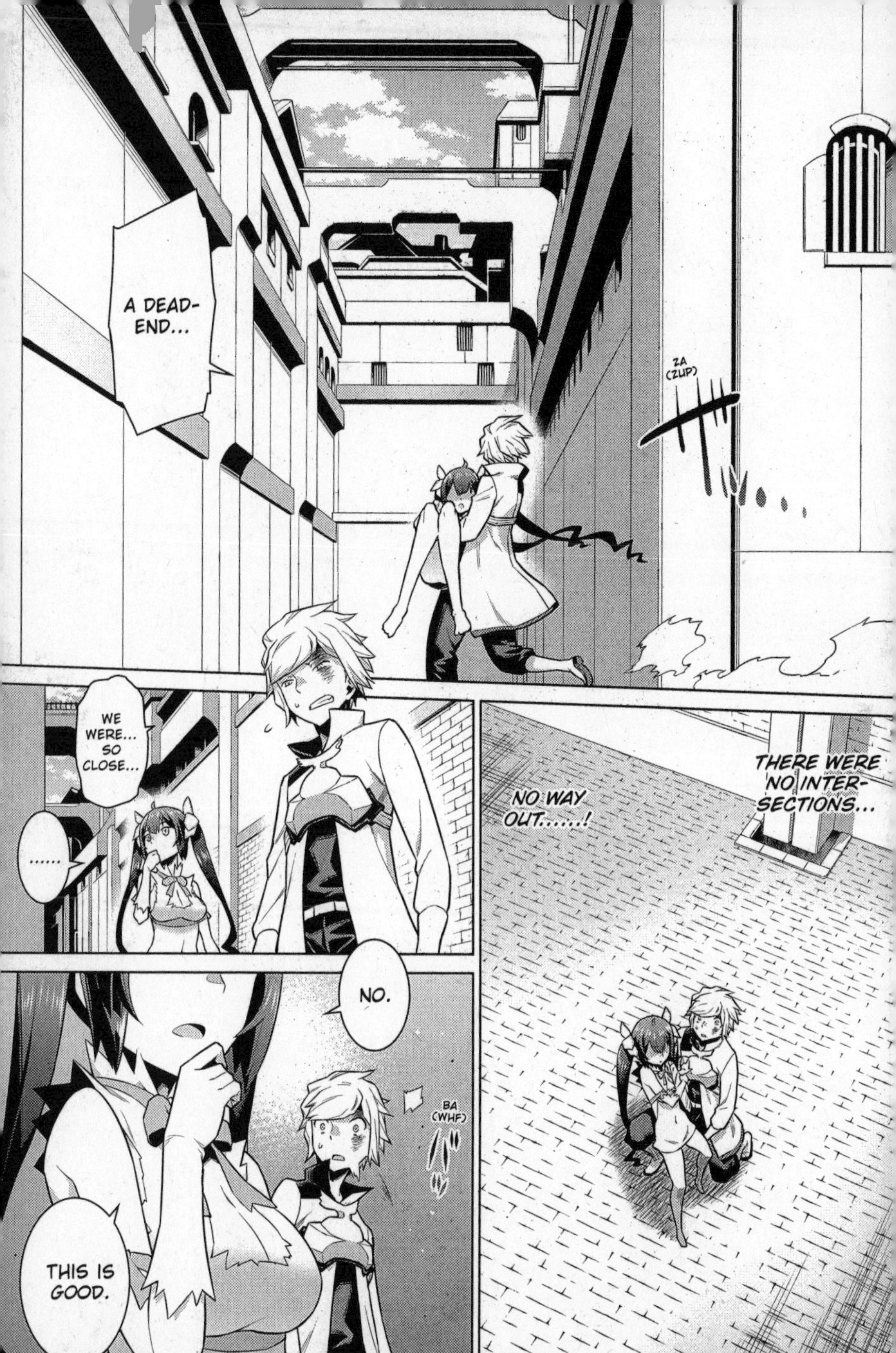
ZA (ZUP)
A DEAD-END...
THERE WERE NO INTER-SECTIONS...
NO WAY OUT......!
WE WERE... SO CLOSE...
......
NO.
BA (WHF)
THIS IS GOOD.

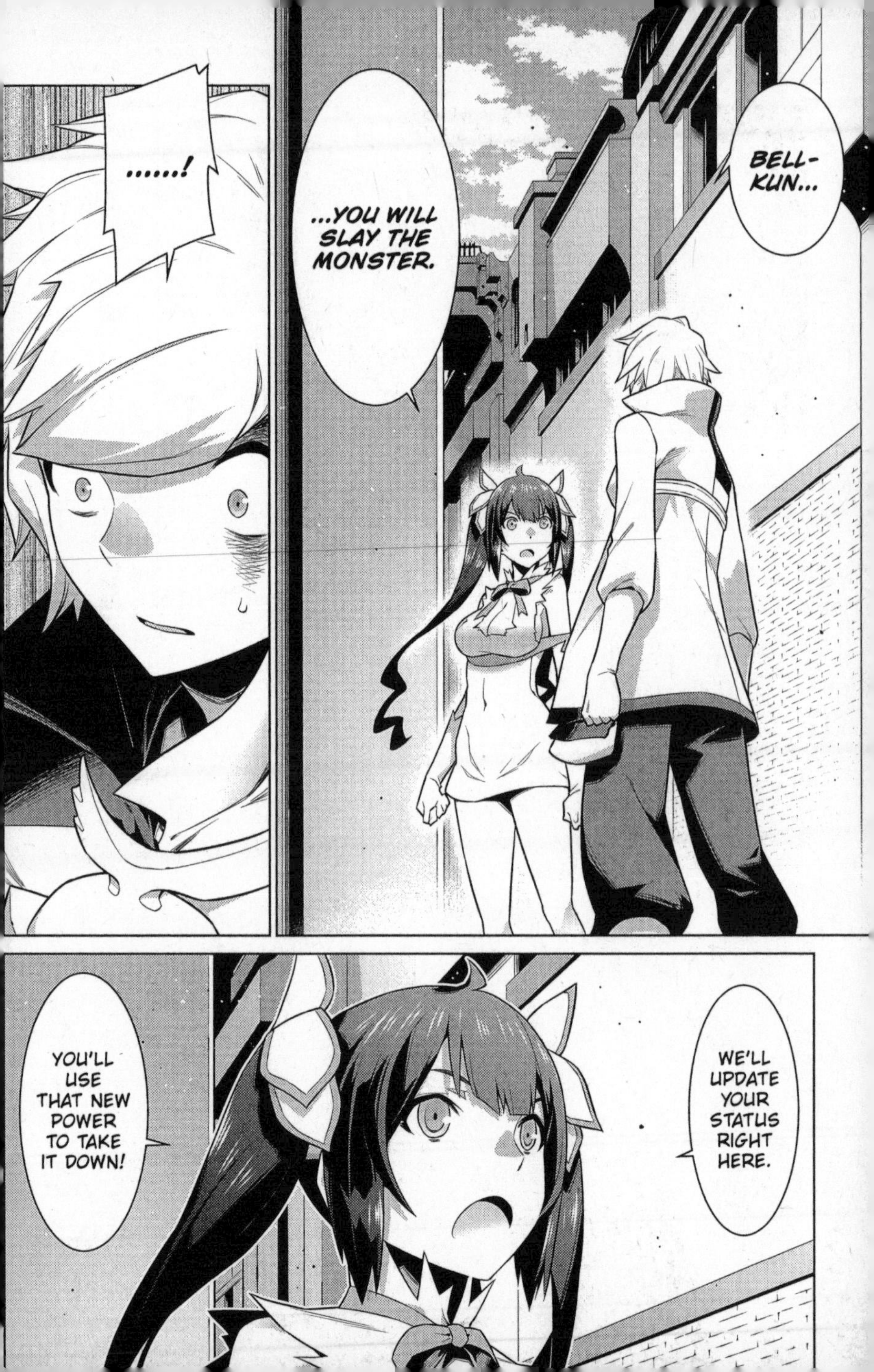
BELL-KUN...
...YOU WILL SLAY THE MONSTER.
......!
WE'LL UPDATE YOUR STATUS RIGHT HERE.
YOU'LL USE THAT NEW POWER TO TAKE IT DOWN!

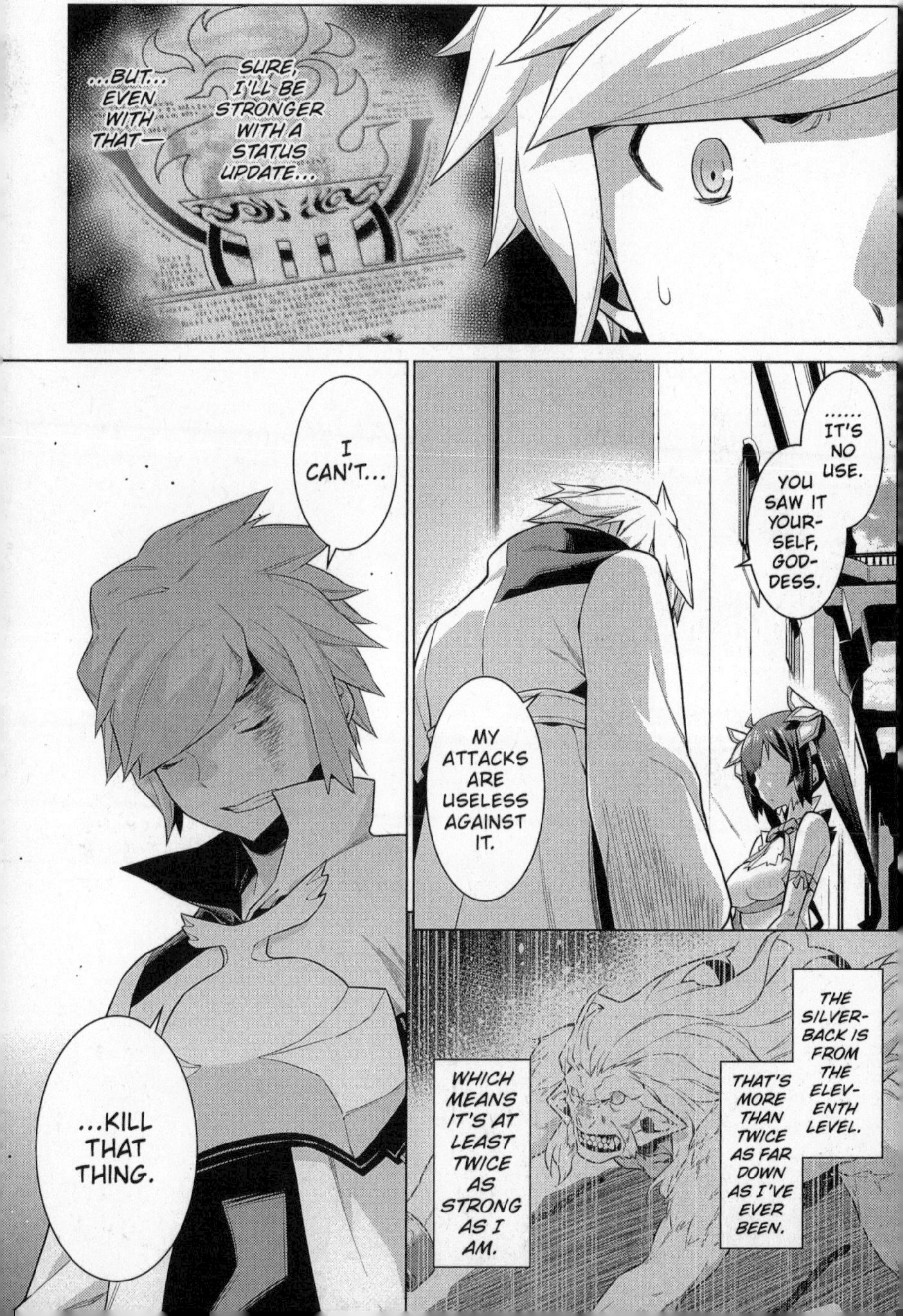
SURE, I'LL BE STRONGER WITH A STATUS UPDATE...
...BUT... EVEN WITH THAT—
...... IT'S NO USE. YOU SAW IT YOURSELF, GODDESS.
MY ATTACKS ARE USELESS AGAINST IT.
THE SILVER-BACK IS FROM THE ELEVENTH LEVEL.
THAT'S MORE THAN TWICE AS FAR DOWN AS I'VE EVER BEEN.
WHICH MEANS IT'S AT LEAST TWICE AS STRONG AS I AM.
I CAN'T...
...KILL THAT THING.

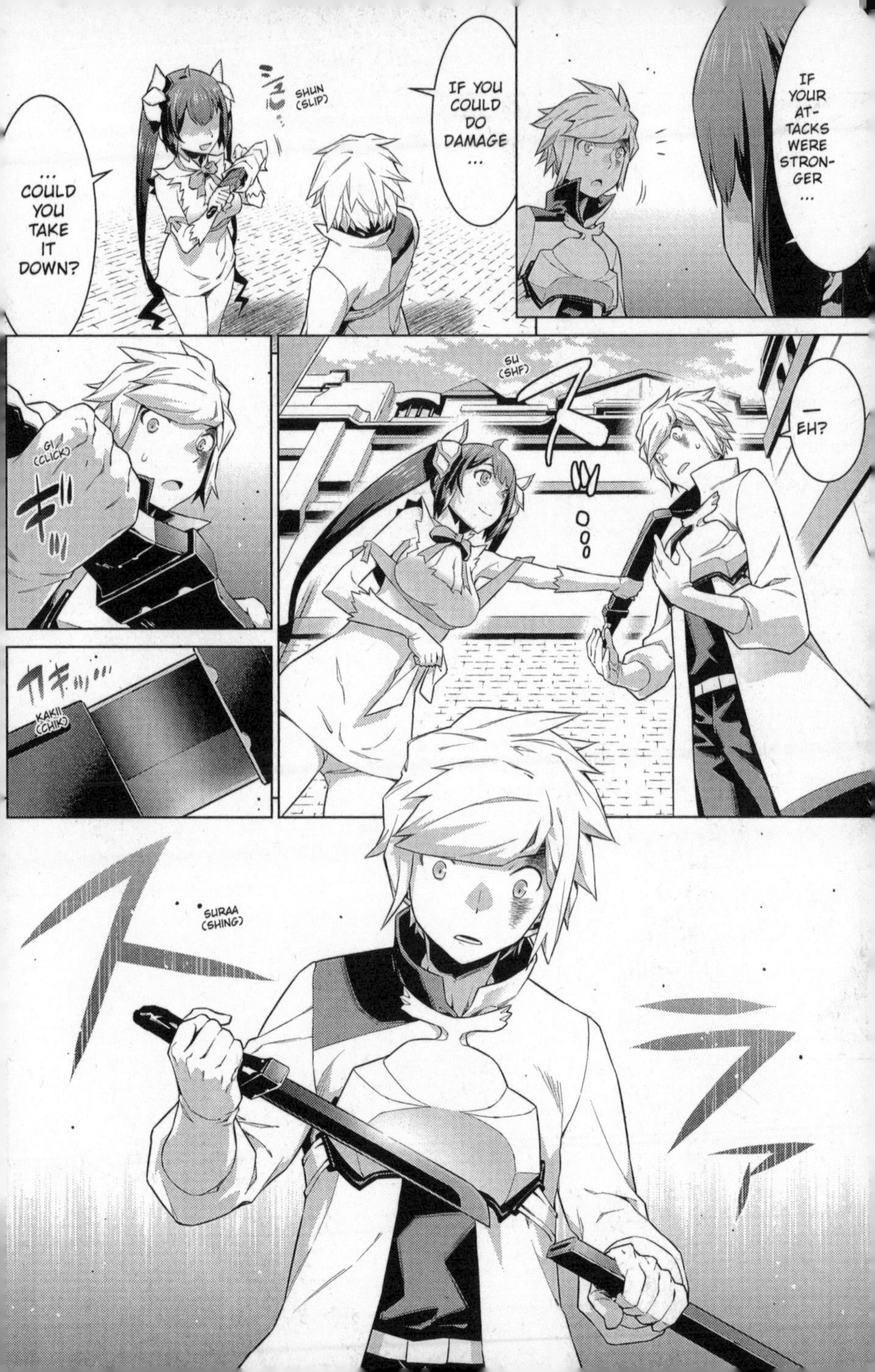

IF YOUR AT-TACKS WERE STRON-GER ...
IF YOU COULD DO DAMAGE ...
SHUN (SLIP)
... COULD YOU TAKE IT DOWN?
—EH?
SU (SHF)
GI (CLICK)
KAKII (CHIK)
SURAA (SHING)

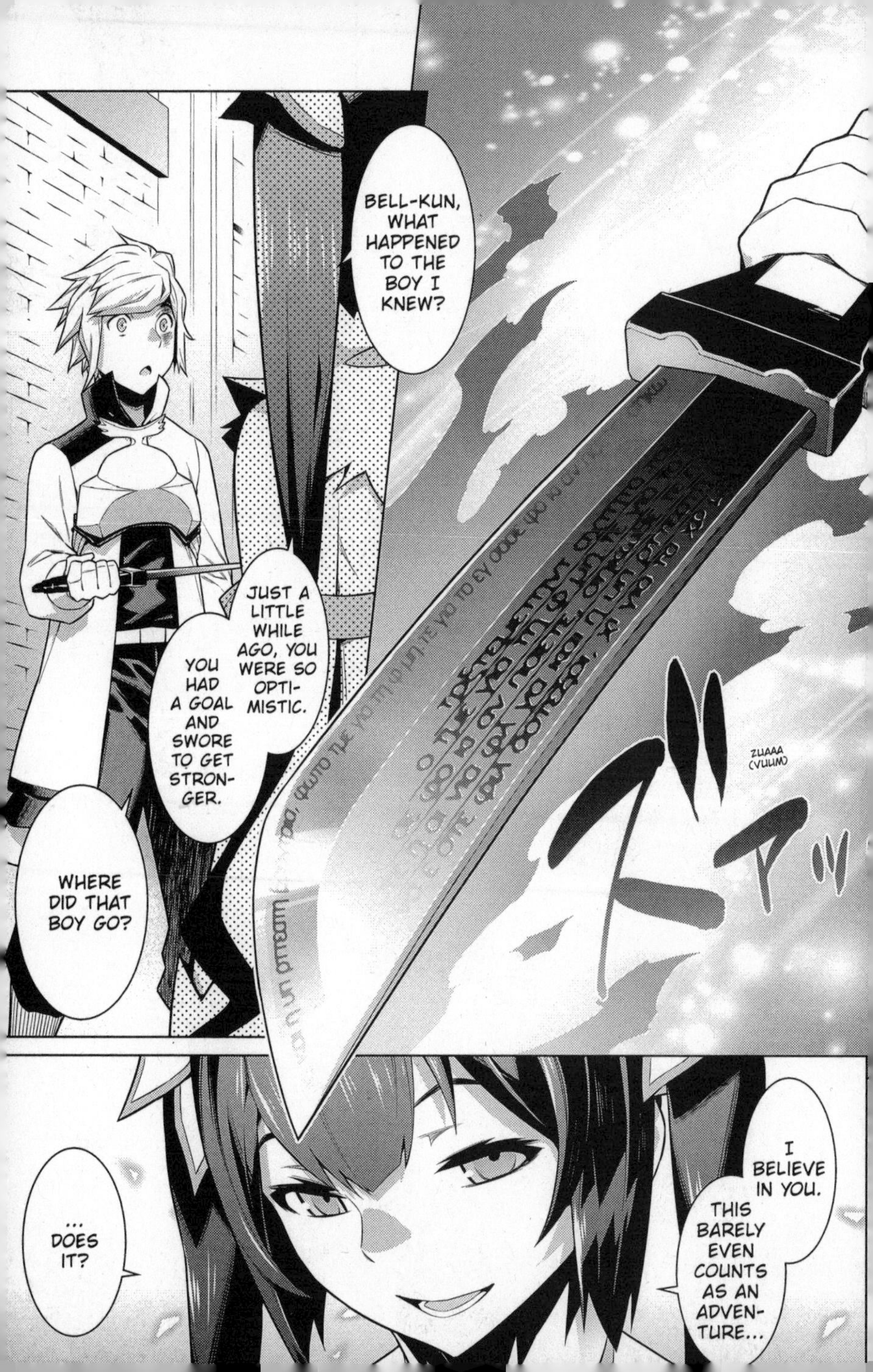
BELL-KUN, WHAT HAPPENED TO THE BOY I KNEW?
JUST A LITTLE WHILE AGO, YOU WERE SO OPTIMISTIC.
YOU HAD A GOAL AND SWORE TO GET STRONGER.
WHERE DID THAT BOY GO?
ZUAAA (VUUM)
I BELIEVE IN YOU.
THIS BARELY EVEN COUNTS AS AN ADVENTURE...
...DOES IT?

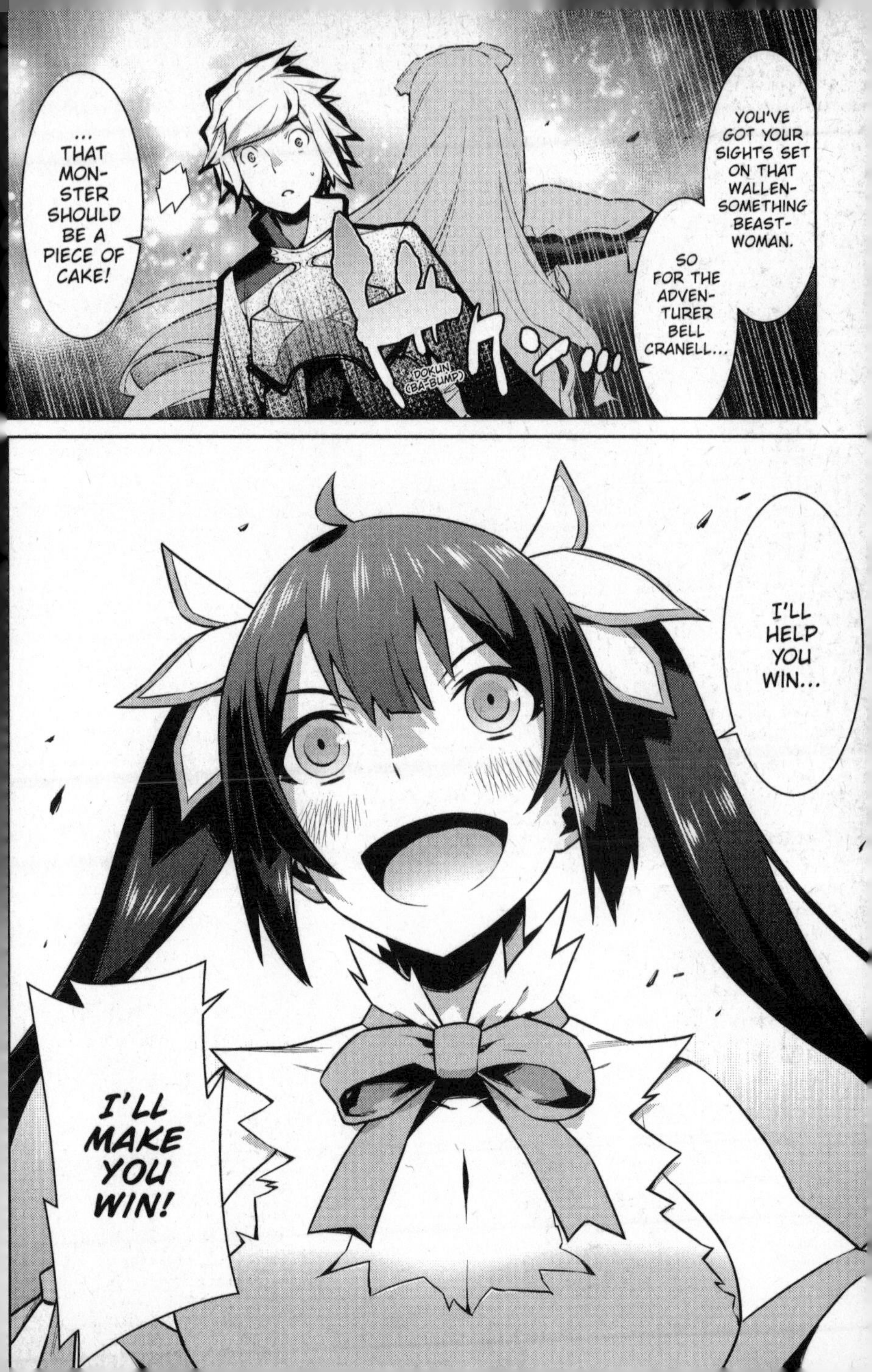
YOU'VE GOT YOUR SIGHTS SET ON THAT WALLEN-SOMETHING BEAST-WOMAN.
SO FOR THE ADVENTURER BELL CRANELL...
DOKUN (BA-BUMP)
... THAT MON-STER SHOULD BE A PIECE OF CAKE!
I'LL HELP YOU WIN...
I'LL MAKE YOU WIN!

CITIZENS OF ORARIO

text by Fujino Omori
character rough by Kunieda

➤File 07

SYR FLOVER

The girl next door. She works at The Benevolent Mistress as a waitress. She's a mild-mannered human girl, who pays a great amount of attention to details.

CITIZENS OF ORARIO

text by Fujino Omori
character rough by Kunieda

➤File 08

MIA GRAND

A particularly large dwarf woman.
Owner of The Benevolent Mistress.
An ex-adventurer, her presence is
larger than life.

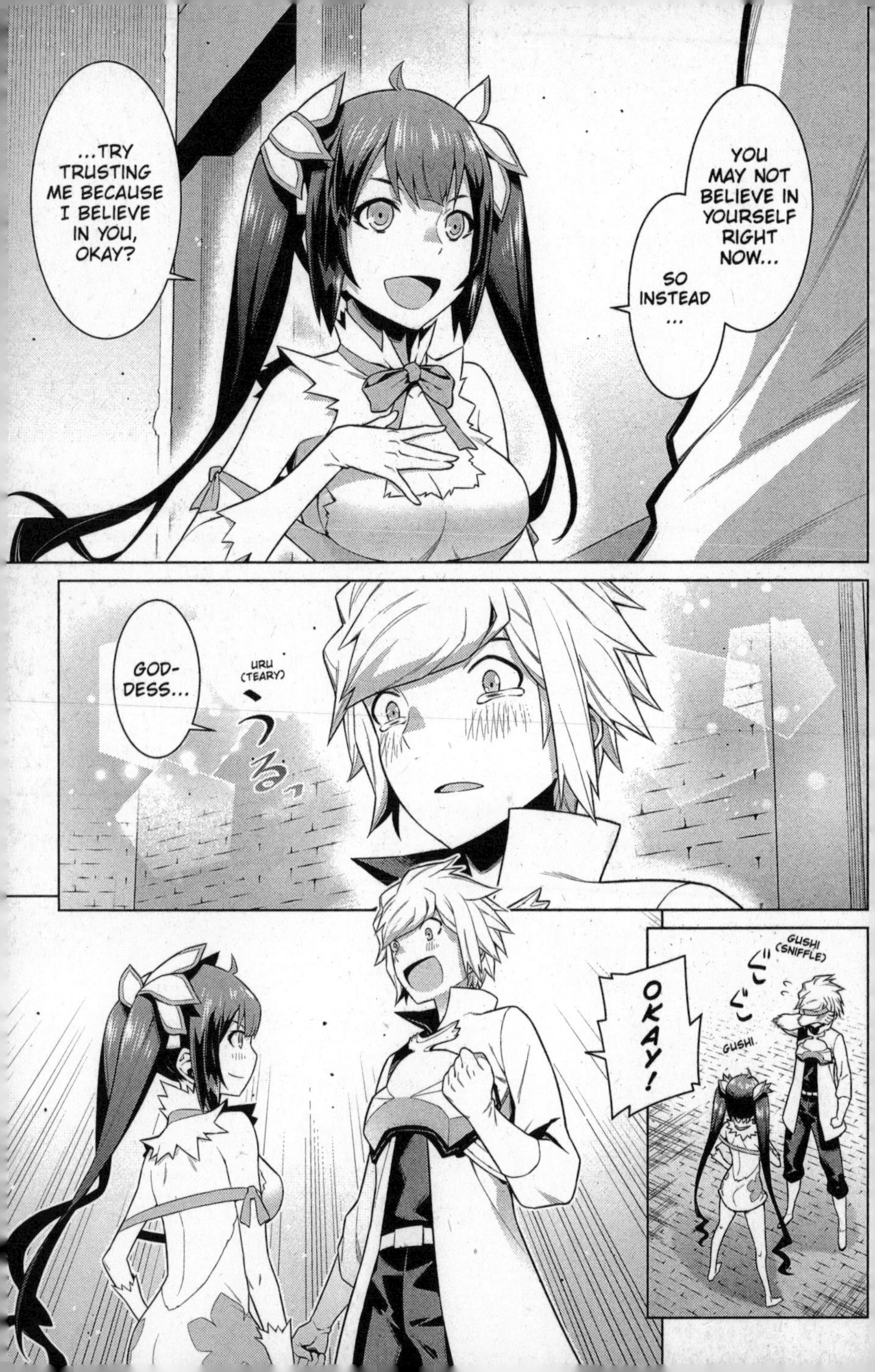
YOU MAY NOT BELIEVE IN YOURSELF RIGHT NOW...
SO INSTEAD ...
...TRY TRUSTING ME BECAUSE I BELIEVE IN YOU, OKAY?
URU (TEARY)
GOD-DESS...
GUSHI (SNIFFLE)
GUSHI
OKAY!

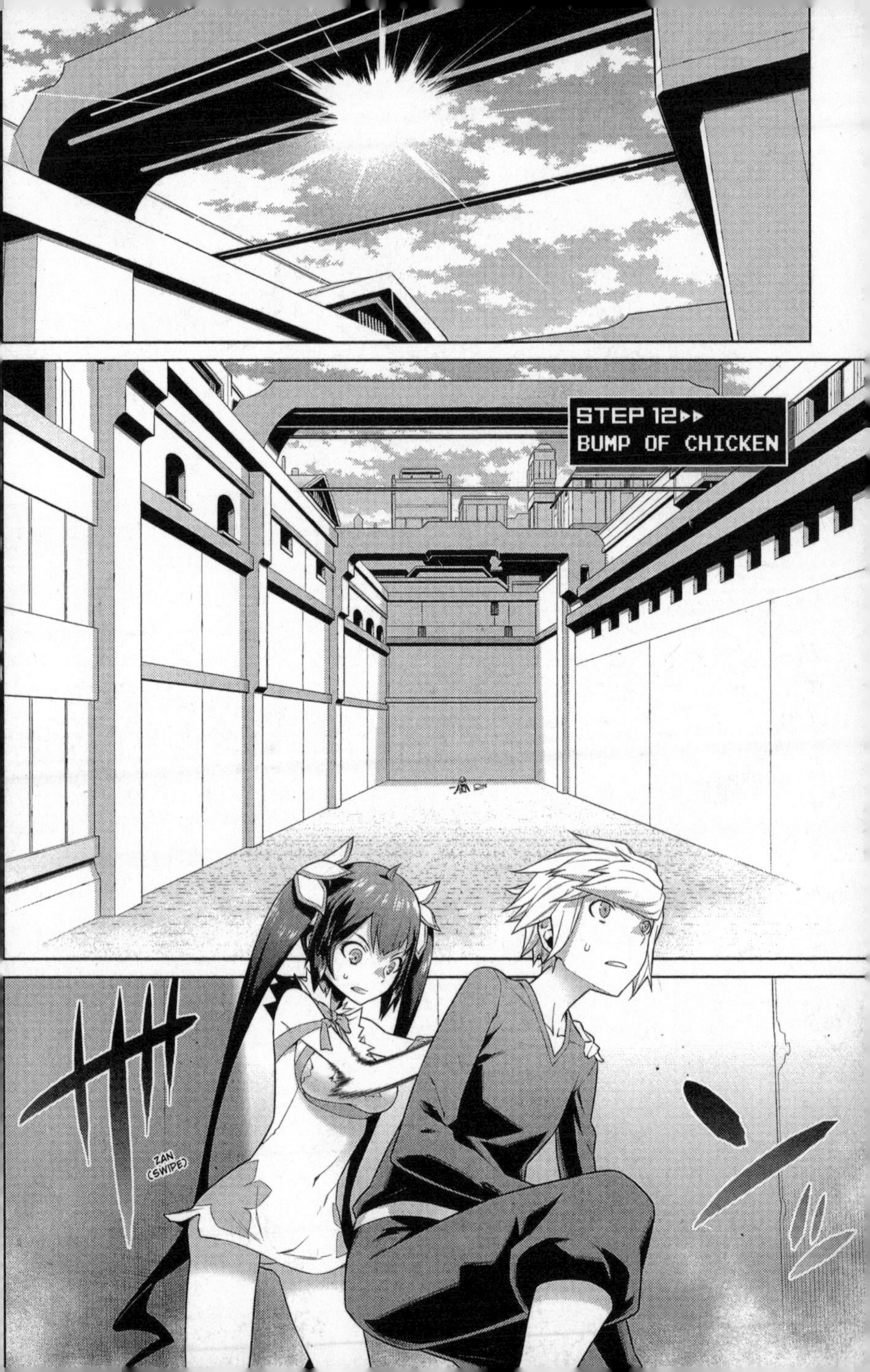
STEP 12▸▸
BUMP OF CHICKEN
ZAN
(SWIPE)

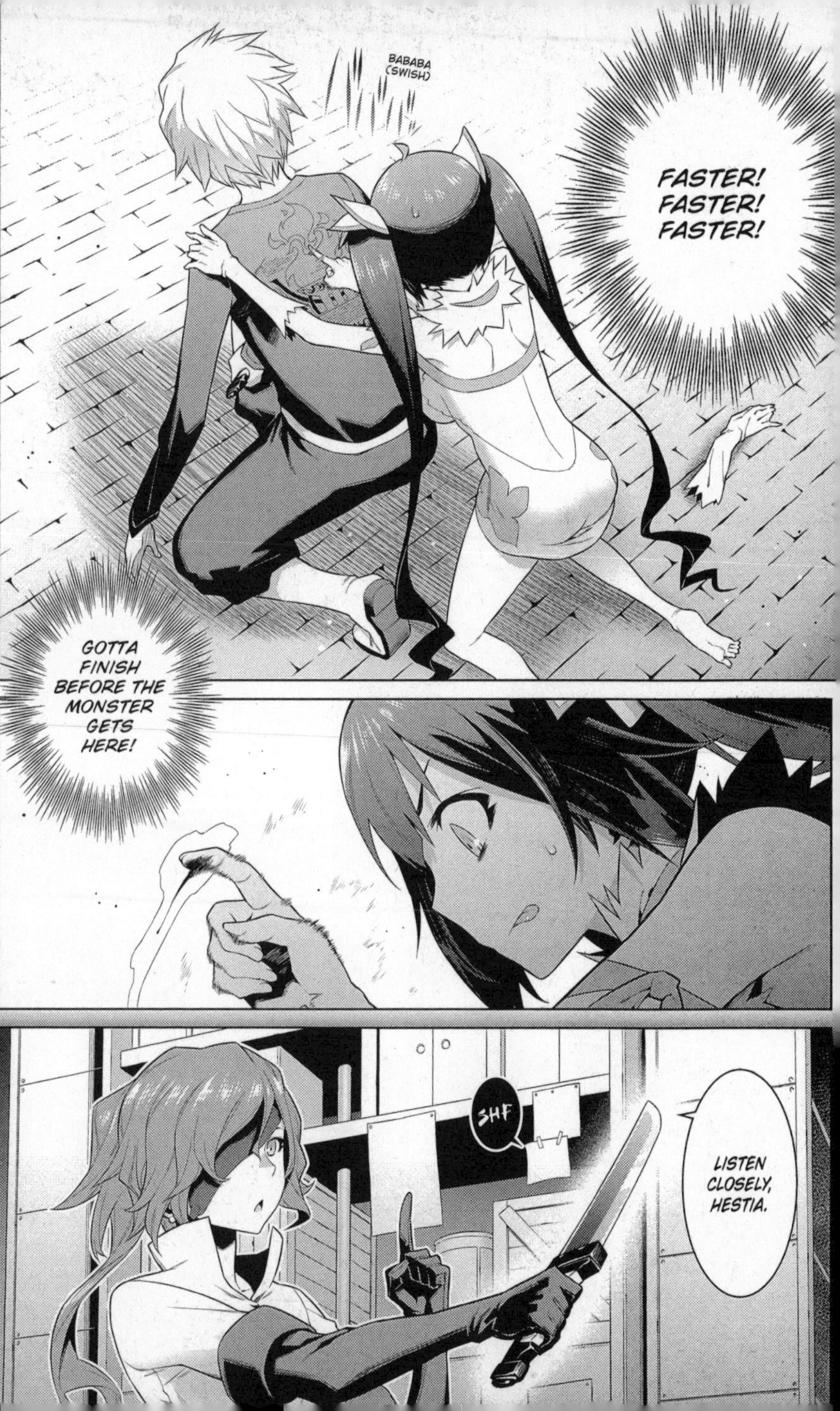
FASTER! FASTER! FASTER!
BABABA (SWISH)
GOTTA FINISH BEFORE THE MONSTER GETS HERE!
LISTEN CLOSELY, HESTIA.
SHF

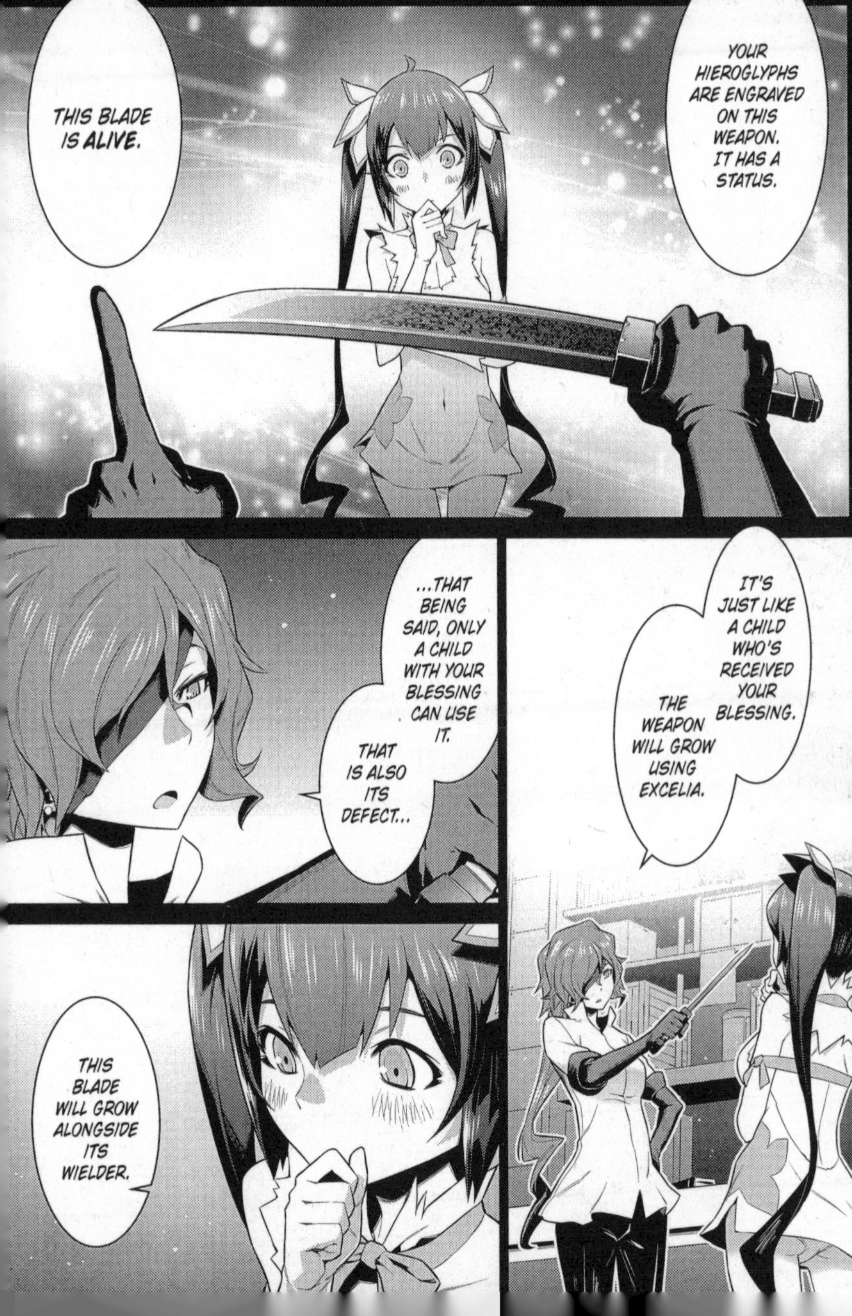
YOUR HIEROGLYPHS ARE ENGRAVED ON THIS WEAPON. IT HAS A STATUS.
THIS BLADE IS ALIVE.
IT'S JUST LIKE A CHILD WHO'S RECEIVED YOUR BLESSING.
THE WEAPON WILL GROW USING EXCELIA.
...THAT BEING SAID, ONLY A CHILD WITH YOUR BLESSING CAN USE IT.
THAT IS ALSO ITS DEFECT...
THIS BLADE WILL GROW ALONGSIDE ITS WIELDER.

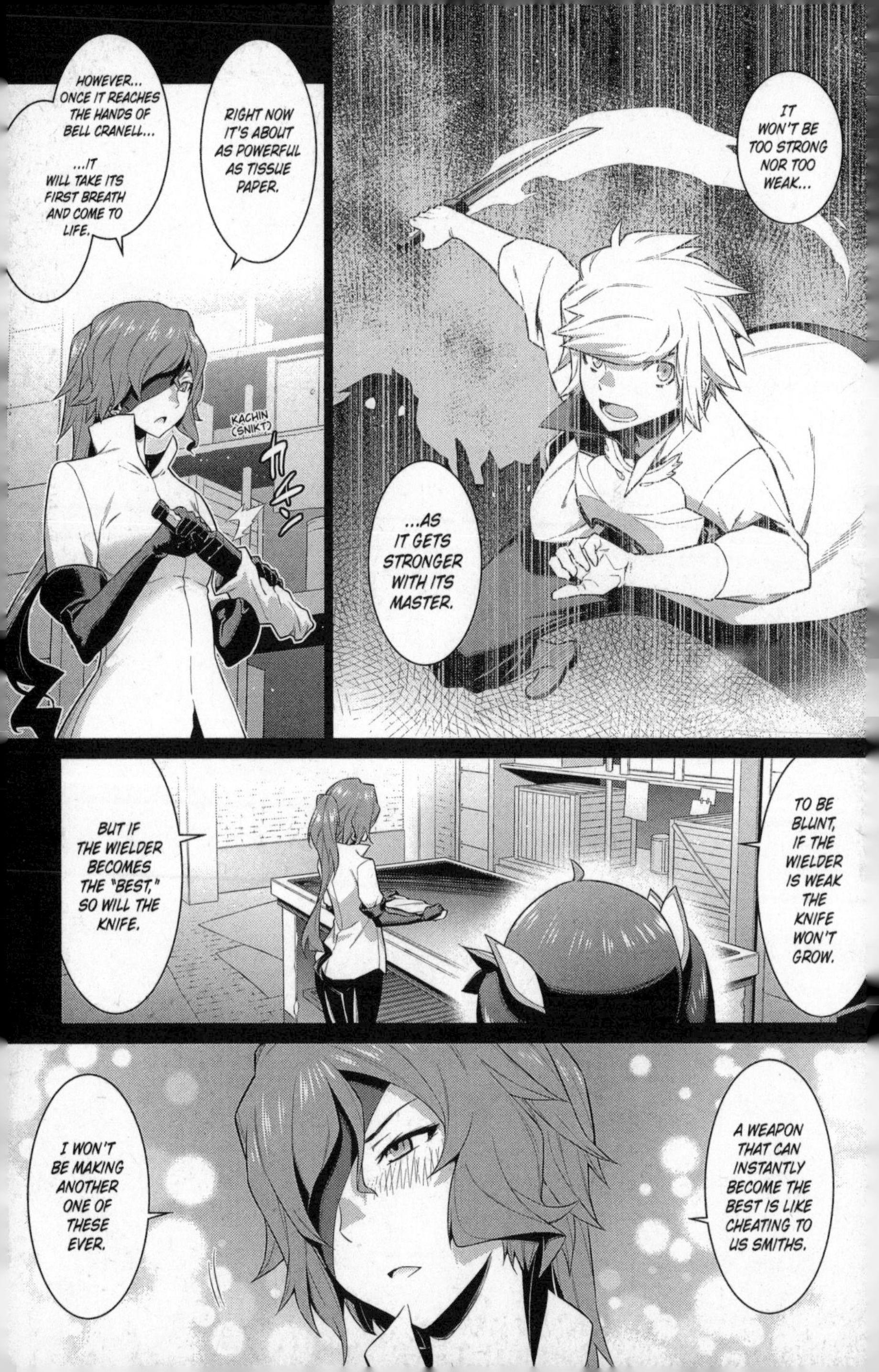
IT WON'T BE TOO STRONG NOR TOO WEAK...
...AS IT GETS STRONGER WITH ITS MASTER.
RIGHT NOW IT'S ABOUT AS POWERFUL AS TISSUE PAPER.
HOWEVER... ONCE IT REACHES THE HANDS OF BELL CRANELL...
...IT WILL TAKE ITS FIRST BREATH AND COME TO LIFE.
KACHIN (SNIKT)
TO BE BLUNT, IF THE WIELDER IS WEAK THE KNIFE WON'T GROW.
BUT IF THE WIELDER BECOMES THE "BEST," SO WILL THE KNIFE.
A WEAPON THAT CAN INSTANTLY BECOME THE BEST IS LIKE CHEATING TO US SMITHS.
I WON'T BE MAKING ANOTHER ONE OF THESE EVER.

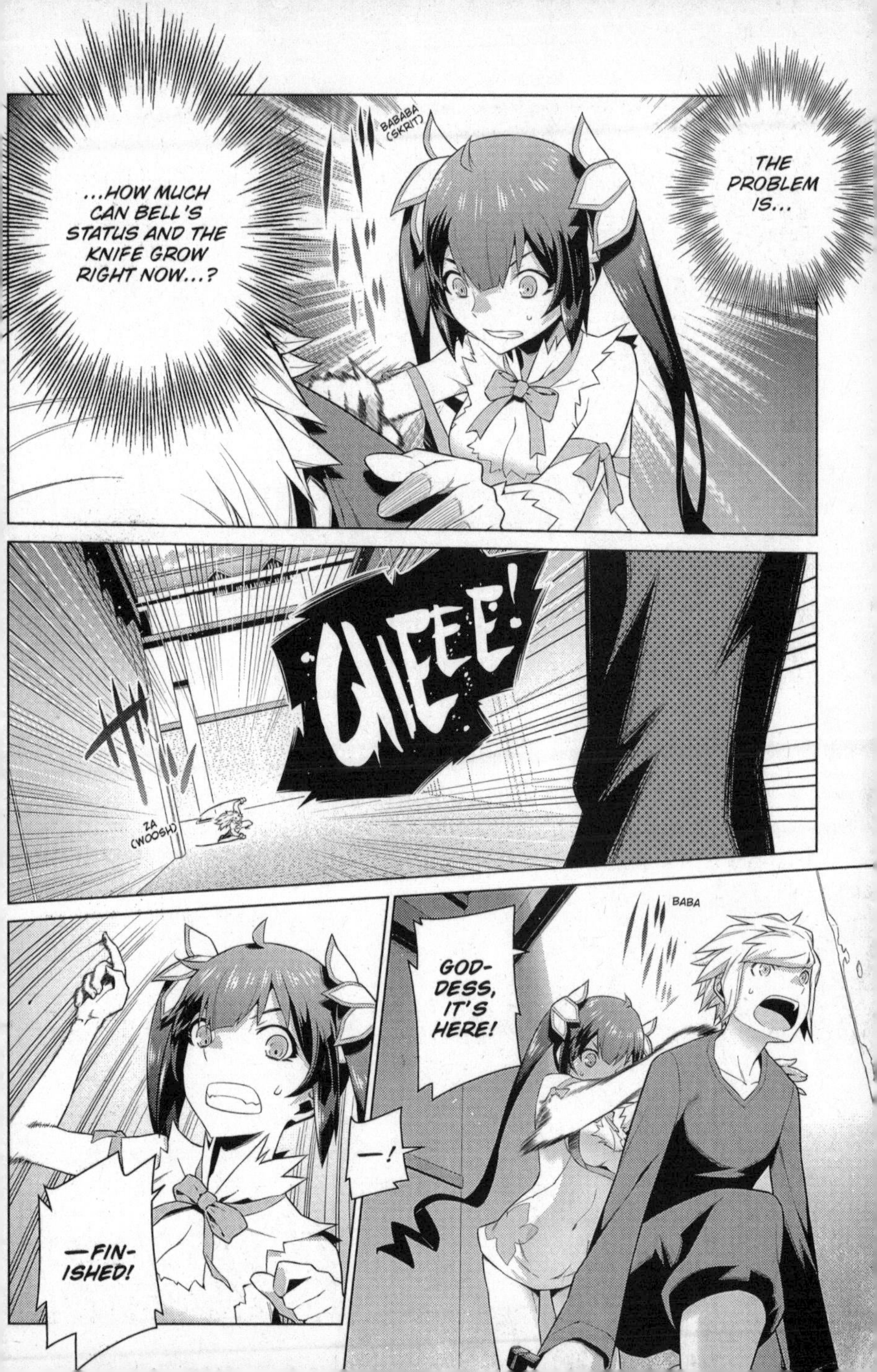
THE PROBLEM IS...
BABABA (SKRIT)
...HOW MUCH CAN BELL'S STATUS AND THE KNIFE GROW RIGHT NOW...?
GIEEE!
ZA (WOOSH)
BABA
GOD-DESS, IT'S HERE!
—!
—FIN-ISHED!

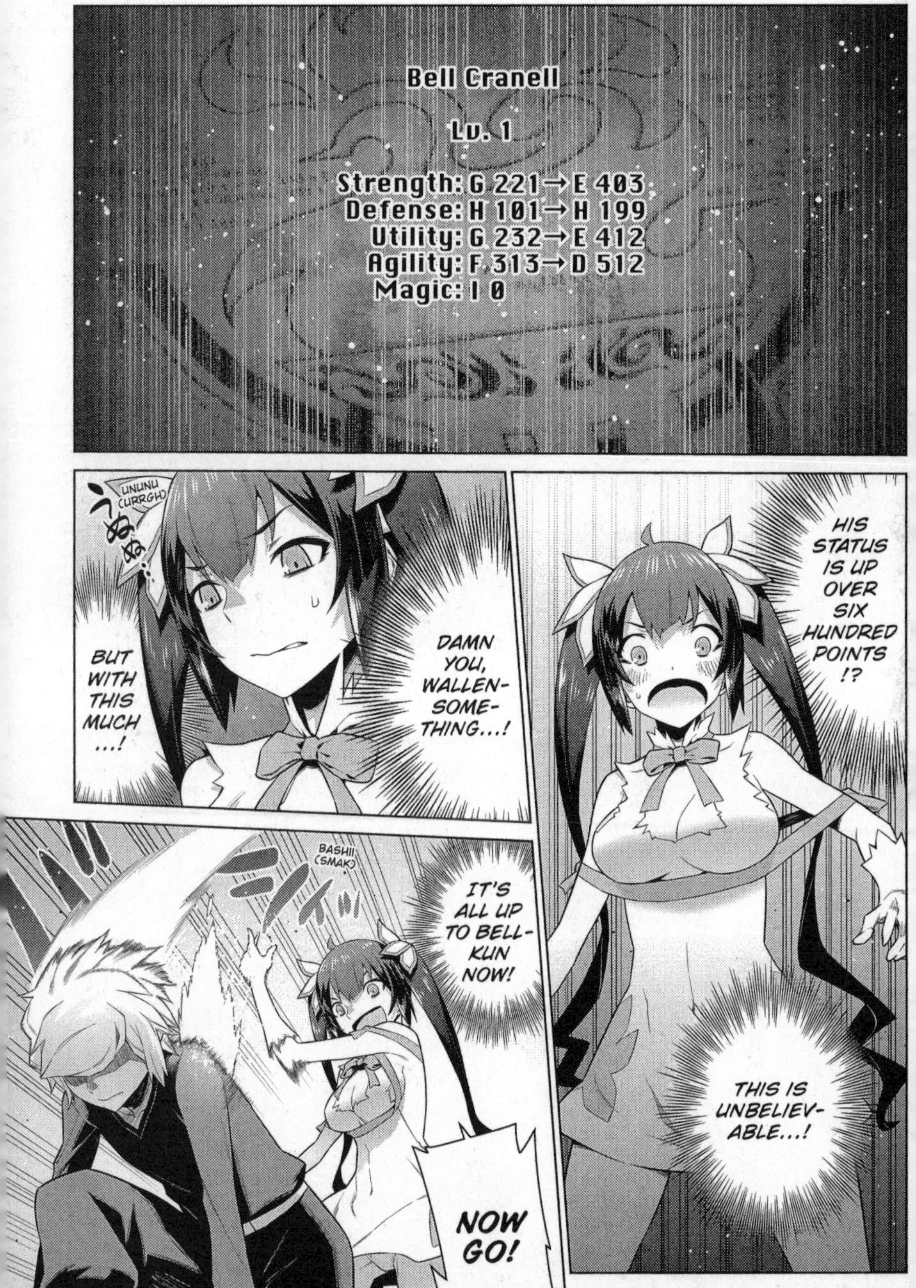
Bell Cranell
Lv. 1
Strength: G 221→E 403
Defense: H 101→H 199
Utility: G 232→E 412
Agility: F 313→D 512
Magic: I 0
HIS STATUS IS UP OVER SIX HUNDRED POINTS!?
THIS IS UNBELIEV-ABLE...!
UNUNU (CURRGH)
DAMN YOU, WALLEN-SOME-THING...!
BUT WITH THIS MUCH...!
BASHI! (SMAK)
IT'S ALL UP TO BELL-KUN NOW!
NOW GO!

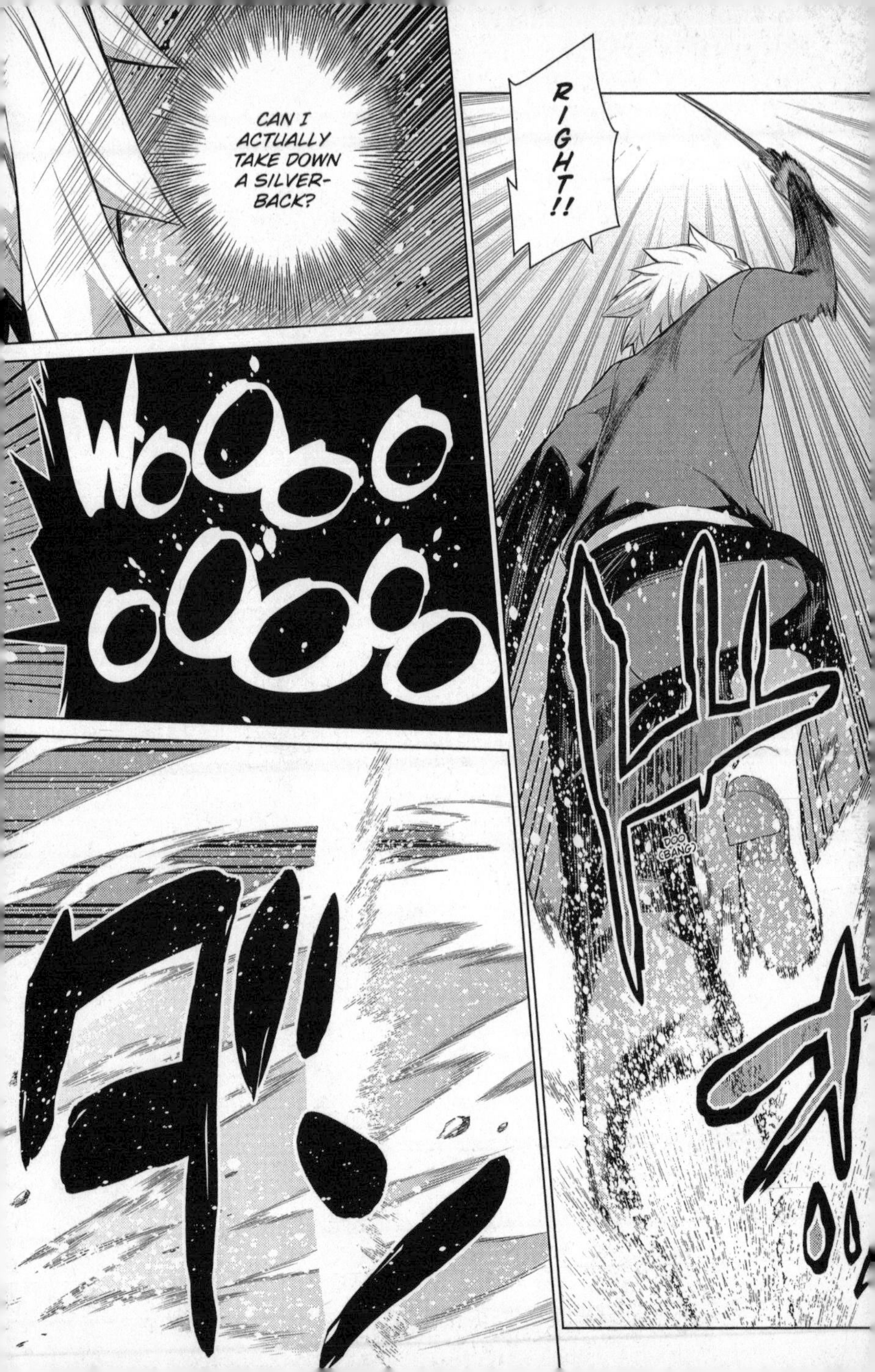
CAN I ACTUALLY TAKE DOWN A SILVER-BACK?
RIGHT!!
DOO (BANG)
WOOOOOOOOOO

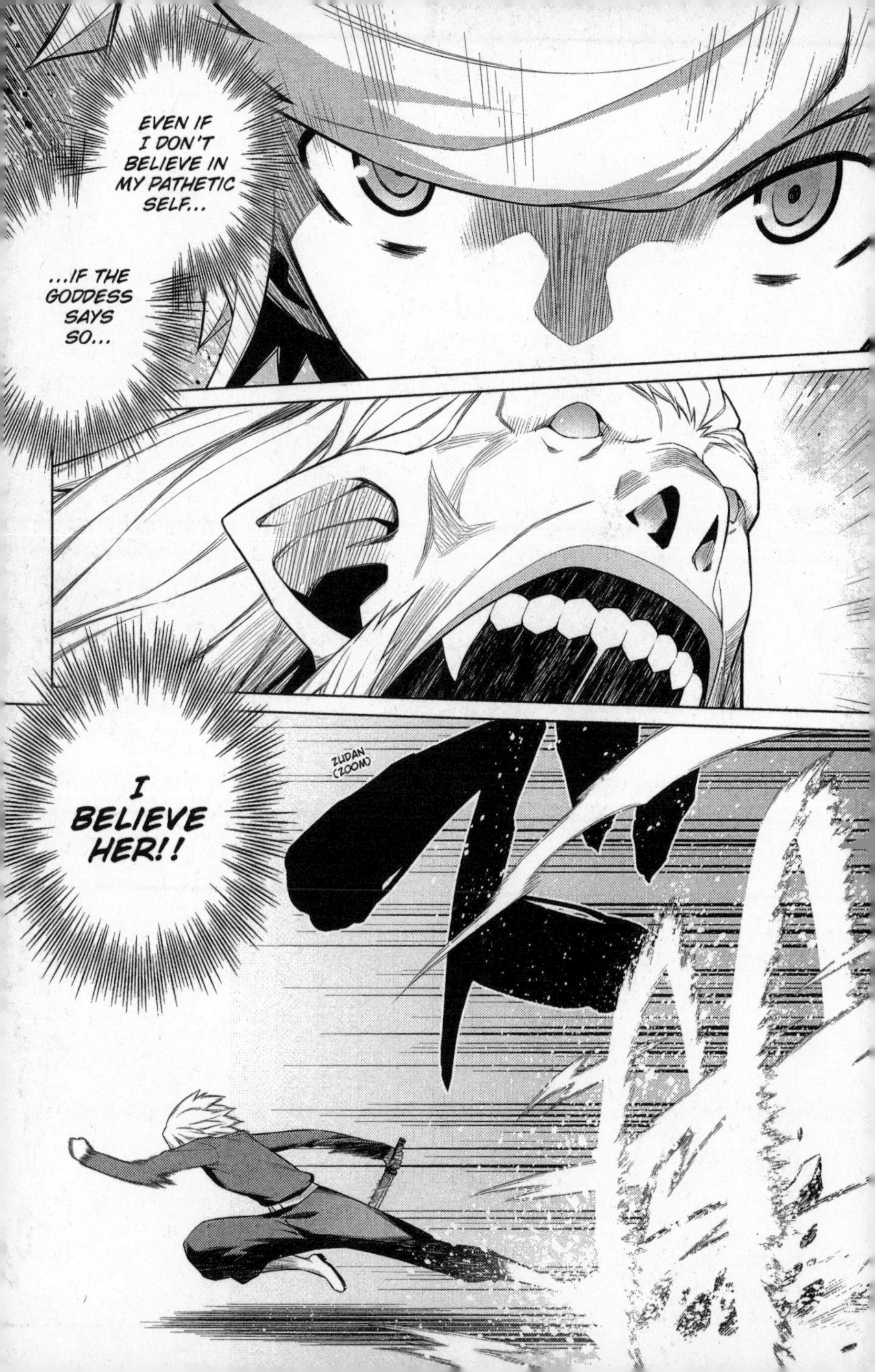
EVEN IF I DON'T BELIEVE IN MY PATHETIC SELF...
...IF THE GODDESS SAYS SO...
ZUDAN (ZOOM)
I BELIEVE HER!!

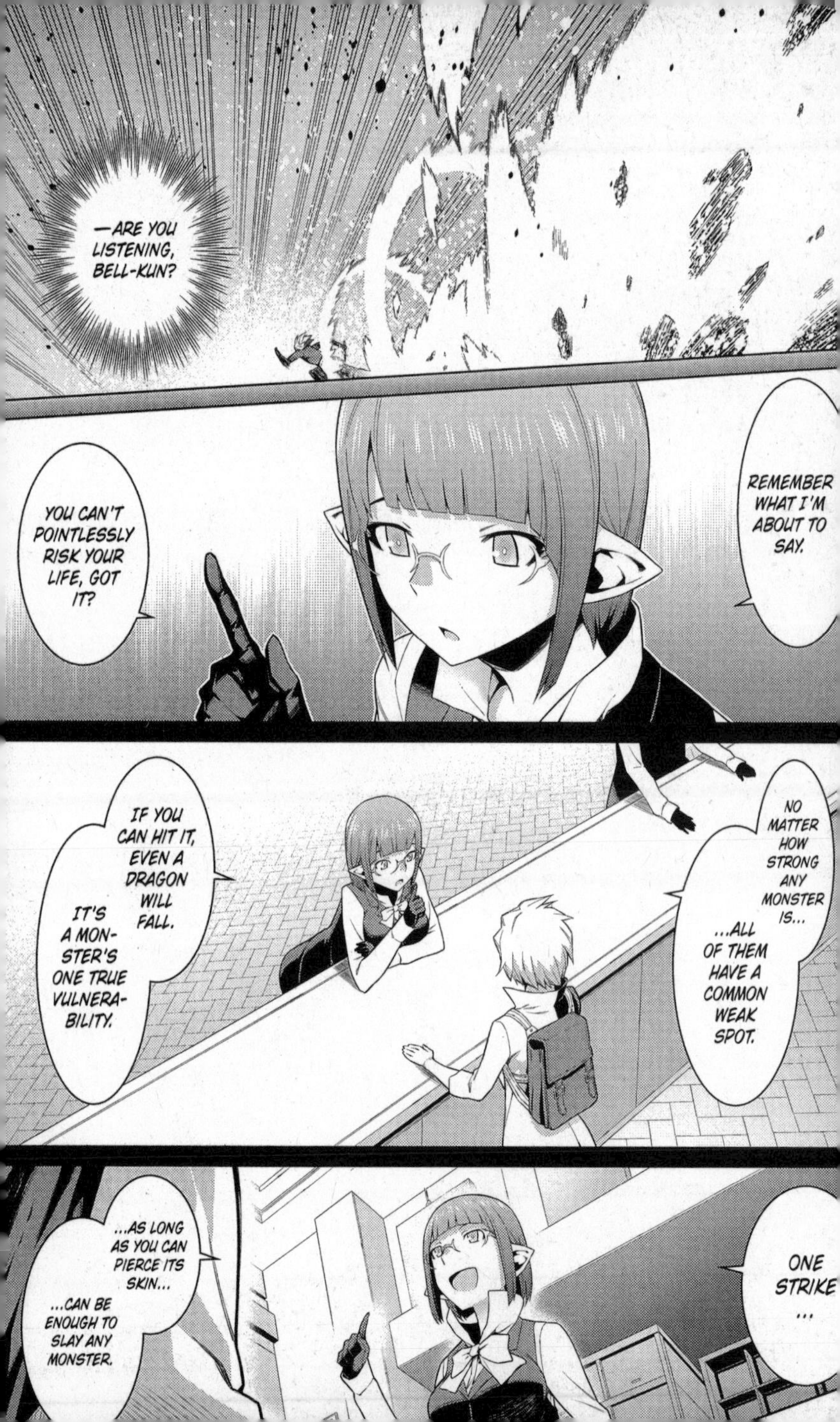
—ARE YOU LISTENING, BELL-KUN?
REMEMBER WHAT I'M ABOUT TO SAY.
YOU CAN'T POINTLESSLY RISK YOUR LIFE, GOT IT?
NO MATTER HOW STRONG ANY MONSTER IS...
...ALL OF THEM HAVE A COMMON WEAK SPOT.
IF YOU CAN HIT IT, EVEN A DRAGON WILL FALL.
IT'S A MONSTER'S ONE TRUE VULNERABILITY.
ONE STRIKE...
...AS LONG AS YOU CAN PIERCE ITS SKIN...
...CAN BE ENOUGH TO SLAY ANY MONSTER.

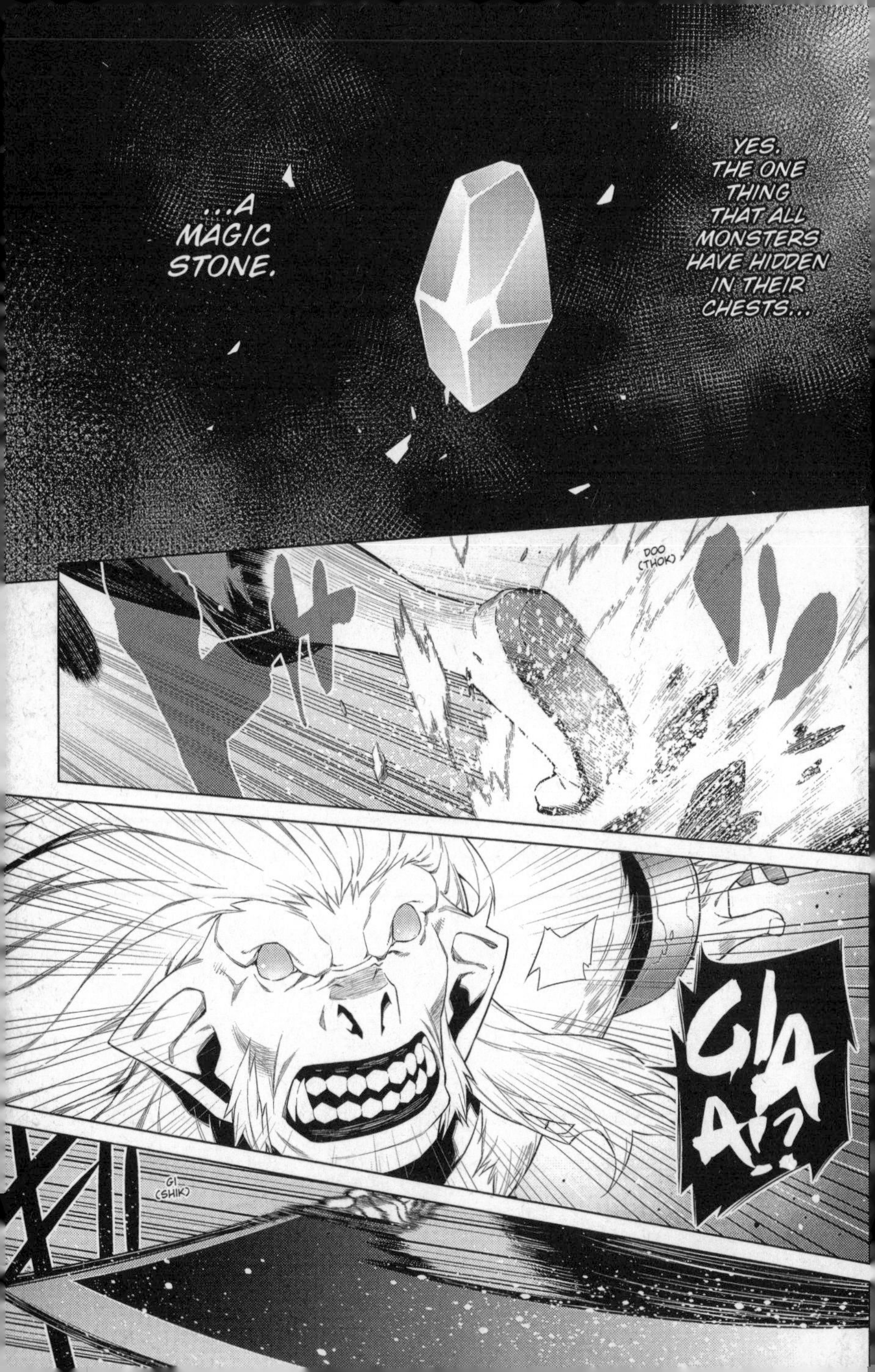
YES. THE ONE THING THAT ALL MONSTERS HAVE HIDDEN IN THEIR CHESTS...
...A MAGIC STONE.
DOO (THOK)
GIAA!?
GI (SHIK)

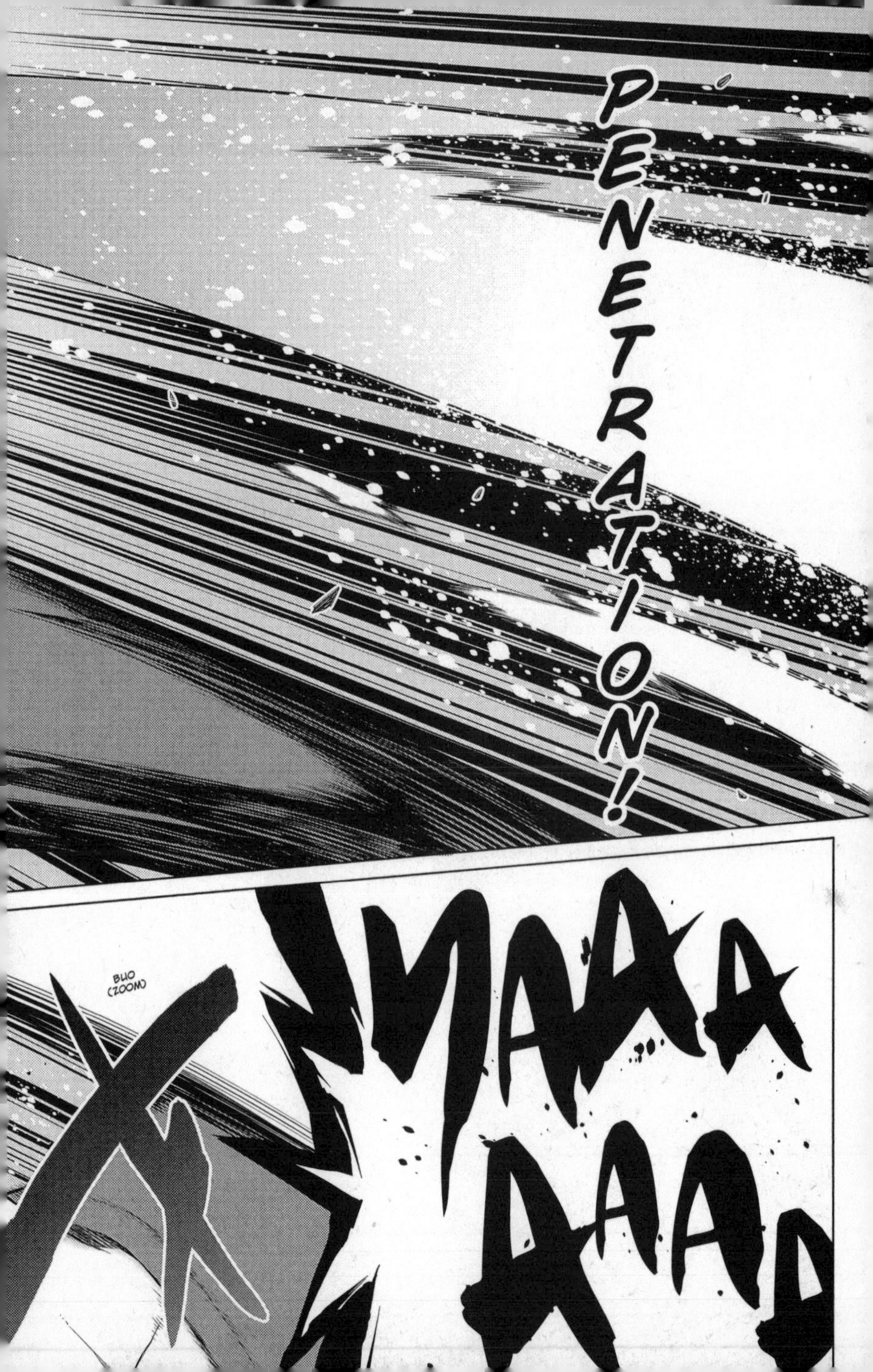
PENETRATION!
BUO (ZOOM)
NAAA
AAAA

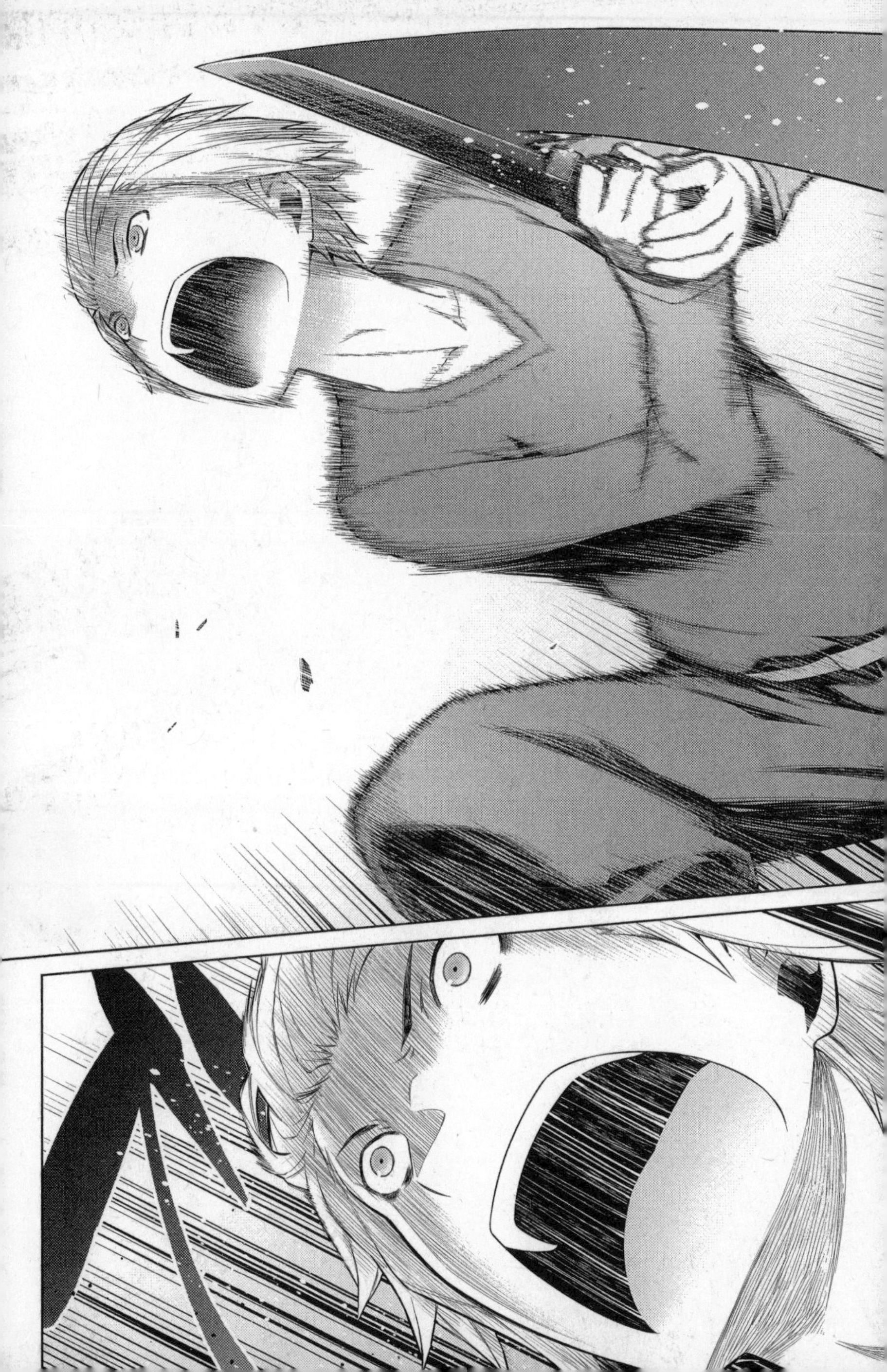

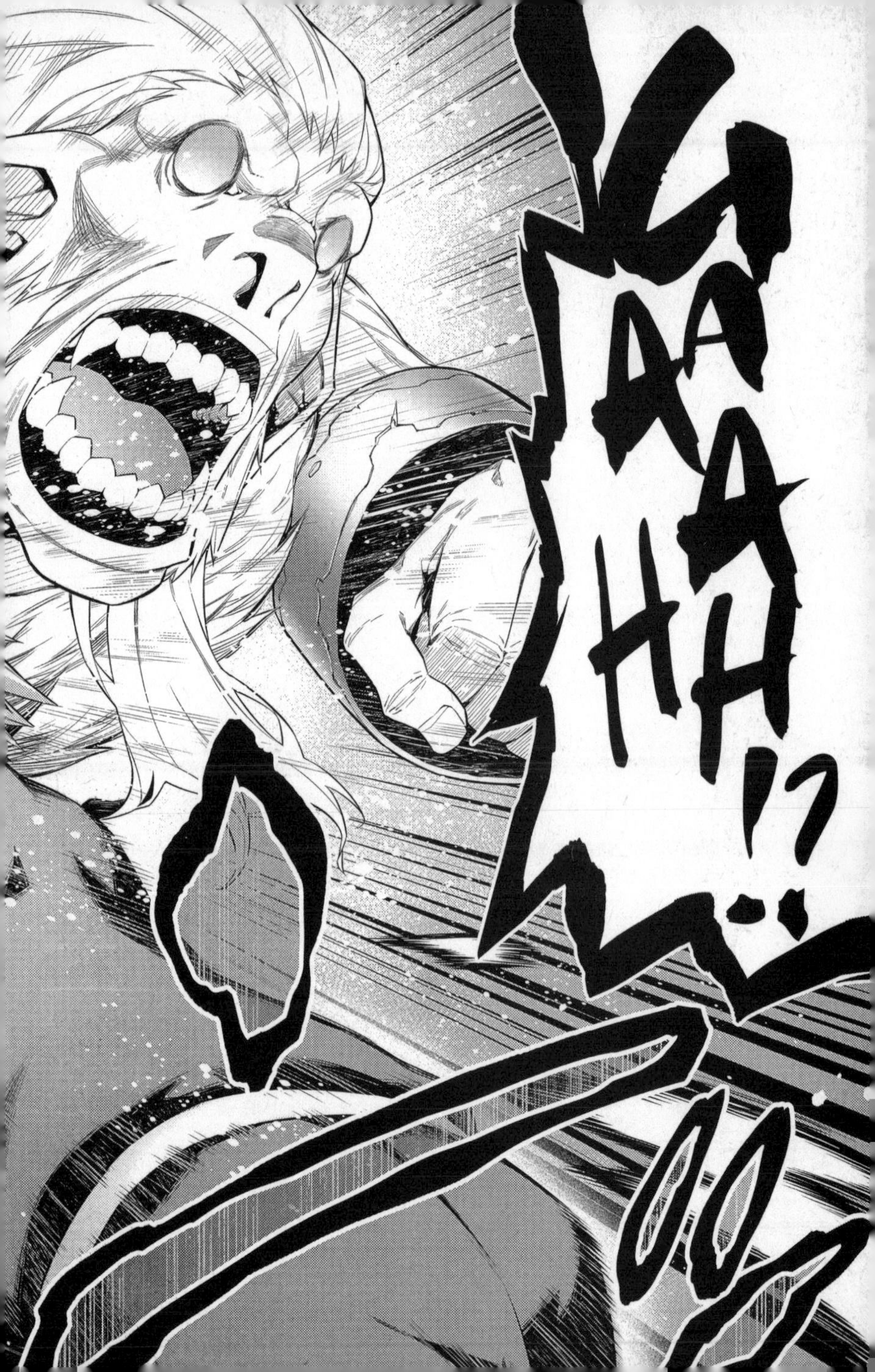
GAAAHH!?

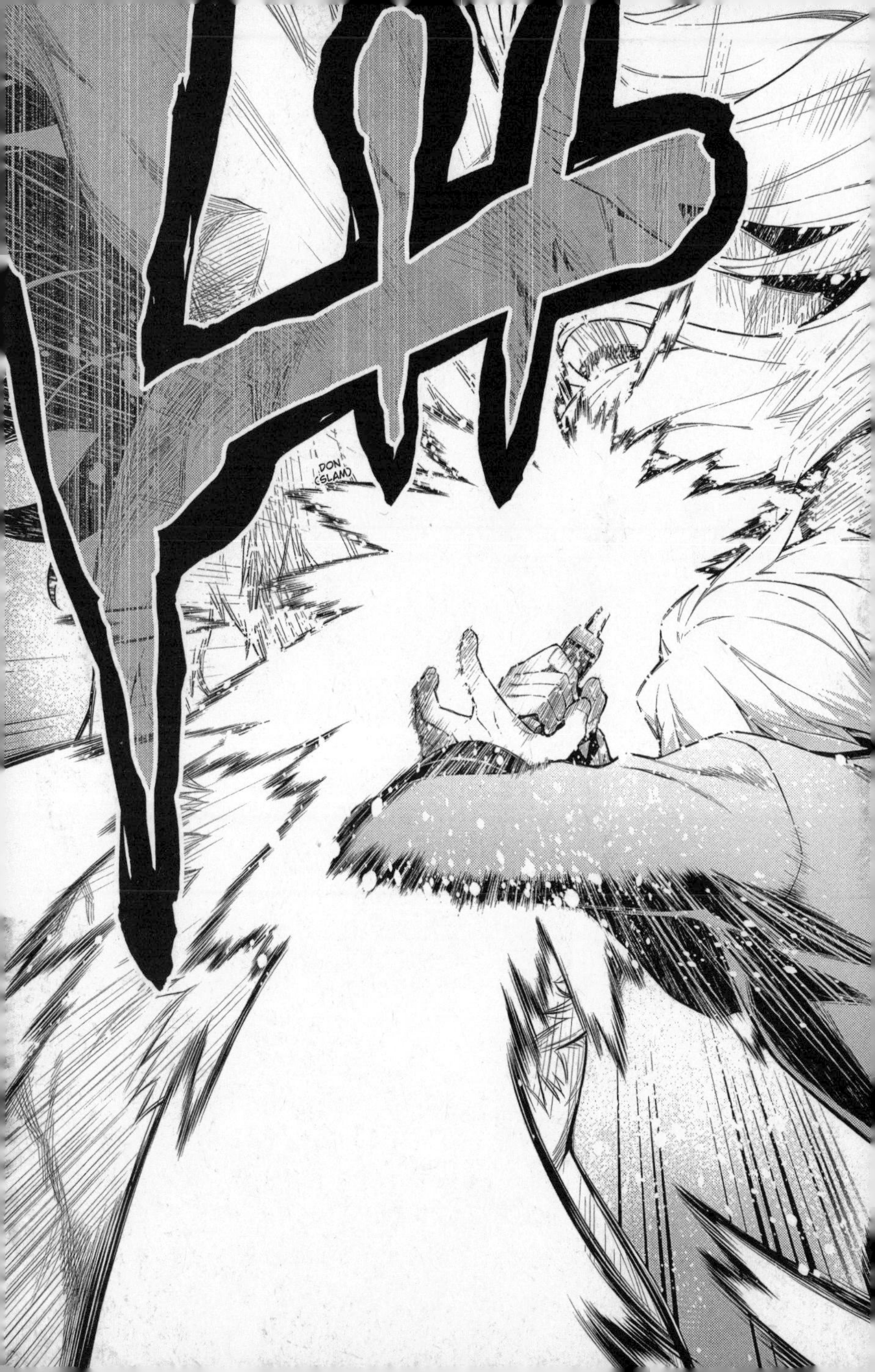
DON
(SLAM)

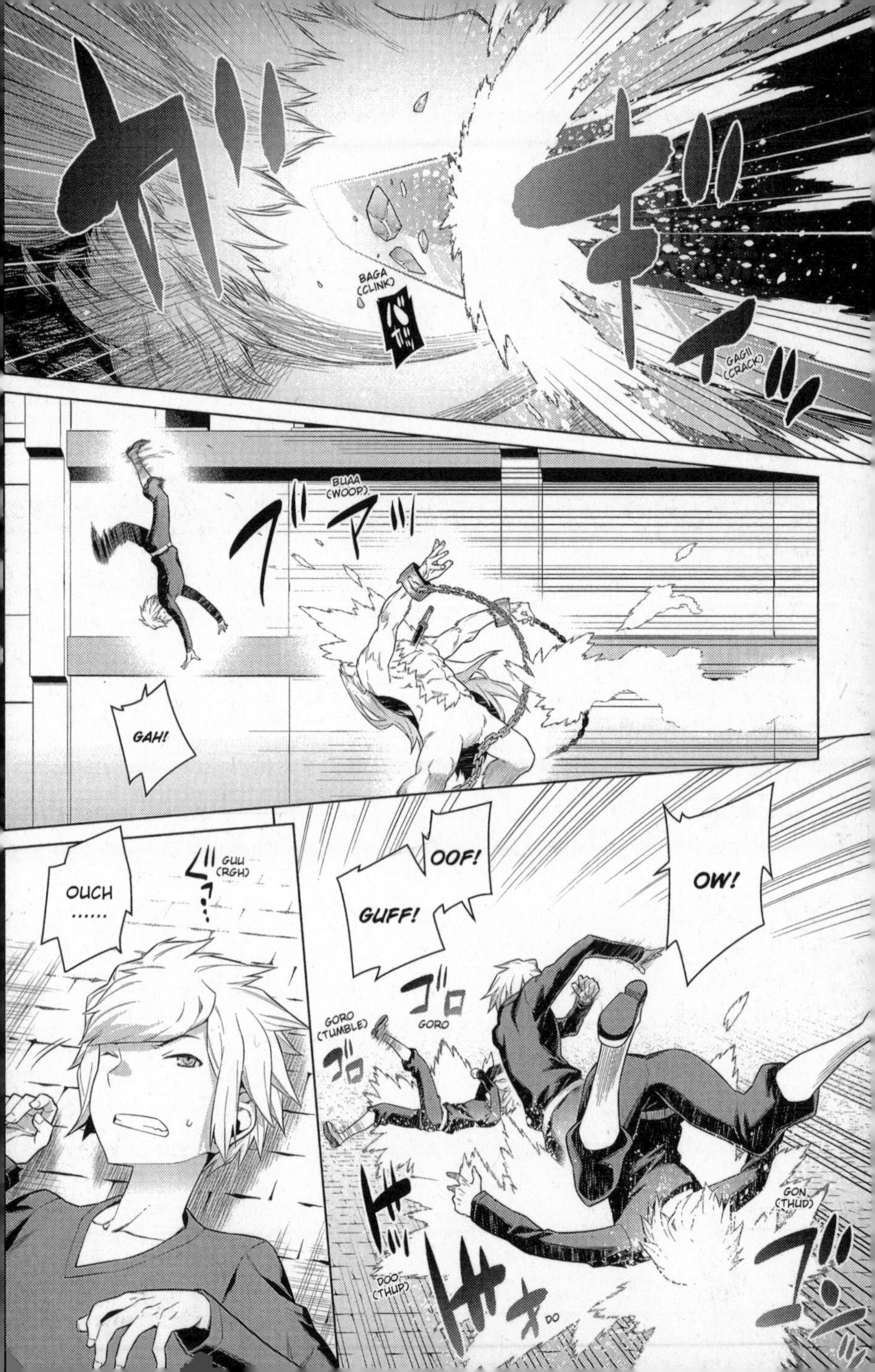
GAGII (CRACK)
BAGA (CLINK)
BUAA (WOOP)
GAH!
OW!
OOF!
GUFF!
GORO
GORO (TUMBLE)
GON (THUD)
DOO (THUD)
DO
GUU (RGH)
OUCH
......

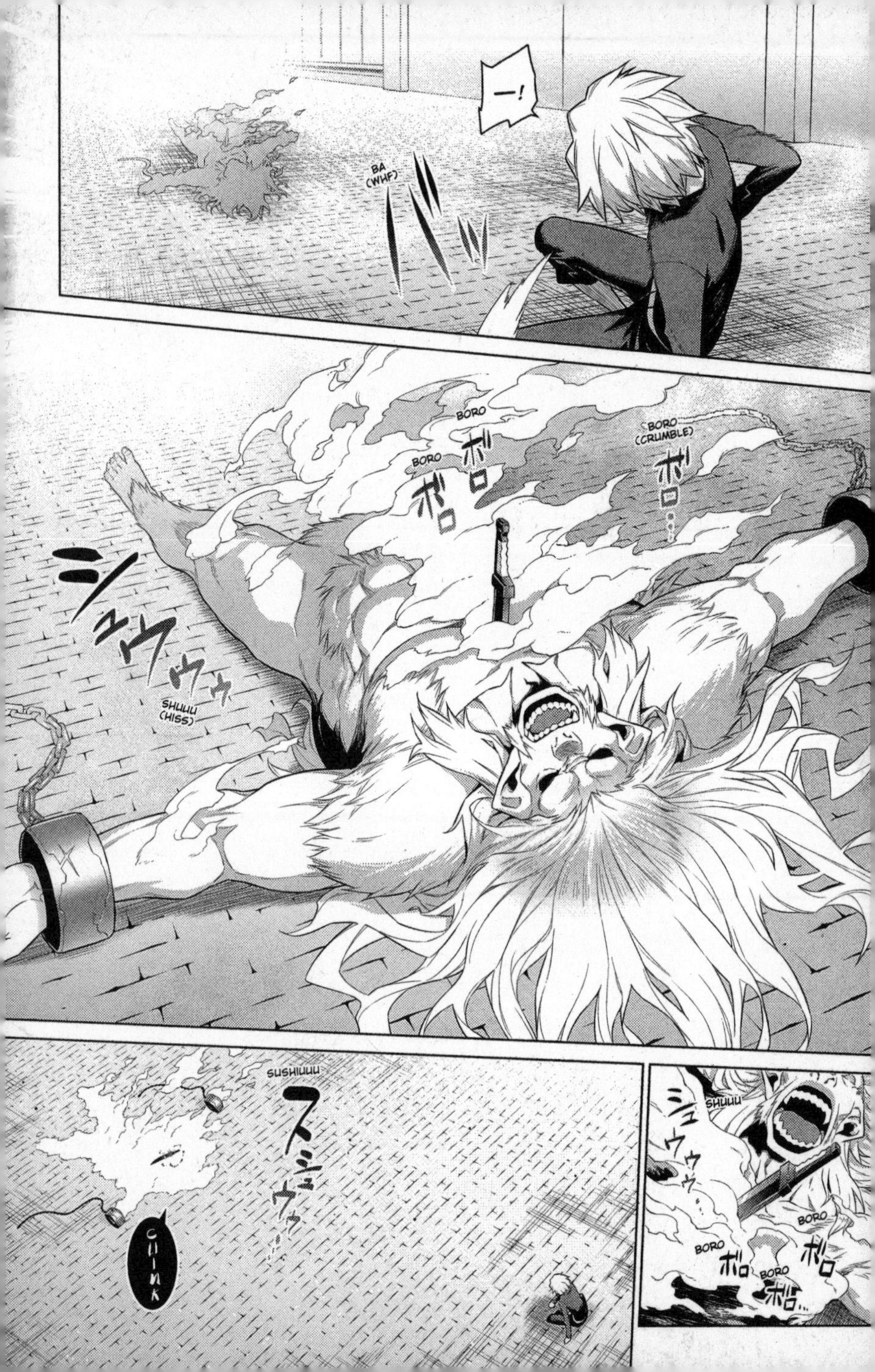
—!
BA (WHF)
バッ
BORO
ボロ
BORO
ボロ
BORO (CRUMBLE)
ボロ…
SHUUU (HISS)
シュウゥゥ
SHUUU
シュウゥ…
BORO
ボロ
BORO
ボロ
BORO
ボロ…
SUSHIUUU
スシュウゥ…
CHINK

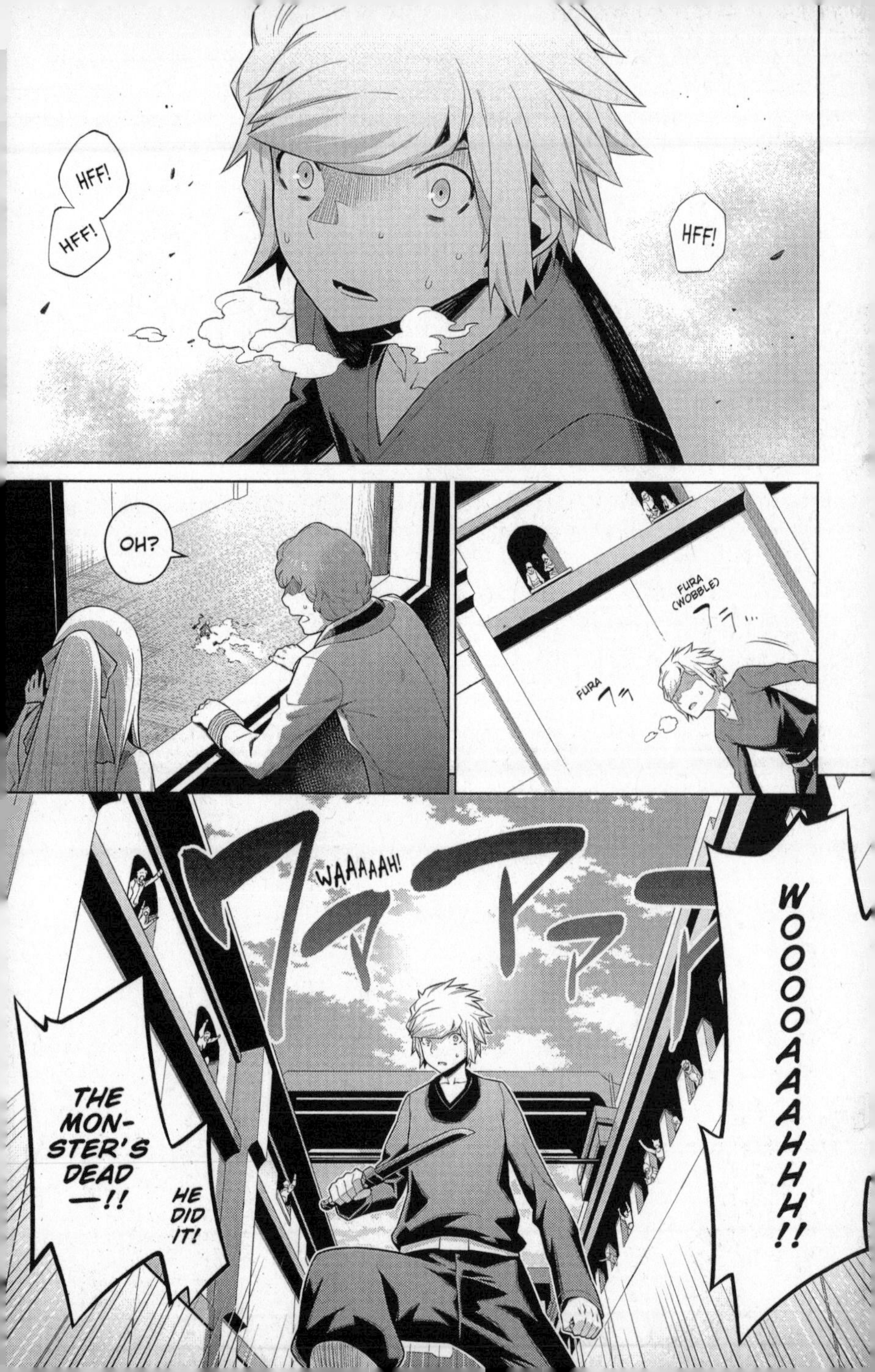
HFF!
HFF!
HFF!
FURA (WOBBLE)
フラ…
FURA
フラ
OH?
WOOOOAAAAHHHH!!
WAAAAAH!
THE MONSTER'S DEAD—!!
HE DID IT!

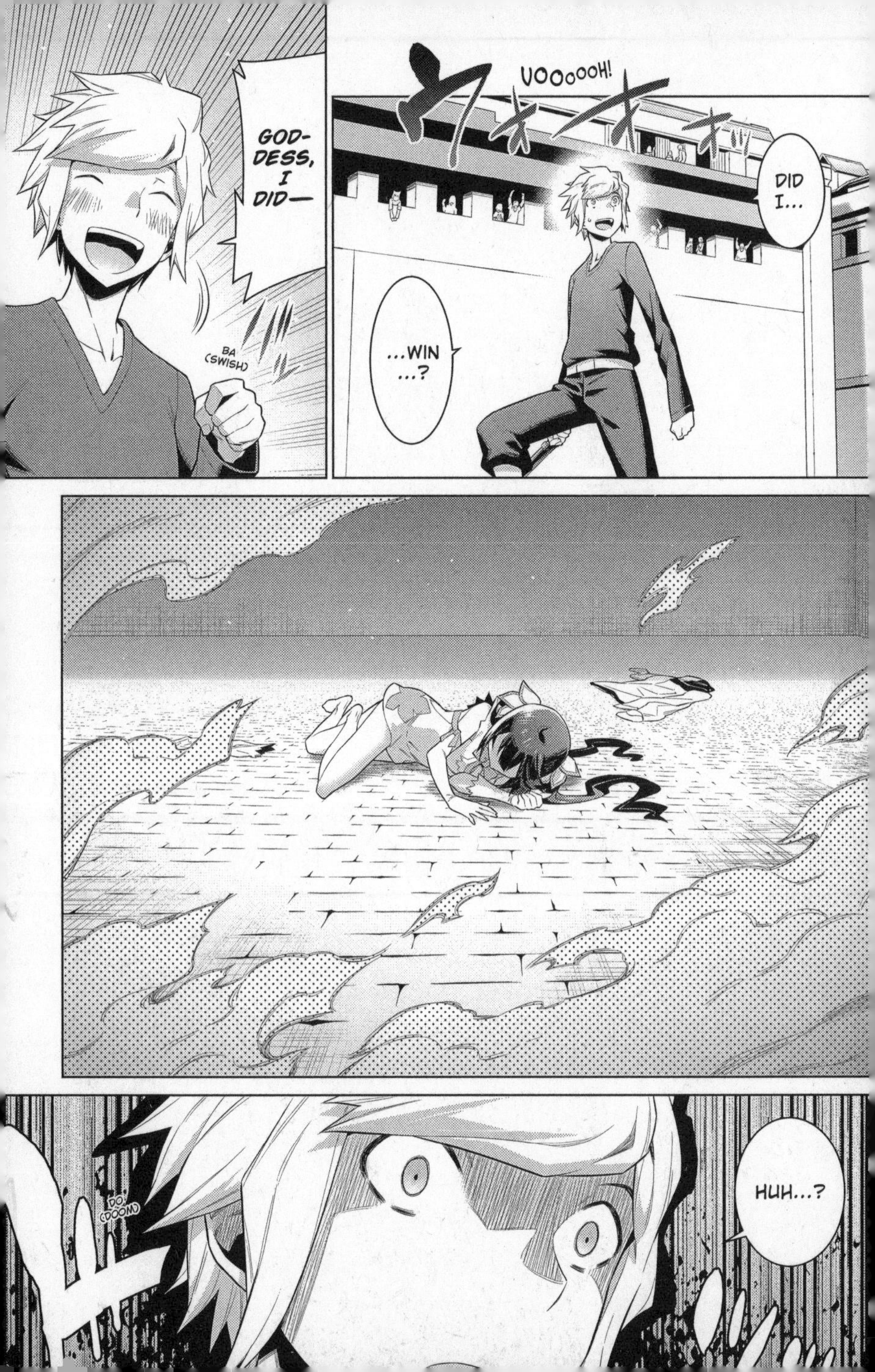
VOOooooH!
DID I...
...WIN ...?
GOD-DESS, I DID—
BA (SWISH)
HUH...?
DO (DOOM)

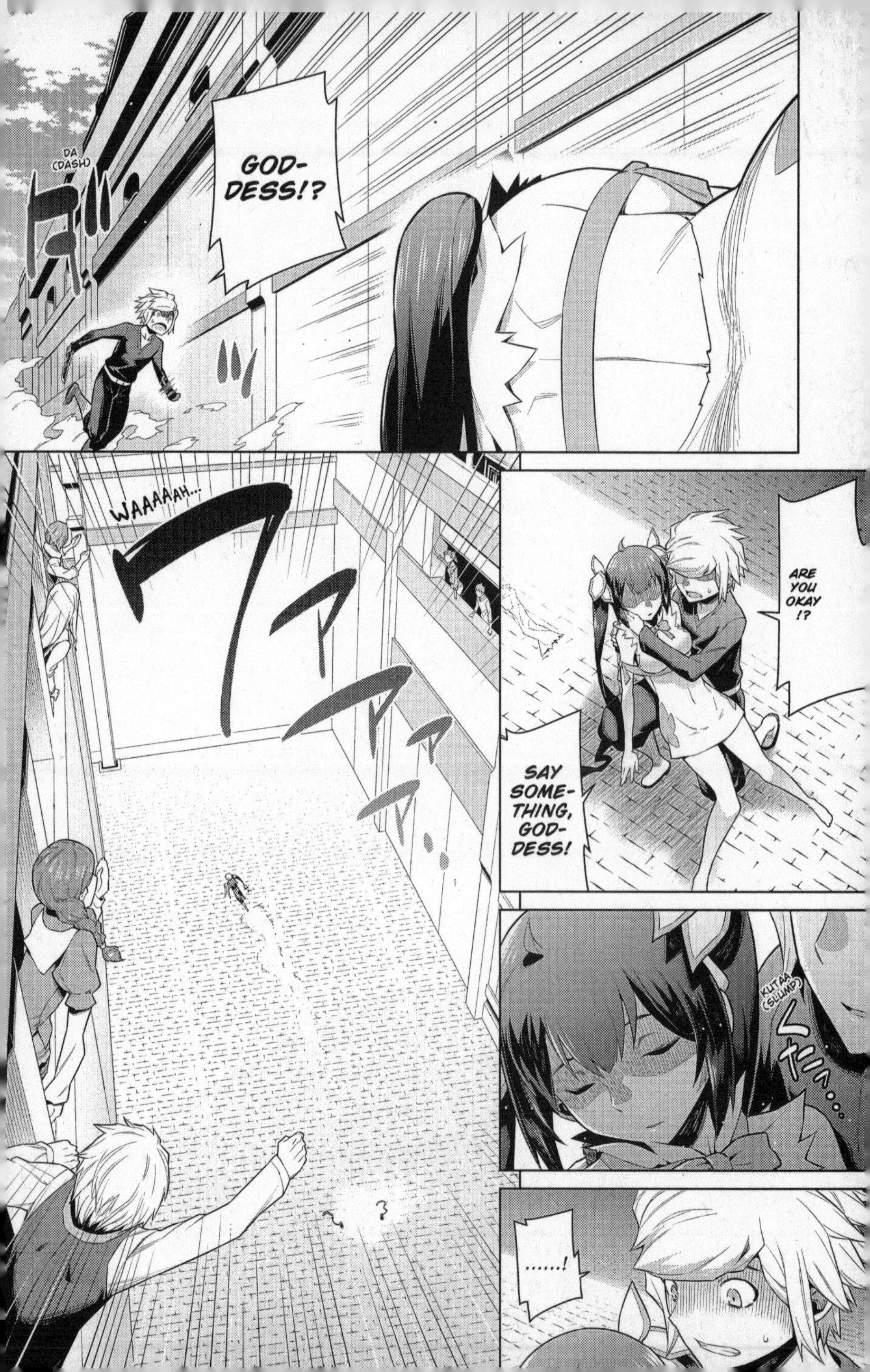
GOD-
DESS!?
DA
(DASH)
ARE YOU OKAY !?
SAY SOME-THING, GOD-DESS!
KUTAA (SLUMP)
......!
WAAAAAH...

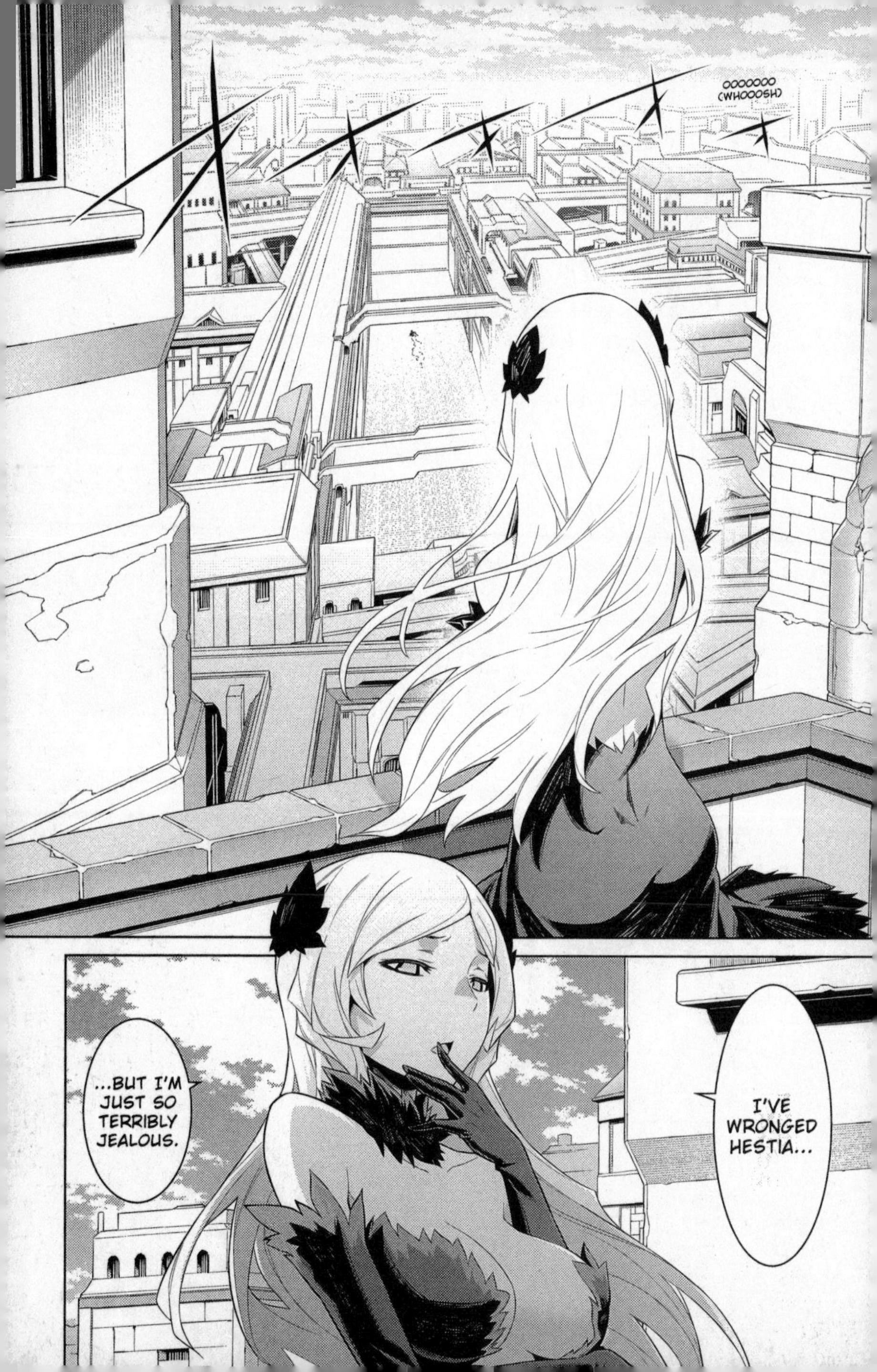
OOOOOOO
(WHOOOSH)
I'VE WRONGED HESTIA...
...BUT I'M JUST SO TERRIBLY JEALOUS.

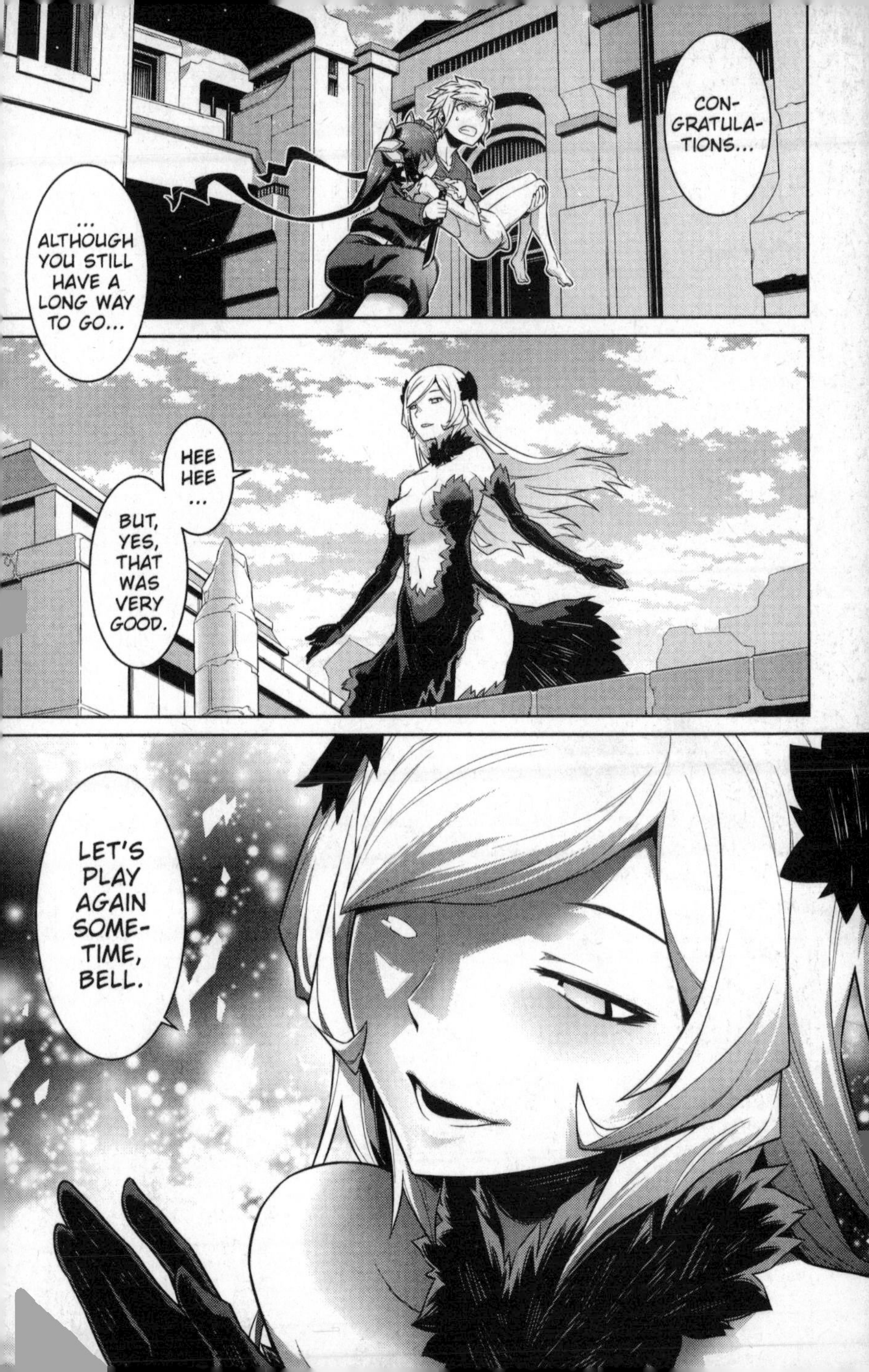
CON-GRATULATIONS...
...ALTHOUGH YOU STILL HAVE A LONG WAY TO GO...
HEE HEE...
BUT, YES, THAT WAS VERY GOOD.
LET'S PLAY AGAIN SOMETIME, BELL.

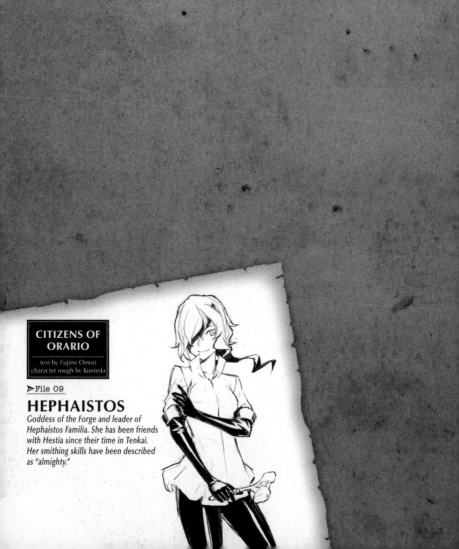

CITIZENS OF ORARIO

text by Fujino Omori
character rough by Kunieda

➤File 09

HEPHAISTOS

Goddess of the Forge and leader of
Hephaistos Familia. She has been friends
with Hestia since their time in Tenkai.
Her smithing skills have been described
as "almighty."

CITIZENS OF ORARIO

text by Fujino Omori
character rough by Kunieda

➤ File 10

MISHA FROT

Human secretary belonging to the Guild.
A good friend of Eina's, they've known
each other since their school days.
Can be a little childish.

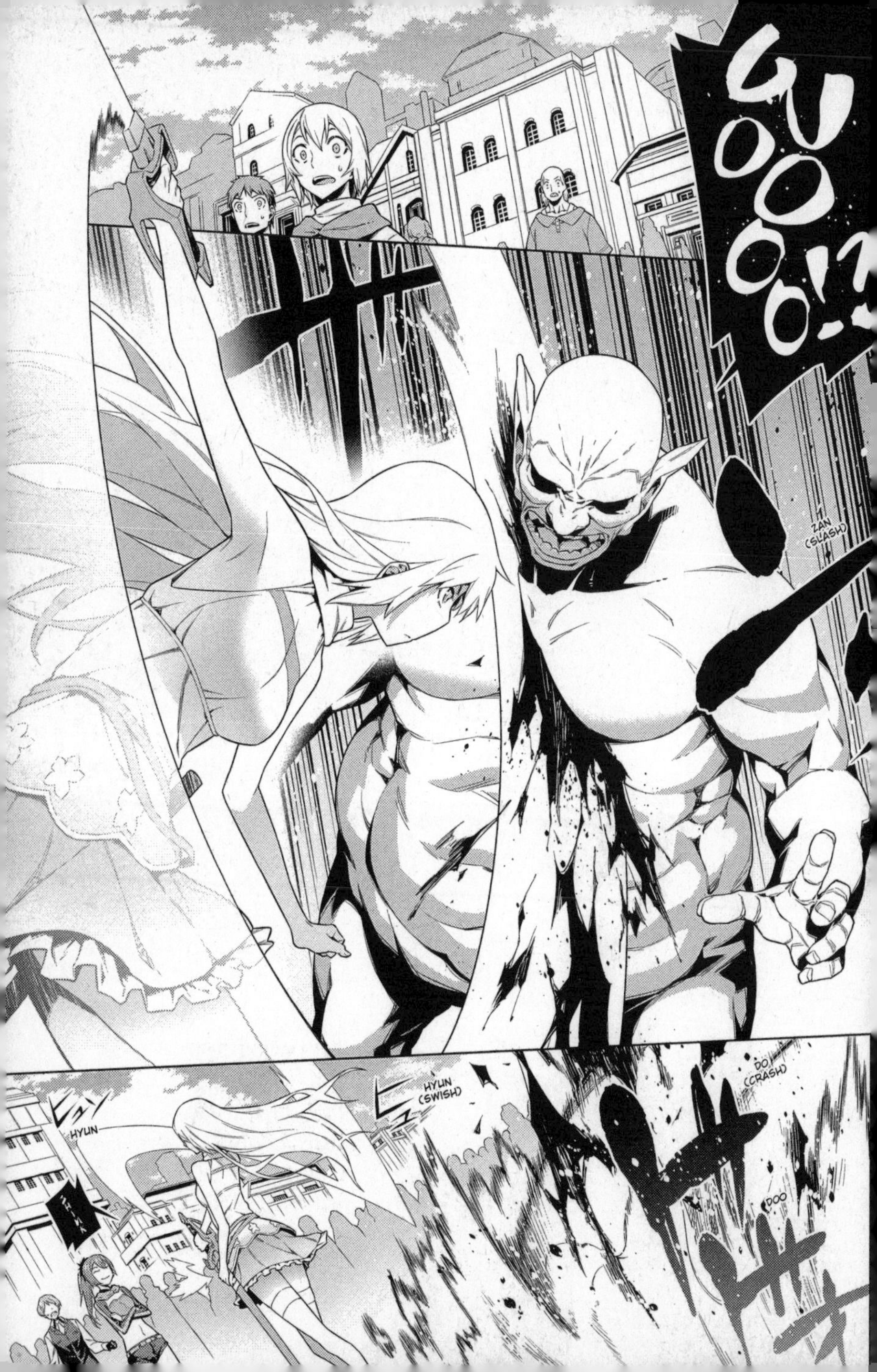
GUOOOOO!!?
ZAN (SLASH)
DO (CRASH)
DOO
HYUN (SWISH)
HYUN
THINK

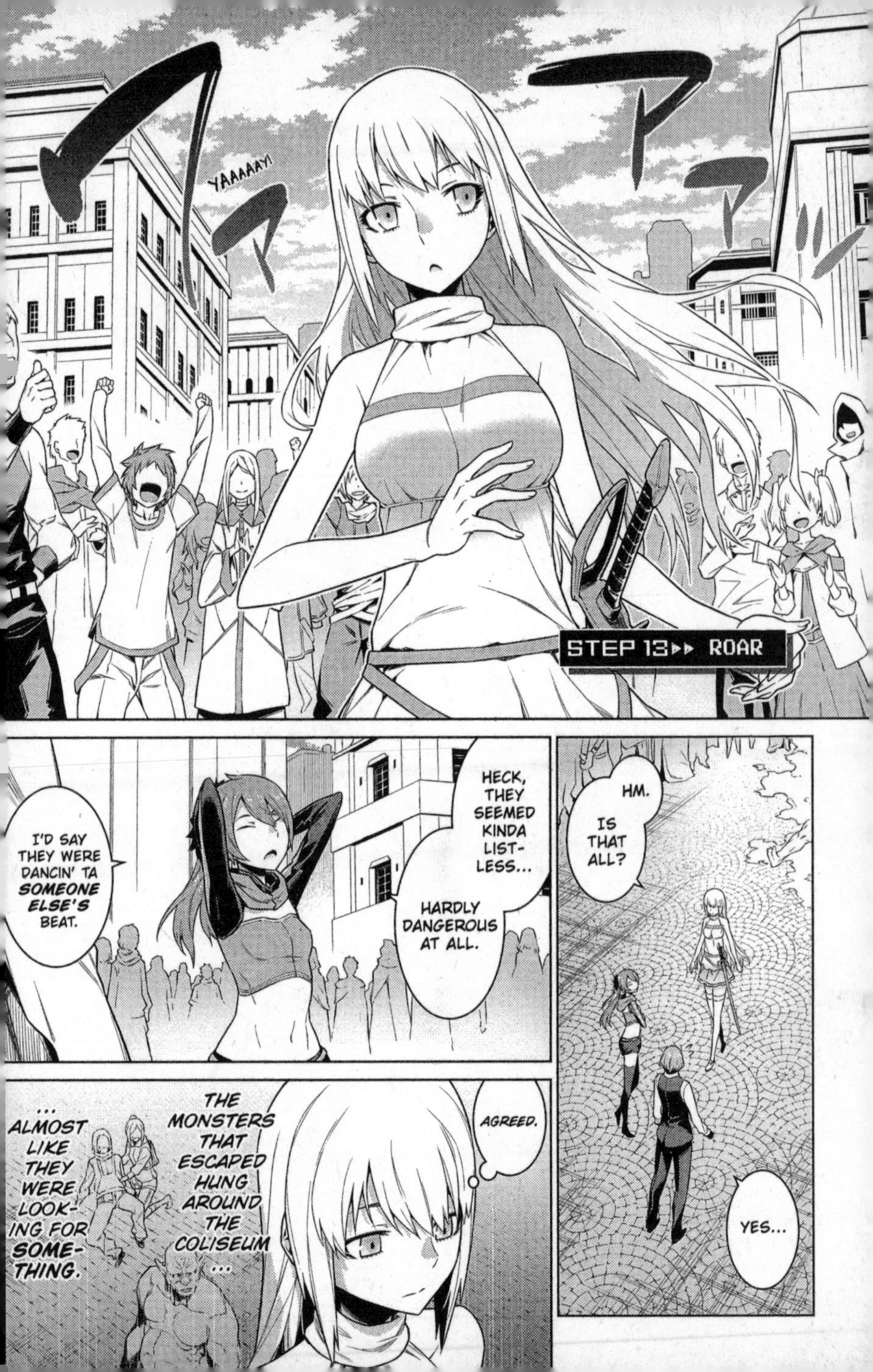
YAAAAAY!
STEP 13 ▸▸ ROAR
HM.
IS THAT ALL?
YES...
HECK, THEY SEEMED KINDA LIST-LESS...
HARDLY DANGEROUS AT ALL.
I'D SAY THEY WERE DANCIN' TA SOMEONE ELSE'S BEAT.
AGREED.
THE MONSTERS THAT ESCAPED HUNG AROUND THE COLISEUM...
...ALMOST LIKE THEY WERE LOOK-ING FOR SOME-THING.

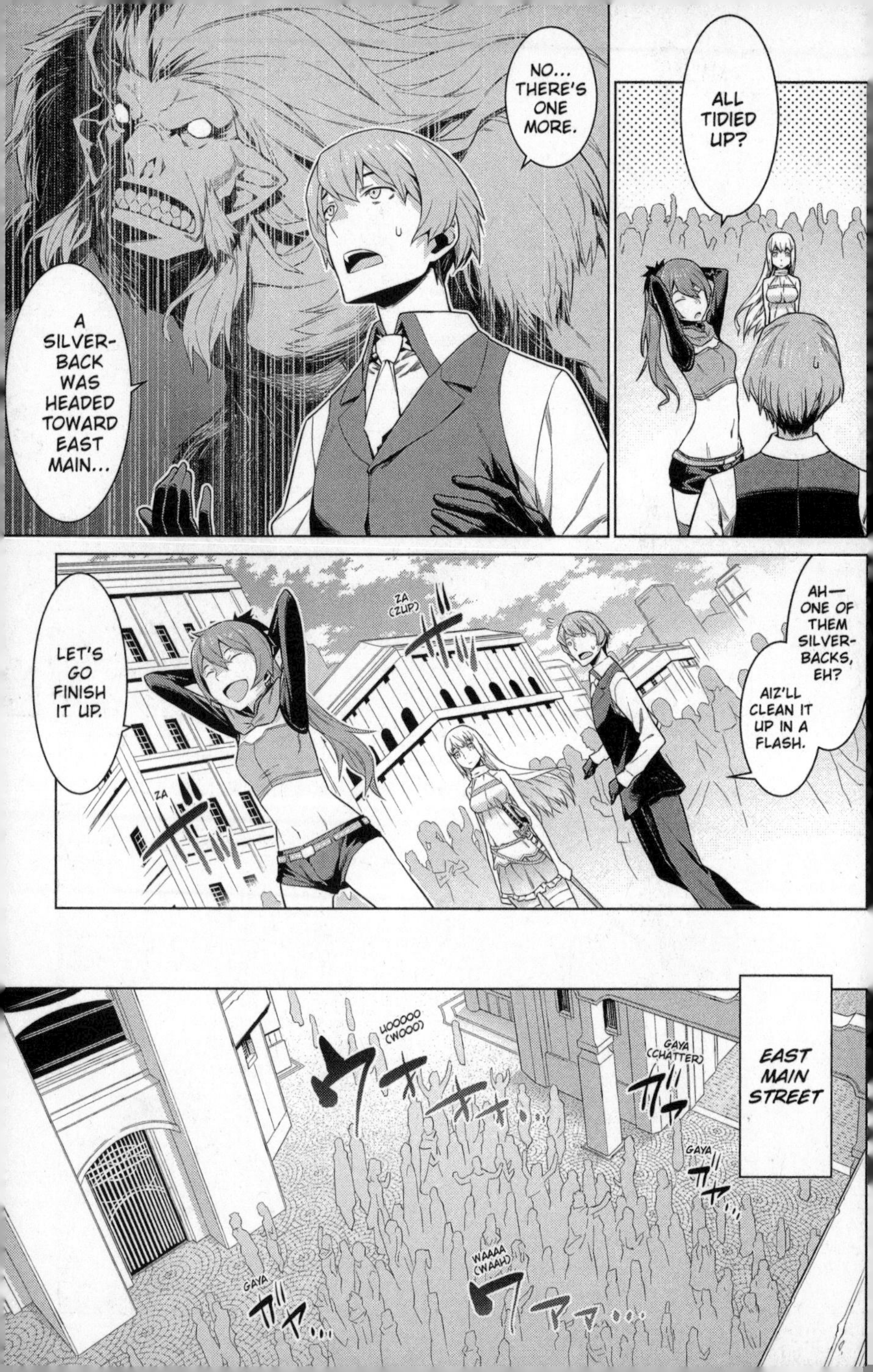
ALL TIDIED UP?
NO... THERE'S ONE MORE.
A SILVER-BACK WAS HEADED TOWARD EAST MAIN...
AH— ONE OF THEM SILVER-BACKS, EH?
AIZ'LL CLEAN IT UP IN A FLASH.
ZA (ZUP)
LET'S GO FINISH IT UP.
ZA
EAST MAIN STREET
GAYA (CHATTER)
GAYA
UOOOOO (WOOO)
WAAAA (WAAH)
GAYA

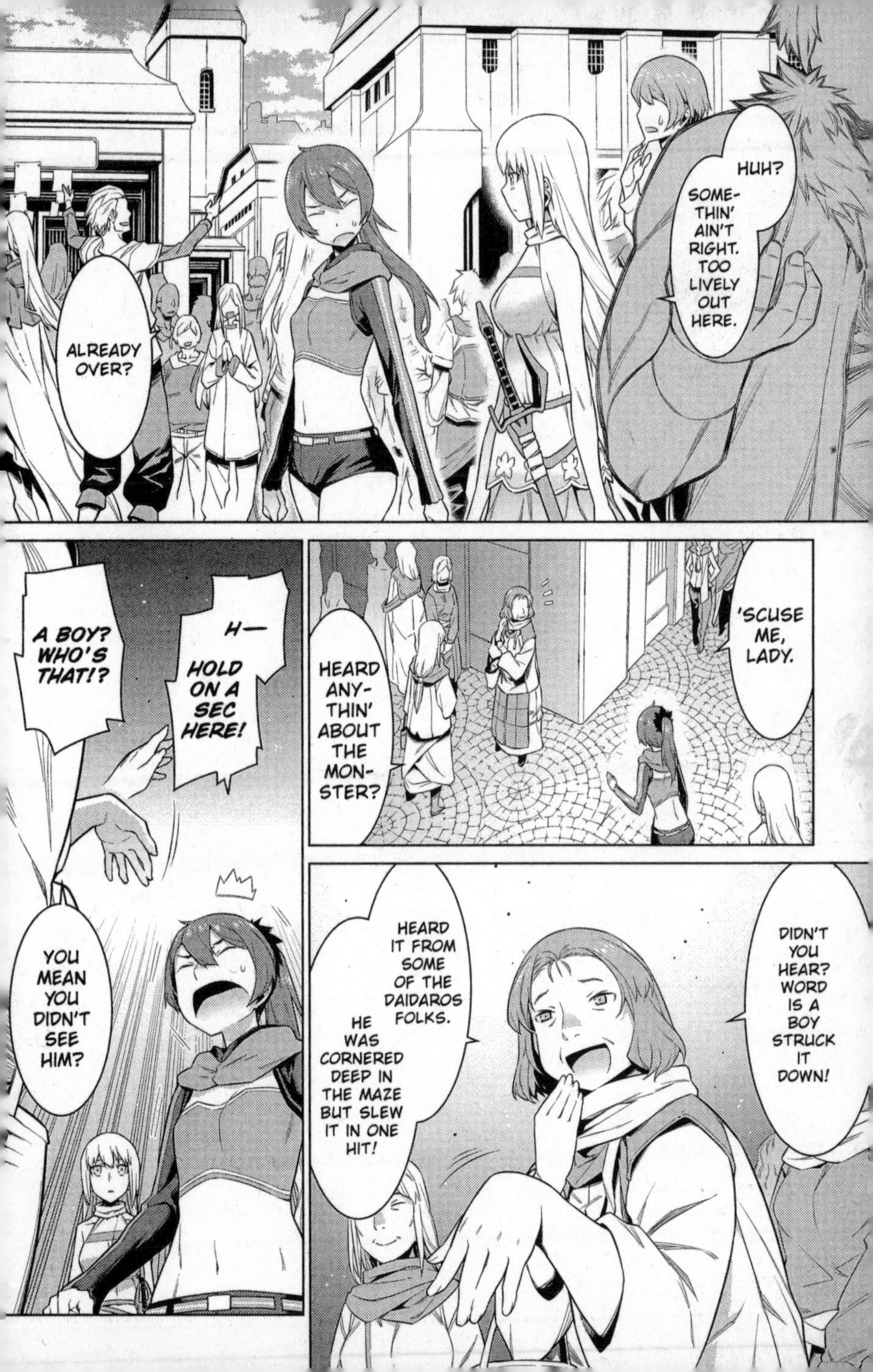
HUH? SOMETHIN' AIN'T RIGHT. TOO LIVELY OUT HERE.
ALREADY OVER?
'SCUSE ME, LADY.
HEARD ANYTHIN' ABOUT THE MONSTER?
DIDN'T YOU HEAR? WORD IS A BOY STRUCK IT DOWN!
HEARD IT FROM SOME OF THE DAIDAROS FOLKS.
HE WAS CORNERED DEEP IN THE MAZE BUT SLEW IT IN ONE HIT!
H— HOLD ON A SEC HERE!
A BOY? WHO'S THAT!?
YOU MEAN YOU DIDN'T SEE HIM?

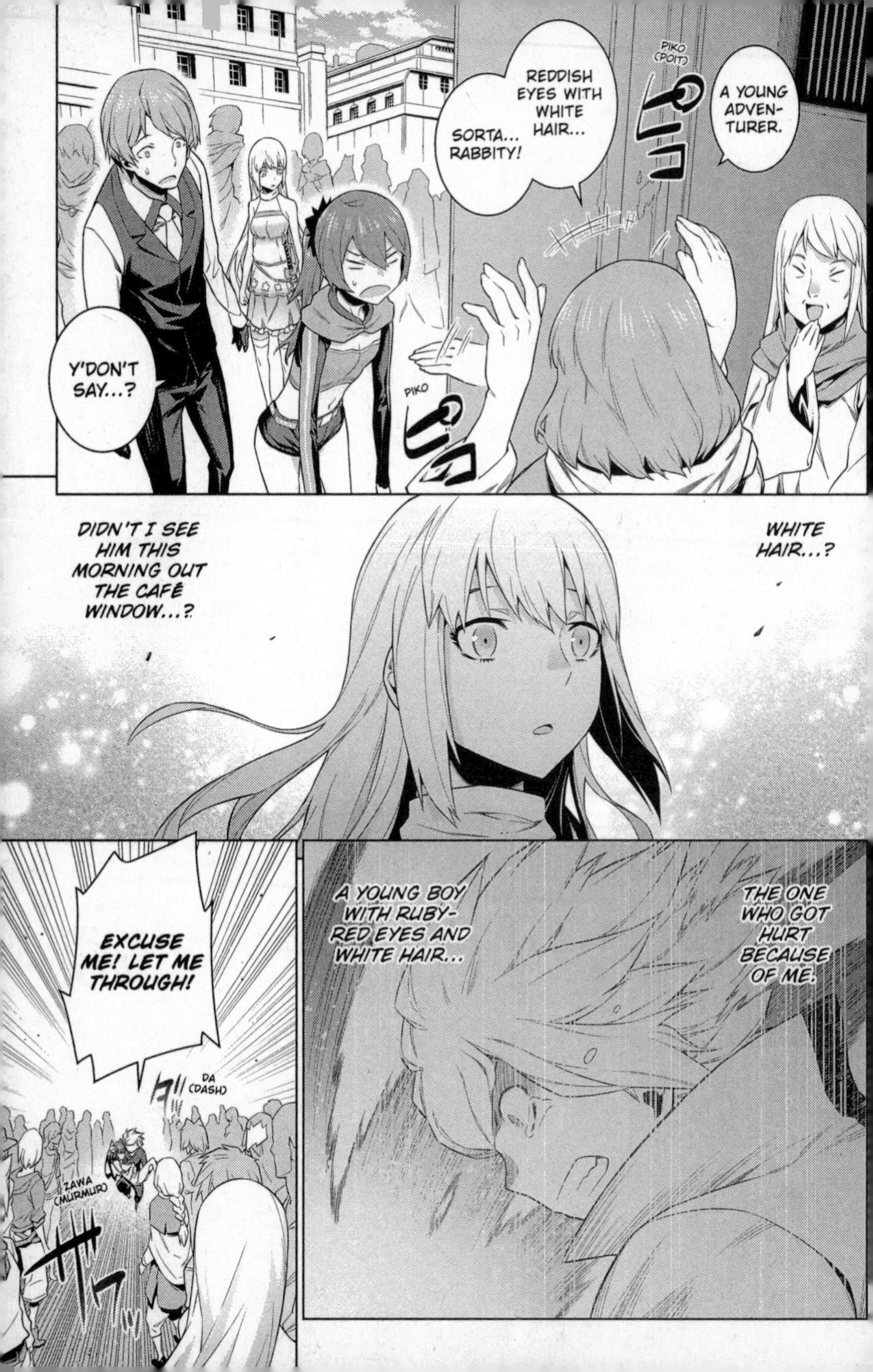
A YOUNG ADVENTURER.
PIKO (POIT)
REDDISH EYES WITH WHITE HAIR...
SORTA... RABBITY!
PIKO
Y'DON'T SAY...?
WHITE HAIR...?
DIDN'T I SEE HIM THIS MORNING OUT THE CAFÉ WINDOW...?
THE ONE WHO GOT HURT BECAUSE OF ME.
A YOUNG BOY WITH RUBY-RED EYES AND WHITE HAIR...
EXCUSE ME! LET ME THROUGH!
DA (DASH)
ZAWA (MURMUR)

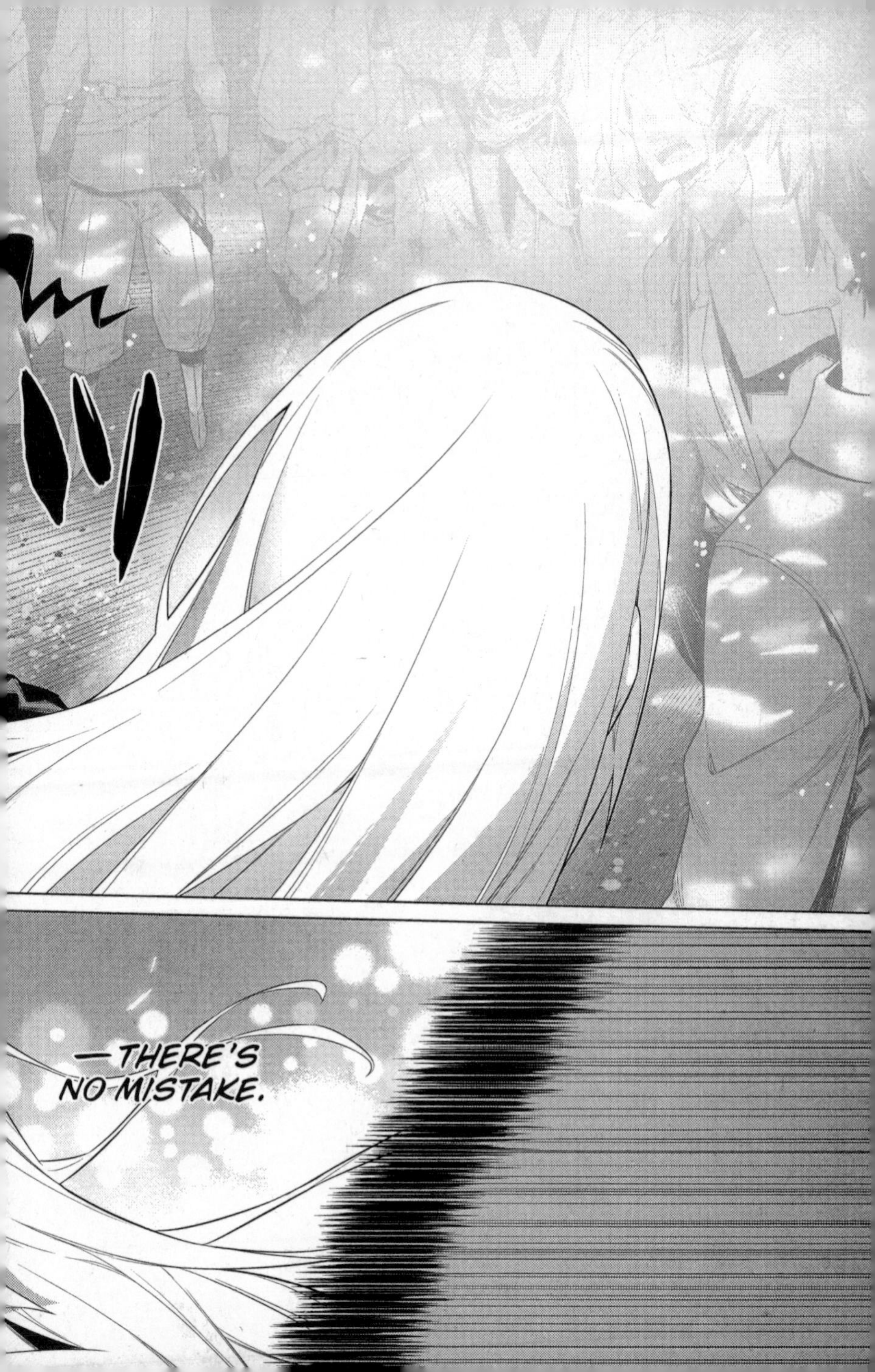
—THERE'S
NO MISTAKE.

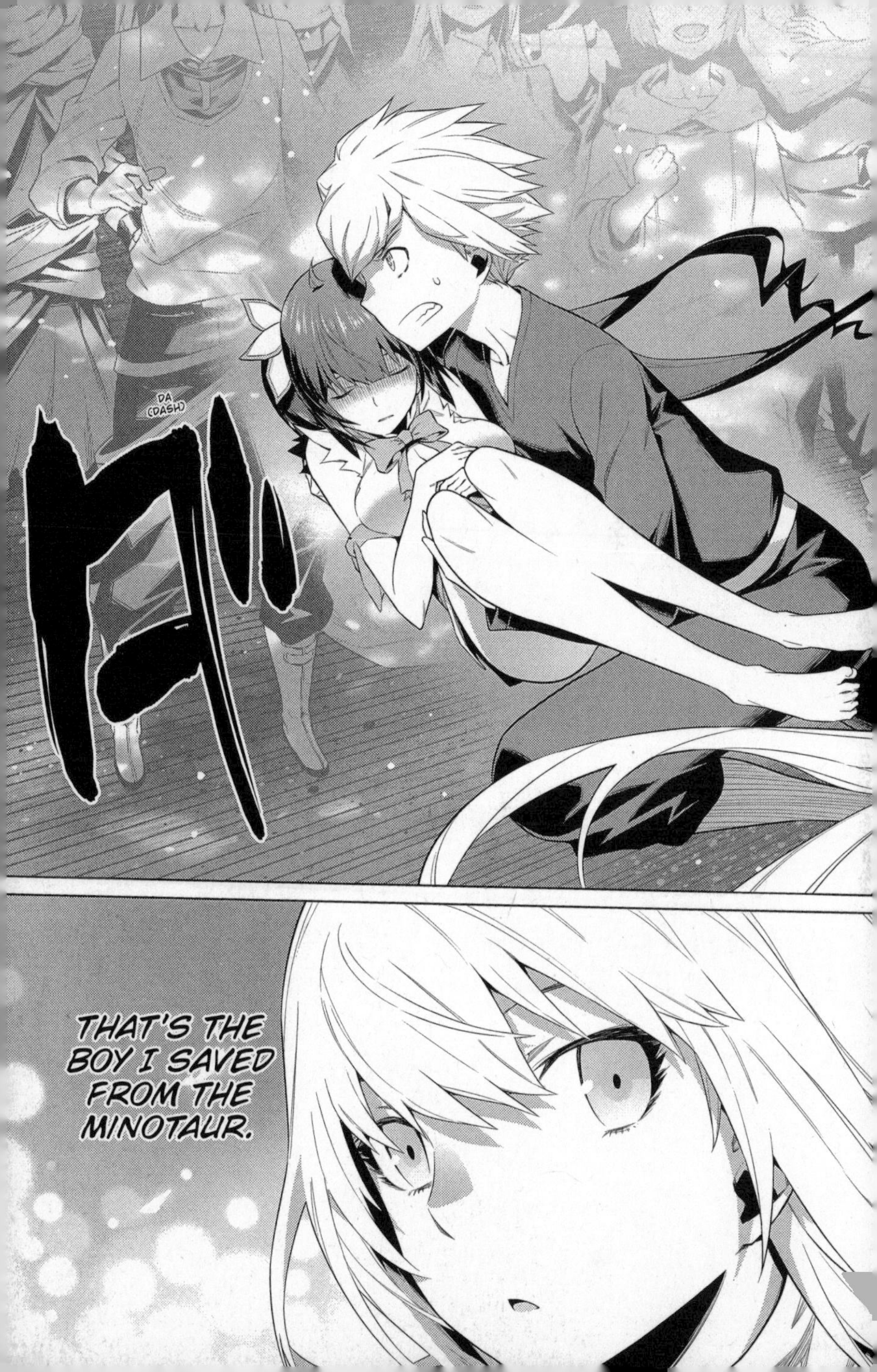
DA
(DASH)
THAT'S THE BOY I SAVED FROM THE MINOTAUR.

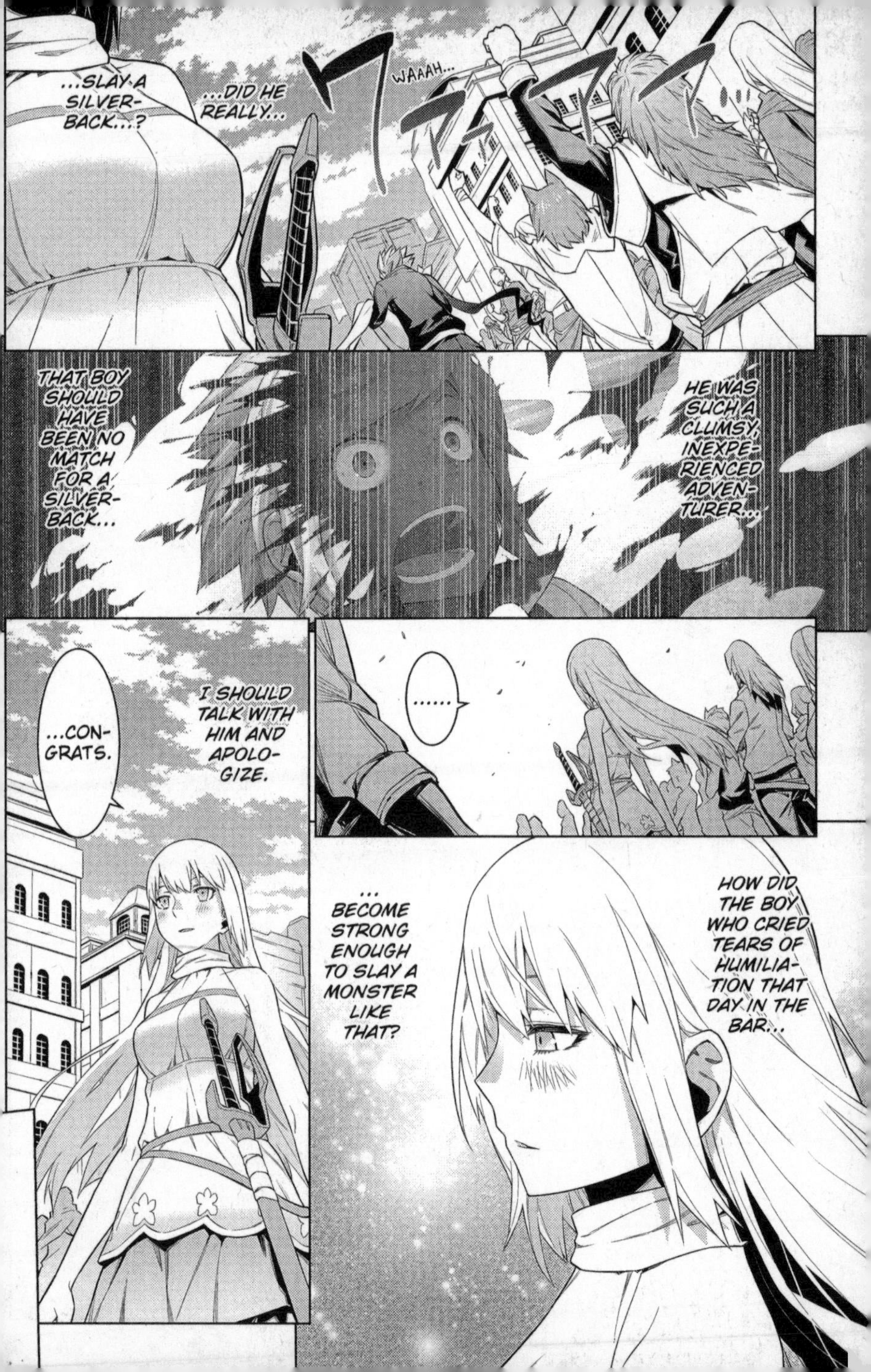
WAAAH...
...DID HE REALLY...
...SLAY A SILVER-BACK...?
HE WAS SUCH A CLUMSY, INEXPE-RIENCED ADVEN-TURER...
THAT BOY SHOULD HAVE BEEN NO MATCH FOR A SILVER-BACK...
......
HOW DID THE BOY WHO CRIED TEARS OF HUMILIA-TION THAT DAY IN THE BAR...
...BECOME STRONG ENOUGH TO SLAY A MONSTER LIKE THAT?
I SHOULD TALK WITH HIM AND APOLO-GIZE.
...CON-GRATS.

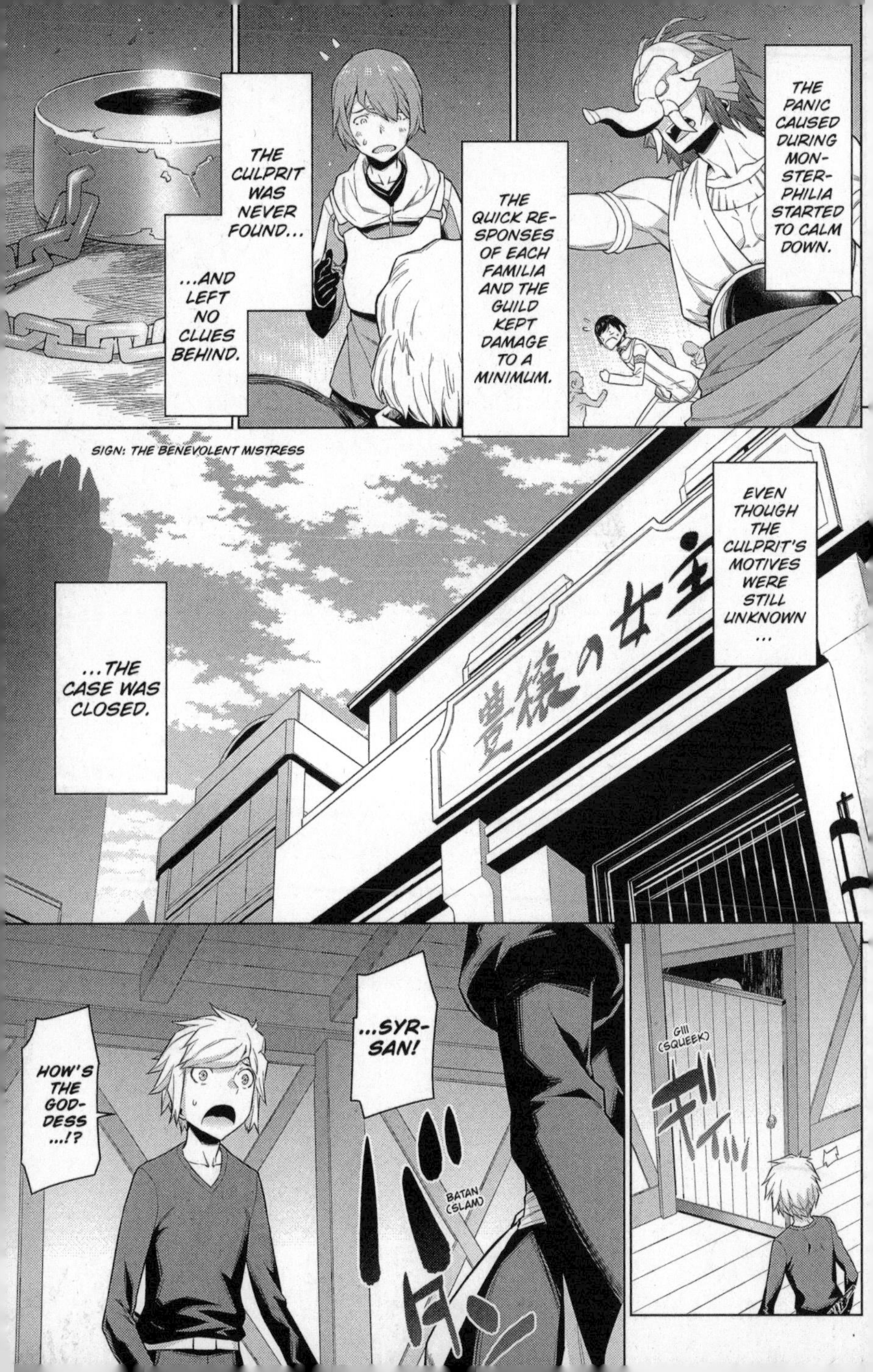
THE PANIC CAUSED DURING MONSTER-PHILIA STARTED TO CALM DOWN.
THE QUICK RESPONSES OF EACH FAMILIA AND THE GUILD KEPT DAMAGE TO A MINIMUM.
THE CULPRIT WAS NEVER FOUND...
...AND LEFT NO CLUES BEHIND.
SIGN: THE BENEVOLENT MISTRESS
EVEN THOUGH THE CULPRIT'S MOTIVES WERE STILL UNKNOWN...
...THE CASE WAS CLOSED.
GIII (SQUEEK)
...SYR-SAN!
HOW'S THE GOD-DESS ...!?
BATAN (SLAM)

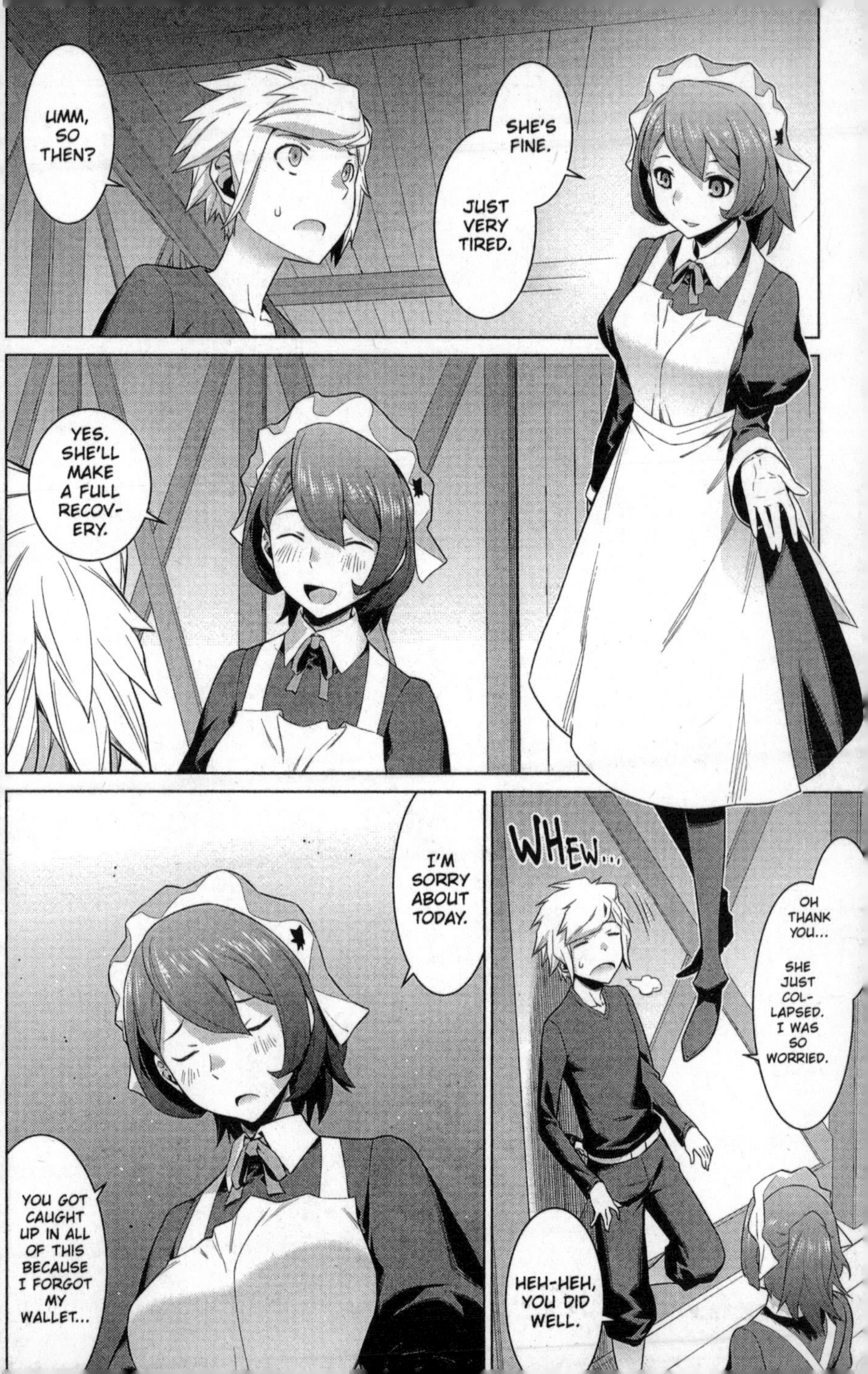
UMM, SO THEN?
SHE'S FINE. JUST VERY TIRED.
YES. SHE'LL MAKE A FULL RECOV-ERY.
WHEW...
OH THANK YOU... SHE JUST COL-LAPSED. I WAS SO WORRIED.
HEH-HEH, YOU DID WELL.
I'M SORRY ABOUT TODAY.
YOU GOT CAUGHT UP IN ALL OF THIS BECAUSE I FORGOT MY WALLET...

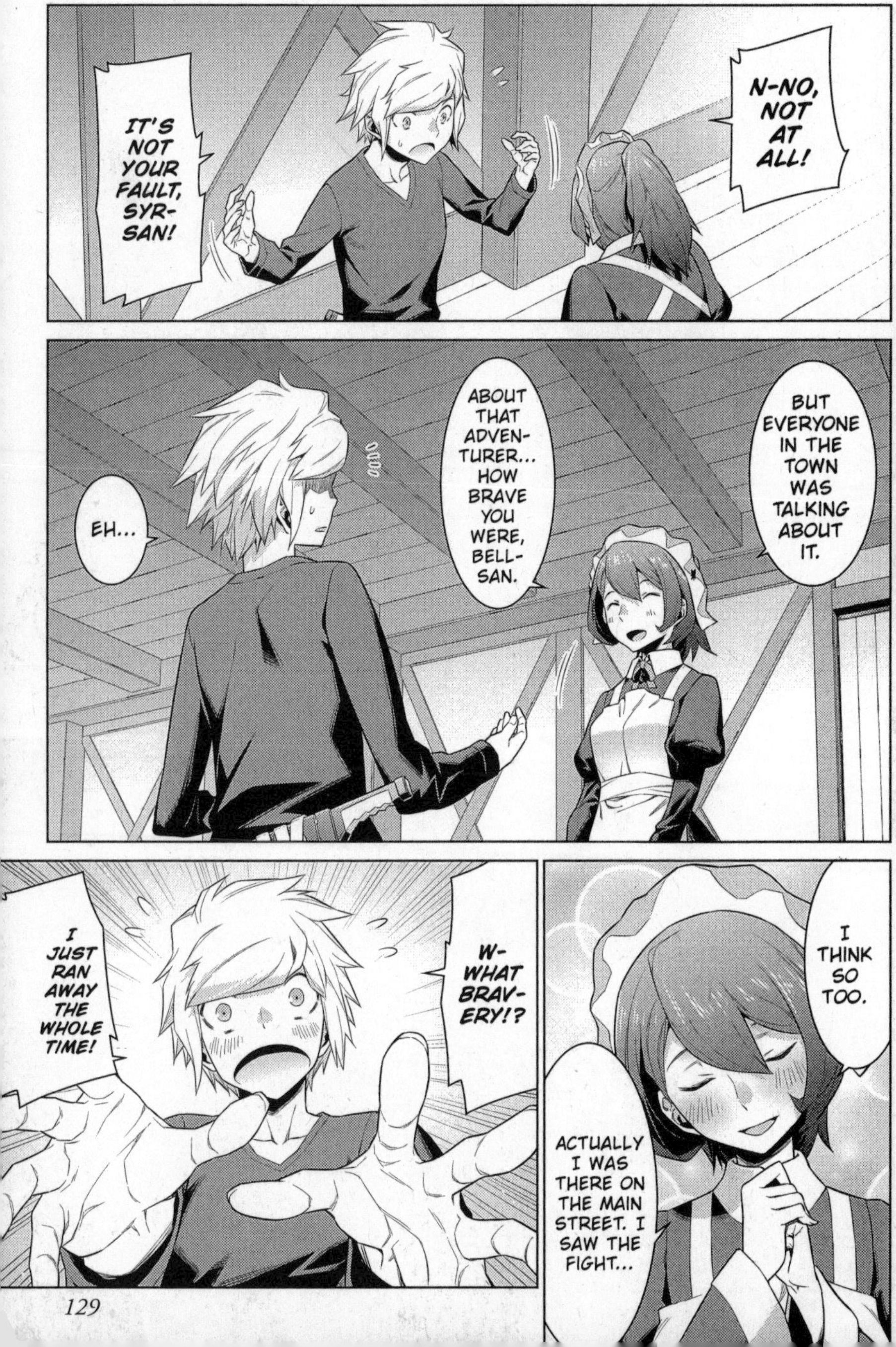
N-NO, NOT AT ALL!
IT'S NOT YOUR FAULT, SYR-SAN!
BUT EVERYONE IN THE TOWN WAS TALKING ABOUT IT.
ABOUT THAT ADVENTURER... HOW BRAVE YOU WERE, BELL-SAN.
EH...
I THINK SO TOO.
ACTUALLY I WAS THERE ON THE MAIN STREET. I SAW THE FIGHT...
W-WHAT BRAVERY!?
I JUST RAN AWAY THE WHOLE TIME!

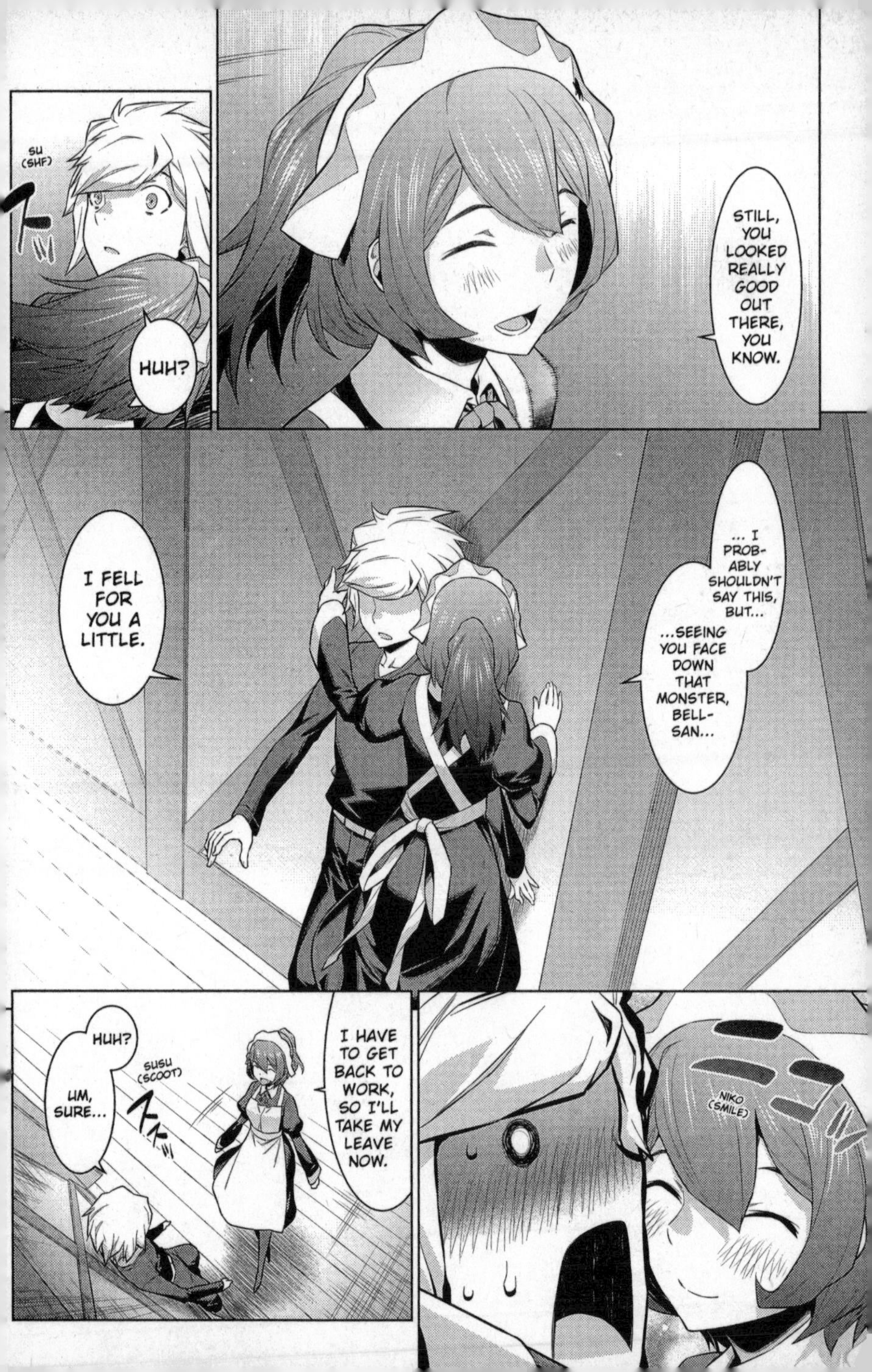
STILL, YOU LOOKED REALLY GOOD OUT THERE, YOU KNOW.
SU (SHF)
HUH?
... I PROBABLY SHOULDN'T SAY THIS, BUT...
...SEEING YOU FACE DOWN THAT MONSTER, BELL-SAN...
I FELL FOR YOU A LITTLE.
NIKO (SMILE)
I HAVE TO GET BACK TO WORK, SO I'LL TAKE MY LEAVE NOW.
HUH?
SUSU (SCOOT)
UM, SURE...

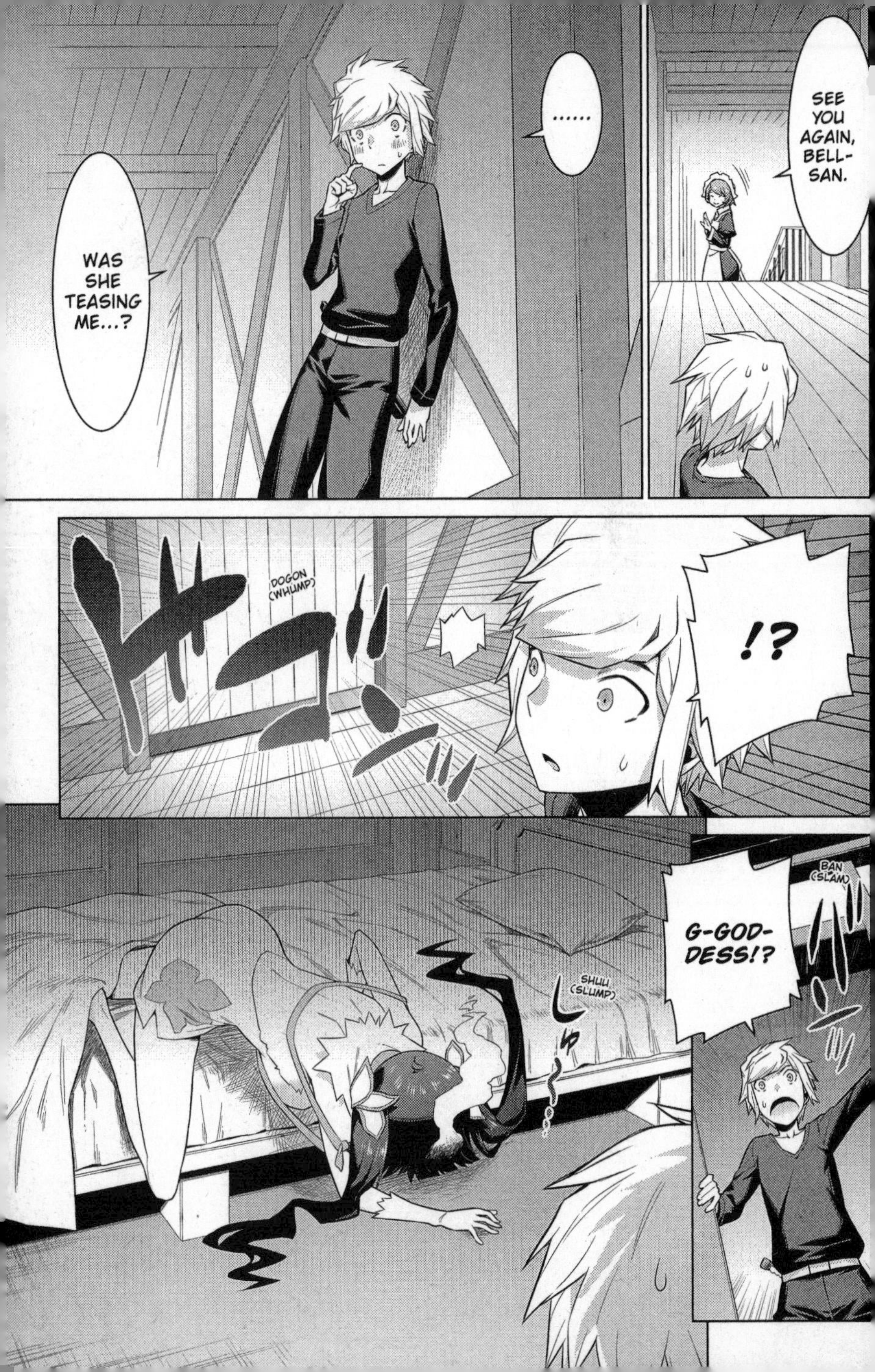
SEE YOU AGAIN, BELL-SAN.
......
WAS SHE TEASING ME...?
!?
DOGON (WHUMP)
BAN (SLAM)
G-GOD-DESS!?
SHUU (SLUMP)

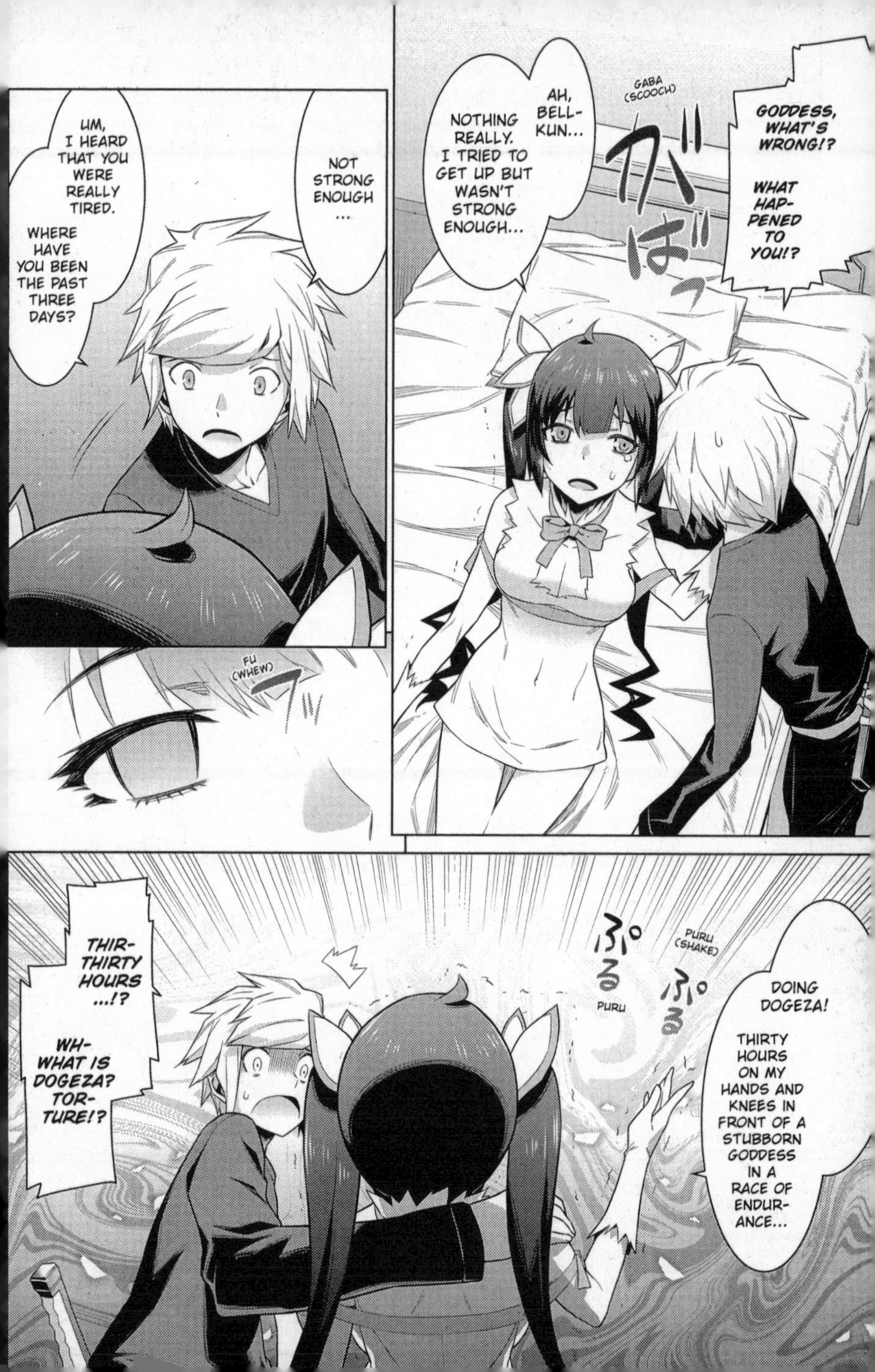
GODDESS, WHAT'S WRONG!?
WHAT HAP-PENED TO YOU!?
がばっ
GABA (SCOOCH)
AH, BELL-KUN...
NOTHING REALLY. I TRIED TO GET UP BUT WASN'T STRONG ENOUGH...
NOT STRONG ENOUGH ...
UM, I HEARD THAT YOU WERE REALLY TIRED.
WHERE HAVE YOU BEEN THE PAST THREE DAYS?
FU (WHEW)
DOING DOGEZA!
THIRTY HOURS ON MY HANDS AND KNEES IN FRONT OF A STUBBORN GODDESS IN A RACE OF ENDUR-ANCE...
ぷる
PURU (SHAKE)
ぷる
PURU
THIR-THIRTY HOURS ...!?
WH-WHAT IS DOGEZA? TOR-TURE!?

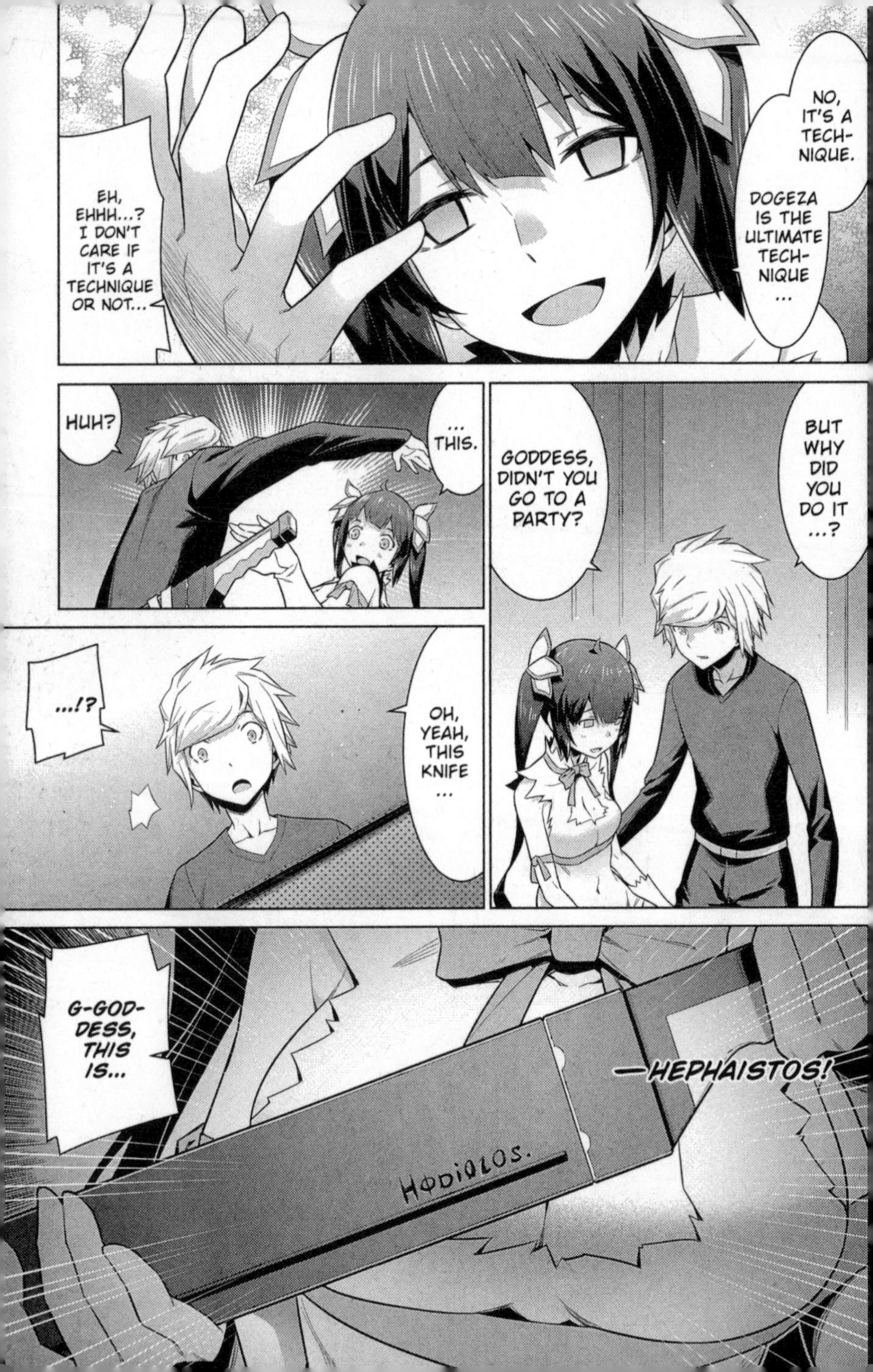
NO, IT'S A TECHNIQUE.
DOGEZA IS THE ULTIMATE TECHNIQUE...
EH, EHHH...? I DON'T CARE IF IT'S A TECHNIQUE OR NOT...
BUT WHY DID YOU DO IT...?
GODDESS, DIDN'T YOU GO TO A PARTY?
...THIS.
HUH?
OH, YEAH, THIS KNIFE...
...!?
—HEPHAISTOS!
G-GODDESS, THIS IS...

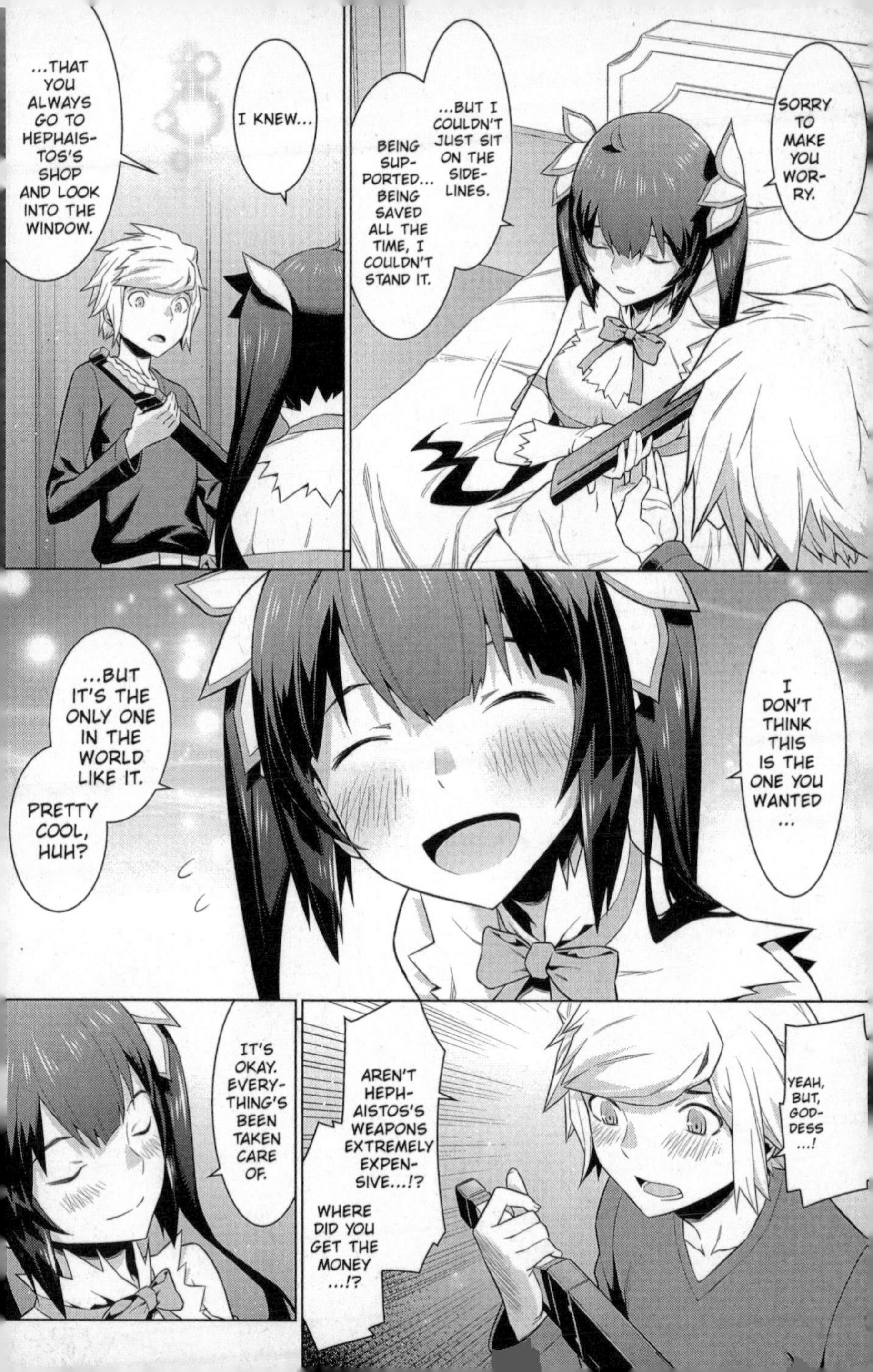
SORRY TO MAKE YOU WORRY.
...BUT I COULDN'T JUST SIT ON THE SIDELINES.
BEING SUPPORTED... BEING SAVED ALL THE TIME, I COULDN'T STAND IT.
I KNEW...
...THAT YOU ALWAYS GO TO HEPHAISTOS'S SHOP AND LOOK INTO THE WINDOW.
I DON'T THINK THIS IS THE ONE YOU WANTED...
...BUT IT'S THE ONLY ONE IN THE WORLD LIKE IT.
PRETTY COOL, HUH?
YEAH, BUT, GODDESS...!
AREN'T HEPHAISTOS'S WEAPONS EXTREMELY EXPENSIVE...!?
WHERE DID YOU GET THE MONEY...!?
IT'S OKAY. EVERYTHING'S BEEN TAKEN CARE OF.

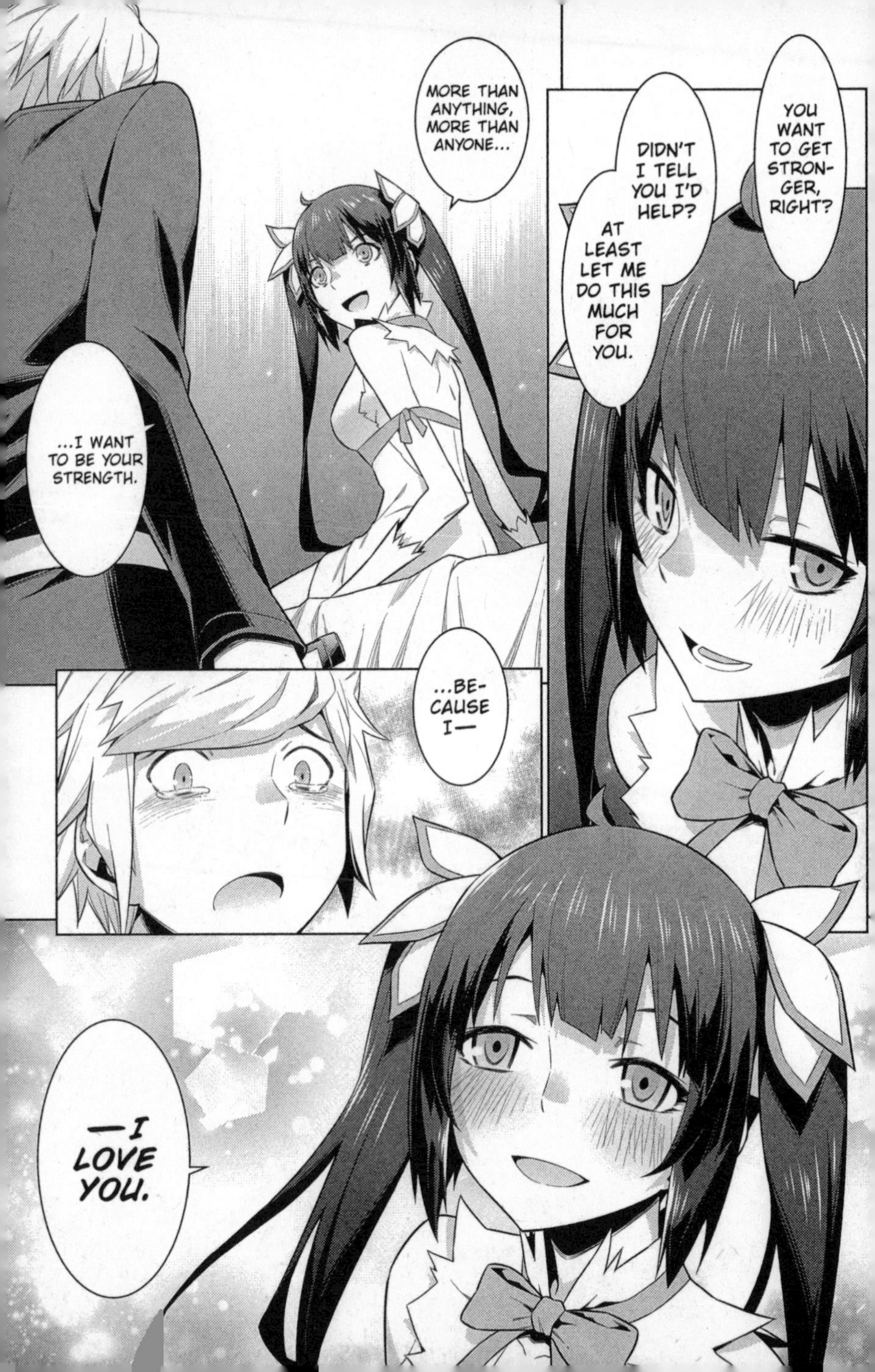
YOU WANT TO GET STRON-GER, RIGHT?
DIDN'T I TELL YOU I'D HELP?
AT LEAST LET ME DO THIS MUCH FOR YOU.
MORE THAN ANYTHING, MORE THAN ANYONE...
...I WANT TO BE YOUR STRENGTH.
...BE-CAUSE I—
—I LOVE YOU.

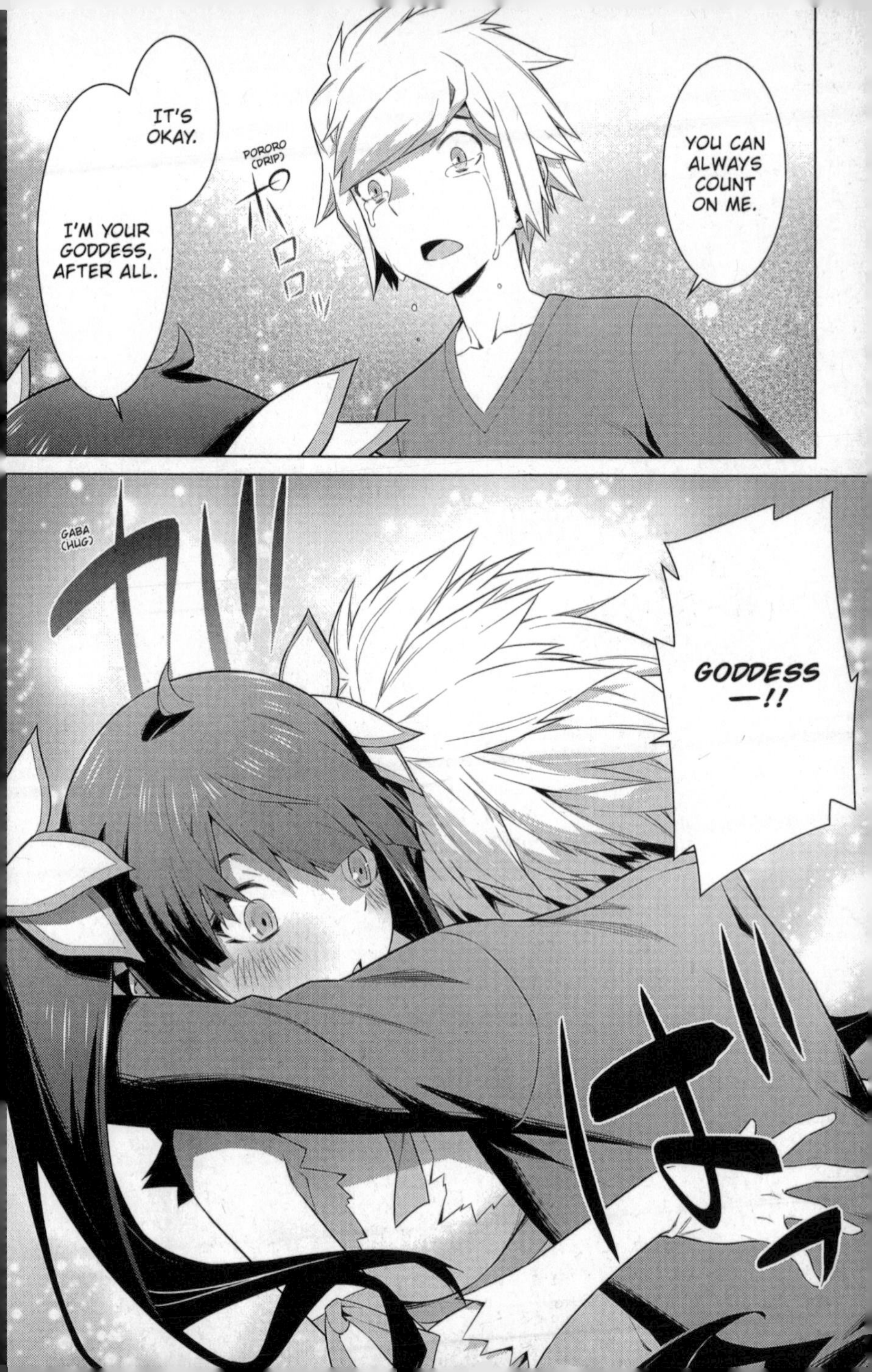
YOU CAN ALWAYS COUNT ON ME.
PORORO (DRIP)
IT'S OKAY.
I'M YOUR GODDESS, AFTER ALL.
GODDESS—!!
GABA (HUG)

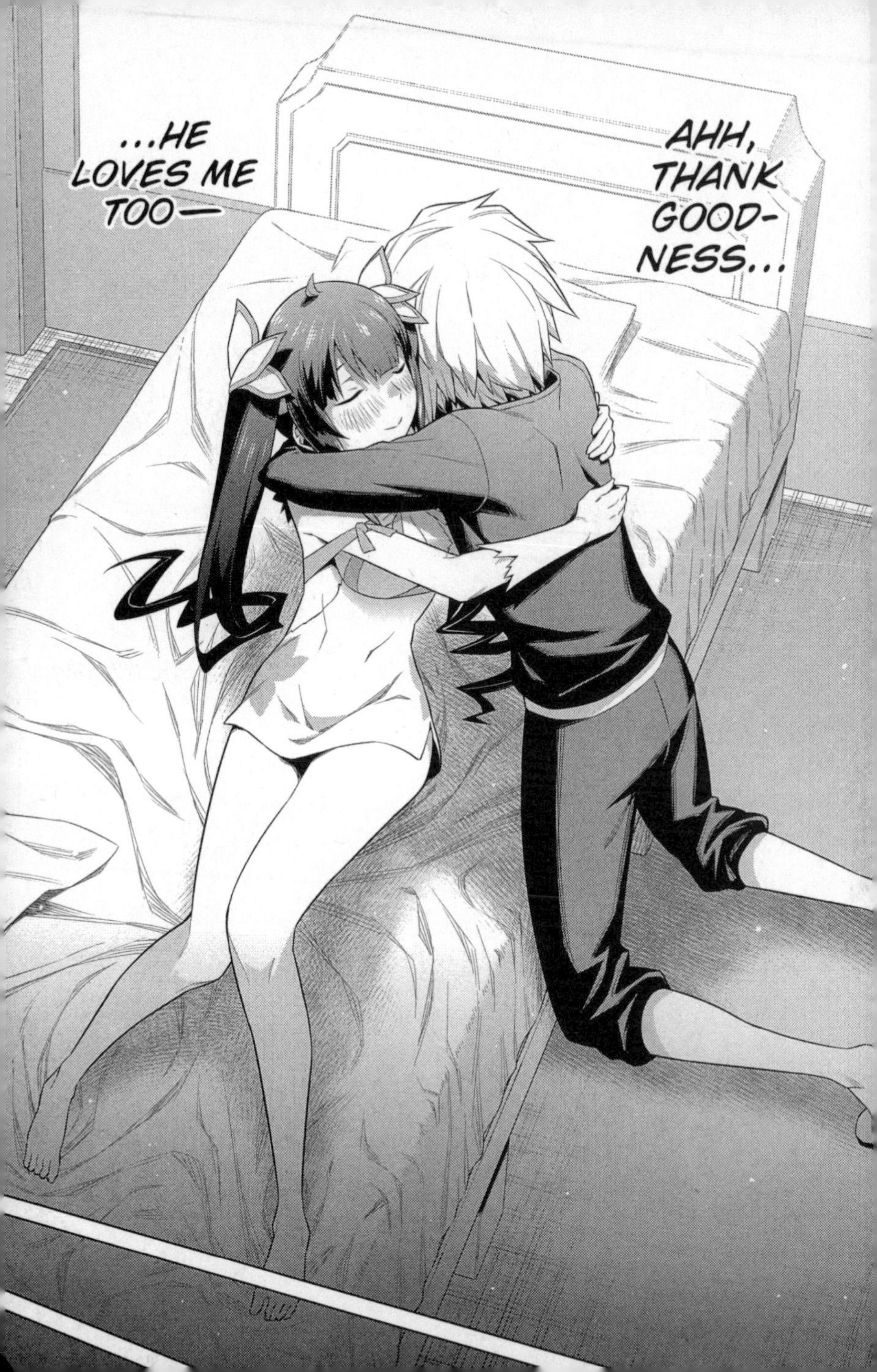
AHH, THANK GOOD-NESS...
...HE LOVES ME TOO—

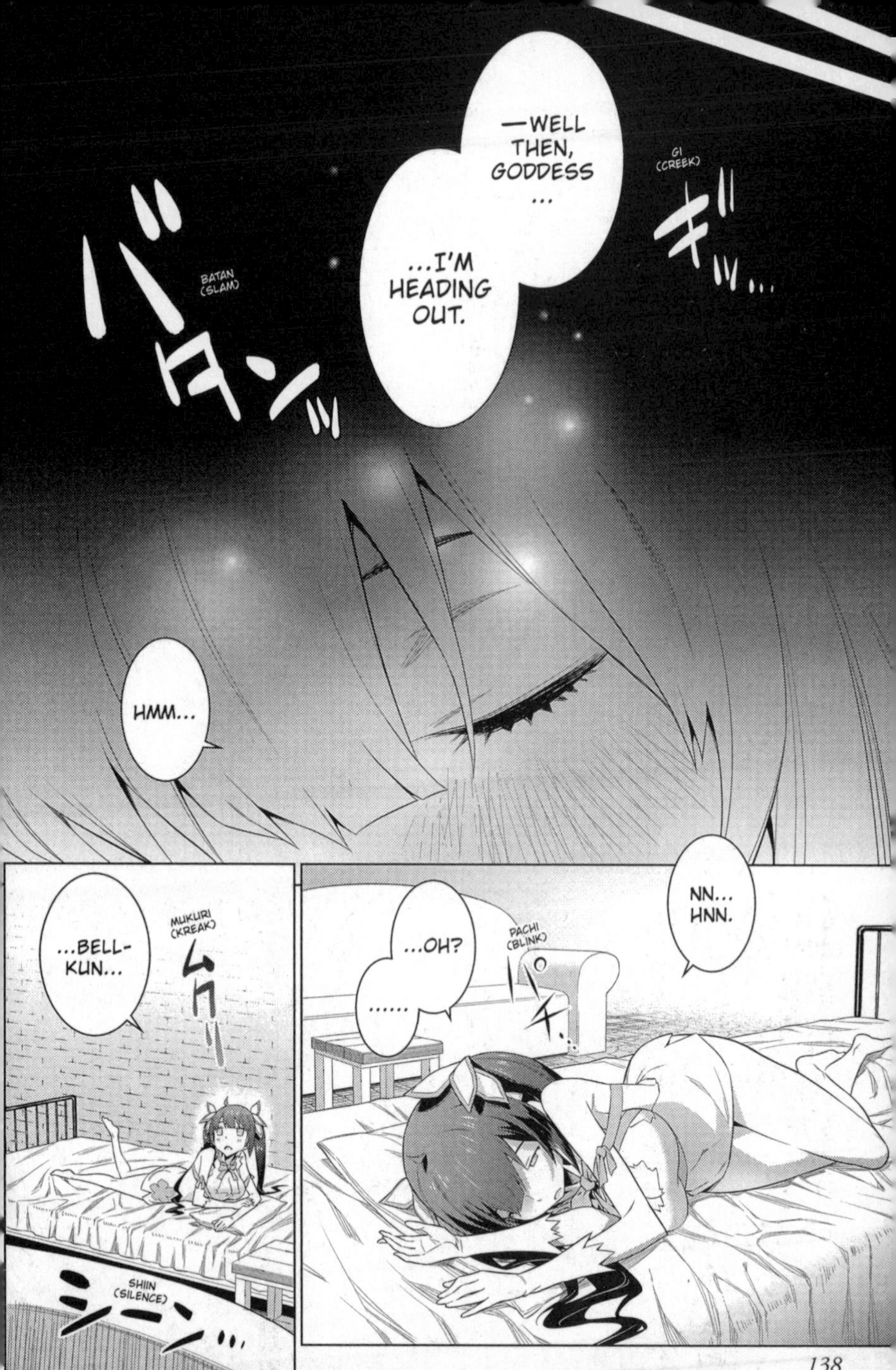
GI
(CREEK)
—WELL THEN, GODDESS...
...I'M HEADING OUT.
BATAN
(SLAM)
HMM...
NN... HNN.
PACHI
(BLINK)
...OH?
......
...BELL-KUN...
MUKURI
(KREAK)
SHIIN
(SILENCE)

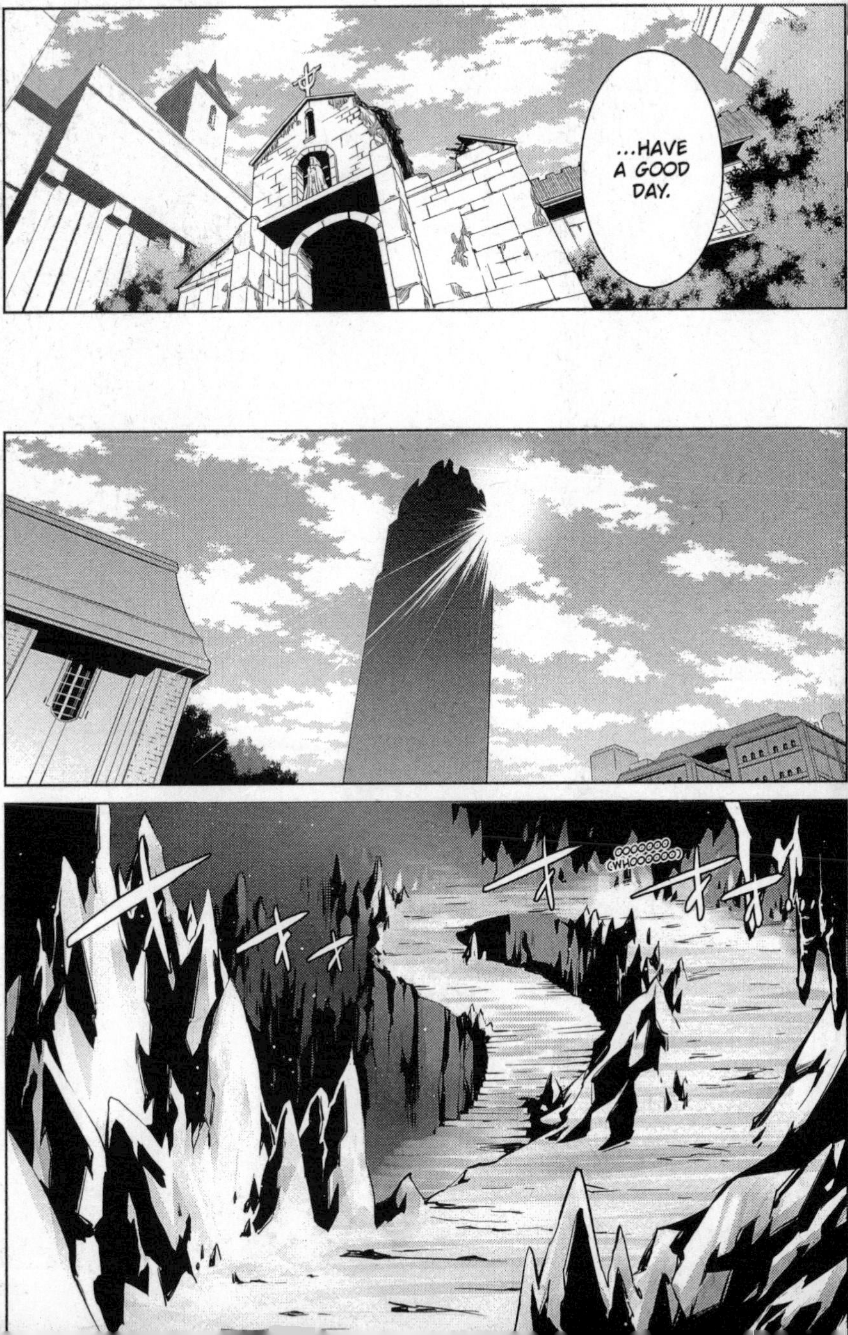
...HAVE A GOOD DAY.
OOOOOOO
(WHOOOOOO)

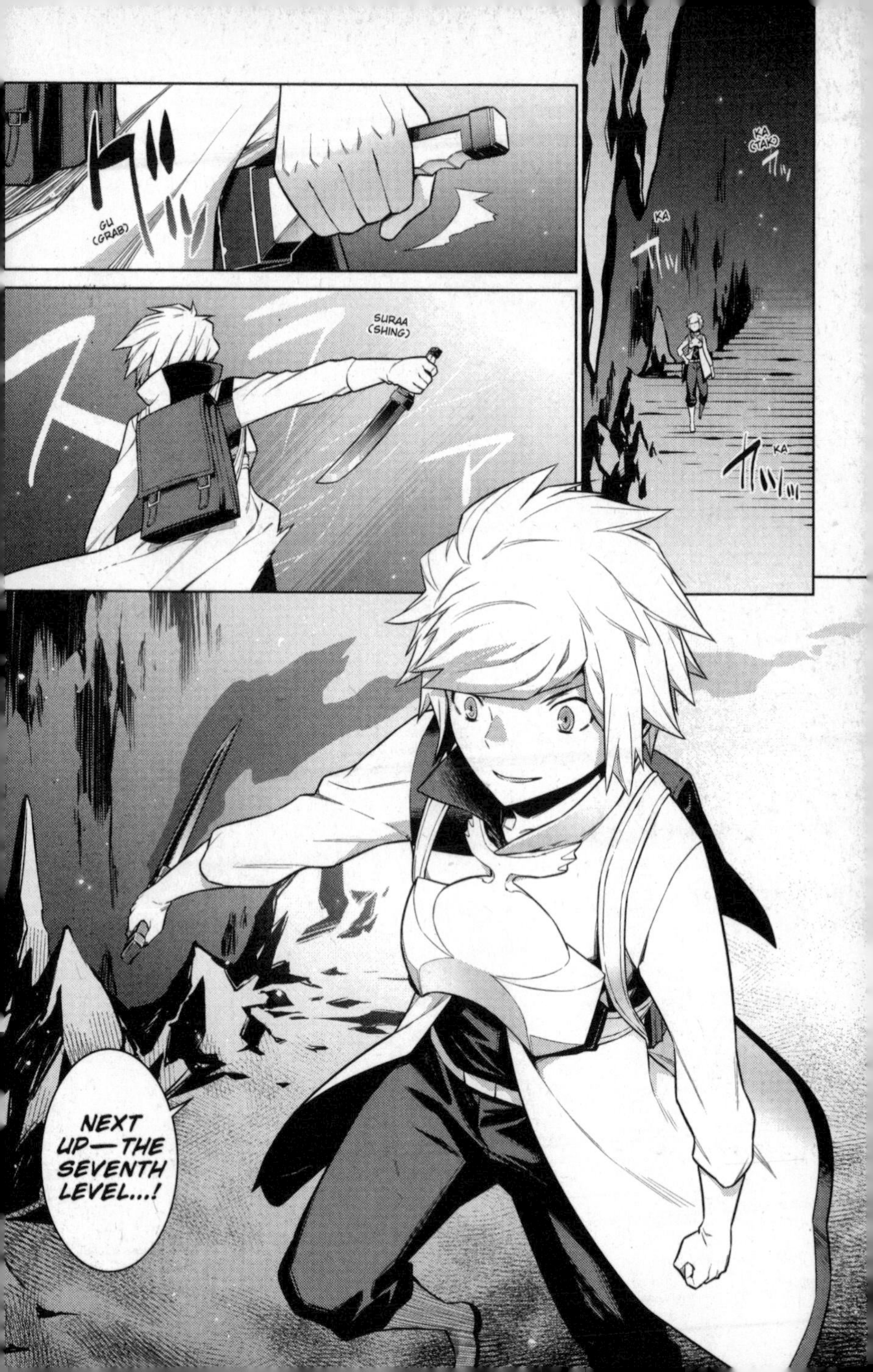
KA (TAK)
KA
KA
GU (GRAB)
SURAA (SHING)
NEXT UP—THE SEVENTH LEVEL...!

CITIZENS OF ORARIO

text by Fujino Omori
character rough by Kunieda

➤File 11

BETE LOGA

A werewolf who belongs to Loki Familia. A warrior with excessive strength, he often looks down on weak adventurers, and he hates weak females most of all.

CITIZENS OF ORARIO

text by Fujino Omori
character rough by Kunieda

➤File 12

REVERIA RIYOS AHRVE

A very proud high elf belonging to Loki Familia. Despite being one of the "children" of the lower world, her beauty rivals many goddesses'. She's known as one of the best magic users in all of Orario.

STEP 14 ▸▸ A CHANCE MEETING

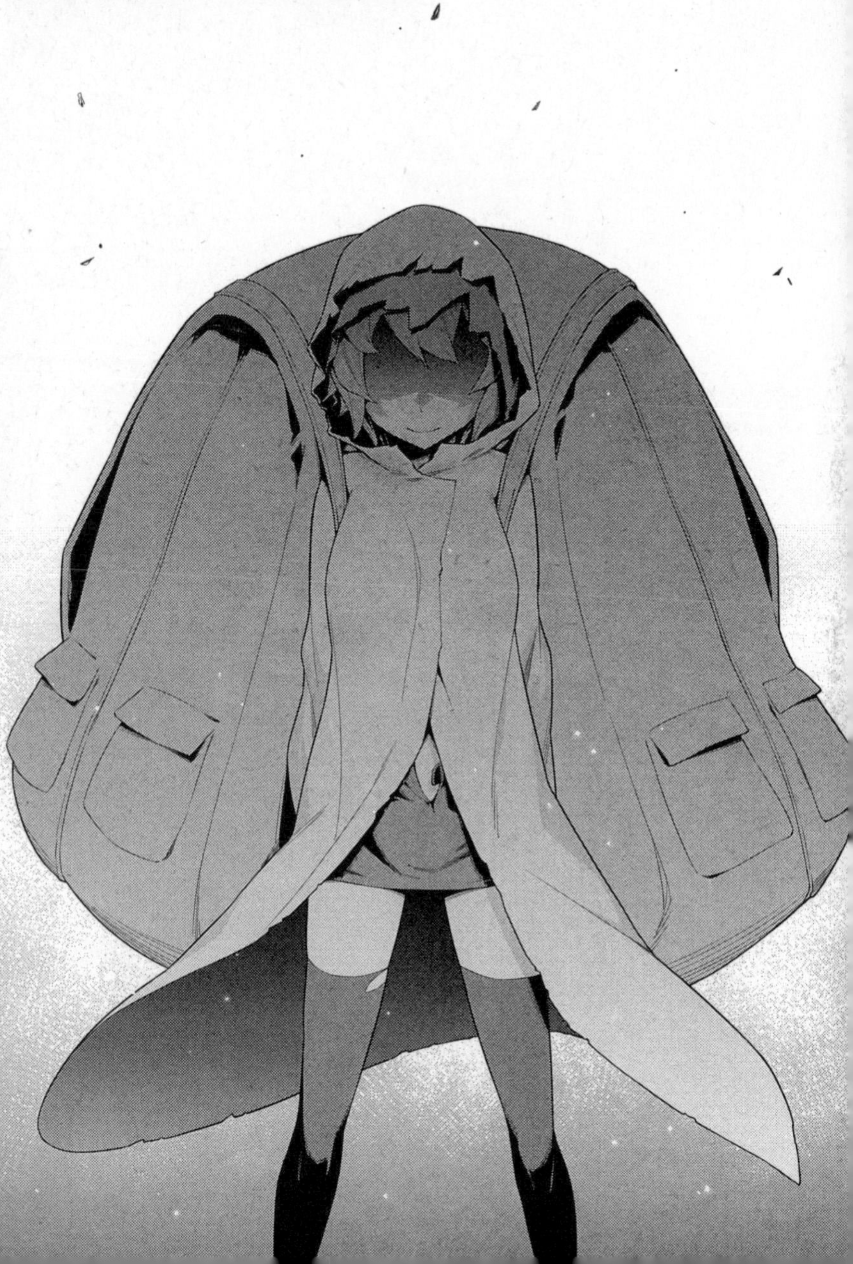

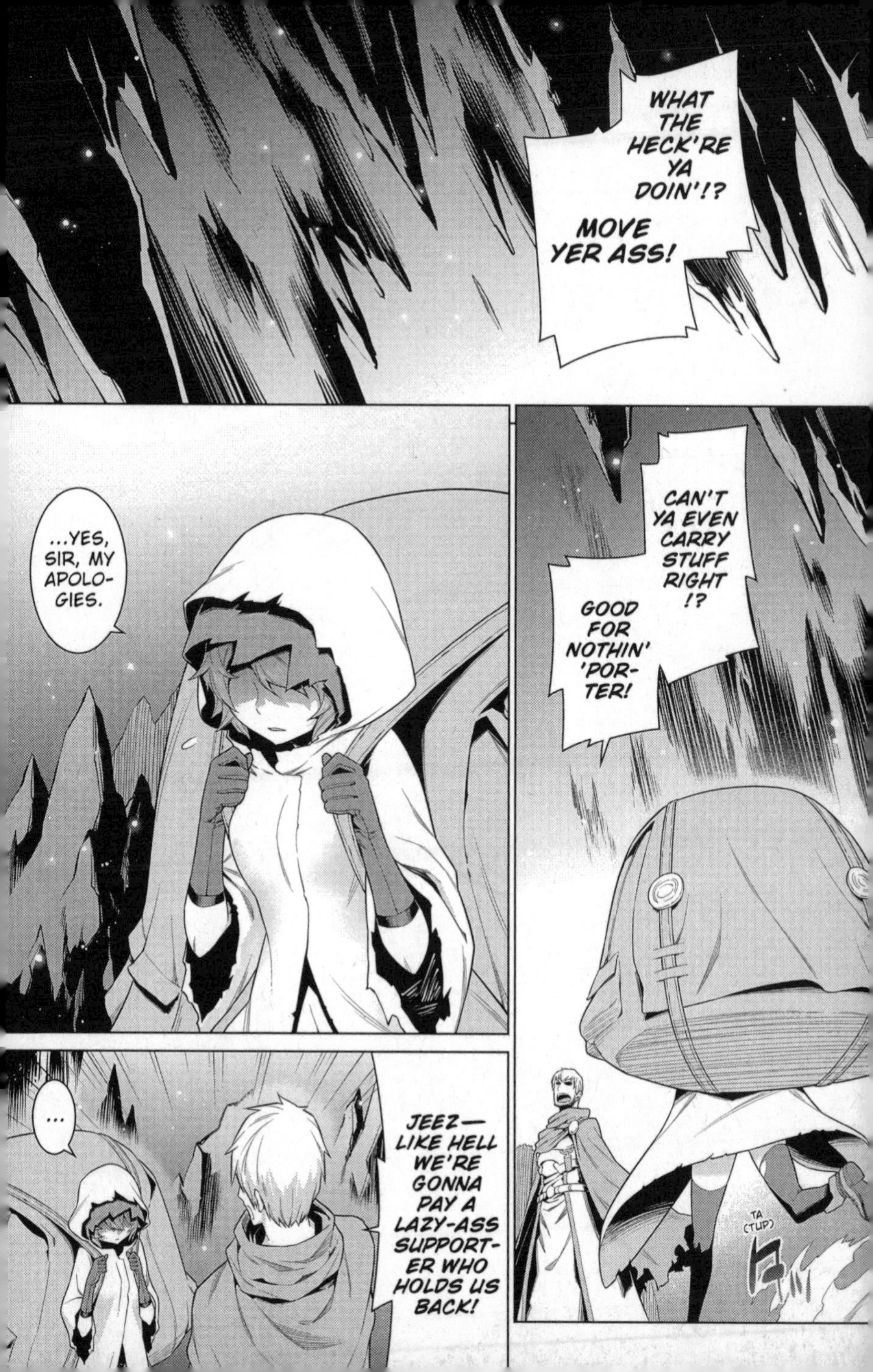
WHAT THE HECK'RE YA DOIN'!?
MOVE YER ASS!
CAN'T YA EVEN CARRY STUFF RIGHT!?
GOOD FOR NOTHIN' 'PORTER!
TA (TUP)
...YES, SIR, MY APOLOGIES.
JEEZ—LIKE HELL WE'RE GONNA PAY A LAZY-ASS SUPPORTER WHO HOLDS US BACK!
...

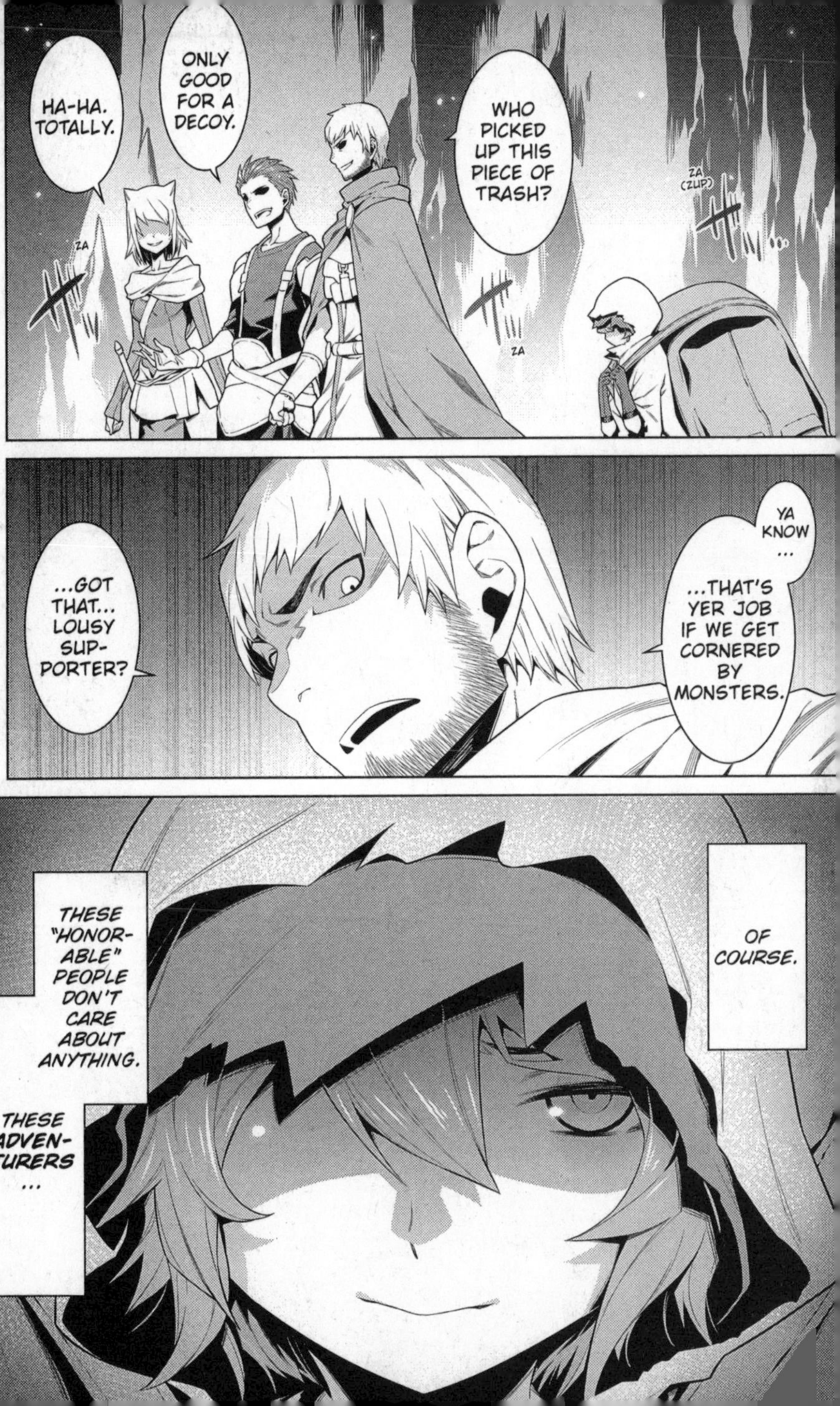
WHO PICKED UP THIS PIECE OF TRASH?
ZA (ZUP)
ONLY GOOD FOR A DECOY.
HA-HA. TOTALLY.
ZA
ZA
YA KNOW...
...THAT'S YER JOB IF WE GET CORNERED BY MONSTERS.
...GOT THAT... LOUSY SUPPORTER?
OF COURSE.
THESE "HONORABLE" PEOPLE DON'T CARE ABOUT ANYTHING.
THESE ADVENTURERS...

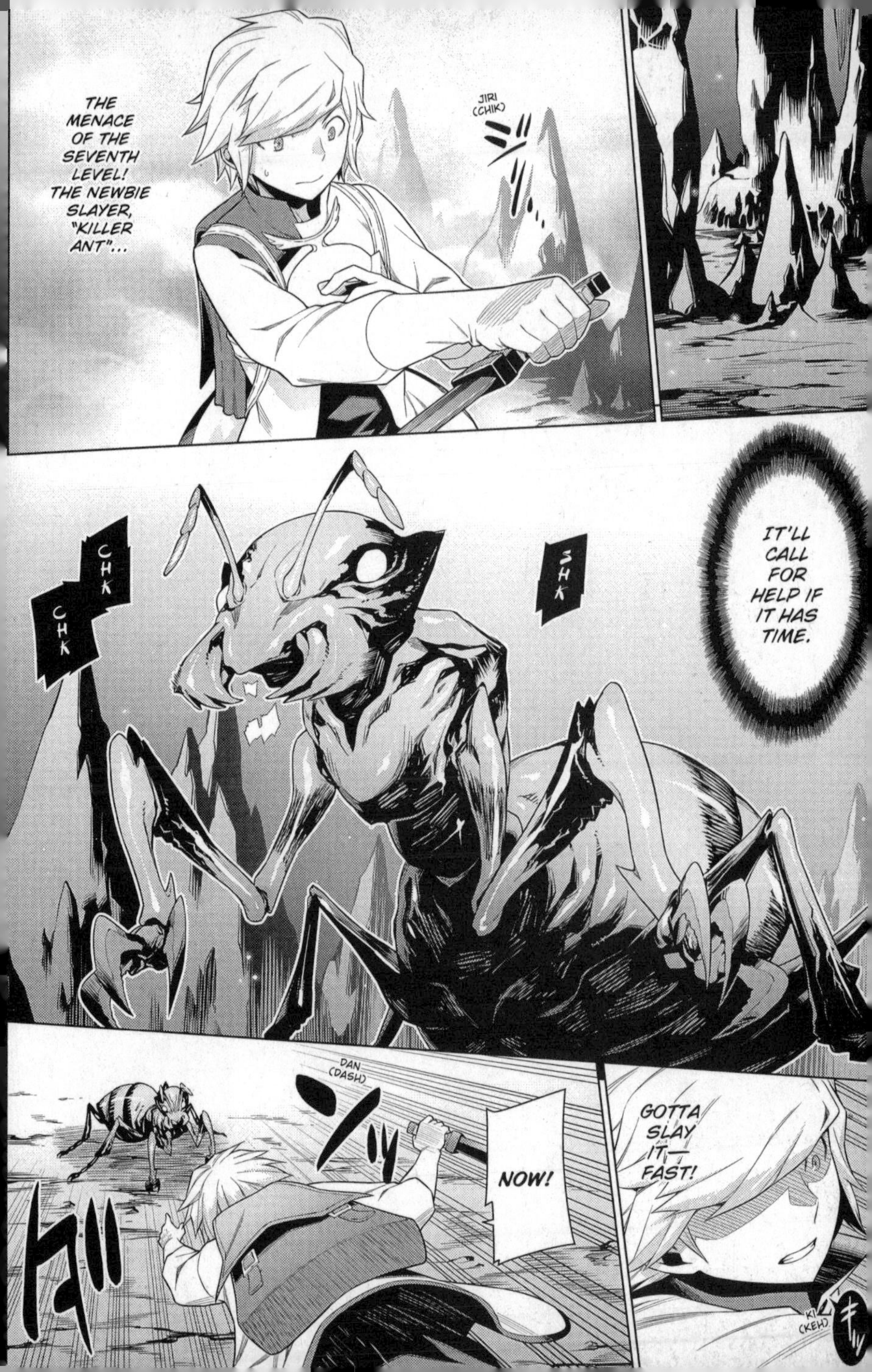
JIRI (CHIK)
THE MENACE OF THE SEVENTH LEVEL! THE NEWBIE SLAYER, "KILLER ANT"...
IT'LL CALL FOR HELP IF IT HAS TIME.
SHK
CHK
CHK
GOTTA SLAY IT— FAST!
KI (KEH)
DAN (DASH)
NOW!

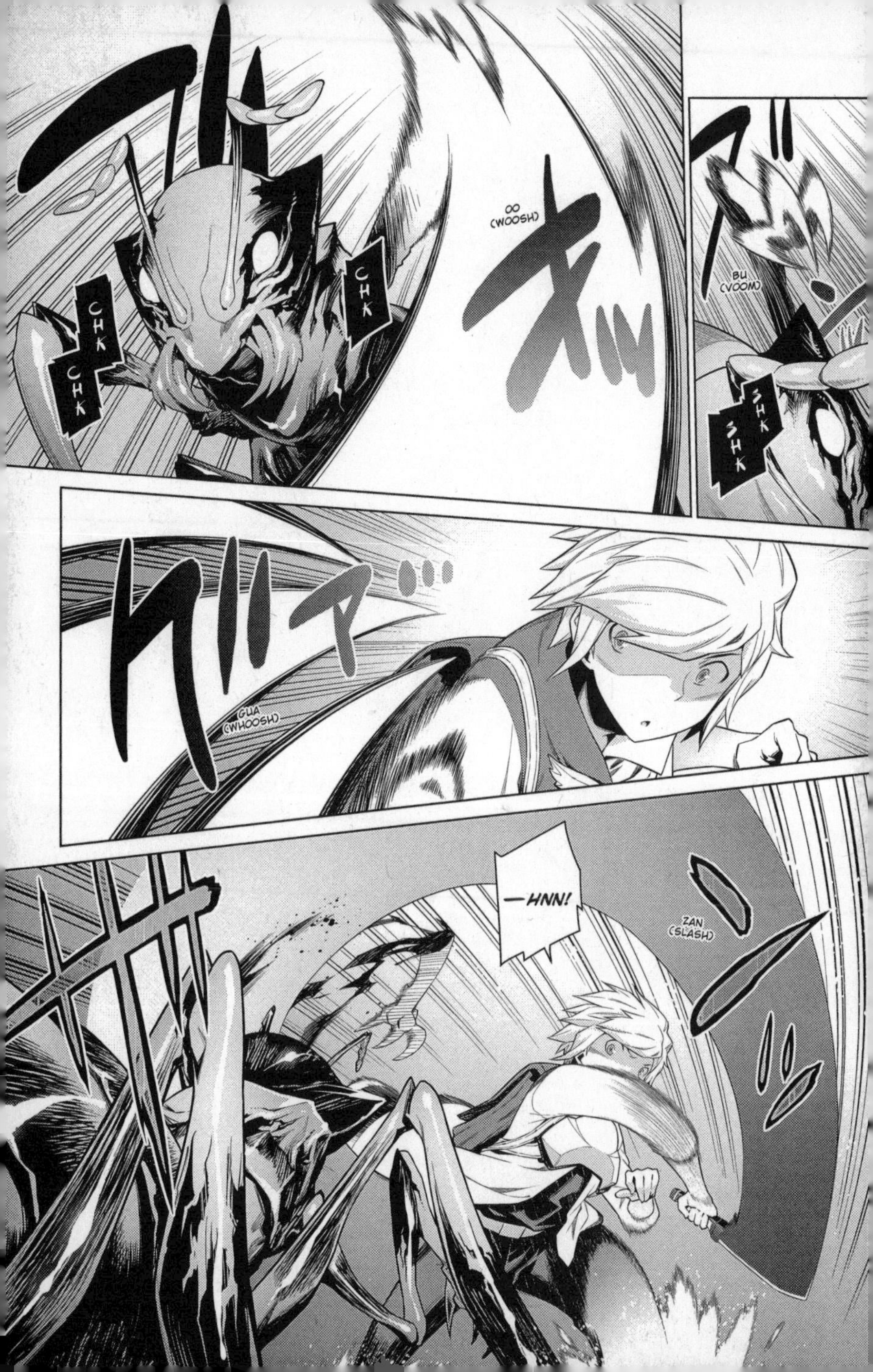
BU
(VOOM)
SHK
SHK
OO
(WOOSH)
CHK
CHK
CHK
CHK
GUA
(WHOOSH)
—HNN!
ZAN
(SLASH)

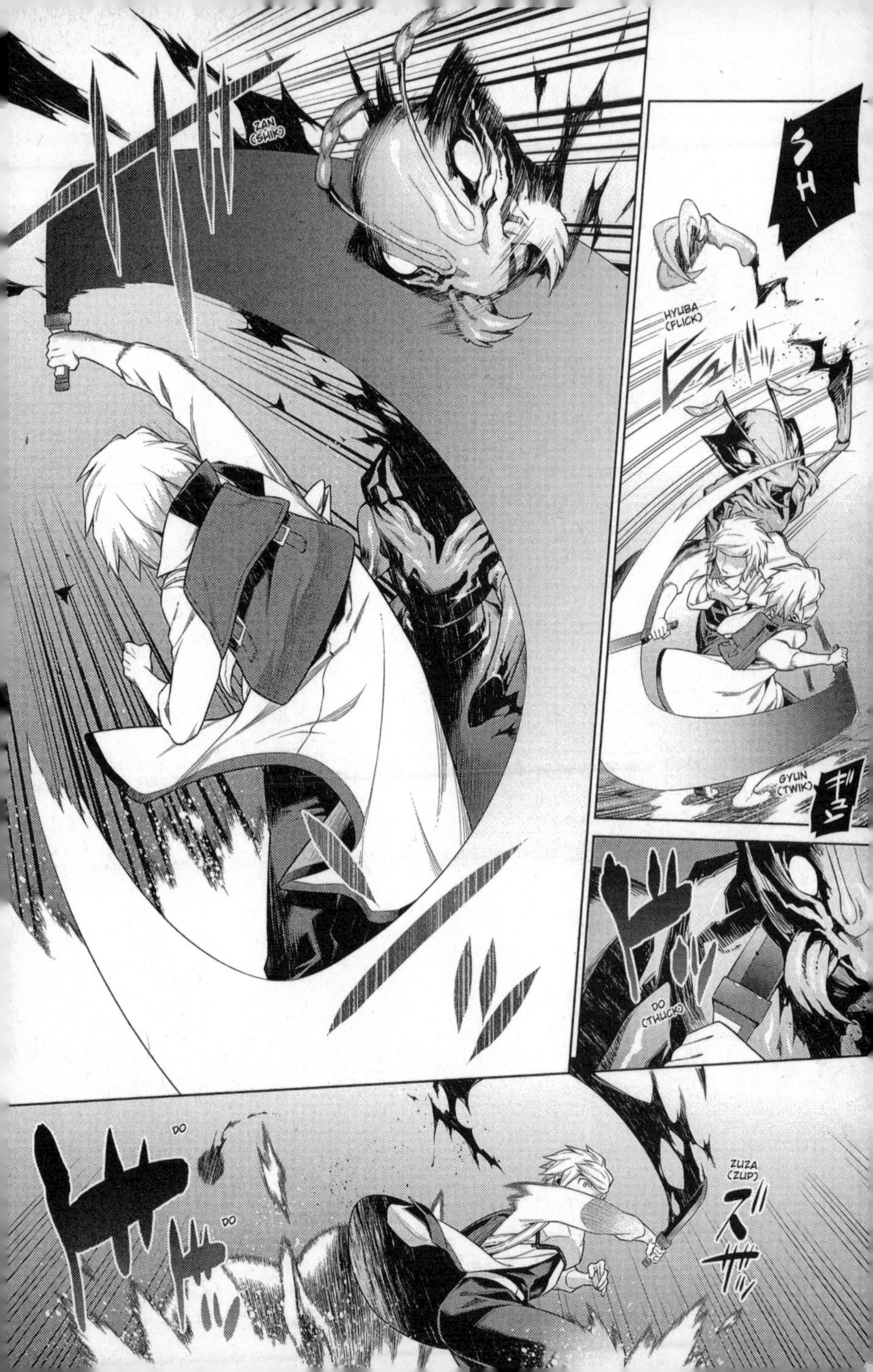
HYUBA (FLICK)
GYUN (TWIK)
DO (THUCK)
ZAN (SHIK)
ZUZA (ZUP)
DO
DO

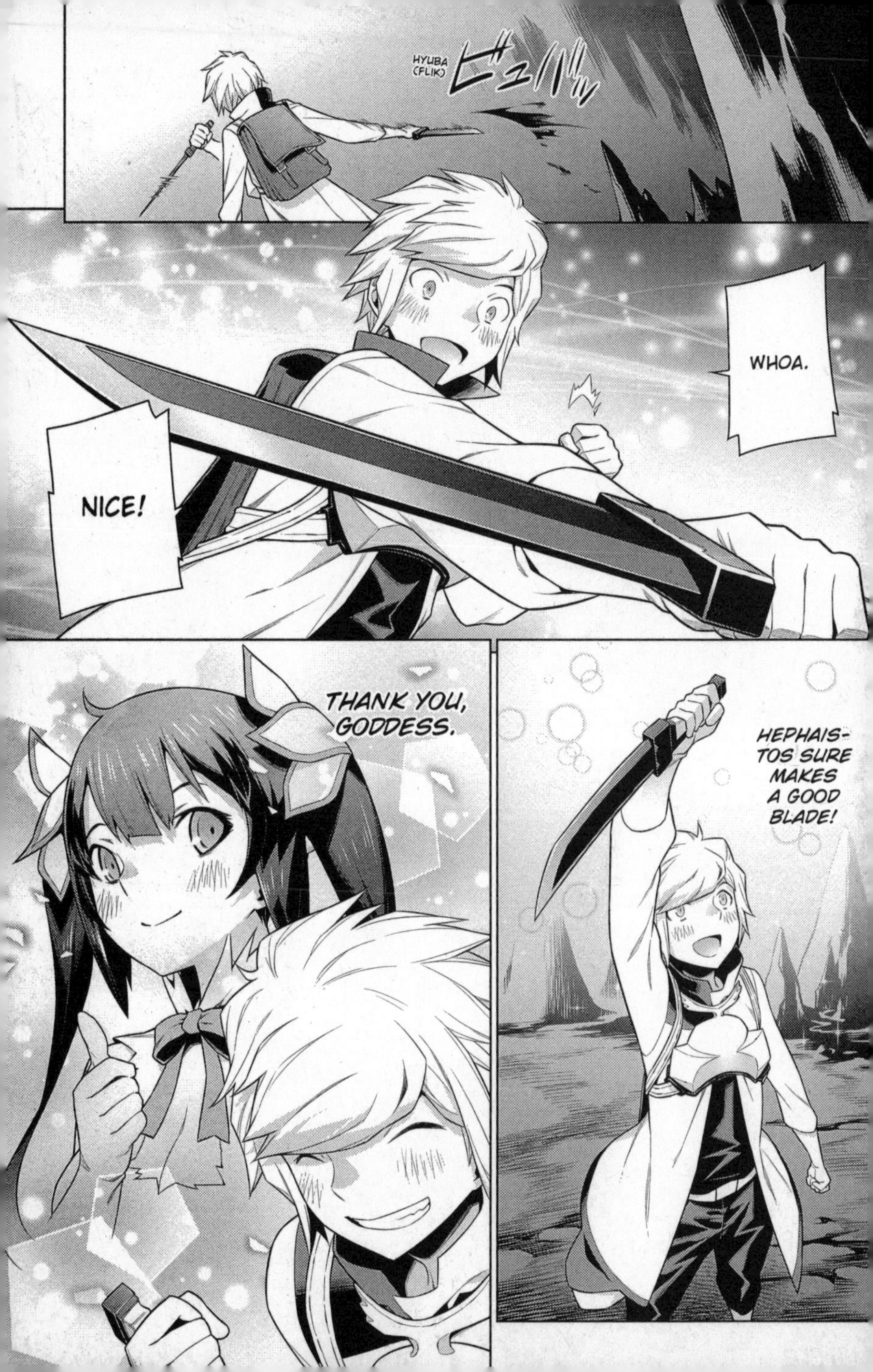

HYUBA (FLIK)
WHOA.
NICE!
HEPHAIS-TOS SURE MAKES A GOOD BLADE!
THANK YOU, GODDESS.

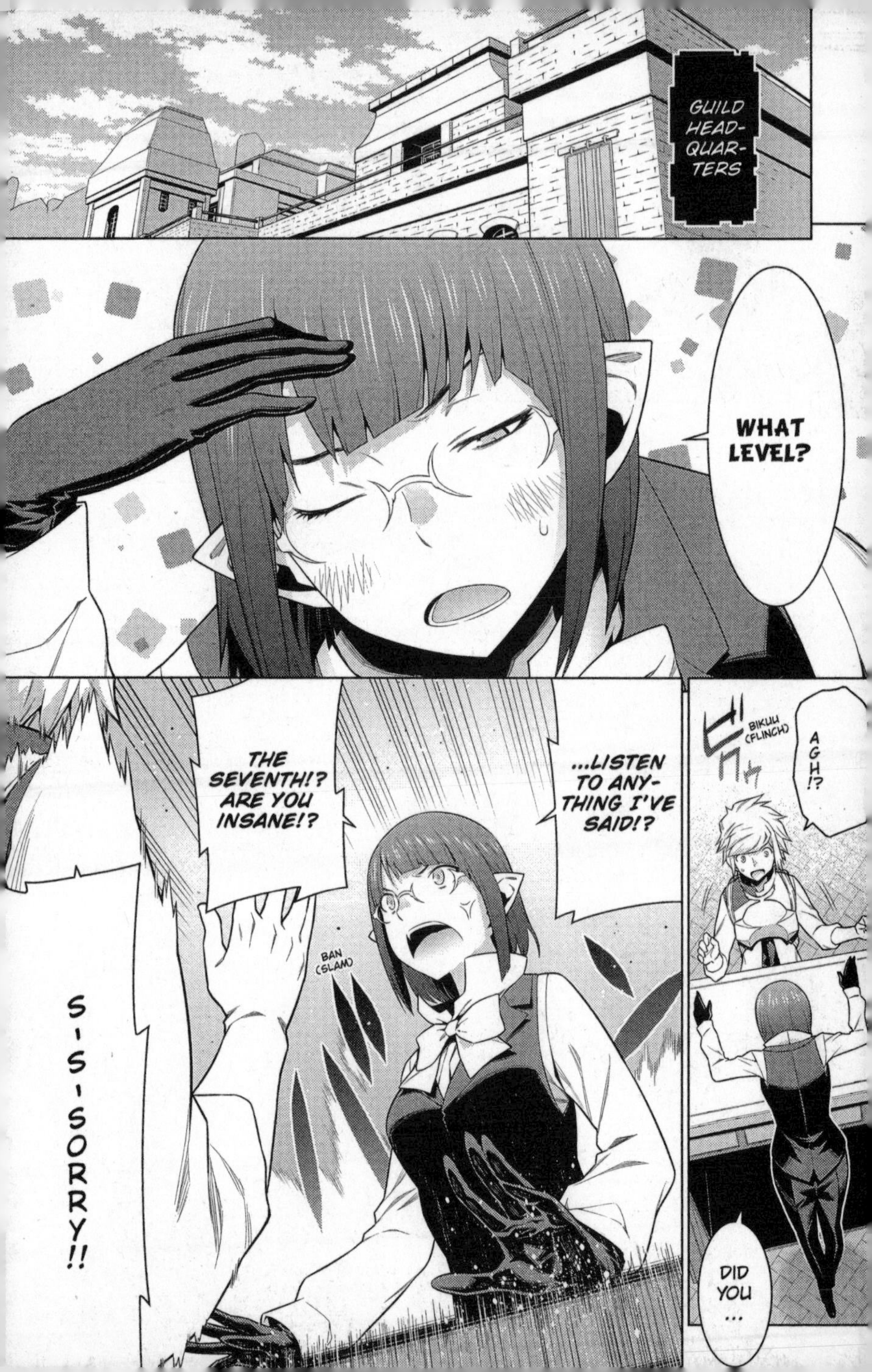
GUILD HEADQUARTERS
WHAT LEVEL?
BIKUU (FLINCH)
AGH!?
DID YOU ...
...LISTEN TO ANYTHING I'VE SAID!?
THE SEVENTH!? ARE YOU INSANE!?
BAN (SLAM)
S-S-SORRY!!

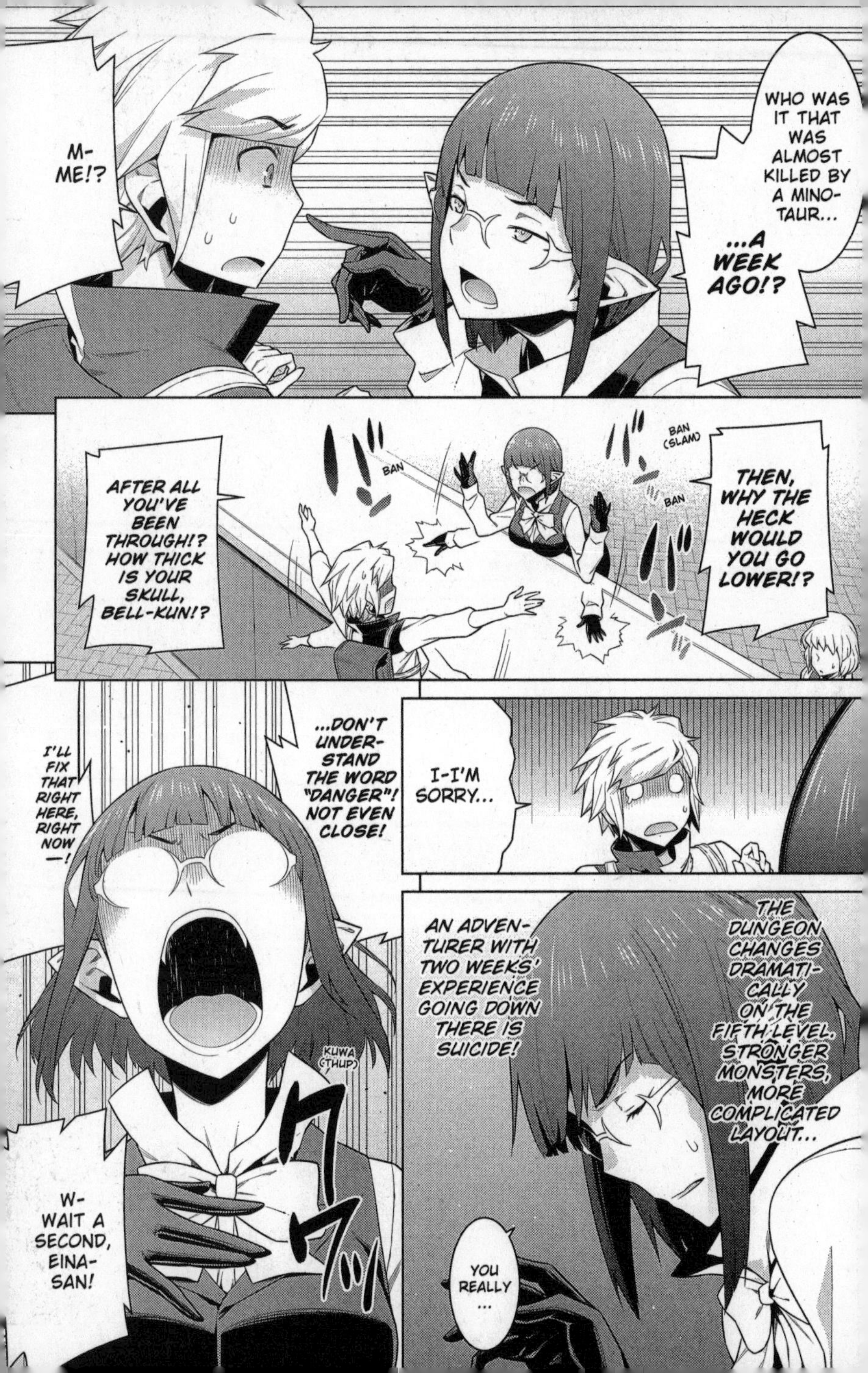
WHO WAS IT THAT WAS ALMOST KILLED BY A MINO-TAUR...
...A WEEK AGO!?
M-ME!?
BAN (SLAM)
THEN, WHY THE HECK WOULD YOU GO LOWER!?
BAN
BAN
AFTER ALL YOU'VE BEEN THROUGH!? HOW THICK IS YOUR SKULL, BELL-KUN!?
I-I'M SORRY...
THE DUNGEON CHANGES DRAMATI-CALLY ON THE FIFTH LEVEL. STRONGER MONSTERS, MORE COMPLICATED LAYOUT...
AN ADVEN-TURER WITH TWO WEEKS' EXPERIENCE GOING DOWN THERE IS SUICIDE!
YOU REALLY ...
...DON'T UNDER-STAND THE WORD "DANGER"! NOT EVEN CLOSE!
I'LL FIX THAT RIGHT HERE, RIGHT NOW —!
KUWA (THUP)
W-WAIT A SECOND, EINA-SAN!

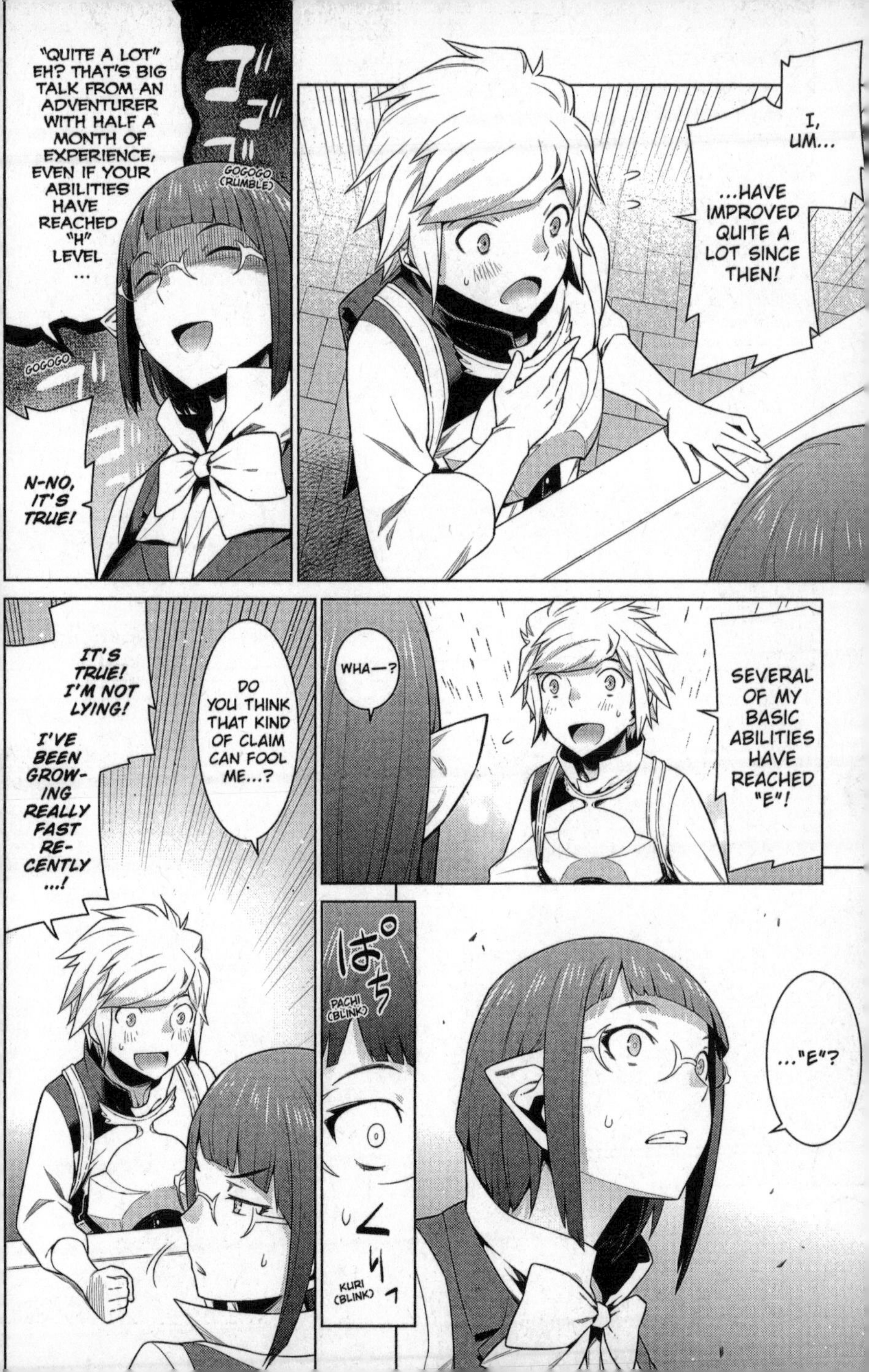
I, UM...
...HAVE IMPROVED QUITE A LOT SINCE THEN!
"QUITE A LOT" EH? THAT'S BIG TALK FROM AN ADVENTURER WITH HALF A MONTH OF EXPERIENCE, EVEN IF YOUR ABILITIES HAVE REACHED "H" LEVEL ...
GOGOGO (RUMBLE)
GOGOGO
N-NO, IT'S TRUE!
SEVERAL OF MY BASIC ABILITIES HAVE REACHED "E"!
WHA—?
..."E"?
PACHI (BLINK)
KURI (BLINK)
DO YOU THINK THAT KIND OF CLAIM CAN FOOL ME...?
IT'S TRUE! I'M NOT LYING!
I'VE BEEN GROWING REALLY FAST RECENTLY ...!

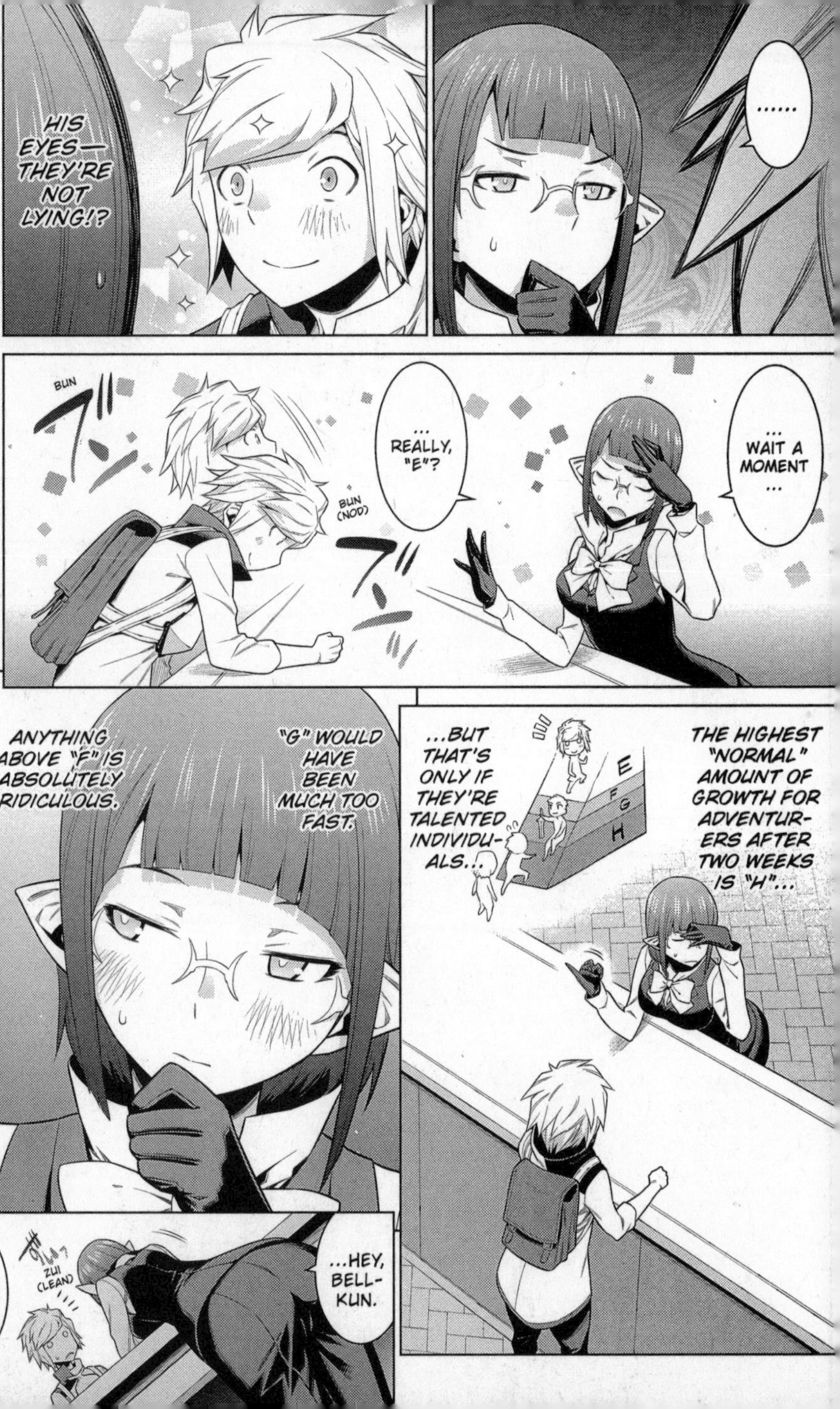
......
HIS EYES—THEY'RE NOT LYING!?
... WAIT A MOMENT ...
... REALLY, "E"?
BUN (NOD)
BUN
THE HIGHEST "NORMAL" AMOUNT OF GROWTH FOR ADVENTURERS AFTER TWO WEEKS IS "H"...
...BUT THAT'S ONLY IF THEY'RE TALENTED INDIVIDUALS...
E
F
G
H
"G" WOULD HAVE BEEN MUCH TOO FAST.
ANYTHING ABOVE "F" IS ABSOLUTELY RIDICULOUS.
...HEY, BELL-KUN.
ZUI (LEAN)
Y-YES?

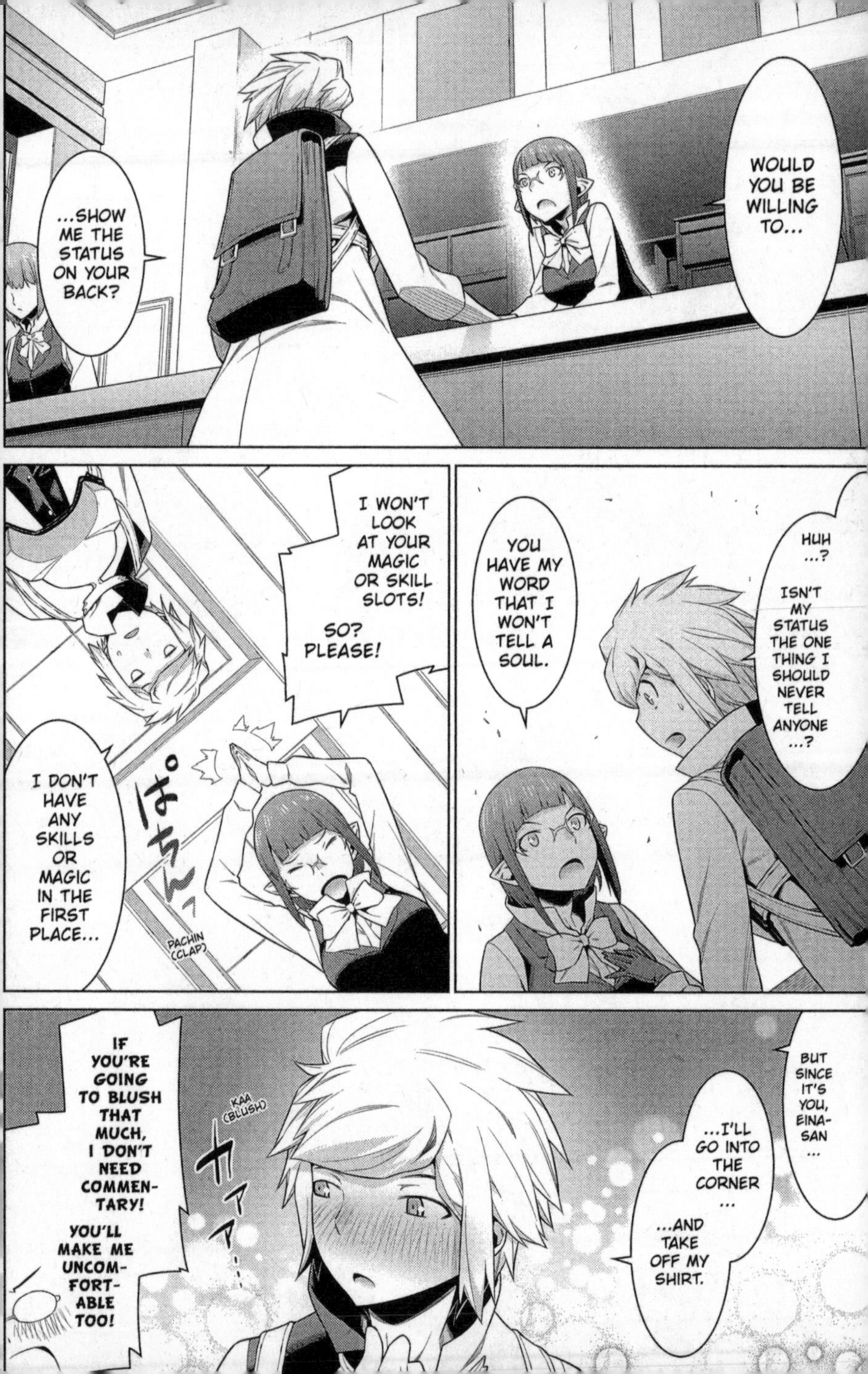
WOULD YOU BE WILLING TO...
...SHOW ME THE STATUS ON YOUR BACK?
HUH ...? ISN'T MY STATUS THE ONE THING I SHOULD NEVER TELL ANYONE ...?
YOU HAVE MY WORD THAT I WON'T TELL A SOUL.
I WON'T LOOK AT YOUR MAGIC OR SKILL SLOTS!
SO? PLEASE!
ぱちん
PACHIN (CLAP)
I DON'T HAVE ANY SKILLS OR MAGIC IN THE FIRST PLACE...
BUT SINCE IT'S YOU, EINA-SAN ...
...I'LL GO INTO THE CORNER ...
...AND TAKE OFF MY SHIRT.
カァ...
KAA (BLUSH)
IF YOU'RE GOING TO BLUSH THAT MUCH, I DON'T NEED COMMENTARY!
YOU'LL MAKE ME UNCOMFORTABLE TOO!

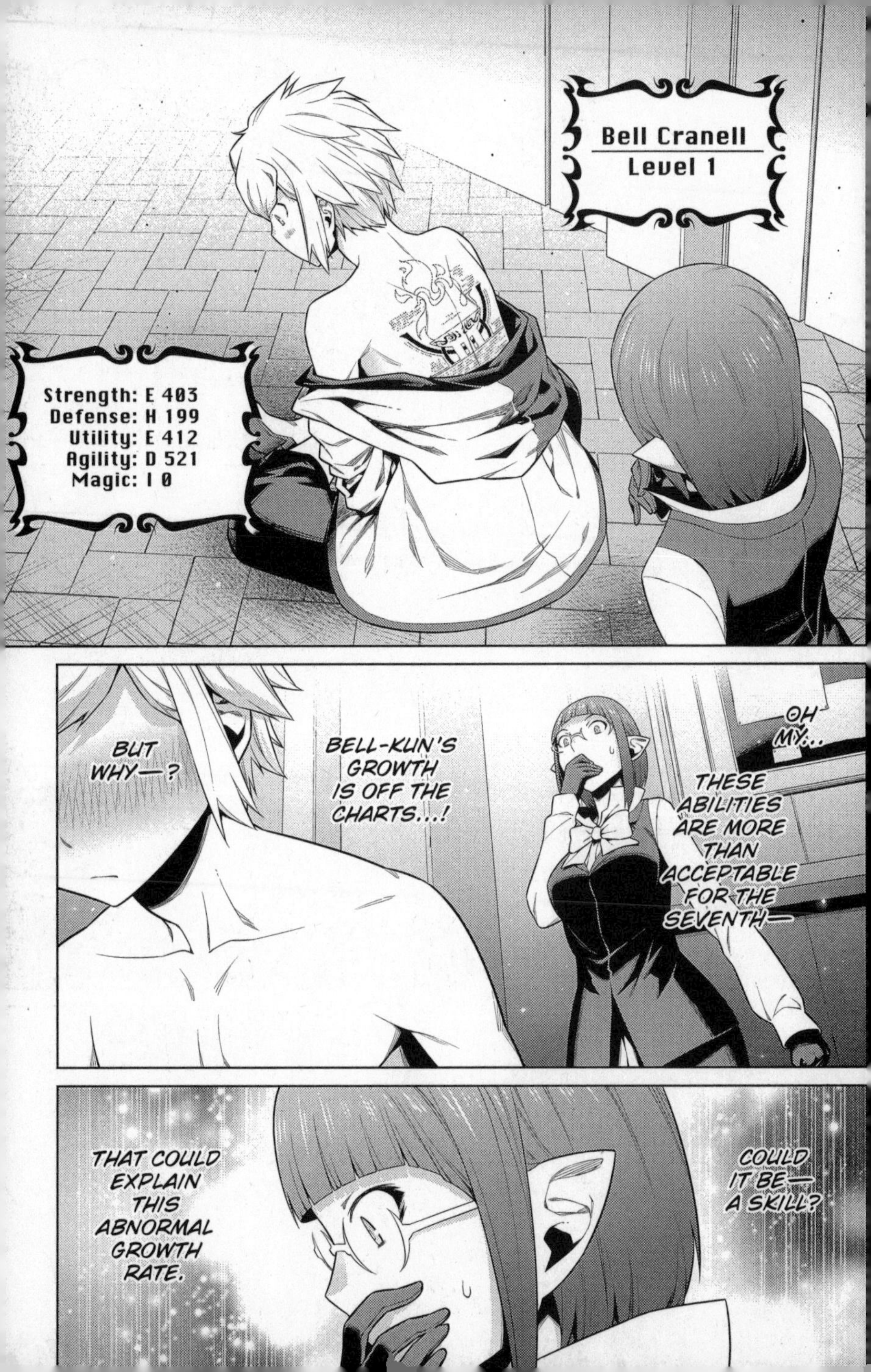
Bell Cranell
Level 1
Strength: E 403
Defense: H 199
Utility: E 412
Agility: D 521
Magic: I 0
OH MY...
THESE ABILITIES ARE MORE THAN ACCEPTABLE FOR THE SEVENTH—
BELL-KUN'S GROWTH IS OFF THE CHARTS...!
BUT WHY—?
COULD IT BE— A SKILL?
THAT COULD EXPLAIN THIS ABNORMAL GROWTH RATE.

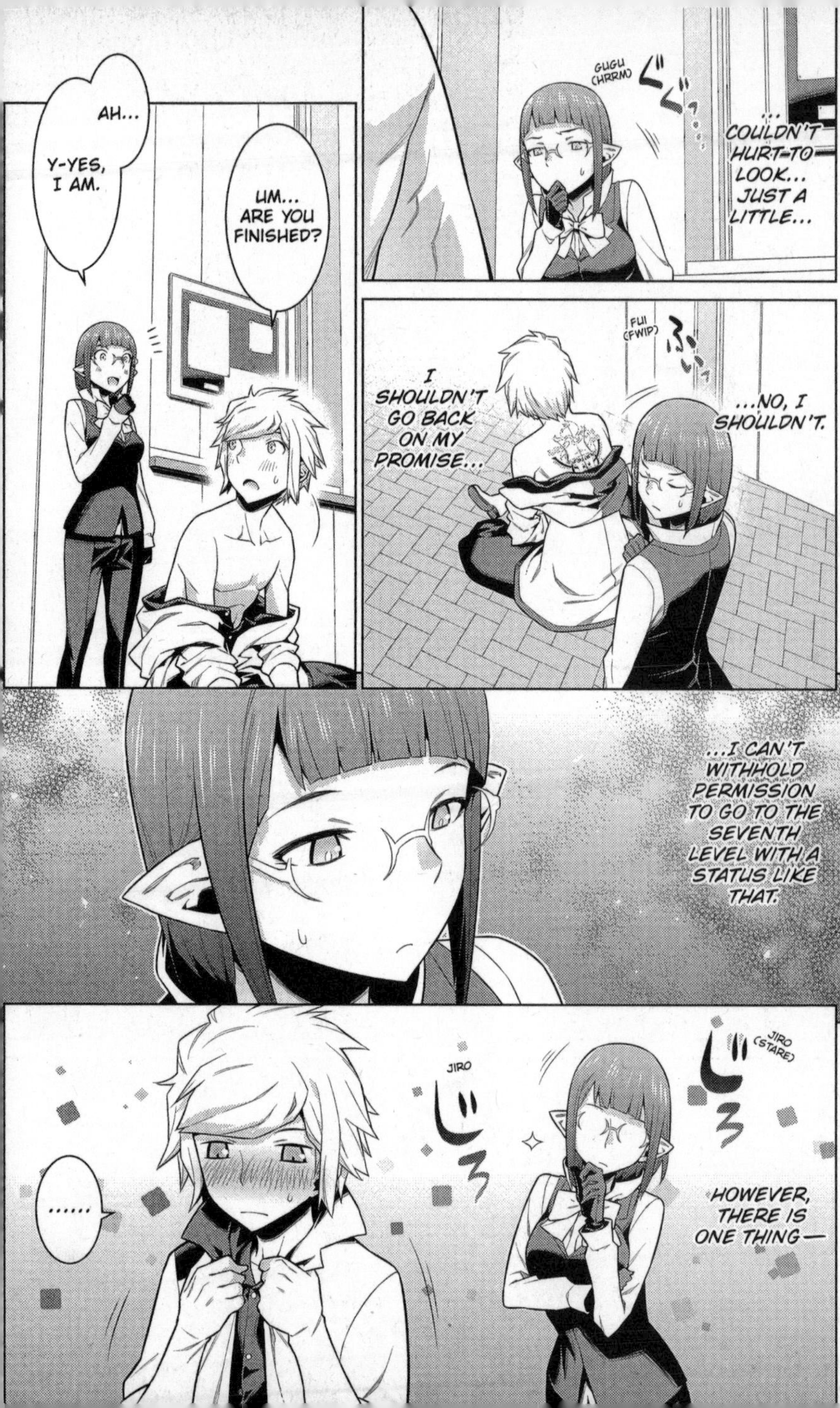
GUGU (HRRM)
...COULDN'T HURT TO LOOK... JUST A LITTLE...
FUI (FWIP)
...NO, I SHOULDN'T.
I SHOULDN'T GO BACK ON MY PROMISE...
UM... ARE YOU FINISHED?
AH...
Y-YES, I AM.
...I CAN'T WITHHOLD PERMISSION TO GO TO THE SEVENTH LEVEL WITH A STATUS LIKE THAT.
JIRO (STARE)
HOWEVER, THERE IS ONE THING—
JIRO
......

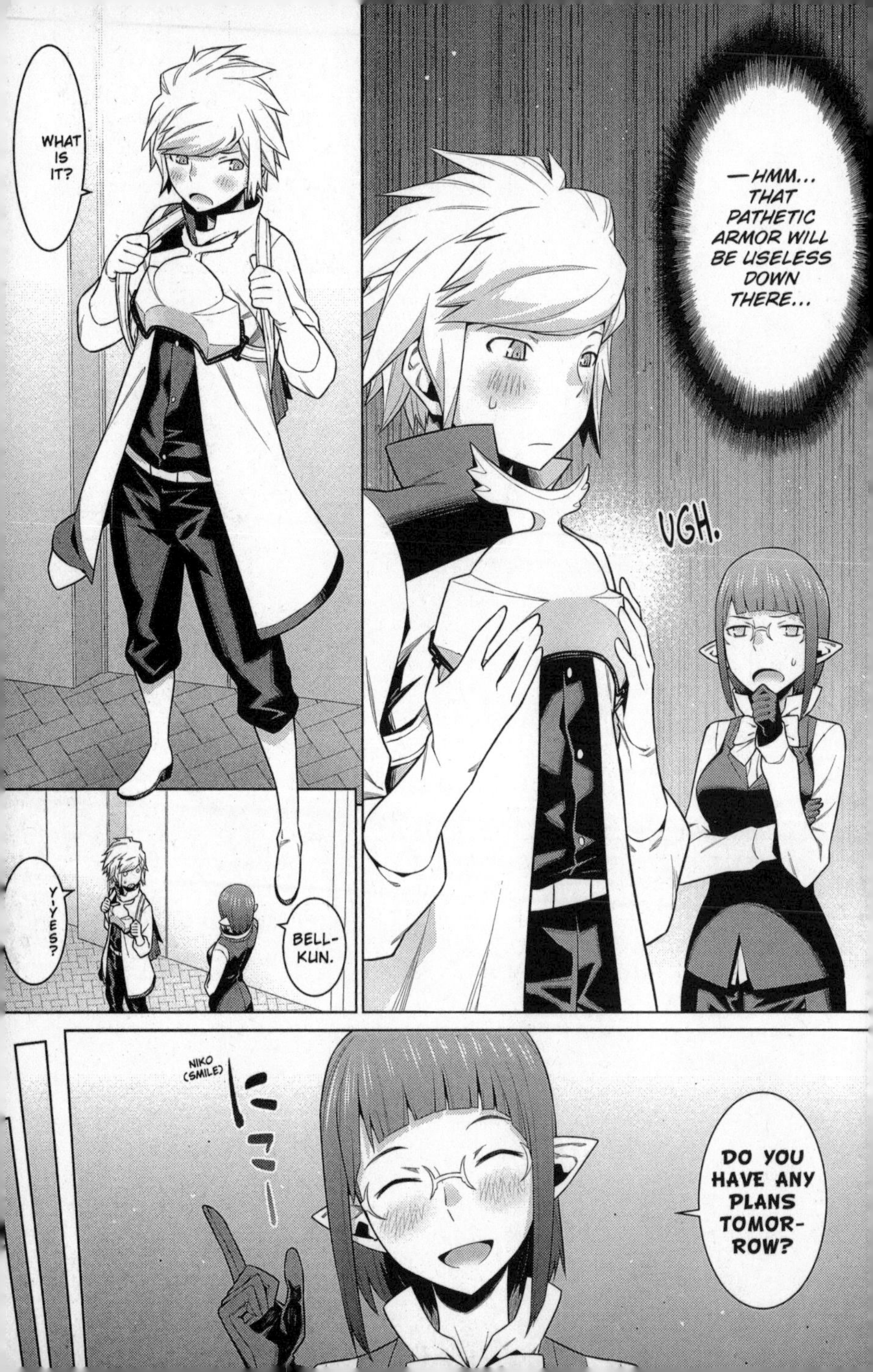
—HMM... THAT PATHETIC ARMOR WILL BE USELESS DOWN THERE...
UGH.
WHAT IS IT?
BELL-KUN.
Y-YES?
DO YOU HAVE ANY PLANS TOMOR-ROW?
NIKO (SMILE)

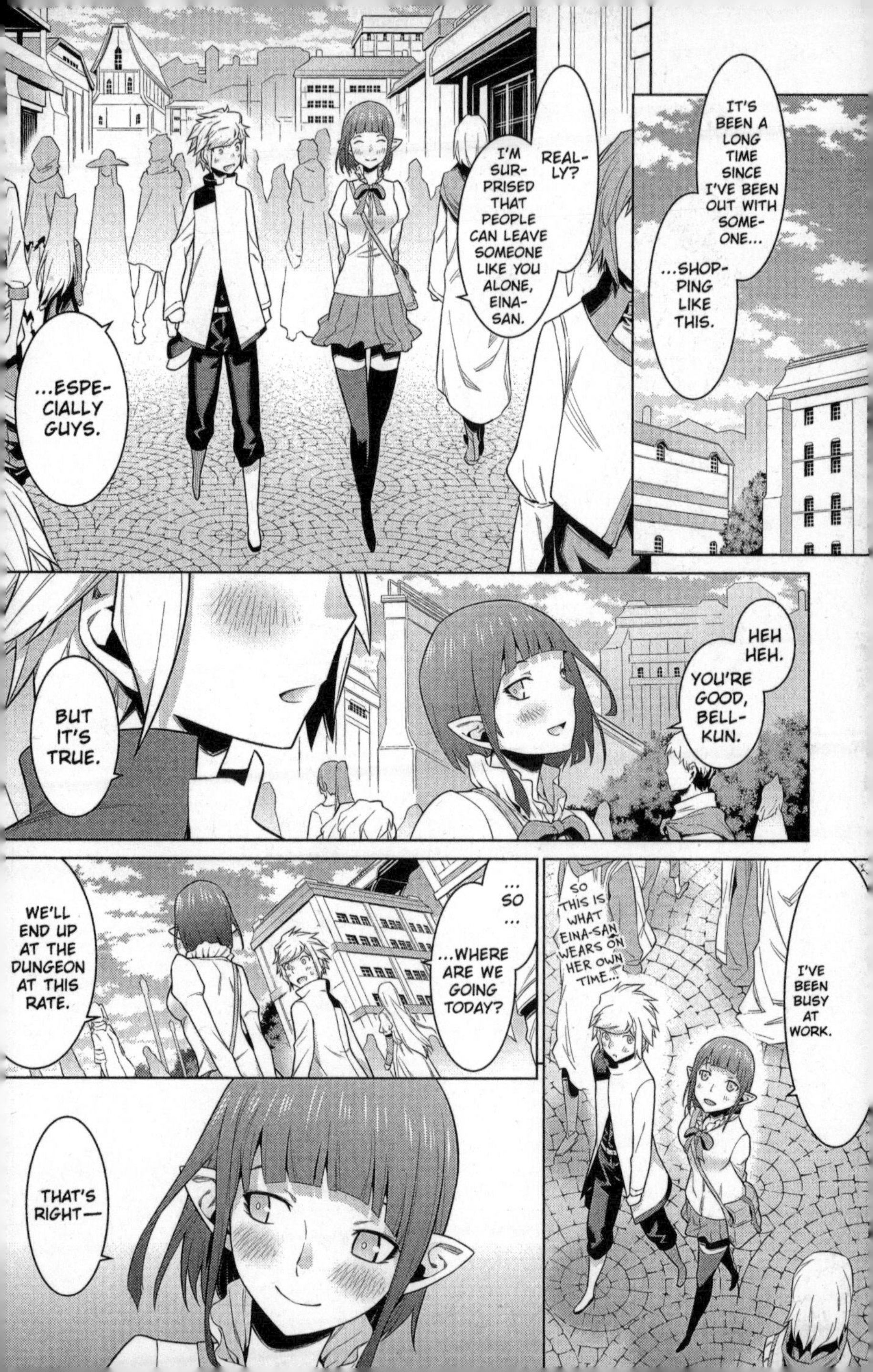
IT'S BEEN A LONG TIME SINCE I'VE BEEN OUT WITH SOMEONE...
...SHOPPING LIKE THIS.
REALLY?
I'M SURPRISED THAT PEOPLE CAN LEAVE SOMEONE LIKE YOU ALONE, EINA-SAN.
...ESPECIALLY GUYS.
HEH HEH. YOU'RE GOOD, BELL-KUN.
BUT IT'S TRUE.
I'VE BEEN BUSY AT WORK.
SO THIS IS WHAT EINA-SAN WEARS ON HER OWN TIME...
...SO...
...WHERE ARE WE GOING TODAY?
WE'LL END UP AT THE DUNGEON AT THIS RATE.
THAT'S RIGHT—

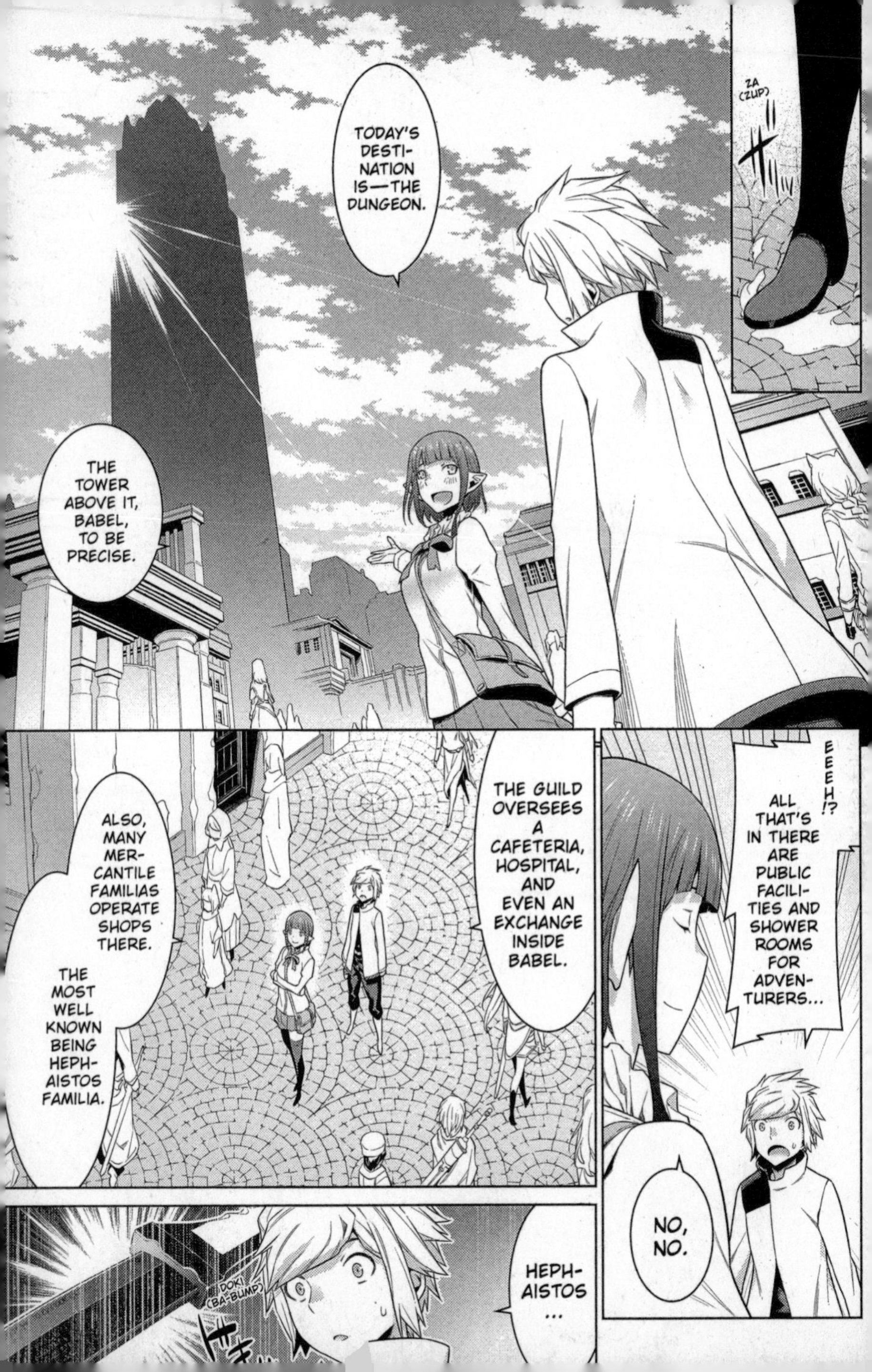
ZA (ZUP)
TODAY'S DESTINATION IS—THE DUNGEON.
THE TOWER ABOVE IT, BABEL, TO BE PRECISE.
EEEEH!?
ALL THAT'S IN THERE ARE PUBLIC FACILITIES AND SHOWER ROOMS FOR ADVENTURERS...
NO, NO.
THE GUILD OVERSEES A CAFETERIA, HOSPITAL, AND EVEN AN EXCHANGE INSIDE BABEL.
ALSO, MANY MERCANTILE FAMILIAS OPERATE SHOPS THERE.
THE MOST WELL KNOWN BEING HEPHAISTOS FAMILIA.
HEPHAISTOS...
DOKI (BA-BUMP)

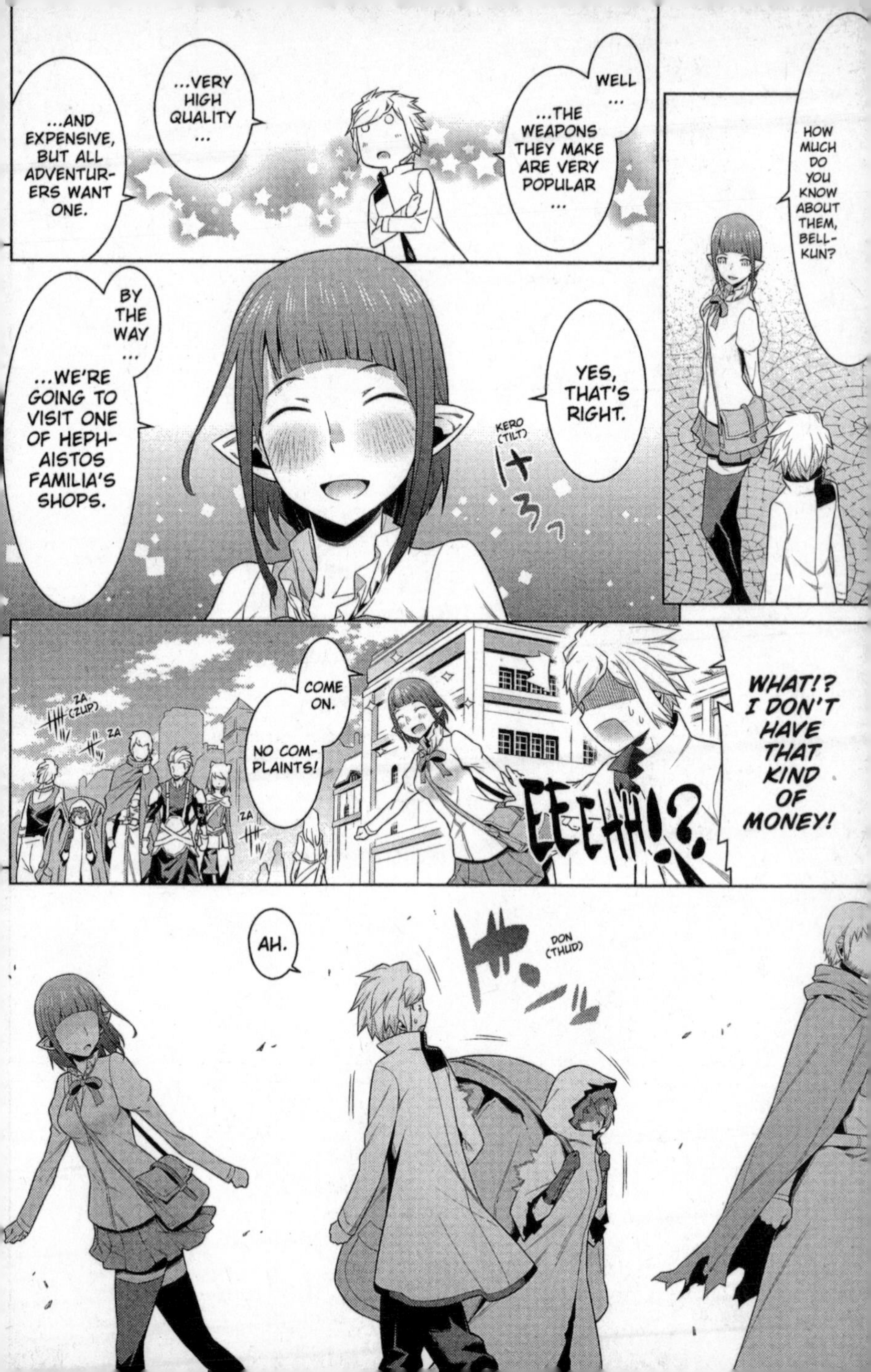
HOW MUCH DO YOU KNOW ABOUT THEM, BELL-KUN?
WELL...
...THE WEAPONS THEY MAKE ARE VERY POPULAR...
...VERY HIGH QUALITY...
...AND EXPENSIVE, BUT ALL ADVENTURERS WANT ONE.
YES, THAT'S RIGHT.
KERO (TILT)
BY THE WAY...
...WE'RE GOING TO VISIT ONE OF HEPHAISTOS FAMILIA'S SHOPS.
WHAT!? I DON'T HAVE THAT KIND OF MONEY!
EEEHH!?
COME ON.
NO COMPLAINTS!
ZA (ZUP)
ZA
ZA
DON (THUD)
AH.

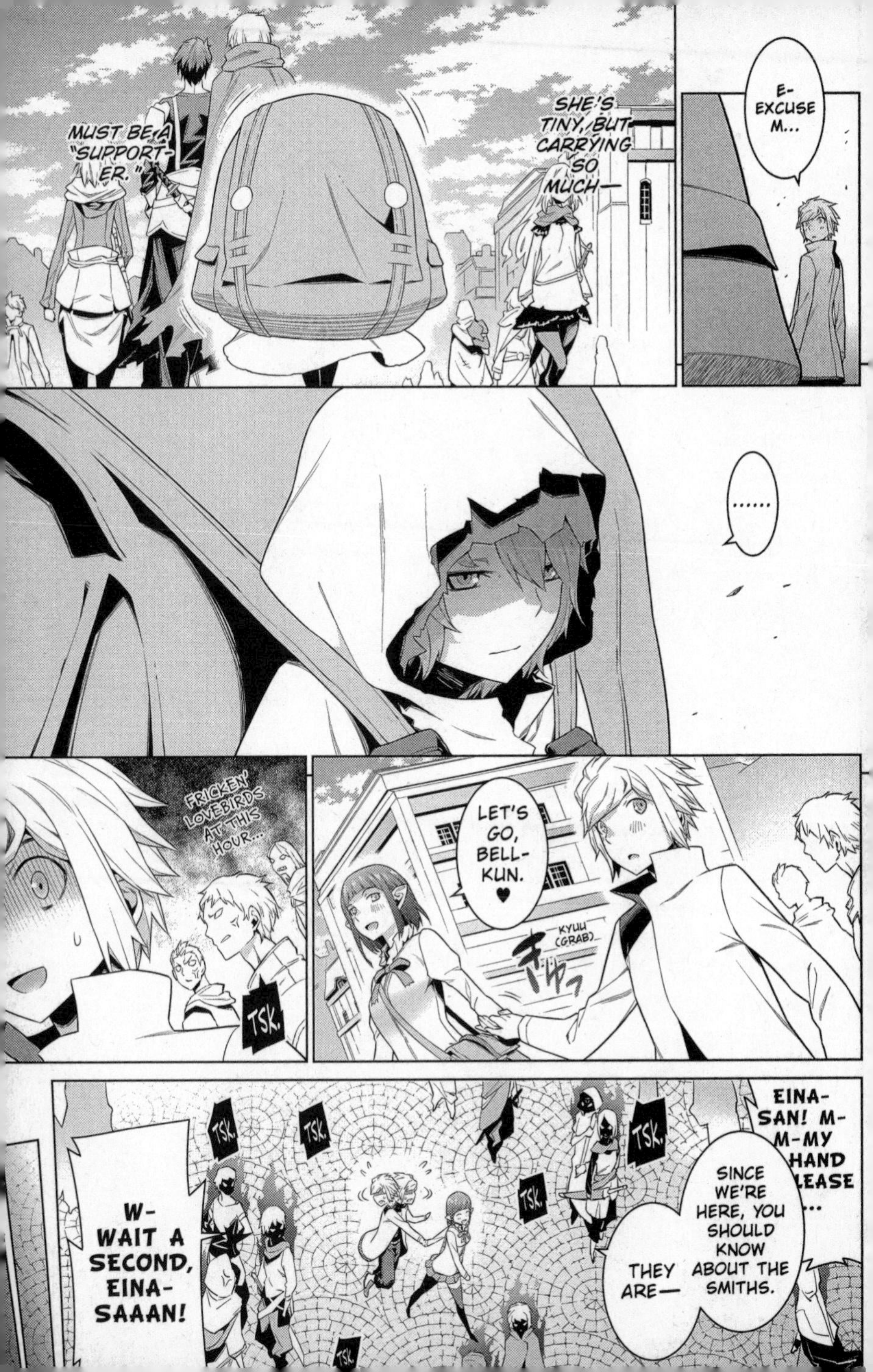
E-EXCUSE M...
SHE'S TINY, BUT CARRYING SO MUCH—
MUST BE A "SUPPORTER."
......
LET'S GO, BELL-KUN. ♥
KYUU (GRAB)
FRICKEN' LOVEBIRDS AT THIS HOUR...
TSK.
EINA-SAN! M-M-MY HAND LEASE ...
TSK.
SINCE WE'RE HERE, YOU SHOULD KNOW ABOUT THE SMITHS.
THEY ARE—
TSK.
TSK.
TSK.
W-WAIT A SECOND, EINA-SAAAN!
TSK.

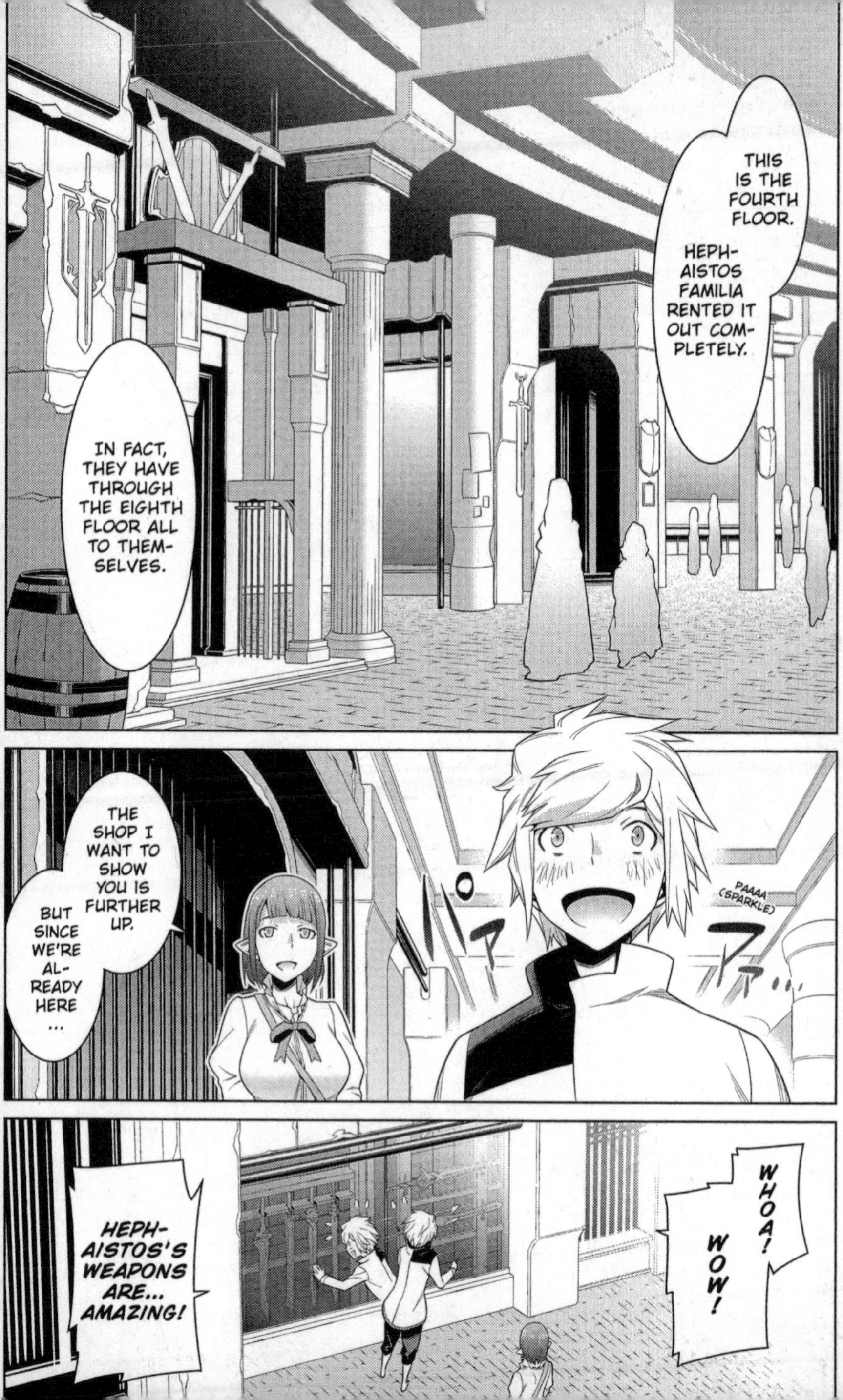
THIS IS THE FOURTH FLOOR.
HEPHAISTOS FAMILIA RENTED IT OUT COMPLETELY.
IN FACT, THEY HAVE THROUGH THE EIGHTH FLOOR ALL TO THEMSELVES.
PAAAA (SPARKLE)
THE SHOP I WANT TO SHOW YOU IS FURTHER UP.
BUT SINCE WE'RE ALREADY HERE...
WHOA! WOW!
HEPHAISTOS'S WEAPONS ARE... AMAZING!

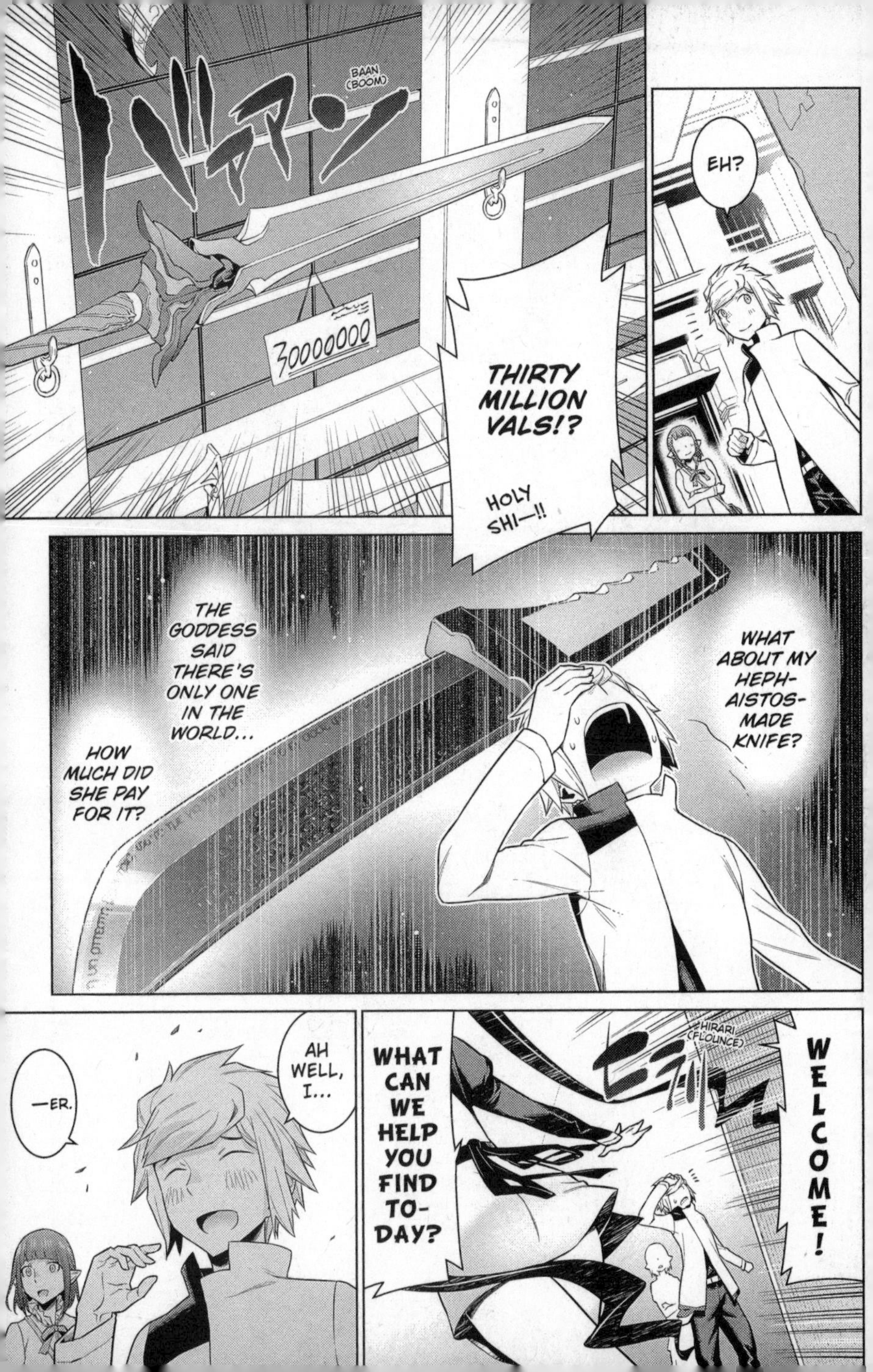
EH?
BAAN (BOOM)
30000000
THIRTY MILLION VALS!?
HOLY SHI—!!
WHAT ABOUT MY HEPH-AISTOS-MADE KNIFE?
THE GODDESS SAID THERE'S ONLY ONE IN THE WORLD...
HOW MUCH DID SHE PAY FOR IT?
WELCOME!
HIRARI (FLOUNCE)
WHAT CAN WE HELP YOU FIND TO-DAY?
AH WELL, I...
—ER.

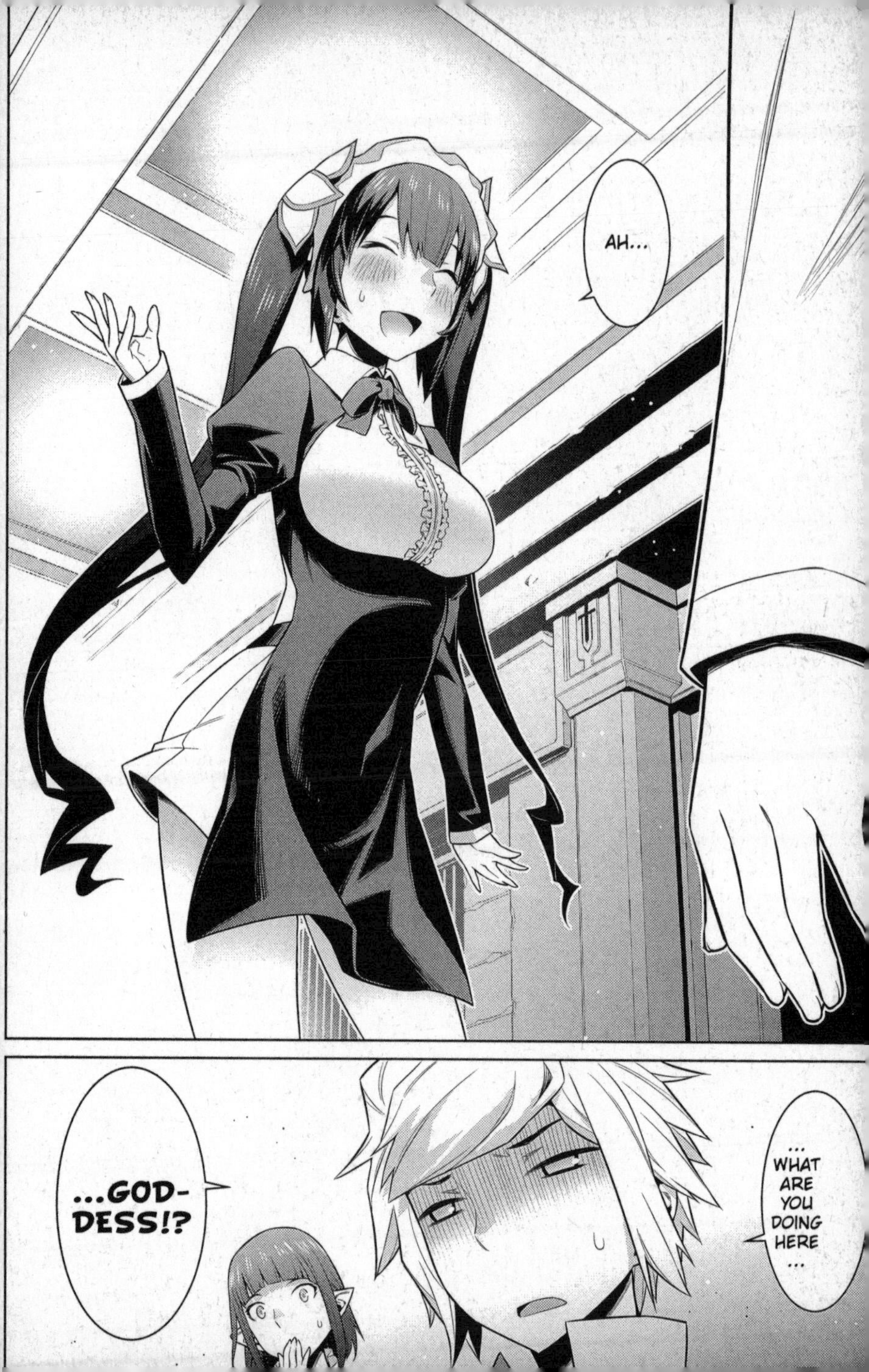
AH...
...WHAT ARE YOU DOING HERE...
...GOD-DESS!?

Is It Wrong to Try to Pick Up Girls in a Dungeon?

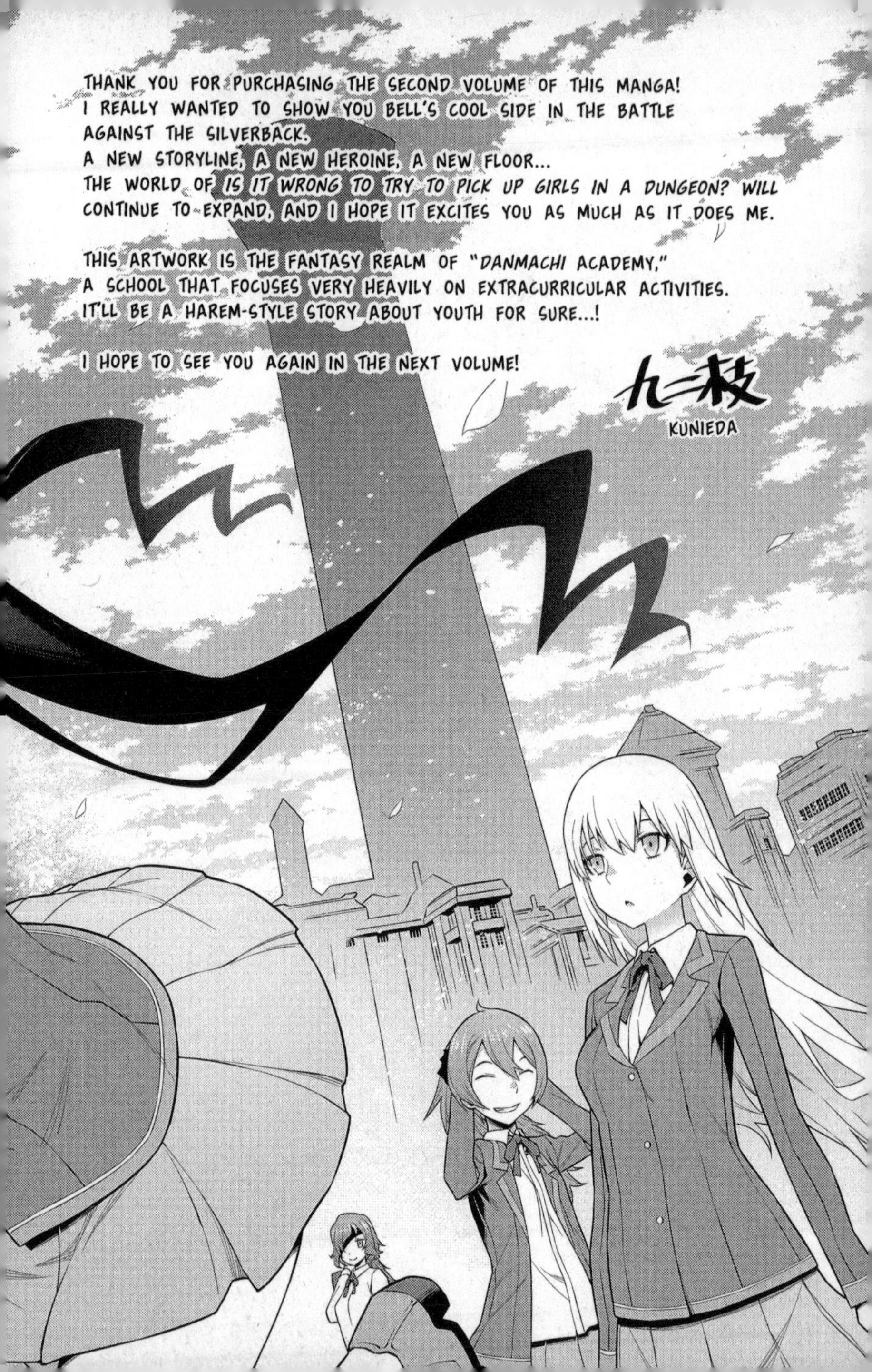
THANK YOU FOR PURCHASING THE SECOND VOLUME OF THIS MANGA!
I REALLY WANTED TO SHOW YOU BELL'S COOL SIDE IN THE BATTLE AGAINST THE SILVERBACK.
A NEW STORYLINE, A NEW HEROINE, A NEW FLOOR...
THE WORLD OF *IS IT WRONG TO TRY TO PICK UP GIRLS IN A DUNGEON?* WILL CONTINUE TO EXPAND, AND I HOPE IT EXCITES YOU AS MUCH AS IT DOES ME.
THIS ARTWORK IS THE FANTASY REALM OF "*DANMACHI ACADEMY*," A SCHOOL THAT FOCUSES VERY HEAVILY ON EXTRACURRICULAR ACTIVITIES.
IT'LL BE A HAREM-STYLE STORY ABOUT YOUTH FOR SURE...!
I HOPE TO SEE YOU AGAIN IN THE NEXT VOLUME!
九二枝
KUNIEDA

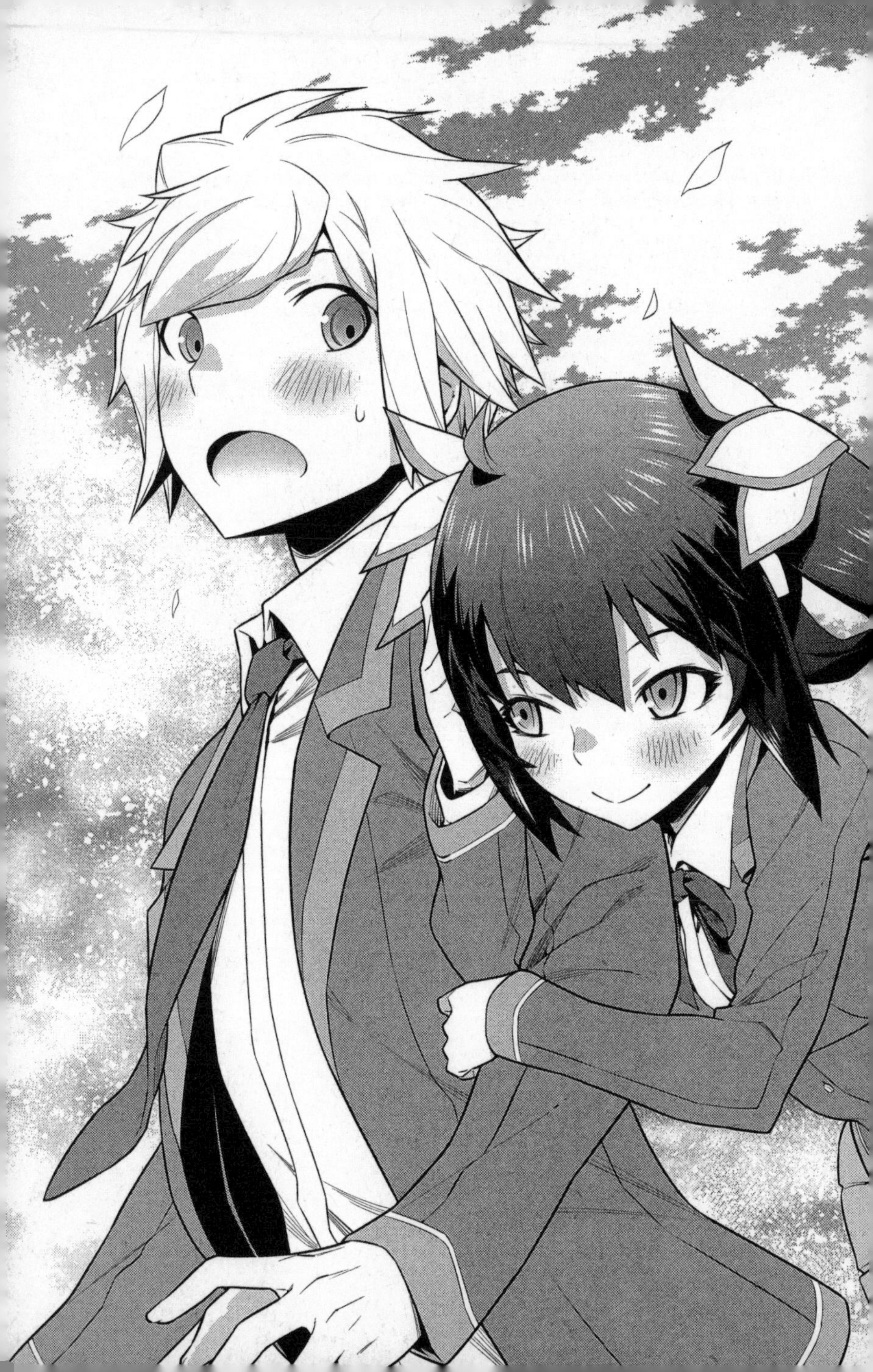

TRANSLATION NOTES

Common Honorifics

no honorific: Indicates familiarity or closeness; if used without permission or reason, addressing someone in this manner would constitute an insult.

-san: The Japanese equivalent of Mr./Mrs./Miss. If a situation calls for politeness, this is the failsafe honorific.

-shi: Not unlike *-san;* the equivalent of Mr./Mrs./Miss but conveying a more official or bureaucratic mood.

-sama: Conveys great respect; may also indicate that the social status of the speaker is lower than that of the addressee.

-kun: Used most often when referring to boys, this indicates affection or familiarity. Occasionally used by older men among their peers, but it may also be used by anyone referring to a person of lower standing.

-chan: An affectionate honorific indicating familiarity used mostly in reference to girls; also used in reference to cute persons or animals of either gender.

PAGE 47
Kenki: "Sword princess." The nickname Aiz Wallenstein's feats have earned her.

PAGE 117
Tenkai: Literally "the heavenly world," this refers to the heavens—the realm from which the gods descended.

PAGE 132
Dogeza: The deepest bow possible in Japanese culture, performing dogeza involves kneeling down and touching one's forehead to the ground.

PAGE 173
Danmachi: A shortened version of the original Japanese title *Dungeon ni Deai Wo Motomeru no wa Machigatteiru Darouka.*

Is It WRONG to TRY to PiCK UP GiRLS iN A DUNGEON?

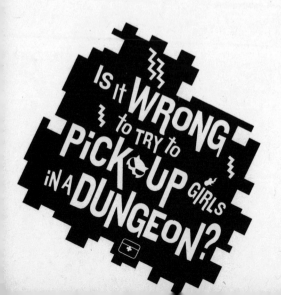

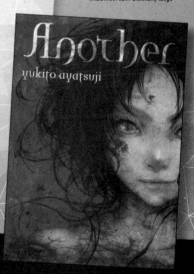

IS IT WRONG TO TRY TO PICK UP GIRLS IN A DUNGEON? ❷

FUJINO OMORI
KUNIEDA
SUZUHITO YASUDA

Translation: Andrew Gaippe • Lettering: Brndn Blakeslee, Lys Blakeslee

DUNGEON NI DEAI WO MOTOMERU NO WA MACHIGATTEIRUDAROUKA vol. 2
© 2014 Fujino Omori / SB Creative Corp.
© 2014 Kunieda / SQUARE ENIX CO., LTD.
First published in Japan in 2014 by SQUARE ENIX CO., LTD.
English Translation rights arranged with SQUARE ENIX CO., LTD.
and Hachette Book Group through Tuttle Mori Agency, Inc.

Translation © 2015 by SQUARE ENIX CO., LTD.

Yen Press
Hachette Book Group
1290 Avenue of the Americas, New York, NY 10104

www.HachetteBookGroup.com
www.YenPress.com

Yen Press is an imprint of Hachette Book Group, Inc. The Yen Press name and logo are trademarks of Hachette Book Group, Inc.

The publisher is not responsible for websites (or their content) that are not owned by the publisher.

First Yen Press Edition: August 2015

ISBN: 978-0-316-34591-0

10 9 8 7 6 5 4 3 2 1

BVG

Printed in the United States of America

HEY! FLIP THE BOOK TO READ
A SPECIAL BONUS SHORT STORY
STRAIGHT FROM FUJINO OMORI!

Is it Wrong to Try to Pick Up Girls in a Dungeon?

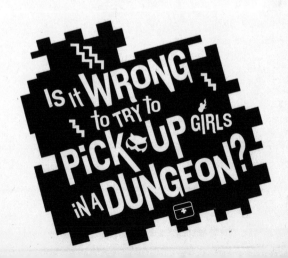

"Stop muttering to yourself and get your rear in gear, new girl. You've been here all of two days. That all you got?" The store manager, a half-dwarf standing three heads taller than Hestia, scolded her.

"Yes, sir," she responded in a weak voice. As if they had been instructed to be as hard on her as possible, the staff of demi-humans hadn't given her a shred of leeway. Evidently, Hephaistos had been extremely clear on how Hestia should be treated. Hestia forced her weak little body forward, raising her head to look at the busy storefront.

Ah, more customers. It looked like a couple.

A human boy and a half-elf girl. *That would be so nice. I'm so jealous. What I wouldn't give to walk around like that with Bell.* With thoughts like these running through her head, she went to the front to meet the new customers.

Her eyes fell on the white-haired boy, who looked rather familiar, her mind checking out as her body went into autopilot and formed the smile that had been drilled into her over the past two days.

"Welcome! What can we help you find today?"

take out a loan.

At this very moment, the details of said loan were being laid out by Hephaistos herself.

"You will be working at one of my shops. All of your pay will go toward your loan, so you will never see any of it nor have to give me a val. I'll let you continue to work at your other part-time job. Therefore, if you want to eat you'd better do both."

"Waahh......"

"You will be working eight-hour shifts. No overtime pay. You may have two days off......per month."

"Demon! You're EVIIIIIILLL!!" Hestia cried out on the spot.

"What are you talking about? Someone in your position doesn't have time to relax, now, does she? You think you can take it easy when you've got a loan to pay? Dream on."

"E-even so... A-are you trying to work me to death, Hephaistos?!"

"I won't deny it."

"Why?!"

"You have a horrible attention span; this will be a good experience for you. Now, work like your life depends on it."

Hephaistos had become judge, jury, and executioner. Her low chilling voice put Hestia in her place.

Hephaistos lifted her crimson bangs, revealing a large eye patch and one angrily squinted crimson eye.

"'I'll prove to you once and for all that my love for him is pure'...... Those were your words. Why don't you show me the power of your love?"

"DAMN IT!!!"

Soon, childish whimpers of "Bell" echoed through the room.

A day later.

"Waah! There's no time to sit down......"

Now on her second day of work, a foggy-eyed Hestia had started complaining to herself.

She had been assigned to work on the fourth floor of an imposing skyscraper in the middle of the city—Babel Tower. The floor was devoted to just one shop, and the flow of customers was endless. It was Hestia's job to greet them. She had never been this busy before, and the continuous motion was starting to get to her.

At least the uniform is cute, she thought to herself with a heavy sigh, looking down at the crimson apron wrapped around her body.

It was the day after the Monsterphilia.

There was something else going on as Bell was having fun tearing through monsters with the Hestia Knife.

Two goddesses stood like pillars as they faced each other.

"Well then, I'll work you to the bone just like I promised I would."

"P-please go easy on me......"

The Goddess of the Forge, Hephaistos, drew herself up to her full height and pursed her lips in front of Hestia.

They were standing inside *Hephaistos Familia's* headquarters. A curtain blocked the sunlight coming in through the windows, keeping the tense room shrouded in a dim glow. It felt somehow oppressive.

Hestia fought to keep her body from shaking as she formed a very weak smile. She looked up at the crimson-haired, crimson-eyed goddess standing before her. Hephaistos's nostrils flared menacingly.

"'Go easy on you'? Those are the words of a fool who took out a loan she couldn't pay back. If it's compassion you're looking for, you'll get none from me."

A wave of fear washed over Hestia as she heard no trace of mercy in the words that came from the coolheaded goddess that was her friend.

It had all started a few days before. Motivated by Bell's newfound determination to get stronger, Hestia had come to *Hephaistos Familia* looking to purchase a weapon for him. Most likely, only the goddess in front of her—a legendary smith even among the gods in the upper world of Tenkai—could make the unique weapon that would be suitable for him.

Her asking price had been obviously steep. It was far beyond what Hestia was capable of paying—high enough to make the recipient of the weapon pass out if he heard it—so Hestia had been forced to

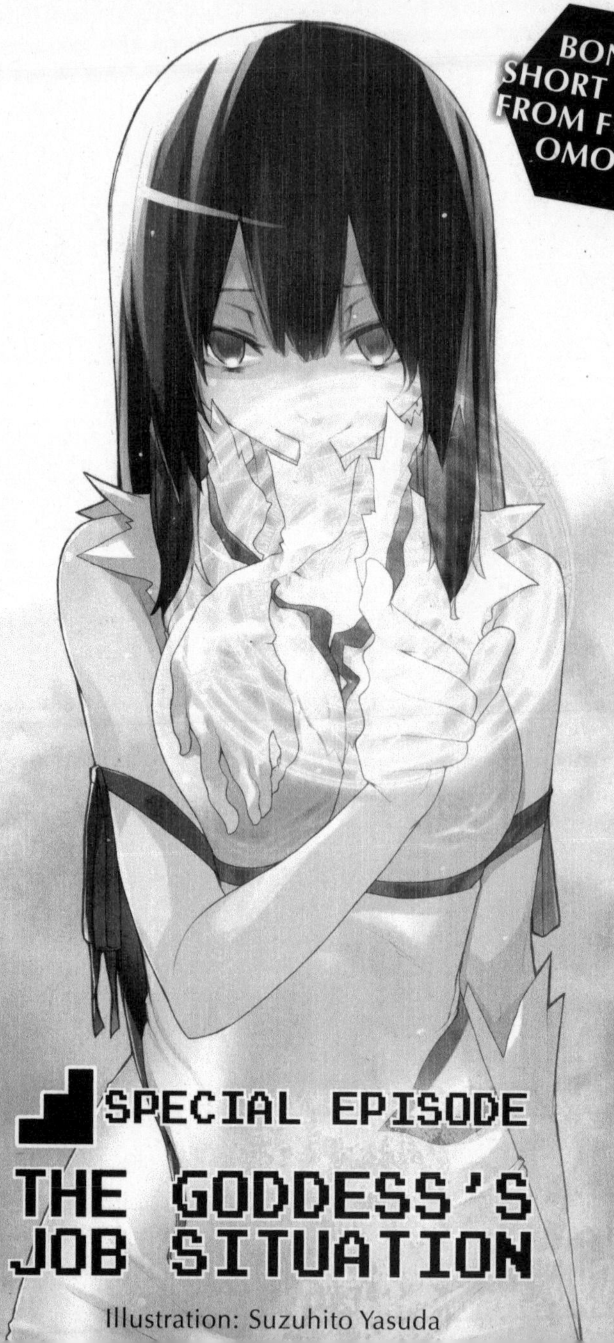

BONUS SHORT STORY FROM FUJINO OMORI!

SPECIAL EPISODE
THE GODDESS'S JOB SITUATION

Illustration: Suzuhito Yasuda